Lynda Weinman's | **Hands-On Training**

Adobe®
Flash® CS3
Professional

Includes Exercise Files and Demo Movies

lynda.com

By Todd Perkins

Adobe® Flash® CS3 Professional Hands-On Training
By Todd Perkins

lynda.com/books | Peachpit Press
1249 Eighth Street • Berkeley, CA • 94710
510.524.2178
510.524.2221(fax)
www.lynda.com/books
www.peachpit.com

lynda.com/books is published
in association with Peachpit Press,
a division of Pearson Education
Copyright ©2008 by lynda.com

ISBN-13: 978-0-321-50983-3
ISBN-10:   0-321-50983-8

0 9 8 7 6 5 4 3 2 1

Printed and bound in the
United States of America

H•O•T Credits

Director of Product Development and Video Production: Tanya Staples

Senior Editor: Karyn Johnson

Production Editor: Tracey Croom

Compositors: Myrna Vladic and David Van Ness

Technical Writer: Lauren Harmon

Copyeditor: Kim Wimpsett

Proofreader: Liz Welch

Interior Design: Hot Studio, San Francisco

Cover Design: Don Barnett

Cover Illustration: Bruce Heavin

Indexer: Jack Lewis

H•O•T Colophon

The text in *Adobe Flash CS3 Professional H·O·T* was set in Avenir from Adobe Systems Incorporated. The cover illustration was painted in Adobe Photoshop and Adobe Illustrator.

This book was created using QuarkXPress and Microsoft Office on an Apple Macintosh using Mac OS X. It was printed on 60 lb. Influence Matte at Courier.

Table of Contents

Table of Contents

Table of Contents

Introduction

A Note from Lynda Weinman

Most people buy computer books to learn, yet it's amazing how few books are written by teachers. Todd Perkins and I take pride that this book was written by experienced teachers who are familiar with training students in this subject matter. In this book, you'll find carefully developed lessons and exercises to help you learn Adobe Flash CS3 Professional—one of the most powerful and popular animation and authoring tools for the Web.

This book is targeted to beginning-level and intermediate-level Web designers and Web developers who need a tool for creating powerful, compelling, and highly interactive digital content for the Web. The premise of the hands-on approach is to get you up-to-speed quickly with Flash CS3 while actively working through the lessons in this book. It's one thing to read about a program, and it's another experience entirely to try the product and achieve measurable results. Our motto is, "Read the book, follow the exercises, and you'll learn the program." I have received countless testimonials, and it is our goal to make sure it remains true for all our hands-on training books.

This book doesn't set out to cover every single aspect of the Flash CS3 program, and it doesn't try to teach you everything this extremely powerful application can do. What we saw missing from the bookshelves was a process-oriented tutorial that teaches readers core principles, techniques, and tips in a hands-on training format.

I welcome your comments at **books-errata@lynda.com**. If you run into any trouble while you're working through this book, check out the technical support link at **www.lynda.com/books/HOT/flcs3**.

Todd Perkins and I hope this book will improve your skills in Flash. If it does, we have accomplished the job we set out to do!

—Lynda Weinman

About lynda.com

lynda.com was founded in 1995 by Lynda Weinman and Bruce Heavin in conjunction with the first publication of Lynda's revolutionary book, *Designing Web Graphics*. Since then, lynda.com has become a leader in software training for graphics and Web professionals and is recognized worldwide as a trusted educational resource.

lynda.com offers a wide range of Hands-On Training books, which guide users through a progressive learning process using real-world projects. lynda.com also offers a wide range of video-based tutorials, which are available on CD-ROM and DVD-ROM and through the lynda.com Online Training Library. lynda.com also owns the Flashforward Conference and Film Festival.

For more information about lynda.com, check out **www.lynda.com**. For more information about the Flashforward conference and film festival, check out **www.flashforwardconference.com**.

Register for a FREE 24-hour Pass

Register your copy of Adobe *Flash CS3 Professional HOT* today, and receive the following benefits:

- **FREE 24-hour pass to the lynda.com Online Training Library** with more than 20,000 professionally produced video tutorials covering more than 300 topics by leading industry experts and teachers

- News, events, and special offers from lynda.com

- The lynda.com monthly newsletter

To register, visit **www.lynda.com/register/ HOT/flcs3**.

Additional Training Resources from lynda.com

To help you master and further develop your skills with Flash CS3, Web design, and Web development, register to use the free 24-hour pass to the lynda.com Online Training Library, and check out the following training resources:

Flash CS3 Professional Essential Training
with Rich Schupe

ActionScript 3.0 in Flash CS3 Professional Essential Training
with Todd Perkins

Illustrator CS3 and Flash CS3 Professional Integration
with Mordy Golding

About the Author

Todd Perkins is an Adobe Certified Instructor and spends much of his time teaching people Adobe Web development software. Todd has several years of experience teaching people of all ages and backgrounds, and he is an expert at teaching complex concepts in a way everyone can understand. Todd is half of the dynamic duo behind All Things Adobe: The Chad and Todd Podcast and has authored a vast array of video training titles. Todd also loves to teach in classrooms, consult with businesses, and train people online, but what he loves most is playing video games with his amazing wife, Jessica.

Acknowledgments from Todd Perkins

I want to give thanks to all the people who helped make this book possible. To my brother Chad: Thanks for introducing me to the amazing folks at lynda.com and inspiring me to learn Flash. Tanya and Lauren, thank you for all your hard work. You guys are awesome! Jessica, thanks for all the support you've given me in writing this book and for motivating me to work hard. Thanks to everyone at lynda.com; I love working with all of you! Last, I want to thank *you* for reading this book.

How to Use This Book

The following sections outline important information to help you make the most of this book.

The Formatting in This Book

This book has several components, including step-by-step exercises, commentary, notes, tips, warnings, and video tutorials. Step-by-step exercises are numbered. File names, folder names, commands, keyboard shortcuts, and Web addresses are in bold so they pop out easily: **filename.htm**, the **images** folder, **File > New**, **Ctrl-click**, **www.lynda.com**.

Commentary is in dark gray text:

This is commentary text.

Interface Screen Captures

Most of the screen shots in the book were taken on a Windows computer using Windows Vista. I also own, use, and love my Mac computers, and I note important differences between the two platforms when they occur.

What's on the HOT CD-ROM?

You'll find a number of useful resources on the **Flash HOT CD-ROM**, including the following: exercise files, video tutorials, and information about product registration. Before you begin the hands-on exercises, read the following sections so you know how to set up the exercise files and video tutorials.

Exercise Files

The files required to complete the exercises are on the **Flash HOT CD-ROM** in a folder called **exercise_files**. These files are divided into chapter folders, and you should copy each chapter folder onto your desktop before you begin the exercises for that chapter. For example, if you're about to start Chapter 5, copy the **chap_05** folder from the **exercise_files** folder on the **Flash HOT CD-ROM** onto your desktop.

On Windows, when files originate from a CD-ROM, they automatically become write-protected, which means you cannot alter them. Fortunately, you can easily change this attribute. For complete instructions, read the "Making Exercise Files Editable on Windows Computers" section later in this introduction.

Video Tutorials

Throughout the book, you'll find references to video tutorials. In some cases, these video tutorials reinforce concepts explained in the book. In other cases, they show bonus material you'll find interesting and useful. To view the video tutorials, you must have Apple QuickTime Player installed on your computer. If you do not have QuickTime Player, you can download it for free from Apple's Web site: **www.apple.com/quicktime**.

To view the video tutorials, copy the videos from the **videos** folder on the **Flash HOT CD-ROM** onto your hard drive. Double-click the video you want to watch, and it will automatically open in QuickTime Player. Make sure the volume on your computer is turned up so you can hear the audio content.

Making Exercise Files Editable on Windows Computers

By default, when you copy files from a CD-ROM to a Windows computer, the files are set to read-only (write-protected), which will cause a problem with the exercise files because you will need to edit and save many of them. You can remove the read-only property by following these steps:

1 Open the **exercise_files** folder on the **Flash HOT CD-ROM**, and copy one of the subfolders, such as **chap_05**, to your **Desktop**.

2 Open the **chap_05** folder you copied to your **Desktop**, and choose **Edit > Select All**.

3 Right-click one of the selected files, and choose **Properties** in the contextual menu.

4 In the **Properties** dialog box, select the **General** tab. Deselect the **Read-Only** option to disable the read-only properties for the selected files in the **chap_05** folder.

Making File Extensions Visible on Windows Computers

By default, you cannot see file extensions, such as **.htm**, **.fla**, **.swf**, **.jpg**, **.gif**, or **.psd** on Windows computers. Fortunately, you can change this setting easily. Here's how:

1 On your **Desktop**, double-click the **My Computer** icon.

Note: If you (or someone else) changed the name, it will not say My Computer.

2 Choose **Tools > Folder Options** to open the **Folder Options** dialog box. Select the **View** tab.

3 Deselect the **Hide extensions for known file types** option to makes all file extensions visible.

Flash CS3 Professional System Requirements

Windows

- 800 MHz Intel Pentium III processor (or equivalent) and newer
- Windows 2000, Windows XP
- 256 MB RAM (1 GB recommended to run more than one Studio 8 product simultaneously)
- 1024 x 768, 16-bit display (32-bit recommended)
- 710 MB available disk space

Mac

- 600 MHz PowerPC G3 and newer
- Mac OS X 10.3, 10.4
- 256 MB RAM (1 GB recommended to run more than one CS3 product simultaneously)
- 1024 x 768, thousands of colors display (millions of colors recommended)
- 360 MB available disk space

Getting Demo Versions of the Software

If you want to try demo versions of the software used in this book, you can download demo versions from the following Web page:

www.adobe.com/downloads

1

Getting Started

Most likely, if you've purchased a copy of Adobe Flash CS3 Professional, you already know why you want to use the program. You may have experience building Web pages or using other graphics programs and want to increase your software skills for today's job market. However, you might not know the benefits of using Flash rather than HTML (**H**yper**T**ext **M**arkup **L**anguage) for authoring a Web site. This chapter outlines the different Flash products and file types and answers the question, "Why use Flash CS3?" It also summarizes the notable new features in Flash CS3, and it outlines some of the ways you can extend Flash CS3 content using other technologies such as CGI (**C**ommon **G**ateway **I**nterface), XML (e**X**tensible **M**arkup **L**anguage), and JavaScript.

Introducing Adobe Flash CS3 Professional

In the previous release of Flash, Macromedia offered two versions of the program, Basic and Professional. However, since acquiring Macromedia, Adobe has decided to develop the program into one distinct solution: Flash CS3 Professional.

Flash CS3 Professional was developed, like Macromedia Flash 8 Basic, so users can create, import, and manipulate many types of media, such as audio, video, and text. But it also integrates some of the complex features previously offered only in Macromedia Flash 8 Professional, built for advanced Web designers and application builders. You can use Flash CS3 to create everything from export-ready slideshows to large-scale, complex projects deployed using the Adobe Flash Player along with a hybrid of HTML content. Flash CS3 also includes a number of valuable enhancements, including superior integration with other Adobe applications such as Adobe Illustrator and Adobe Photoshop, rich drawing tools, and full support for ActionScript 3.0 development.

This chapter summarizes the new and enhanced features of Flash CS3 Professional.

Why Use Flash CS3?

Flash has several key benefits, including small file sizes, fast download speeds, precise visual control, advanced interactivity, the capability to combine bitmap and vector graphics and include video and animation, and scalable and streaming content.

File Size and Download Speed

If you want to design a Web site containing an abundance of visual content, download speed can be a major problem. As you probably know, nothing can be more frustrating than a slow-loading site. Even limited use of compressed bitmap graphic file formats (GIF and JPEG) can result in slow Web sites that frustrate visitors. Because of this, Web developers are often forced to use less visual but faster-downloading designs.

Flash content is often smaller than HTML content because it uses its own compression scheme, which optimizes vector and bitmap content differ-

ently than GIFs or JPEGs. For this reason, Flash has become the delivery medium of preference for graphic-intensive Web sites.

Visual Control

Another benefit of Flash is that it frees Web designers from many of the restraints of traditional HTML. Flash CS3 gives you complete and accurate control over position, color, fonts, and other aspects of the screen regardless of the delivery platform (Windows or Mac) or browser (Internet Explorer, Firefox, Netscape, Safari, and others). This is a radical and important departure from traditional HTML authoring, which requires precise planning to ensure that graphics and content appear reliably and consistently on different computer platforms and with various browsers. Flash CS3 lets designers focus on design instead of HTML workarounds.

Enhanced Interactivity

Although Flash is often known as an animation program, it also provides powerful interactivity tools so you can create buttons or free-form interfaces for site navigation that include sound and animation. Flash CS3 provides powerful scripting capabilities that make it possible to create complex presentations well beyond the capability of standard HTML or JavaScript. This book covers interactivity in a number of later chapters.

Combine Vectors and Bitmaps

Most graphics on the Internet are bitmap images, such as GIFs or JPEGs. The size of a bitmap file depends on the number of pixels it contains; as the image dimensions increase, so does the file size and download time. In addition to file size disadvantages, bitmap images that are enlarged beyond their original size often appear distorted, out of focus, and pixelated.

In contrast, graphics created within Flash are composed of vectors. **Vector images** use mathematical formulas to describe the images; **bitmap images** record information pixel by pixel and color by color. Vector graphics offer much smaller file sizes and increased flexibility for certain types of images, such as those with solid color fills and typographic content. Some images will have a smaller file size as bitmaps, and some will be smaller as vectors. The great aspect of Flash CS3 is that you can use either type of image.

A bitmap graphic, shown in the illustration on the left, is built pixel by pixel and color by color; a vector graphic, shown in the illustration on the right, is built from mathematical formulas. A vector graphic remains the same file size regardless of its physical dimensions, whereas a bitmap graphic increases and decreases depending on its size. As a result, you can use Flash CS3 to create and display large vector images and animations without increasing file size.

Video

Embedding video in SWF files is a huge plus for creating media-rich Web sites, and Adobe has enhanced the video capabilities even further in this release of Flash. Incorporating video increases the types of projects you can create using Flash CS3. You will get the chance to learn about the video features in Flash CS3 in Chapter 16, *"Video."*

Scalability

Because Flash movies can use vectors, they can be resized in any browser window and still retain their original scale and relative position. Most important, the file size of a vector graphic is independent of the display size, making it possible to create full-screen vector animations displaying at any resolution that are only a fraction of the file size of a comparable bitmap graphic.

You can set Flash CS3 content to scale dynamically within the browser window, as shown in the illustration on the next page.

Does all this mean you should use only vectors in your Flash CS3 movies? Absolutely not. Although Flash CS3 is known for its vector capabilities, its support of bitmap images is excellent and far exceeds the support offered by HTML. Specifically, if you scale a bitmap image larger than its original size in HTML, the graphic will become distorted and unattractive. Flash CS3 lets bitmaps scale, animate, and transform (skew, distort, and so on) without much image degradation, which means you can, and often will, combine bitmap and vector images in your movies. Delivering both

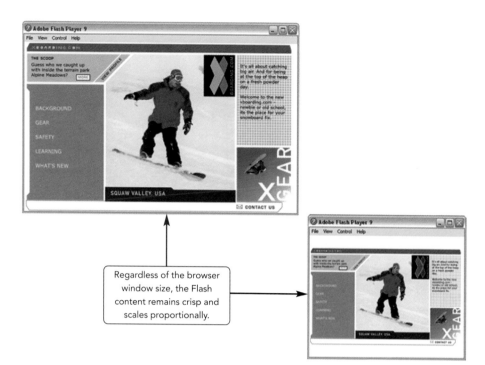

Regardless of the browser window size, the Flash content remains crisp and scales proportionally.

bitmap and vector graphics together lets you create movies that look good at different resolutions and still deliver a bandwidth-friendly file size. You can even use Flash CS3 to convert bitmap images into vectors, which you will learn to do in Chapter 9, *"Working with Bitmaps."*

Streaming Content

Vectors are not the only way Flash CS3 makes itself more bandwidth friendly. Flash CS3 files download to browsers in small units so that the files display some content while the rest is still downloading in the background. Ideally, the content will play more slowly than it downloads so that the viewing experience is not interrupted. This method of playing one part of an entire Web site while the rest is still downloading is called **streaming**. It differs significantly from the way HTML files are downloaded and displayed in a browser, which takes place one page at a time.

With HTML, all content is organized into **pages** (HTML files). When you load a page, all the parts

of its content are downloaded to the browser and then displayed. Flash CS3 movies, on the other hand, can be organized in a very different way.

Imagine a Web site with four or five pages. If it were a pure-HTML site, each time you traveled from one page to another you would have to wait for the new page to download before being displayed. With a site built in Flash CS3, however, all the "pages" could be contained in a single movie. When you visit the site, the first page would download and be displayed. While you were reading the first page, the other pages would be downloading in the background. When you clicked a link to go to another page, you would see it displayed immediately! This is the real beauty of streaming. When used correctly, it lets you build a site that eliminates a lot of unwanted waiting plaguing much of the Internet. You'll learn more about how to optimize your Flash CS3 content for streaming in Chapter 17, *"Publishing and Exporting."*

What's New in Flash CS3?

Flash CS3 offers many upgraded and new features providing a more efficient workflow, greater control over the look and feel of your finished projects, enhanced text support, scripting improvements, and improved video support. The following chart outlines the new features:

Flash CS3 New Features	
Feature	**Description**
New, improved interface	Flash CS3 is now consistent with the rest of the Adobe applications in the new CS3 suite, including Photoshop and Illustrator. Panels and docks are now fully collapsible, and you can save your workspace setup preferences. Save one workspace for animation and another for drawing. (See Chapter 2, "*Understanding the Interface.*")
Seamless integration with other Adobe applications	Photoshop and Illustrator files can now be imported intact with the advanced import wizard. With the wizard, you can individually convert layers to vectors, bitmaps, or editable text and import them as either Flash layers or individual keyframes.
Advanced drawing tools	Flash CS3 now includes a more advanced Pen tool, with the features previously found only in Illustrator and Adobe InDesign. You can copy and paste artwork directly from Illustrator and modify it using the same keyboard shortcuts. I discuss the drawing tools in detail in Chapter 3, "*Using the Drawing and Color Tools.*"
Adobe Device Central	With this new application in the CS3 suite, you can preview your projects on a variety of mobile devices, working with the actual device interfaces. This makes it easier than ever to customize your Flash projects for maximum cross-compatibility.
Scripting improvements	Flash CS3 now includes a new ActionScript debugger offering improved flexibility and feedback and is consistent with Adobe's Flex 2 debugger. You can also convert animations directly to ActionScript and copy and paste ActionScript animation properties from one object to another.
Improved QuickTime export	Now you can export Flash projects containing ActionScript, nested movie clips, and even effects such as drop shadows to the Apple QuickTime (.mov) format.
New video encoder	The new stand-alone video encoder application, Flash Video Encoder, significantly improves the video production workflow by providing an easy way to convert video files to the Flash Video (FLV) format. This encoder application can also batch process video files. (See Chapter 16, "*Video.*")

Flash, Flash Player, or Flash Lite?

Flash as a term can be confusing. Adobe uses the word to mean Flash as an authoring tool, Flash as a player, and Flash Lite (the player for mobile devices). The following chart should help you understand the differences among the authoring tool and the different players:

Adobe Flash Applications	
Application	**Description**
Flash	The Flash software application creates and edits artwork, animation, audio, and other interactive elements, storing the results in the Flash project file format (FLA). Any changes to the Flash movie must be edited in the production FLA file. FLA files are exported the SWF file format, which is typically embedded in an HTML document and published to the Web.
Flash Player	The Flash Player plays the published SWF files. The Flash Player plug-in for browsers must be installed in order for users to see Flash content on the Web. This plug-in comes preinstalled in most current browsers. If for some reason you do not have the current Flash Player, you can download it from the Adobe Web site for free.
Flash Lite	Flash Lite is a version of the Flash Player for use on mobile devices. The latest version (2.0) supports ActionScript 2.0.

File Types Associated with Flash CS3

You can save and output Flash CS3 media in many formats. The most common types of Flash CS3 files are project files, movie files, and published files. The file types can become very confusing, because all of them are commonly referred to as

movies. The following table explains the three most prominent Flash CS3 formats. You will learn about all the file types that Flash CS3 can produce in Chapter 17, *"Publishing and Exporting."*

Flash File Types	
File Type	**Description**
ActionScript file (.as) Script-1.as Flash ActionScript File 3 bytes	The file containing source code for a project file or movie. ActionScript can also reside directly within a SWF file, but on occasion it will be exported separately.
Project file (.fla) Untitled-1.fla Flash Document 32.0 KB	The master project file format, sometimes referred to as the *production file.* This stores all the settings and resources for your Flash CS3 project. You can reopen and reedit the FLA file at any time using the Flash CS3 authoring tool. (.fla stands for **FLA**sh.)
Video file (.flv) Untitled-1.flv Flash Video File 1.05 MB	The Flash video file format, which is usually embedded in a SWF file. Encoding video as an FLV file, using Flash's stand-alone Video Encoder or another program, results in better compatibility with your Flash project.
Movie file (.swf) Untitled-1.swf Flash Movie 36 bytes	The movie format, sometimes referred to as the *published file* or the *optimized file.* This can be embedded in Web pages for Web-based Flash presentations. These files are generally not editable in Flash. (.swf stands for **S**mall **W**eb **F**ile.)
Windows Projector file (.exe) and MacProjector file (.app) Untitled-1.exe Adobe Flash Player 9.0 r45 Adobe Systems, Inc.	A stand-alone projector file that can play on any computer without the need for the Flash Player. Flash CS3 writes both Windows and Mac format projector files.

Caution: Player Required!

Flash content is not visible in a browser unless either the Flash Player or the Shockwave Player has been installed in that browser. In the past, this has been seen as a serious limitation of the format, although over the past few years the number of Internet users who have the Flash Player has increased exponentially because current browsers now come with it preinstalled. The Shockwave Player is for viewing content created with Adobe Director, which has not reached quite the same level of popularity as Flash.

Adobe has hired an independent consulting firm to maintain an estimate of the number of the Flash Players in use. At the time of this writing, the Flash Player was installed on 98 percent of Internet-enabled desktops globally, and more 200 million Flash-enabled mobile devices are in existence. Flash Player 9 comes preinstalled on all new browsers shipped by AOL, CompuServe, Microsoft, and Netscape. Additionally, all versions of Microsoft Windows 98 and newer and Apple Mac OS 8 and newer include the plug-in.

The following chart describes the two players and where you can download them:

Adobe Players	
Player	**Description**
Flash Player	The Flash Player is used for viewing Flash content on the Web. You can download the latest version of the Flash Player at **www.adobe.com/downloads/**. This player installs in the player folder for your browser of choice.
Shockwave Player	The Shockwave Player is used for viewing Director content on the Web. You can download the latest version of the Shockwave Player at **www.adobe.com/downloads/**.

Beyond Flash CS3

Flash CS3 is an incredibly powerful tool by itself. However, it can't perform a few functions. Here are some of the Web technologies you should know about if you want to extend Flash CS3 beyond its basic capabilities.

What's Apollo?

Apollo is the code name for a new project under development by Adobe. It is a cross-operating system runtime, or a framework that works along with the operating system to support applications written specifically for the framework. C++ is an example of an existing popular runtime. For years, Web developers have been developing RIAs (**R**ich **I**nternet **A**pplications) for the Web. With Apollo, these developers can use the programming knowledge they already have (such as HTML, Flash, Ajax, and so on) to build and publish desktop applications. Unlike Web applications, Apollo applications will not have to run within a browser environment and can support traditional desktop application features, such as drag-and-drop interactivity, desktop shortcuts, Clipboard access, and integration with other desktop applications. It's an exciting prospect and one that Flash users are eagerly anticipating.

For further information about Apollo, please check out the following URLs:

http://labs.adobe.com/technologies/apollo/

www.codeapollo.com/

What's CGI?

A CGI script is a program that defines a standard way of exchanging information between a browser and a server. You can write CGI scripts in any number of languages (Perl, C, ASP, and others). If you plan to create a complex Web application that requires using something like CGI, it is recommended that you work with a Web engineer who has experience creating these kinds of scripts. Flash CS3 can communicate with CGI scripts, although that topic is beyond the scope of this book.

For further information about using CGI, please check out the following URLs:

www.cgidir.com/

www.cgi101.com/

www.icthus.net/CGI-City/

What's XML?

XML is a standard that handles the description and exchange of data. With XML, developers can define markup languages that in turn define the structure and meaning of information. Therefore, an XML document is much like a database presented in a text file. You can transform XML content into a variety of formats, including HTML, WML (**W**ireless **M**arkup **L**anguage), and VoiceXML.

XML differs from HTML in that it is not predefined—you create the tags and attributes. You can also use XML to create your own data structure and modify it for the data you want it to carry. In Flash CS3, you can use the XML object to create,

manipulate, and pass that data. Using ActionScript, a Flash CS3 movie can load and process XML data. As a result, an XML-savvy Flash CS3 developer can develop a movie that dynamically retrieves data from the external XML document instead of creating static text fields within a project file.

Just as HTML provides an open, platform-independent format for distributing Web documents, XML has become the open, platform-independent format for exchanging any type of electronic information. Like CGI, XML is also a topic beyond the scope of this book.

For further information about XML, take a look at the following URLs:

www.ait-usa.com/xmlintro/xmlproject/article.htm

www.xml.com/

www.xmlfiles.com/

JavaScript and Flash CS3

The Flash CS3 scripting language is ActionScript, which is based on JavaScript, another scripting language. Although they share a similar syntax and structure, ActionScript and JavaScript are two different languages. One way to tell them apart is that ActionScript uses scripts processed entirely within the Flash Player, independently of the browser used to view the file. JavaScript, on the other hand, uses external interpreters that vary according to the browser used.

You can use ActionScript and JavaScript together because Flash CS3 lets you call JavaScript commands to perform tasks or to send and receive data. A basic knowledge of JavaScript can make learning ActionScript easier, because the basic syntax of the scripts and how objects are handled are the same in both languages. However, JavaScript is not a requirement for learning ActionScript.

You will be introduced to ActionScript in Chapter 12, *"ActionScript Basics,"* which gives you hands-on experience in applying the powerful scripting language. For further information and tutorials about JavaScript and how to use it in conjunction with Flash CS3, check out the following URLs:

www.javascript.com/

http://javascript.internet.com/

www.flashkit.com/links/Javascripts/

That's a wrap for this chapter. You've familiarized yourself with the new features of Flash CS3 and how to extend Flash content using various technologies. Now it's time to learn more about the Flash interface. On to the next chapter!

2

Understanding the Interface

If you are new to Adobe Flash CS3 Professional, don't skip this chapter. Although you might be tempted to jump right in with the hands-on exercises, take the time to read this chapter first so you can get a "big picture" look at the Flash CS3 interface.

This chapter begins with an overview of the main interface elements: the **Timeline**, the **Stage**, the **Stage pasteboard**, and the various panels in Flash CS3. This will be a relatively short overview so you can get to the actual exercises as quickly as possible. After all, hands-on exercises are the best way to learn how these tools work.

If you are a veteran of Macromedia Flash 8, feel free to skim this chapter, but be sure to check out the new features in the **Actions** panel and the **Tools** panel.

Exploring the Welcome Screen

When you open Flash CS3 for the first time, you will see the **Welcome Screen**, which gives you a quick way to open a recent file, create a new file, or create a file from a template. To use the features of the **Welcome Screen**, click any of the text links, such as **Flash File (ActionScript 3.0)**.

Note: Your **Welcome Screen** will look a bit different from the one shown here, depending on which files you opened last.

If you prefer not to see the **Welcome Screen**, click the **Don't show again** check box on the bottom left of the **Welcome Screen**.

If you choose not to show the **Welcome Screen** but later want to see it, you can do so by choosing **Edit > Preferences** (Windows) or **Flash > Preferences** (Mac), then choosing **General** on the **Category** tab, and finally choosing **Welcome Screen** from the **On launch** pop-up menu.

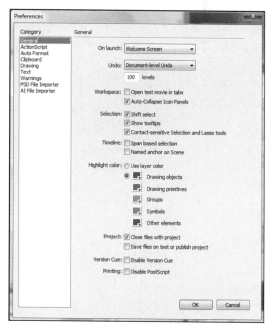

Interface Overview

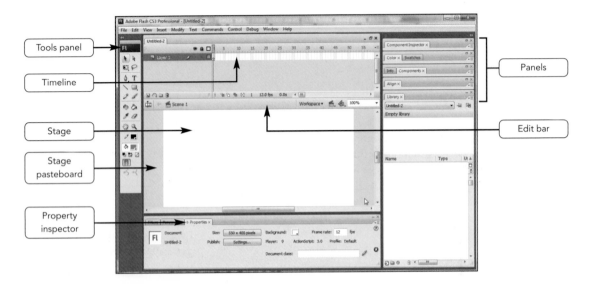

Tools panel

Timeline

Stage

Stage pasteboard

Property inspector

Panels

Edit bar

Each time you create a new document in Flash CS3, you are presented with a blank document window, which is divided into seven main components:

Timeline: The **Timeline** controls all the elements in a project file, including layers, frames, the playhead, and the status bar. You'll learn more about these features later in this chapter. By default, the **Timeline** is docked above the **Stage**, but you can undock and move the **Timeline** to any location onscreen. You'll learn how later in this chapter.

Stage: The **Stage** displays your animations, images, and other content. It is the area visible to users after you publish or export a finished project. You'll learn how to modify the properties of the **Stage**, such as size, color, and frame rate, in Chapter 4, "Animating in Flash," and how to export and publish projects in Chapter 17, "Publishing and Exporting."

Stage pasteboard: The **Stage pasteboard** is the light gray area around the **Stage**. The contents of the **Stage pasteboard** are not visible to users when you export or publish your projects. As a result, you can place objects here and animate them onto the **Stage** so they enter and exit from offstage. You can also store objects with no graphic

representation, such as data elements, on the **Stage pasteboard**, keeping the **Stage** uncluttered.

Edit bar: The **edit bar** displays your current location inside the project file, including the name of the current scene. It also provides controls for editing scenes and symbols and lets you change the magnification using the **Zoom** box. The **edit bar** changes location depending on whether the **Timeline** is docked or undocked. (You'll learn how to dock and undock the **Timeline** later in this chapter.)

Tools panel: The **Tools** panel contains tools for creating and editing artwork. This long vertical bar gives you access to just about every tool you need in order to create and modify objects.

Panels: Each panel has a unique set of tools or information for viewing or modifying specific file elements. For example, the fill and stroke colors in the **Color** panel will change based on the object selected on the **Stage**, letting you make changes to the current selection quickly, right in the panel. You'll learn more about panels later in this chapter.

Property inspector: The **Property inspector** is not just another panel in Flash. It opens at the bottom of the **Stage** in the default Flash CS3 workspace, and you'll find yourself accessing it more often than any other panel. You'll use the **Property inspector** for naming object instances, adding animations and sounds to the **Timeline**, and much, much more. To really understand its importance, you have to use it; therefore, you'll spend a lot of time working with the **Property inspector** throughout this book.

Exploring the Tools Panel

The **Tools** panel contains tools for creating and editing artwork. You will learn more about the various tools in the **Tools** panel in Chapter 3, *"Using the Drawing and Color Tools,"* and in various exercises throughout the book.

Each of the main tools has an associated keyboard shortcut. When you position the cursor over a tool icon, a small tool tip appears with the name and keyboard shortcut for the tool, which is listed in parentheses next to the tool name in the illustration. You can disable the tool tips feature in the **Preferences** dialog box by choosing **Edit > Preferences >** (Windows) or **Flash > Preferences >** (Mac).

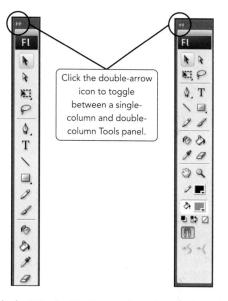

Click the double-arrow icon to toggle between a single-column and double-column Tools panel.

In Flash CS3, the **Tools** panel can be displayed in either a two-column view (traditional) or a one-column view. To toggle between views, click the double-arrow icon at the top left of the **Tools** panel.

TIP:

Using the Tools Panel Pop-Up Menus

When you see a small arrow on the lower-right corner of a tool in the Flash CS3 **Tools** panel, it indicates hidden tools in pop-up menus. To access the hidden tools, click the arrow and hold your mouse down until the pop-up menu appears, and then select a tool from the menu.

Working with the Panels

Panels are windows containing tools and information to help you work in your project file more efficiently. You can use each panel to view and modify elements within your project file. The options within the panels let you change settings, such as color, type, size, rotation, and many others. You can display, hide, move, resize, group, and organize the panels in any way you want. In the next few sections, you'll learn how to dock, resize, and work with panels.

Undocking and Docking Panels

In the default workspace, all the panels are docked, or fitted to, one side of the stage or another. However, by clicking and dragging panels away from the docks, you can create undocked or free-floating panels. You can dock and undock panels to create new combinations that better fit your workflow preferences.

To undock a panel or panel group, position your cursor over the panel title bar. Click and drag to undock the panel(s) to any location onscreen. (To undock a single panel in a group, position your cursor just over that panel's tab.) After you undock a panel, you can move it around the work area by clicking and dragging the panel's title bar.

To redock a panel or add it to another panel group, position your cursor over the panel's title bar. Click and drag the panel onto another panel until you see a dark outline over the panel. When you release the mouse, Flash CS3 adds the panel to the panel group.

Resizing Panels

You can resize panels by clicking and dragging the panel's border or by dragging the size box in the lower-right corner, as shown in the resizing illustration to the right.

Note: You cannot resize some of the panels, such as the **Property inspector** and the **Tools** panel. In the case of the **Property inspector**, the cursor will turn into the resize arrows when you move it over the border, but you cannot resize it as a floating panel. You can resize the **Property inspector** only

when it is docked below the **Stage**, in which case you have to resize both elements together.

Tip: If you have resized or moved your panels and want to return to the default workspace layout, simply choose **Window > Workspace > Default**.

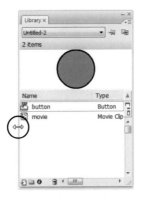 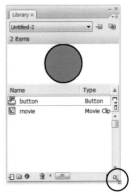

Resize from border   *Resize from corner handle*

Expanding, Collapsing, Hiding, and Closing Panels

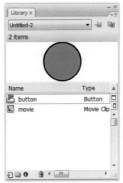

Panel expanded   *Panel collapsed*

To expand and collapse the contents of a panel, double-click the panel name.

To show or hide all the panels in your document, press **F4**; to close all the panels, choose **Window > Hide Panels**.

To close a panel, click the **X** by the panel name or in the upper-right corner of the panel.

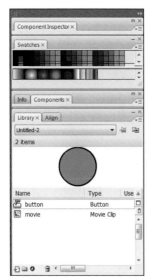

Click once here to expand or collapse the panel dock.

Panel dock expanded

Panel dock collapsed to icons

A new feature in Flash CS3 is the ability to collapse the entire dock by clicking the **Collapse to Icons** double-arrow icon above the dock. Once you are familiar with the different panels and their icons, you may want to use this feature to save screen real estate. You can display individual panels from the collapsed view by clicking the panel's icon once. You can reduce the dock even further by dragging the left border so that only the icon (not the panel name) appears in the dock.

Using the Panel Options Menu

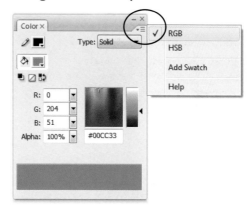

Many panels have an **Options** menu in the upper-right corner, as shown in the illustration above. To display the contents of the menu, simply click it.

Note: If a panel is collapsed, you can still open this menu.

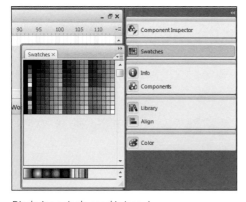

Displaying a single panel in Icon view

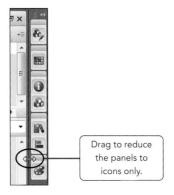

Drag to reduce the panels to icons only.

Icon view collapsed to just panel icons

Creating and Saving Workspace Layouts

With Flash CS3, you can create custom workspace layouts, which you can save and use at any time. This feature lets you quickly organize your workspace for specific tasks. For example, you can create different workspace layouts for drawing, animating, or working with ActionScript. The following steps walk you through the process of saving a custom workspace layout:

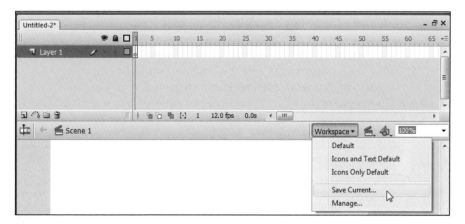

1 Click the **Workspace** button in the **edit bar**, and choose **Save Current** (this option is new in Flash CS3). Or, choose **Window > Workspace > Save Current** to open the **Save Workspace Layout** dialog box.

---

2 Type a name in the **Name** field, and click **OK**. That's all there is to it!

Switching Workspace Layouts

To switch between different workspace layouts, click the **Workspace** button in the **edit bar**, and choose a workspace layout; alternatively, choose **Window > Workspace**, and choose a workspace layout.

Note: To return the panels to their default locations, click the **Workspace** button in the **edit bar**, and choose **Default** (or choose **Window > Workspace > Default**).

Renaming and Deleting Workspace Layouts

You can rename or delete workspace layouts from the **Manage Workspace Layouts** dialog box:

1 Click the **Workspace** button in the **edit bar** and choose **Manage** (or choose **Window > Workspace > Manage**) to open the **Manage Workspace Layouts** dialog box.

---

2 To delete a workspace layout, select it, and then click **Delete.** Click **Yes** to accept the change, and then click **OK** to close the **Manage Workspace Layouts** dialog box.

---

3 To rename a workspace layout, select it, and then click **Rename**. This opens the **Rename Workspace Layout** dialog box. Type a new name in the **Name** field, and click **OK** to close the dialog box. Click **OK** again to close the **Manage Workspace Layouts** dialog box.

Creating a New Custom Keyboard Shortcut Set

If you're a keyboard shortcut junkie, you'll want to learn the shortcuts to using the tools in the various panels. For a listing of the keyboard shortcuts for each of the tools in the **Tools** panel, refer to Chapter 3, *"Using the Drawing and Color Tools."* To further streamline your workflow, you can create, modify, duplicate, and delete sets of custom keyboard shortcuts. Flash CS3 has an entire interface dedicated to making this process easier. One of its niftiest features lets you assign keyboard shortcuts in Flash CS3 that match those used in other programs, including Adobe Fireworks, Adobe Freehand, Adobe Photoshop, and even earlier versions of Flash! You may be thinking, "Hey, this is only for power users," but you'll be a power user in no time, right? This exercise outlines the process of creating, modifying, and deleting custom keyboard shortcuts. This isn't an exercise you have to complete now; if you'd like, just make a mental note of it for later use.

---

1 Choose **Edit > Keyboard Shortcuts** (Windows) or **Flash > Keyboard Shortcuts** (Mac) to open the **Keyboard Shortcuts** dialog box.

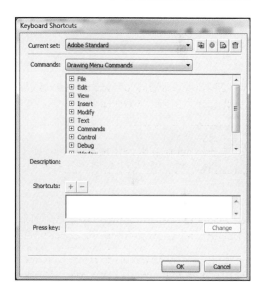

---

2 In the upper-right corner of the dialog box, click the **Duplicate Set** button to open the **Duplicate** dialog box. From here, you can create a copy of the current keyboard shortcut set, ensuring you don't make permanent changes to the original keyboard shortcut set.

---

3 Type a name for new the keyboard shortcut set in the **Duplicate name** field. Try to stick to a meaningful name you can recall later. Click **OK**.

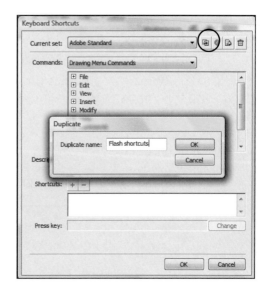

4 Back in the **Keyboard Shortcuts** dialog box, choose an option (such as **Drawing Menu Commands**) from the **Commands** pop-up menu. A view of the first-level commands will appear. Click the **plus sign** (Windows) or the **arrow** (Mac) next to a command to drill down and display additional commands. Click to select the command for which you want to change the keyboard shortcut.

5 Click the **+** (**Add Shortcut**) or **–** (**Remove Shortcut**) button to add or delete the currently selected keyboard shortcut.

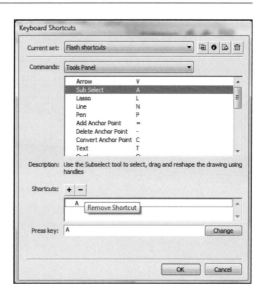

6 Press the keys you want to use as the keyboard shortcut to assign the shortcut to the option. Notice the shortcut key appears in the **Press key** text box. Click **Change** to confirm your selection and assign it to the menu item. Click **OK** to close the **Keyboard Shortcuts** menu.

Note: If the key combination you selected is already in use, you will get an error message at the bottom of the dialog box. You must select another key combination or find and replace the key combination that's in use for the other command before reassigning it.

Well, that's a quick run-through of the Flash CS3 interface. Now that you are more familiar with the "big picture," let's narrow the focus to specific interface elements. In the next chapter, you'll work with the drawing and coloring tools in the Tools panel. Flash CS3 has a powerful set of graphics tools for creating any kind of artwork and animation imaginable. So go ahead—turn to the next page to get started.

3

Using the Drawing and Color Tools

Adobe Flash CS3 Professional has a powerful set of drawing and color tools to help you create artwork for your animations. In addition to creating drawings from scratch, you can import existing artwork into Flash CS3 from other programs such as Adobe Fireworks, Adobe Photoshop, or Adobe Illustrator. You'll learn how in Chapter 19, *"Integration."*

In this chapter, you'll learn how to create drawings from scratch in Flash CS3 using the drawing and color tools. You'll also learn how to apply complex gradients to objects, and you'll learn about the Object Drawing model, which makes it easier to work with and modify shapes.

Drawing Tools Defined

Flash CS3 contains a set of powerful drawing tools. Although many of the tools may be familiar to you from other programs, you'll find some of them are quite unique. The following chart outlines the behavior of each drawing tool, including the associated keyboard shortcuts. Don't feel compelled to read through everything here. If you want to jump into the exercises, go right ahead. Either way, you'll be comfortable drawing in Flash CS3 in a very short time!

	Drawing Tools in Flash CS3	
Icon	Name	What Does It Do?
	Selection (V)	Selects, moves, and edits shapes and drawings.
	Subselection (A)	Modifies the anchor points and tangent handles of a shape's path or outline.
	Free Transform (Q)	Freely transforms objects, groups, instances, or text blocks. With this tool, you can move, rotate, scale, skew, and distort individual transformations or combine several transformations all at once.
	Gradient Transform (F)	Modifies the gradient fills of shapes and is stored in the pop-up menu with the **Free Transform** tool. With the **Gradient Transform** tool, you can adjust the size, direction, or center of the fill; precisely control the location of the gradient focal point; and apply other parameters to your gradients.
	Lasso (L)	Creates irregular-shaped selections of your artwork by drawing a freehand selection around it. Use the **Lasso** options to fine-tune and adjust your selections.
	Pen (P)	Creates straight or curved line segments and is the only drawing tool in Flash CS3 that lets you create Bézier curves, which gives you precise control of your line segments.
	Text (T)	Creates static text or text fields. With text fields, you can accept user input and even display HTML (**H**yper**T**ext **M**arkup **L**anguage)–formatted text that has been loaded from an external text file into a movie.
	Line (N)	Draws straight lines. Holding down the **Shift** key lets you constrain the lines to 45-degree angles. You can modify the lines drawn with this tool by using the **Ink Bottle** tool or by using the controls in the **Property inspector**.

continues on next page

Drawing Tools in Flash CS3 *continued*

Icon	Name	What Does It Do?
	Oval (O)	Creates circles and ovals composed of fills and strokes, just fills, or just strokes. Holding down the **Shift** key lets you create perfect circles. Holding down the **Alt** key (Windows) or the **Opt** key (Mac) lets you draw a circle or oval from the center.
	Rectangle (R)	Creates rectangles and squares composed of strokes and fills, just strokes, or just fills. Holding down the **Shift** key creates perfect squares. Holding down the **Alt** key (Windows) or the **Opt** key (Mac) draws a rectangle or square from the center.
	Pencil (Y)	Creates lines in one of three modes: Straighten, Smooth, or Ink.
	Brush (B)	Creates shapes with fills only. You can adjust the size, style, and behavior of the brush by adjusting the tool options or by using the **Property inspector**.
	Ink Bottle (S)	Changes the color or width of a line or adds a stroke to a shape. The **Ink Bottle** tool has no effect on the fill of a shape.
	Paint Bucket (K)	Adds a fill inside a shape and can change the color of a fill. The **Paint Bucket** tool has no effect on the stroke of a shape.
	Eyedropper (I)	Copies the fill or stroke attributes of an object so you can apply them to another object. This tool is especially useful when you want to copy the color of one object and use it on another object.
	Eraser (E)	Removes any unwanted image areas on the **Stage**. Holding down the **Shift** key lets you erase in perfect horizontal and vertical lines.

Lines, Strokes, and Fills Defined

In addition to learning how each of the drawing tools behave, you need to understand the difference between fills, strokes, lines, and shapes. These differences can be confusing because the interface refers to both lines and strokes. The following chart provides an example and a brief explanation of each:

	Lines, Strokes, and Fills	
Element	**Example**	**Description**
Lines and strokes		Create line drawings with the **Pencil**, **Pen**, and **Line** tools. Create strokes or outlines with the **Rectangle** and **Oval** tools. The terms *stroke* and *fill* are used interchangeably in the Flash CS3 documentation and throughout this book because you can modify both shapes and strokes using the same tools. Lines and strokes are independent of fills, and you can modify them using the **Ink Bottle** tool, the **Color** and **Tool** modifiers in the **Tools** panel, the **Color** panel, or the **Stroke Color** in the **Property inspector**.
Fills		Create fills with the **Brush** and **Paint Bucket** tools. You can create fills without strokes, as shown in the illustration here. You can modify fills using the **Paint Bucket** tool, the **Color** and **Tool** modifiers in the **Tools** panel, the **Color** panel, or the **Property inspector**.
Strokes, lines, fills, and shapes	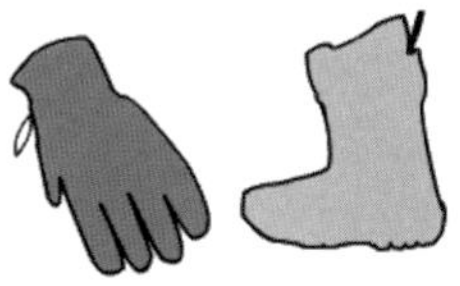	Attach strokes and lines to fills, as shown in the illustration here, with the **Ink Bottle** tool. Modify them using the **Ink Bottle** tool, the **Color** and **Tool** modifiers in the **Tools** panel, the **Color** panel, or the **Property inspector**. Flash CS3 refers to strokes, lines, and fills, or a combination thereof, as *shapes*. Shapes appear as a dotted mesh on the **Stage** and display the word *shape* in the **Property inspector**.

1 | Drawing with the Pencil Tool

The **Pencil** tool creates freehand line drawings. By selecting one of the three modes—Straighten, Smooth, or Ink—you can control how the lines are drawn. In this exercise, you will draw a circle with the **Pencil** tool using each of the three modes so you can better understand how each one behaves.

---

1 Copy the **chap_03** folder from the **Flash HOT CD-ROM** to your desktop. Open **pencil.fla** from the **chap_03** folder.

As you can see, pencil.fla is a blank file with the Stage dimensions set to 400 x 200 pixels, which should be enough space for you to draw some shapes.

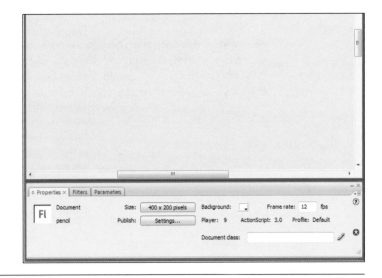

2 Select the **Pencil** tool in the **Tools** panel, and choose **Straighten** from the **Pencil Mode** pop-up menu.

As you can see, the Pencil Mode pop-up menu is located in the Options section of the Tools panel. The Options section is context-sensitive based on the tool selected in the Tools panel.

NOTE:

About the Pencil Tool Modes

In Flash CS3, the **Pencil** tool is similar to tools in other graphics programs, such as Illustrator and Photoshop. One of the great features of the **Pencil** tool in Flash CS3 is the different drawing modes—Straighten, Smooth, and Ink—which give you more precise control over your drawings.

Straighten:
Perfect look

Smooth:
Smooth look

Ink:
Hand-drawn look

As shown in the illustration here, drawing with the Straighten mode creates perfect, geometric shapes; drawing with the Smooth mode smoothes the edges of shapes; and drawing with the Ink mode represents the line exactly as you draw it, giving it the most hand-drawn appearance of the three modes.

The circles as you draw in Straighten mode

The circle when you finish drawing in Straighten mode

3 Click and drag to draw a circle on the **Stage**.

Notice when you release the mouse, the shape automatically snaps to a perfect circle. The Straighten mode guesses what shape you are trying to draw and automatically creates a perfect geometric shape.

4 In the **Tools** panel, choose **Smooth** from the **Pencil Mode** pop-up menu.

The circle as you draw in Smooth mode

The circle when you finish drawing in Smooth mode

5 Click and drag to draw another circle on the **Stage**.

Notice when your release the mouse, the circle gets smoother, but the change is less significant than when you used Straighten mode.

The circle as you draw in Ink mode

The circle when you release the mouse

6 In the **Tools** panel, choose **Ink** from the **Pencil Mode** pop-up menu. Click and drag to draw a third circle on the **Stage**.

Notice when using the Ink mode there is very little change in the circle when you release the mouse.

---

7 Tired of drawing circles? Go ahead and practice drawing other simple shapes, such as squares, triangles, polygons, and so on, with each of the **Pencil Mode** options. You'll get an even better idea of how each drawing mode works and how each one can help you create artwork in Flash CS3.

Tip: To clear the Stage, press Ctrl+A (Windows) or Cmd+A (Mac) to select everything on the Stage, and then press the Delete key.

---

8 When you are done experimenting with the **Pencil** tool, close **pencil.fla**. You don't need to save your changes.

---

2 | Using the Oval and Rectangle Tools

The **Oval** and **Rectangle** tools are ideal for creating geometric shapes, such as ovals, circles, rectangles, and squares. You can create simple shapes with independent lines and fills quickly and effortlessly. In this exercise, you'll learn how to use these tools.

---

1 Open **shapes.fla** from the **chap_03** folder.

The shapes.fla file is a blank file you can use to draw shapes.

---

2 Select the **Oval** tool from the **Rectangle** tool pop-up menu in the **Tools** panel. At the bottom of the **Tools** panel are two options: **Object Drawing**, which lets you choose which drawing model to use (you will learn about drawing models later in this chapter), and **Snap to Objects**, which makes it easier to align objects on the **Stage**. Click the **Snap to Objects** button.

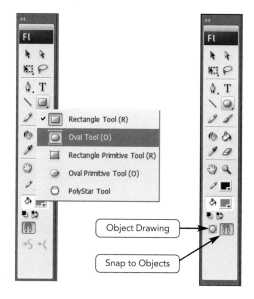

Notice how the Property inspector has updated to show options for drawing an oval. New in Flash CS3, you can control the inner and outer radii of ovals you create with the Oval tool. You must set these options *before* you draw an oval, unless you use the Oval Primitive tool. (You'll learn about the Oval Primitive tool in Step 5.)

In this exercise, you'll learn how to create shapes using the Merge Drawing model (the default drawing model) and the Snap to Objects feature. Later in this chapter, you'll create shapes using the Object Drawing model.

---

3 Hold down the **Shift** key, and click and drag to draw a circle on the **Stage**.

Holding down the Shift key while drawing creates a perfect circle. Notice Flash CS3 automatically uses the current fill and stroke colors to create the circle.

---

4 Click and drag to create an oval on the **Stage**.

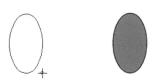

When you don't hold down the Shift key while drawing, Flash CS3 doesn't constrain the shape as a perfect circle. Also, the drawing cursor is different from how it appeared in Step 3. The cursor change is a visual clue you are drawing an oval or a circle.

5 Select the **Oval Primitive** tool from the **Oval** tool pop-up menu in the **Tools** panel.

The Oval Primitive tool differs from the Oval tool in that it allows you to modify an oval's radii before *or* after the oval is created.

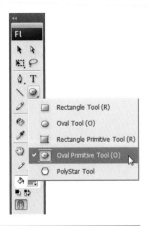

6 In the **Property inspector**, set the **End Angle** property to **60**.

Adjusting the Start Angle or End Angle setting will give you a pie shape. Adjusting the Inner Radius setting will result in a doughnut shape.

7 Click and drag to create a pie shape on the **Stage**.

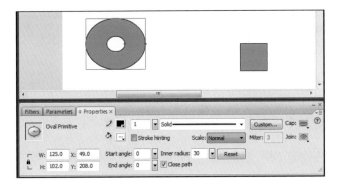

8 Click anywhere on the **Stage** to deselect the pie shape. In the **Property inspector**, change **End Angle** to **0**, change **Inner Radius** to **30**, and click and drag to create a doughnut shape on the **Stage**.

Notice the circular handles on the shape you just created. You can also click and drag these handles with the Selection tool to adjust the radii of your shape.

9 Select the **Rectangle** tool in the **Tools** panel. In the **Options** area of the **Tools** panel, leave the **Snap to Objects** button turned on and the **Object Drawing** button turned off.

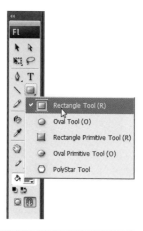

10 Hold down the **Shift** key, and click and drag to create a square on the **Stage**.

Notice the cursor indicates you are drawing a "perfect shape," the same as it did when you created a circle in Step 3. Again, just as when you created the circle and oval, Flash CS3 uses the selected fill and line colors.

Take a look at the corners of the square you just drew. Notice they are square, 90-degree corners. What if you want to create rounded corners? Not to worry, you can easily create rounded corners using the Set Corner Radius feature. You'll learn how in the next steps.

11 At the bottom of the **Property inspector**, set the upper-left **Rectangle Corner Radius** field to **25**. This option will add rounded corners with a 25-point radius to the next rectangle you draw. You can enter a value from -100 to 100. The higher the number, the more rounded the corners.

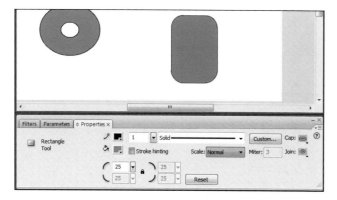

12 Click and drag to draw another rectangle on the **Stage**.

Notice the corners of the rectangle are rounded, reflecting the value you entered in the Property inspector. Nice!

13 Select the **Rectangle Primitive** tool in the **Rectangle** tool pop-up menu in the **Tools** panel.

With the Rectangle Primitive tool, you can modify the corner radii of your rectangles before *and* after you create them! You can even set a different radius for each corner!

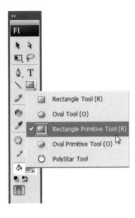

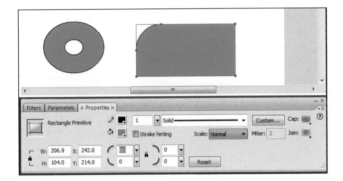

14 Click and drag on the **Stage** to create a rectangle primitive, and then modify the corner radius in the **Property inspector**.

Tip: To set a different radius for each corner, click the lock icon. This will unlock the other three radii fields. Also note that in Flash CS3, you can set a negative corner radius.

TIP:

Rounding Corners As You Draw

You may find it difficult to decide on the exact radius of a corner before you draw a rectangle, and unfortunately, you can't use the **Set Corner Radius** option after you draw a rectangle. Luckily, a handy keyboard shortcut helps you interactively create rounded corners as you draw rectangles in Flash CS3. As you click and drag to draw a rectangle, press the **down arrow** key to increase the corner radius, or press the **up arrow** key to increase the corner radius. This is a very cool little shortcut you'll use often!

Oval and Rectangle Settings

If you want to create a specific-sized oval or rectangle, you may find it difficult to do so with the **Oval** tool or **Rectangle** tool. Fortunately, you can also specify the width and height of ovals and rectangles, as well as the corner radii of rectangles, by using the controls in the **Oval Settings** and **Rectangle Settings** dialog boxes.

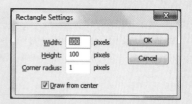

With either the **Oval** tool or the **Rectangle** tool selected in the **Tools** panel, **Alt-click** (Windows) or **Opt-click** (Mac) an empty area on the **Stage** where you want to create the oval or rectangle. In the **Oval Settings** or **Rectangle Settings** dialog box, specify your settings, and click **OK**. Flash CS3 automatically draws an appropriate-sized oval or rectangle where you clicked.

15 Save your **shapes.fla** file by choosing **File > Save**. Close the file.

3 | Using the Brush Tool

You can use the **Brush** tool to paint shapes with solid colors, gradients, and even bitmap fills. In this exercise, you'll learn how to use the **Brush** tool to create and modify shapes.

---

1 Open **paint.fla** from the **chap_03** folder.

The paint.fla file is a blank file you can use to draw shapes.

---

2 Select the **Brush** tool in the **Tools** panel.

Notice the Brush tool has several options—Object Drawing, Lock Fill, Brush Mode, Brush Size, and Brush Shape. You'll learn about these options in this exercise.

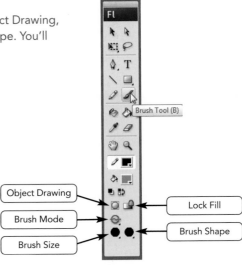

---

3 Draw a circle on the **Stage**.

Notice Flash CS3 uses the fill color for this shape, not the stroke color. The Brush tool creates shapes that are fills and, therefore, uses only the fill color.

---

4 At the bottom of the **Tools** panel, click to expand the contents of the **Brush Size** pop-up menu. Select the fourth size from the top.

As you can see from the preview, this is a smaller brush tip than the default brush tip you worked with in Step 3. You'll see how it works in the next step.

5 Draw a smaller circle inside the large one on the **Stage**.

Notice the smaller brush size creates a narrower fill shape than the shape you drew in Step 3.

6 At the bottom of the **Tools** panel, click to expand the contents of the **Brush Shape** pop-up menu. Select the fifth shape from the bottom.

As you can see from the preview, this tip has a different shape than the default, round brush you've been using. You'll see how it works in the next step.

7 Draw another circle on the **Stage**.

Notice the different result between this brush shape and the one you used in Steps 3 and 5. You can produce some very nice calligraphy effects with this brush shape because it changes thickness depending on the direction of your brush stroke—just like working with a calligraphy pen or a flat paintbrush.

Working with a Wacom Tablet

Flash CS3 offers support for most pressure-sensitive graphics tablets, including Wacom tablets. Using a tablet can help you create natural-looking shapes with a hand-drawn look. As you increase pressure on the tablet, the width of the shape will increase, whereas less pressure will create a thinner shape. For more information, refer to the Wacom Web site at **www.wacom.com**.

8 Experiment with the other brush shapes and sizes so you are more comfortable with the **Brush** tool. If you have a graphics tablet, try the pressure sensitivity with the **Brush** tool.

Note: The Brush tool sizes are relative to the magnification of your Stage. To experiment, zoom in to 400 percent and draw a line; then zoom out to 100 percent and draw another line without modifying the size of your brush.

Adding Strokes to Brush Shapes

Because the **Brush** tool creates shapes that are fills, you can use the **Ink Bottle** tool to easily add a stroke to the shapes you create. You'll learn how to use the **Ink Bottle** tool in Exercise 4.

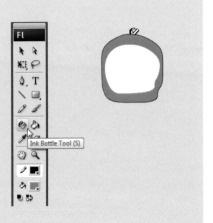

9 When you are done experimenting with the **Brush** tool, close **paint.fla**. You don't need to save your changes.

painting.mov

In the previous exercise, you learned how to create and edit brush strokes. You can use a number of other useful features with the **Brush** tool, such as **Paint Fills**, **Paint Selections**, **Paint Behind**, and **Paint Inside**. To learn more about these features, check out **painting.mov** in the **videos** folder on the **Flash HOT CD-ROM**.

4 | Modifying Lines and Shapes

In the previous three exercises, you learned how to draw lines and create shapes with the **Brush**, **Oval**, and **Rectangle** tools. You'll learn how to modify these shapes in this exercise and the next one. In this exercise, you'll learn how to use the **Property inspector** and **Ink Bottle** to modify the appearance of existing lines. In addition, you will learn some of the nuances involved in selecting lines and when to use the **Ink Bottle** tool versus the **Property inspector**.

---

1 Open **strokes.fla** from the **chap_03** folder.

This file contains shapes created with lines and fills, which you'll use to modify lines and add strokes to shapes.

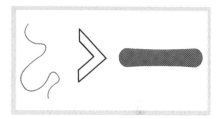

---

2 Select the **Selection** tool in the **Tools** panel, and click the squiggle drawing to select it.

Notice when you select the line, it gets a bit thicker, and a dotted mesh appears over it, indicating the line is selected.

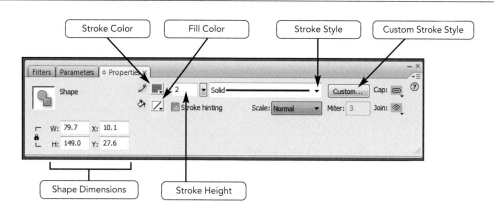

3 Make sure the **Property inspector** is visible. If it's not, choose **Window > Properties > Properties**.

Note: You must select a line before you can modify its stroke settings using the Property inspector.

The Property Inspector

When you're working in Flash CS3, you'll constantly use the **Property inspector** because it conveniently displays, and lets you change, the settings associated with the currently selected object on the **Stage**, including text, symbols, video, frames, and even tools, all in one easy-to-use interface.

4 With the line still selected, choose the dotted line from the **Stroke Style** pop-up menu (the fourth style from the top). Click a blank area on the **Stage** to deselect the line so you can clearly see the change you just made.

Use the Property inspector as a quick, easy way to modify selected artwork. When you have a line selected, the Property inspector displays the current settings for that line. This is helpful when you need to know what the line settings are for a particular object. The default stroke settings are a 1-point, solid black line.

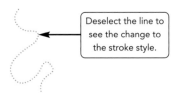

Deselect the line to see the change to the stroke style.

Hiding Selections

When lines are selected, it can be hard to see the changes you've made. To temporarily hide the dotted mesh so you can better see the changes, press **Ctrl+H** (Windows) or **Shift+Cmd+E** (Mac) to hide and show the selection.

5 With the line still selected on the **Stage**, click the **arrow** icon next to **Stroke Height** in the **Property inspector** to reveal the **Stroke Height** slider. Drag the slider to a setting of **4** to increase the thickness of the line. (You can choose a line thickness from **0.25** to **10**.) Deselect the line by clicking a blank area on the **Stage** to see the changes.

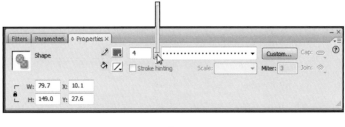

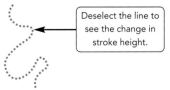

Deselect the line to see the change in stroke height.

6 Click to select the line on the **Stage**. In the **Property inspector**, click the **Stroke Color** box, and choose another color. As you can probably guess, changing the stroke color changes the color of the line. Deselect the line by clicking a blank area on the **Stage** to clearly see the changes.

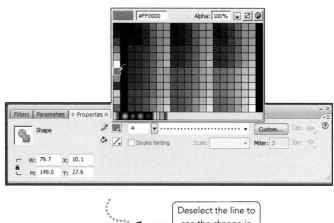

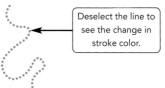

You've now learned how to select and modify the style, height, and color of an entire stroke. Next you'll learn how to modify these properties for just a line segment.

Deselect the line to see the change in stroke color.

TIP:

Creating Custom Line Styles

You can create your own custom line styles in the **Stroke Style** dialog box. With the line selected on the **Stage**, click the **Custom** button in the **Property inspector**. When the **Stroke Style** dialog box opens, you can create your own line style using the different options. The changes you make to the settings here are temporary. They will return to their default settings once you close Flash CS3.

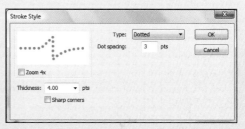

---

7 With the **Selection** tool, position your cursor over the bottom line of the arrow.

As you position the cursor over the line, notice the cursor changes to an arrow with a short, curved line, indicating you're over a line segment.

---

8 Click the lower-right line segment.

Notice a dotted mesh appears over the line segment you selected.

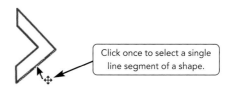

Click once to select a single line segment of a shape.

9 In the **Property inspector**, use the **Stroke Height** slider to change the line width to **5**.

Notice only the selected line segment changed. To modify a line segment, you must select it before you change the settings in the Property inspector. In this case, you selected only one of the six line segments of the arrow shape.

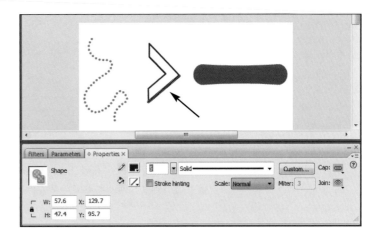

TIP:

Selecting Line Segments

Unlike other drawing programs, Flash CS3 breaks lines with hard angles into separate line segments. For example, clicking the bottom line of the arrow shape selects only the bottom portion of the shape because the shape has six hard angles, creating six separate lines. If you want to select the entire shape, *double-click* only one of the line segments.

---

10 With the line segment still selected, type **2.75** in the **Stroke Height** field in the **Property inspector**.

If you know the exact value you want to use, you can change the width of a line by typing a specific numeric value in the field next to the Stroke Height slider.

---

11 Click anywhere on the **Stage** to deselect the line segment. Double-click any part of the arrow to select all six line segments.

This shortcut is essential when you need to select entire shapes composed of multisegmented lines.

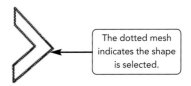

The dotted mesh indicates the shape is selected.

---

12 Practice changing the style, width, and color of the selected lines using the controls in the **Property inspector**. Choose any setting you like—the point here is to become more comfortable with selecting lines and line segments and changing their properties with the **Property inspector**.

Now you know how to modify an existing line using the Property inspector, but what do you do when your object doesn't have a line or a stroke? You add one using the Ink Bottle tool. You'll learn how in the following steps.

13 Select the **Ink Bottle** tool in the **Tools** panel.

The Ink Bottle tool lets you add a stroke around an object with no stroke or make changes to the color, width, and texture of existing lines. With the Ink Bottle tool, you can set the stroke color using the Property inspector or the Stroke Color options in the Tools panel. Since you have used the Property inspector quite a bit in this exercise, next you'll get a chance to use the color settings in the Tools panel.

N O T E : 	**Property Inspector or Tools Panel?** In Flash CS3, you can often access and work with the same tools in several different ways. In most situations, you'll find the **Property inspector** will streamline your work-flow, because it gives you quick access to the properties of the currently selected object or tool in one convenient panel. In contrast to the **Property inspector**, which is useful for modifying the properties of existing shapes, you can use the **Tools** panel to set object properties before creating new shapes.

14 In the **Tools** panel, click the **Stroke Color** box, and choose a light gray in the color palette.

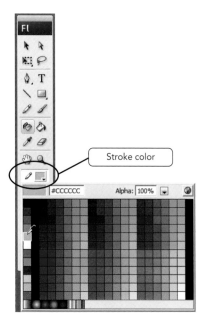

Stroke color

15 Click the outer edge of the snowboard shape to add a stroke to the outside of the shape.

The Ink Bottle Tool

The **Ink Bottle** tool serves many purposes. You can add a stroke to an object, as you did in the previous step, or you can modify the color, size, and style of the stroke for several objects at once. To modify more than one object, hold down the **Shift** key to multiple-select the objects on the **Stage**. You'll find multiple-selecting objects saves you a lot of time when you have several objects to add or modify.

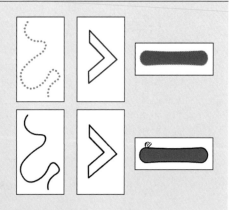

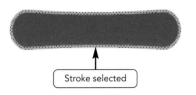

Stroke selected

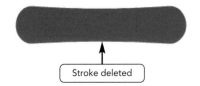

Stroke deleted

16 Select the **Selection** tool in the **Tools** panel, and double-click to select the stroke around the snowboard shape. The dotted mesh appears, confirming you have selected the stroke. Press the **Delete** key to remove the stroke.

Now you know how to add and remove strokes—it's that easy!

Complex Artwork

Complex objects containing numerous lines and shapes add to the file size of your final movie, so if your design allows, use complex artwork sparingly.

17 Close **strokes.fla**. You don't need to save your changes.

5 | Modifying Strokes and Fills

You can change the stroke and fill of a shape in several ways. You can specify the stroke and fill colors before you create the shape; you can use the **Paint Bucket** tool to modify fill colors and the **Ink Bottle** tool to modify strokes; or you can use the **Color** panel to create solid, gradient, and bitmap strokes and fills, which you can apply to the shapes you create. In this exercise, you'll learn how to use the **Paint Bucket** tool and the **Color** panel to modify strokes and fills of a shape.

---

1 Open **modifyFills.fla** from the **chap_03** folder.

As you can see, this file contains one layer with a vector graphic of a snowboard.

---

2 Select the **Selection** tool in the **Tools** panel. Click to select the blue background of the snowboard.

When a shape is selected, a dotted mesh appears over the shape. Make sure *only* the background is selected.

---

3 Choose Window > Color to open the Color panel.

NOTE:

What Is the Color Panel?

The **Color** panel gives you precise control over color, all in one panel. The next exercise will show you how to use the **Color** panel to create gradient fills.

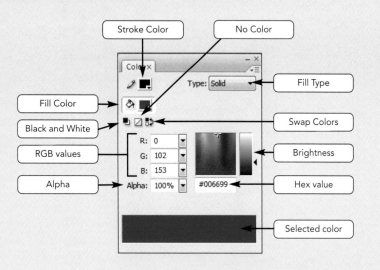

4 In the **Color** panel, click the **Fill Color** box, and select a shade of red in the palette.

Notice the background color of the snowboard changes to red. Unfortunately, the insides of the letters are still blue. Not to worry, you'll fix this in the next step.

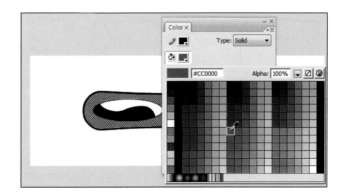

NOTE:

Why Didn't Everything Turn the Color You Selected?

Flash CS3 treats shapes that are one continuous color as a single shape. Each time a new color appears, it is a new shape, which means you must modify it individually. In the previous step, the middle parts of the letters were treated as separate shapes because they were surrounded by white. Next, you will learn how to quickly fill these remaining blue shapes with the **Paint Bucket** tool.

5 Select the **Paint Bucket** tool in the **Tools** panel, and click each of the blue shapes inside the letters to change the color to match the currently selected color (the red background color you selected in Step 4).

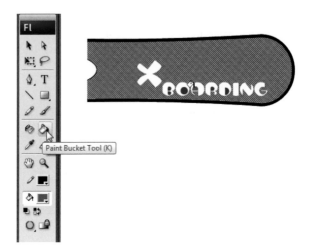

Unlike the Color panel method, you don't need to select the artwork before you color it with the Paint Bucket tool. If you are having trouble clicking the small blue regions inside the type, you may want to magnify the contents on the Stage using the Zoom tool. You can also use shortcut keys to zoom in and out by pressing Ctrl+ and Ctrl– (Windows) or Cmd+ and Cmd– (Mac).

Tip: As a safeguard, you can always press Ctrl+Z (Windows) or Cmd+Z (Mac) to undo any mistakes you make.

TIP:

Applying Fills

Using the **Fill Color** box in the **Color** panel or using the **Paint Bucket** tool in the **Tools** panel are two ways to change the solid fill color of an object. Both methods yield the same results, but using the **Property inspector** can help speed up your workflow, since you can change and access many features using only one panel. You will use this third method of changing fill colors shortly, but note that you *must* have the object selected first if you want to change the fill color using the **Property inspector**.

6 Select the **Selection** tool in the **Tools** panel. Click the letter *B* on the snowboard to select it. You'll know it's selected when you see the dotted mesh.

You could select and change the color of each letter individually, but that would be a time-consuming process. Instead, you'll use the Shift key to multiple-select all the letters in the word *BOARDING* so you can fill all the letters at the same time.

---

7 Hold down the **Shift** key, and click each of the remaining letters in the word *BOARDING* to multiple-select all the letters. If you make a mistake and want to start over, press the **Esc** key to clear all selections, or click a blank area on the **Stage** to deselect.

---

8 Make sure the **Property inspector** is visible. If it's not, choose **Window > Properties > Properties**. In the **Property inspector**, click the **Fill Color** box, and select black in the **Fill Color** palette.

Notice all the letters changed to the new color you selected! Now that you've mastered changing fills, it's time to learn how to modify strokes. You'll learn how in the next few steps.

---

9 With the **Selection** tool still selected in the **Tools** panel, double-click the snowboard to select it.

Double-clicking will select the entire object, including both strokes—the one around the snowboard and also the one around the yin and yang design.

Tip: To select a single stroke, double-click the stroke.

---

10 In the **Property inspector**, click the **Stroke Color** box, and select a shade of yellow in the **Stroke Color** palette. Choose a different stroke style from the **Stroke Style** pop-up menu. When you're finished, click a blank area on the **Stage** to deselect your artwork so you can see your changes clearly.

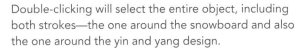

11 Double-click the stroke of the yin and yang design on the snowboard to select it. In the **Property inspector**, select a new **Stroke Color** and **Stroke Height** for the outline. When you're finished, click a blank area on the **Stage** to deselect your artwork so you can see your changes clearly.

---

12 Close **modifyFills.fla**. You don't need to save your changes.

Understanding the Flash Drawing Models

Now that you've mastered how to use the drawing tools in Flash CS3, it's time to learn about the two drawing models in Flash CS3: the Merge Drawing model and the Object Drawing model. The drawing models define how multiple shapes interact with each other, particularly when you create overlapping shapes.

The Merge Drawing model, which has been the default drawing model in previous versions of Flash, automatically merges overlapping shapes. As a result, if you create overlapping shapes and then move the shapes away from the each other, you end up with broken or merged shapes. For

many users, the Merge Drawing model was difficult to understand because it was so different from models in other drawing programs.

Fortunately, Flash CS3 has another drawing model—the Object Drawing model—that provides more control and flexibility when creating multiple or overlapping objects. The Object Drawing model behaves the way models in other drawing programs behave. Before you get started with the hands-on exercises, take some time to review the following chart, which will help you understand the differences and benefits of each of the two drawing models:

Flash Drawing Models Defined

Merge Drawing Model	Object Drawing Model	Description
Selecting Objects		
  Selection displayed as dotted mesh	 Selection displayed as bounding rectangle	When selecting a shape created with the Merge Drawing model, the selection appears as a dotted mesh. When you select a shape created using the Object Drawing model, Flash CS3 surrounds the shape with a rectangular bounding box.
Overlapping Objects		
  Shapes on the same layer interact with each other.	 Shapes on the same layer do not interact with each other.	The Merge Drawing model automatically merges shapes when they overlap. The Object Drawing model creates separate objects you can manipulate individually and that do not automatically merge when overlapped.
Stroke and Fill		
  Stroke and fill independent	 Stroke and fill integrated	Merge shapes contain separate strokes and fills, which you can manipulate independently. Object shapes contain integrated strokes and fills. To manipulate them, double-click the shape to enter Object Drawing mode.

EXERCISE 6

Using the Merge and Object Drawing Models

In this exercise, you will create shapes with each drawing model using the **Oval** tool to learn the differences, benefits, and nuances of working with each.

1 Open a new file in Flash CS3 by choosing **File > New > Flash File (ActionScript 3.0)**. Choose a light gray color in the **Fill Color** palette and black in the **Stoke Color** palette in the **Tools** panel. Make sure **Object Drawing** is deselected. Draw two circles or ovals on the **Stage**.

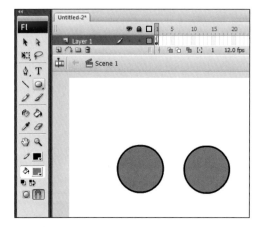

2 Select the **Selection** tool in the **Tools** panel. Double-click one of the oval shapes on the **Stage** to select it. Drag to reposition the oval so it overlaps the other oval.

The dotted mesh indicates the selected merge object.

The Merge Drawing model is the default drawing model. When selected, the merge object displays a dotted mesh.

3 Deselect the oval by clicking the **Stage** anywhere. Double-click the oval to select it again, and click and drag it away from the circle.

Notice the selected oval left a hole in the other oval where the two shapes overlapped. When you overlap objects using the Merge Drawing model, they automatically merge to create a single shape. When you move the shapes apart, the shapes do not return to their original, unmerged states. If you want to keep the objects as separate, unmerged objects when overlapped, you must use the other drawing model in Flash CS3—the Object Drawing model. You will do this next.

4 Deselect the oval by clicking anywhere on the **Stage**. Choose a green color in the **Fill Color** palette. Select the **Oval** tool in the **Tools** panel. At the bottom of the **Tools** panel, click the **Object Drawing** button to switch from the default Merge Drawing model to the Object Drawing model.

---

5 Drag with the **Oval** tool to create a third oval, adjacent to the first two, on the **Stage**.

You've just created an object shape. Object shapes behave a bit differently than the merge shapes you have worked with up to this point.

---

6 Select the **Selection** tool in the **Tools** panel. Click the green oval to select it. Move it so it overlaps one of the gray merge object ovals.

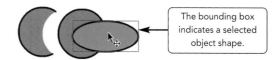

The bounding box indicates a selected object shape.

Notice the green oval shape, which was created using the Object Drawing model, is surrounded by a rectangular bounding box, rather than the dotted mesh you saw for the gray merge object ovals.

---

7 Click and drag the green oval away from the gray oval. Deselect the green oval by clicking anywhere on the **Stage**.

Unlike in Step 3, the objects did not merge where they overlapped. When you create shapes with the Object Drawing model, they behave independently from other shapes.

---

8 Double-click the green oval.

The other gray ovals on the Stage dim, and you cannot select them! Notice the edit bar indicates you are no longer on Scene 1 but are on something called a *drawing object*.

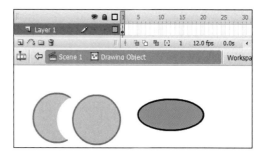

9 Click the green oval, and move it around the **Stage**.

Stroke

A dotted mesh replaces the bounding rectangle, and the stroke is left behind. The shape no longer looks or behaves as an object shape but as a merge shape! When you double-click an object shape, you automatically exit the Object Drawing model and enter the Merge Drawing model. As a result, object shapes are automatically converted to merge shapes, which in some circumstances are easier to use. However, this isn't a permanent change—you can return merge shapes to object shapes easily. You'll learn how in the next step.

---

10 In the **edit bar**, click the **Scene 1** button to return to the Object Drawing model. The shape no longer behaves as a merge shape but as an object shape. See for yourself by manipulating the graphics on the **Stage** again.

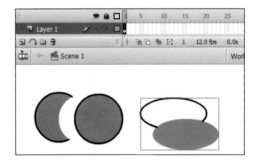

You now have a good overview of the differences between the two drawing models in Flash CS3. If you're new to Flash, you may think the Object Drawing model is the best way to create your Flash artwork, because it behaves like the models in most other graphics programs and because usually you won't want objects merging with each other. However, you can achieve some interesting effects using the Merge Drawing model, which you'll learn about in the following tip.

---

11 Close your Flash file. You don't need to save your changes.

Creating Negative Space with Merge Objects

You can use the unique behavior of merge objects, described in the previous exercise, to create some interesting artwork, such as artwork that takes advantage of "negative" space. For example, if you place a different-colored merge object shape over the glove shape, deselect it, reselect it, and then move it away, it will cut an X shape in the fill of the glove, as illustrated here. This is a quick and easy way to add an interesting logo to the snowboarding glove!

Note: If the X shape were exactly the same color as the glove, it would not have cut through the glove and made an X shape. Instead, it would have just combined with the glove into one shape.

Other than starting out with Object Drawing model shapes, you can overlap shapes in additional ways without having them cut into or combine them with one another. You can convert the shapes to symbols, which you will learn more about in Chapter 6, "Creating Symbols and Instances." You can also select multiple shapes and group them (Modify > Group), which you will learn about in the next exercise. Grouping shapes also makes it easier to work with shapes you want to keep together or modify in the same way.

7 | Grouping Objects

Now that you have a good idea of how the drawing features behave in Flash CS3, this exercise shows you how to group objects so you can modify and work with them all together.

1 Open **multiple.fla** from the **chap_03** folder.

This file contains some simple shapes created with the merge object model that you will combine into a group.

2 Double-click the blue glove object to select both its shape and fill. Notice that it displays a dotted mesh. **Shift+double-click** the boot to select its stroke and fill as well. Choose **Modify > Group**. A thin blue line appears around both shapes, indicating they are part of the same (grouped) object. You can also group an object by using the keyboard shortcuts, **Ctrl+G** (Windows) or **Cmd+G** (Mac).

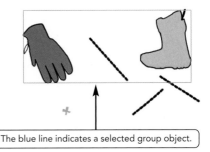

The blue line indicates a selected group object.

3 Select the **Selection** tool in the **Tools** panel. Drag the group over one of the other merge objects on the **Stage**.

The two shapes move as one grouped object on the Stage.

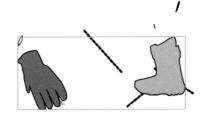

4 Deselect the group by clicking any blank area on the **Stage**. Click the group again, and move it off the objects. Notice that the grouped objects do not interact with the other Merge Drawing objects on the **Stage**.

As you can see, grouping objects, even single objects, is a quick way of protecting them from being affected by or affecting other objects. In addition to being able to move grouped objects together, you can also modify them as a single object, which you'll learn how to do next.

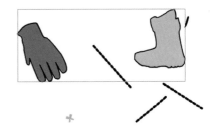

5 Select the **Free Transform** tool in the **Tools** panel, and click the group to select it. Position the cursor over the lower-right corner of the selection bounding box until the cursor changes to a double-headed arrow. Drag toward the lower right to scale both objects in the group.

You can also rotate, skew, flip, and make other modifications to all the members of a selected group. Next, you will learn how to modify single elements of a group, independent of the other members of the group.

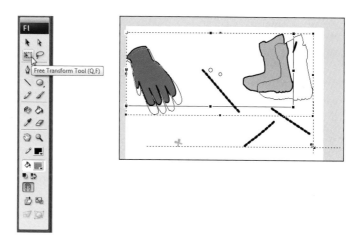

6 Double-click the blue glove with the **Selection** tool. Flash exits **Scene 1** and enters the Timeline for the group. Deselect both objects by clicking any blank area on the **Stage**. Select just the glove so only it is highlighted with a dotted mesh (which indicates you can now edit the object independent of the other objects in the group). Select a different color in the **Fill Color** palette. Notice only the glove changes color.

The edit bar shows you are in the Group Timeline.

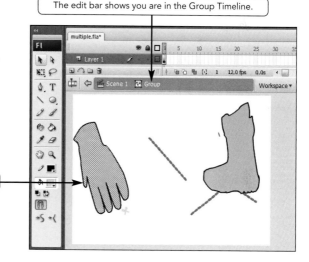

The dotted mesh indicates a selected shape.

7 Click the **Scene 1** link above the **Timeline** to exit from the group Timeline and return to **Scene 1**. The group should still be selected. Choose **Modify > Ungroup** to return each object to its original ungrouped status.

The ease with which you can group and ungroup combinations of shapes (object shapes as well as merge shapes) and the power and flexibility provided by this grouping capability make this an important workflow-enhancing skill.

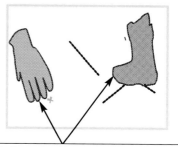

The dotted mesh indicates the objects are no longer grouped.

8 Save your **multiple.fla** file by choosing **File > Save**. Close the file.

8 | Creating Gradients

Gradients help you create cool, interesting effects. Flash CS3 lets you create two types of gradient fills: linear and radial. In this exercise, you'll learn how to use the **Color** panel and **Swatches** panel to create, apply, and change the shape and color of linear and radial gradients. Flash CS3 has really beefed up its gradient capabilities since version 8, both in the **Color** panel and in the **Gradient Transform** tool.

---

1 Open **newGradient.fla** from the **chap_03** folder.

This file contains one layer with two snowboards. You will be applying gradients to both of these shapes in this exercise.

---

2 Select the **Selection** tool in the **Tools** panel. Click the blue fill on the snowboard on the left to select it.

---

3 Make sure the **Color** panel is open. If it is not, choose **Window > Color**. Choose **Radial** from the **Type** pop-up menu.

As you can see, the selected shape is now filled with a radial gradient, using black and white, which are the default colors. A radial gradient radiates outward from the center. In this case, black is in the center, and the gradient radiates to white.

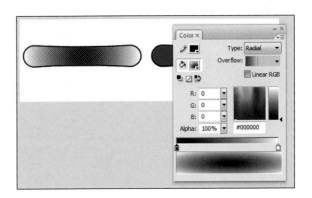

---

4 Double-click the black color pointer in the **Color** panel. This opens a color palette that lets you define the fill color for the selected color pointer.

Tip: It may take several tries to get the color palette to appear. Double-click the black color pointer carefully!

Fill color

Pointer

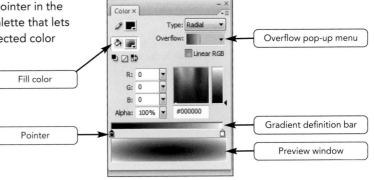

Overflow pop-up menu

Gradient definition bar

Preview window

---

5 Select a shade of red in the color palette.

As you can see, the appearance of the radial gradient changes to range from red to white instead of ranging from black to white. You have just created your first custom gradient! Next you will use the Gradient Transform tool to edit the appearance of the gradient.

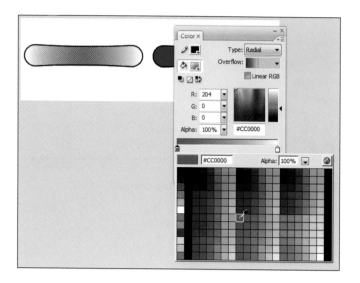

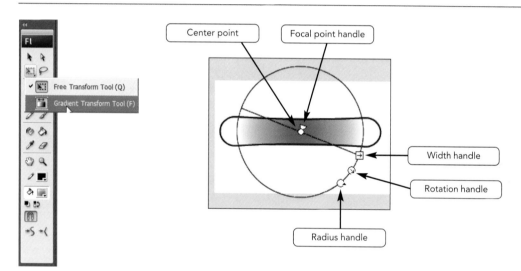

6 Select the **Gradient Transform** tool from the **Free Transform** pop-up menu in the **Tools** panel. Use the various edit handles to change the center point, width, radius, rotation, and focal point of the gradient fill. Experiment with each of the edit handles to get the hang of how each controls the appearance of the gradient fill.

Next you will make a linear gradient.

7 Select the **Selection** tool in the **Tools** panel. Click the blue fill on the snowboard on the right side on the **Stage** to select it.

8 In the **Color** panel, choose **Linear** from the **Type** pop-up menu.

As you can see, this option creates a linear gradient using the same colors you used for the previous gradient.

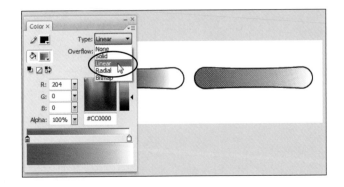

9 Make sure the **Swatches** panel is visible. If it's not, choose **Window > Swatches**. Choose **Add Swatch** from the **Color Options** menu to save the currently selected gradient in the **Color Swatches** panel so you can access it easily.

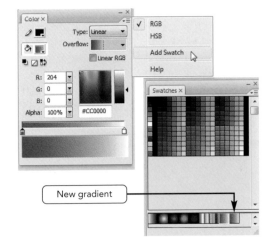

New gradient

10 Select the **Gradient Transform** tool in the **Tools** panel. Modify the width, rotation, and center point handles to become familiar with how they modify the appearance of the linear gradient fill.

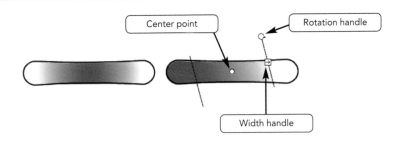

Center point

Rotation handle

Width handle

11 When you're finished, close **newGradient.fla**. You don't need to save your changes.

NOTE:

New Gradient Features in Flash CS3

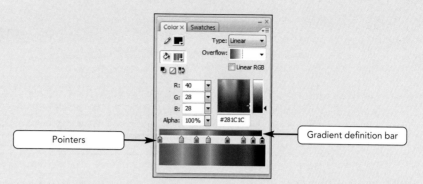

Pointers

Gradient definition bar

In addition to new features in the **Gradient Transform** tool, Flash CS3 now supports the use of gradients containing up to 15 colors, which lets you create much more complicated and colorful gradients. Create additional colors in your gradients by clicking below the **Gradient Definition** bar in the **Color** panel. A new color, represented by the color pointer, will appear after each click.

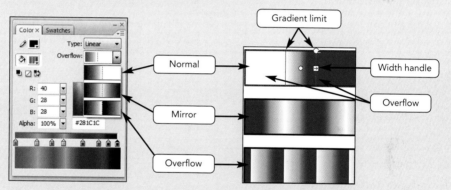

Gradient limit

Normal

Width handle

Overflow

Mirror

Overflow

Flash CS3 provides three new options for controlling how gradient overflow, the colors that extend beyond the limits of the gradient, should be handled. The options are **Normal** (Windows) or **Extend** (Mac), which is the default; **Mirror** (Windows) or **Reflect** (Mac); and **Repeat**. You can generate an overflow in your gradients by selecting them with the **Gradient Transform** tool and decreasing their widths by dragging the width handles.

9 | Drawing with the Pen Tool

The **Pen** tool creates more complex shapes by combining both straight and curved lines in the same shape. Shapes created with the **Pen** tool consist of paths, anchor points, and tangent handles, which you can modify with the **Subselection** tool. (You'll learn more about the **Subselection** tool in Exercise 10.)

If you've used other vector-based drawing programs, such as FreeHand or Illustrator, you'll be instantly comfortable with the **Pen** tool in Flash CS3 because it works the same way. If you haven't used the **Pen** tool before, it can take some practice before you become really comfortable with it.

In this exercise, you will start by learning how to use the **Pen** tool to draw a few basic geometric shapes. By the end of this exercise, you will be more comfortable working with the **Pen** tool to create more complex shapes of your own.

---

1 Open **pen.fla** from the **chap_03** folder.

As you can see, this file has two layers: the shapes layer contains a series of outlines you'll use as a guide for drawing shapes in this exercise, and the draw here layer is an empty layer you'll use to draw shapes with the Pen tool. The shapes layer is locked so you can't edit the artwork, but have fun drawing on the draw here layer.

Note: Since you will be using the Pen tool in this exercise, it will be easier to see the results if you use the default settings for this tool. If you just completed the previous exercises in this chapter, use the Property inspector to set the stroke settings to their default values (black, solid, 1 point).

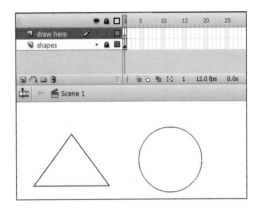

---

2 Click the **draw here** layer on the **Timeline** to select it. You'll know it's selected when you see a pencil icon next to the layer name.

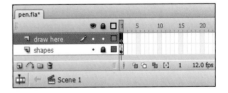

---

3 Select the **Pen** tool in the **Tools** panel.

---

4 Move your cursor to the lower-left corner of the triangle outline, and click.

A small circle appears. This is the first anchor point, indicating the beginning of your line. Line segments are created between pairs of anchor points to create shapes.

---

5 Click the top corner of the triangle to add the second anchor point.

The line segment appears as a red line with two square anchor points on either end on top of the line segment, which is the stroke color in the Property inspector and in the Tools panel you set in Step 1. The red line indicates the line segment is selected.

---

6 Click the lower-right corner of the triangle to create a second line segment between the upper-right and lower-right anchor points.

---

7 Position the cursor over the lower-left corner of the triangle where you created the first anchor point in Step 4. A small circle appears beside the cursor, indicating the path will be closed if you click. Click to close the path and create the shape.

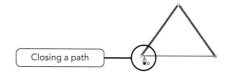

Note: In Flash CS3, when you close a path, the shape will not automatically fill with the currently selected fill color in the Property inspector or in the Tools panel. You must apply fill colors separately.

Next, you'll learn to draw a circle with the Pen tool, which can be a bit more complicated than drawing a triangle and may take some time to master. Don't worry if you have to do this exercise a few times before you get the hang of things.

Pen Preferences

When you are working with the **Pen** tool, you can change a number of preferences to make using it a bit easier. Choose **Edit > Preferences** (Windows) or **Flash > Preferences** (Mac) to open the **Preferences** dialog box. Select the **Drawing** category to see the **Pen** preferences. You may find these three helpful:

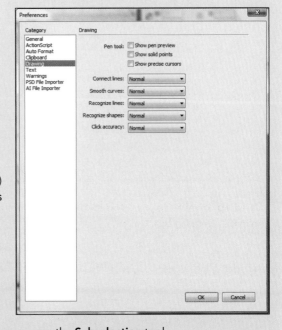

Show pen preview (off by default) lets you preview the line segments as you draw with the **Pen** tool. A stretchy line will appear as a preview of the line segment you will create when you click.

Show solid points (off by default) displays selected anchor points as solid points and unselected anchor points as hollow points when you use the **Subselection** tool.

Show precise cursors (off by default) causes the **Pen** cursor to appear as a crosshair. This can be helpful for precise drawing and works great with the grid feature.

8 Using the **Pen** tool, click at the top center of the circle outline to create the first anchor point.

9 Click the middle-right edge of the circle and drag down to add another anchor point. As you drag, you will see two tangent handles appear. Move the mouse around, and watch how the angle of the line changes as you do this. Don't release the mouse just yet.

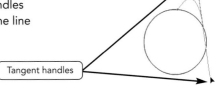

Tangent handles

10 Drag down toward the lower right until the line segment seems to match the outline of the circle. Now release the mouse. The circle you draw doesn't have to be perfect here; just try to get comfortable working with the **Pen** tool.

11 Click the middle-bottom edge of the circle to add another anchor point. The line will curve when you add the third anchor point to complete half of the circle shape.

12 Drag up on the middle-left edge of the circle to add another anchor point. As you drag, you will see two tangent handles appear. Don't release the mouse just yet.

13 Drag up toward the top left until the line segment seems to match the outline of the circle. Release the mouse.

14 Move the cursor to the first anchor point you created at the top of the circle. When you see the small circle appear next to the **Pen** tool pointer, click to close the path, and drag the handles until the line matches the outline of the circle.

15 Select the **Paint Bucket** tool, and fill the circle with the currently selected fill color.

16 Save your changes, and keep **pen.fla** open for the next exercise. Don't worry if the circle you created isn't perfect.

Next you'll learn how to modify lines using the shapes you just made.

10 | Modifying Paths

In the previous exercise, you learned how to create shapes using the **Pen** tool. Next, you'll learn how to reshape them using the **Selection** and **Subselection** tools to modify paths using their anchor points or tangent handles.

---

1 If you just completed Exercise 9, **pen.fla** should still be open. If it's not, complete Exercise 9, and then return to this exercise.

---

2 Select the **Paint Bucket** tool in the **Tools** panel. Click inside the triangle to fill it with the currently selected fill color.

---

3 Choose the **Selection** tool. Position the cursor over the left side of the triangle.

Notice the cursor changes to a small curved line. This line indicates you are over a line segment.

---

4 Drag the line segment to the left. The shape will start to distort and stretch as you continue to drag. When you release the mouse, notice both the line and the fill have changed their shapes.

The Selection tool offers a free-form way of transforming shapes. Although it can be fun to use, it lacks the precision you sometimes need when creating complex shapes. When you need pinpoint precision, use the Subselection tool. The Subselection tool lets you manipulate the anchor points and tangent handles of paths after you have added them.

TIP:

What Do the Icons Associated with the Subselection Tool Mean?

The **Subselection** tool edits paths and anchor points created with the **Pen** tool. As you learn to edit paths, anchor points, and tangent handles with the **Subselection** tool, you will notice that the cursor often changes as you work with it. The following chart outlines the cursors associated with the **Subselection** tool:

▶	
▶	Selects a path
▶	Selects an anchor point
▶	Modifies the tangent handle(s)

5 Select the **Subselection** tool in the **Tools** panel.

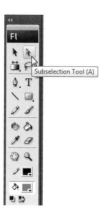

6 Position the cursor over the edge of the circle shape. A small black square appears, indicating you are over a line.

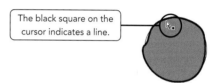

The black square on the cursor indicates a line.

7 Click the edge of the circle to select it. Notice the anchor points are now visible. The anchor points are represented by small red squares along the line of the circle.

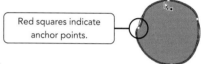

Red squares indicate anchor points.

Note: Flash CS3 adds anchor points, if necessary, to create curves, which is why you might see more than four anchor points on your artwork.

8 Position the cursor over the middle-right anchor point. A small white square appears next to the cursor when you are directly over the anchor point.

9 Click to select the middle-right anchor point. When you do, the tangent handles for that anchor point appear.

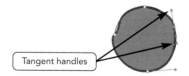

Tangent handles

10 Click and drag the top tangent handle of the middle-right anchor point to the right. When you release the mouse, you'll notice the top and bottom portions of the curve change together. This is the normal behavior of tangent handles.

11 Click to select the middle-left anchor point.

12 Hold down the **Alt** key (Windows) or the **Opt** key (Mac), and click and drag the top tangent handle of the middle-left anchor point to the left. When you release the mouse, you'll notice only the top portion changes.

As you can see, holding down the Alt key (Windows) or the Opt key (Mac) lets you modify one part of a curve without affecting the other.

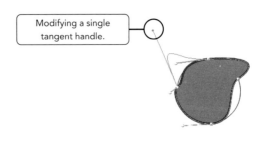

Modifying a single tangent handle.

13 Click the anchor point on the middle right of the circle, and drag down to try to match the circle image in the background. You can click and drag an anchor point to make the circle more perfect in shape.

Now you know how to use the Selection and Subselection tools to modify the lines you create in Flash CS3. With the Selection tool, you can reshape straight or curved lines by dragging the lines themselves. The Subselection tool lets you reshape by clicking and moving the anchor points and tangent handles. Next you will learn how to add, remove, and convert anchor points.

14 Select the **Subselection** tool in the **Tools** panel. Position the tool over the rounded side of the triangle shape. Click to select the path.

In addition to drawing shapes, the Pen tool can add anchor points to a line.

TIP:

What Do the Icons Associated with the Pen Tool Mean?

As you create paths, anchor points, and tangent handles with the **Pen** tool, the cursor will change. The following chart outlines each of the cursor icons associated with the **Pen** tool:

 Draws straight and curved paths to create objects

 Adds anchor points to paths

 Deletes anchor points from paths

 Closes a path

 Converts a corner point to a curve point, and vice versa

15 Select the **Pen** tool in the **Tools** panel. Notice that when you move the **Pen** tool directly over the selected path, a small plus sign appears next to the cursor. Click to add a new anchor point.

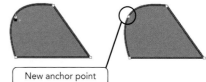

New anchor point

Note: You can also add an anchor point by selecting the Add Anchor Point tool from the Pen tool pop-up menu in the Tools panel.

Converting curves to straight lines is a rather simple process and one you should know how to do. You'll learn how in the following steps.

---

16 Position the cursor over the newly added anchor point, and notice that a small caret (^) symbol appears, indicating you will convert the curve point to a corner point if you click.

Note: You can also convert an anchor point by selecting the Convert Anchor Point tool from the Pen pop-up menu in the Tools panel.

---

17 Double-click the anchor point to convert the anchor point to a corner point, transforming the curve into a straight-edged shape. Because you converted the anchor point to a corner point, you'll no longer have access to any tangent handles.

Converting a corner point to a curve point is even easier to do—you'll do that next.

---

18 Select the **Subselection** tool in the **Tools** panel. Click the anchor point to select it. Hold down the **Alt** key (Windows) or the **Opt** key (Mac), and click and drag up the anchor point you just modified. When you do this, you will convert the corner point to an anchor point.

Note: Make sure the anchor point is still selected before you drag it. Selected anchor points are filled.

---

19 With the anchor point still selected, press **Delete** to remove the anchor point.

---

20 Close **pen.fla**. You don't need to save your changes.

By now, you should feel pretty comfortable working with the drawing and color tools in Flash CS3. If you aren't quite there yet, feel free to practice and play some more with the different tools and color settings. You might try drawing some artwork for a project you want to create in Flash CS3. Nothing will ever replace good old-fashioned practice.

4

Animating in Flash

Flash has a reputation as a powerful and robust animation tool. If you know other animation tools, such as Adobe After Effects or Adobe Director, you might be looking for similarities. It's actually easier to learn the animation capabilities of Adobe Flash CS3 Professional if you don't know other animation programs, because you'll have no preconceived notions of how you think it might work.

This chapter introduces you to the **Timeline**, which plays a significant role in producing animations. The **Timeline** lets you work with keyframes, blank keyframes, frame-by-frame animation, and onion skinning. If these are new terms to you, they won't be for long. This chapter also covers setting the frame rate (and how it affects playback speeds). By the end of this chapter, things should really get moving for you, all puns intended!

Understanding the Timeline

Understanding and working with the **Timeline** is essential to creating animations in Flash CS3. The illustration shown here identifies the elements of the **Timeline** you'll be working with in this chapter.

The following chart describes the **Timeline** features:

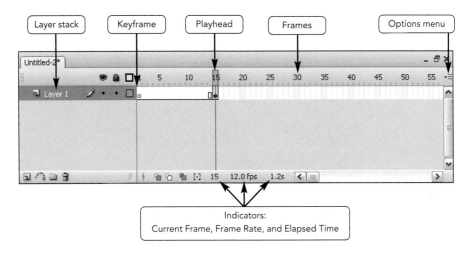

The following chart describes the **Timeline** features:

Timeline Features	
Feature	**Description**
Frame	Represents a unit of time in an animation. Just like film, Flash CS3 divides lengths of time into frames. Frames with no content are represented by white squares. Frames with content are shaded. Frames carry the content of the previous keyframe. The frame rate determines how much time each frame takes up. For example, if your movie's frame rate is 12 fps (**f**rame **p**er **s**econd), one frame will take up 1/12 of 1 second. If an object is on the **Stage** for 24 frames, it will appear visible for 2 seconds in the movie. You'll learn more about frame rates later in this chapter.
Keyframe	Defines a moment on the **Timeline** when content is inserted or actions or animation changes occur. A keyframe with content is represented by a solid dot; a blank keyframe is represented by an empty dot. See the **Working with Frames and Keyframes** chart following Exercise 1 for more information on keyframes.
Playhead	Indicates the currently selected keyframe. Drag (or **scrub**) the playhead, which is the red rectangle with the long red line, back and forth on the **Timeline** to quickly preview your animation.

continues on next page

Timeline Features *continued*

Feature	Description
Options menu	Gives you several options for changing the size and therefore the number of frames visible at one time on the **Timeline**. The default view, Normal, displays the frames at an appropriate size for most projects. However, when you start creating longer animations, you will need to set the Frame view to **Small** or **Tiny** so you can see more frames at one time. You can also use the **Placement** options to dictate whether the **Timeline** appears above, below, left, or right of the document.
Layer stack	Organizes the elements of an animation and controls the order in which they stack on top of each other. In Flash, you can animate layers independently. Each layer has options for hiding or showing the layer, locking it, and displaying its contents as outlines. Immediately below the layer stack are buttons to insert a new layer, add a layer folder, and delete a layer. You'll learn more about layers in Chapter 5, *"Shape Tweening."*
Current Frame	Displays the current position of the playhead and the frame number of the currently selected frame.
Frame Rate	Displays the number of frames per second at which the movie attempts to play on the user's browser or computer. Double-clicking the frame rate value is a quick way to access the **Document Properties** dialog box.
Elapsed Time	Displays the time elapsed (at the selected frame rate) from **Frame 1** to the current playhead location.

1 | Setting Document Properties

The document properties are general specifications—such as **Stage** dimensions, background color, and frame rate—that affect your entire project. When you start a new project in Flash CS3, you should set the document properties. This exercise shows you how.

---

1 Copy the **chap_04 folder** from the **Flash HOT CD-ROM** to your desktop. Open a new file by choosing **File > New > Flash File (ActionScript 3.0)**. Choose **File > Save**.

2 In the **Save** dialog box, name the file **movie.fla**, and save it in the **chap_04** folder. Make sure the **Property inspector** is visible. If it's not, choose **Window > Properties > Properties**.

Notice the following default document properties: the default Stage dimensions are 550 x 400 pixels, the default movie background is white, and the default frame rate is 12 frames per second. You'll learn how to change each setting in the following steps. Document class is empty by default; you'll learn more about this document property in Chapter 12, *"ActionScript Basics."*

---

3 In the **Property inspector**, type **24** in the **Frame rate** field.

For every second of your animation, 24 frames will play. You'll learn more about frame rates in the next exercise.

---

4 In the **Property inspector**, click the **Background** color box to display the default color palette. Select a light blue to change the background color of your movie.

---

5 In the **Property inspector**, click the **Size** button to open the **Document Properties** dialog box.

In the Document Properties dialog box, you can enter a title and brief description of your movie, as well as set frame rate preferences, movie dimensions, background color, and rule measurements for your entire movie.

---

6 Type **700** in the **width** field and **350** in the **height** field.

These fields control the absolute pixel dimensions of the Stage. You will learn other ways to control the size of your movie in Chapter 17, *"Publishing and Exporting."*

7 Click the **Ruler units** pop-up menu, which contains several ways to display the ruler units on your **Stage**. Leave this option set to the default—**Pixels**.

8 Click **OK** to close the **Document Properties** dialog box.

Notice the values in the Property inspector—the dimensions, background color, and frame rate have changed to reflect the settings you specified in the Document Properties dialog box.

You can quickly use the Property inspector at any point to change the movie's background color or frame rate. In addition, you can use the Size button to access the Document Properties dialog box, where you can change the Stage dimensions and ruler units. However, avoid changing dimensions once you have started adding content to your Stage. Changing Stage dimensions at this point offsets the position of your artwork, which can be difficult to fix.

9 Save your changes, and leave **movie.fla** open for the next exercise.

Understanding Keyframes and Frames

Before you start creating animations, you need a better understanding of two terms—frames and keyframes. As mentioned previously, in Flash CS3, the **Timeline** represents the passing of time, with each slot on the **Timeline** representing an individual **frame**. **Keyframes** are a special type of frame that represent a change in the content of your movie.

When you open a new document, Flash always inserts a blank keyframe at **Frame 1**. If you add artwork to **Frame 1** and insert 20 new regular frames, the image on **Frame 1** will persist until the last frame (**Frame 21**). To change the appearance of an animation, you must add new keyframes. If you want to change your artwork on **Frame 2**, you first insert a new keyframe on **Frame 2** and then make the change on the **Stage**. Again, a keyframe will indicate a change in content between two frames.

If you've never worked with animation before, these concepts may seem foreign to you. Not to worry, you'll have lots of opportunities to work with frames and keyframes in this chapter.

Before you start the rest of the hands-on exercises, you need to identify and create frames and keyframes on the **Timeline**. The following chart describes each in more detail, including keyboard shortcuts where available:

Frames and Keyframes

Feature	Description
Frame	Although the **Timeline** in Flash CS3 has *slots* for frames, you have to define them as frames or keyframes in order for the content to exist at that point in the movie. Different layers can have different numbers of frames. For example, **Layer 1** could have ten frames while **Layer 2** has only one. There cannot be gaps between frames; when you insert a frame, all of the previous slots are also defined as frames. If you insert frames between keyframes, you will lengthen the time of your animation without affecting the contents. To insert frames, select any slot(s) or existing frame(s) on the **Timeline** and press **F5**, or choose **Insert > Timeline > Frame**.
Keyframe	A keyframe indicates a change in content or motion between frames. A keyframe containing artwork is represented by a solid black circle. By default, when you add a new keyframe in Flash CS3, the content (except for actions and sounds) is copied from the previous keyframe. Adding a keyframe will not, by itself, change the artwork. To insert a new keyframe, select any slot or frame on the **Timeline** to select it, and then press **F6** or choose **Insert > Timeline > Keyframe**. (Note: A keyframe will be added if you have artwork in a previous frame or keyframe. If the previous frame is blank, pressing F6 will add only a blank keyframe.)
Blank keyframe	A blank keyframe is a keyframe without any artwork. By default, when you create a new document, the **Timeline** contains one blank keyframe, which you can identify by the empty circle icon. (As soon as you create or place artwork on the **Stage**, it becomes a regular keyframe, and the empty circle icon changes to a solid black circle.) A blank keyframe can contain actions and sounds. You will learn more about sound in Chapter 14, *"Sound,"* and more about actions in Chapter 12, *"ActionScript Basics."* Inserting a blank keyframe on the Timeline will remove any content, including actions and sounds, in that layer from the **Stage** at that point. To insert a blank keyframe, select any slot or frame on the **Timeline**, and then press **F7** or choose **Insert > Timeline > Blank Keyframe**.
Clearing frames	Clearing a frame removes the contents of the frame but leaves the frame itself. This process will not reduce the number of frames in a layer. To clear a frame or frames, select the frame(s), and then press **Alt+Backspace** (Windows) or **Opt+Delete** (Mac) or choose **Edit > Timeline > Clear Frames**.
Clearing keyframes	If you clear a keyframe, this process will simply convert a keyframe to a regular frame. Choose **Edit > Timeline > Clear Frames**, or press **Shift+F6**. You can also clear a keyframe by **right-clicking** (Windows) or **Ctrl-clicking** (Mac) a frame and choosing **Clear Keyframe** from the contextual menu.
Removing frames	If you need to delete frames, keyframes, or blank keyframes, select the frames on the **Timeline**, and then press **Shift+F5** or choose **Edit > Timeline > Remove Frames**. You can also remove frames by **right-clicking** (Windows) or **Ctrl-clicking** (Mac) a frame and choosing **Remove Frames** from the contextual menu.

2 | Creating Frame-by-Frame Animations with Keyframes

A common animation technique is to make a word appear as though it is being written before your eyes. You can achieve this effect easily using keyframes. When you insert a keyframe, Flash CS3 copies the content of the previous keyframe to the newly created keyframe, which you can then change to create an animation. In this exercise, you'll learn how to make the word *xboard!* animate on the **Stage** using frame-by-frame animation.

1 Open **movieFinal.fla** from the **chap_04** folder.

The easiest way to understand animations is to look at a finished example, such as the one in movieFinal.fla.

2 Press **Enter** (Windows) or **Return** (Mac) to preview the animation on the **Stage**.

Notice the animation creates the word *xboard!* magically before your eyes! Although it may seem complicated, you'll see how easy it is to create a frame-by-frame animation with keyframes in this exercise.

3 Close **movieFinal.fla**. If you completed Exercise 1, **movie.fla** should still be open. If it's not, complete Exercise 1, and then return to this exercise.

Notice movie.fla contains a single layer with a single blank keyframe. This is the minimum you need to start drawing. This also happens to be the way all new documents appear by default in Flash.

4 On the **Timeline**, double-click the **Layer 1** name. When the bounding box appears, rename the layer **xboard!**, and press **Enter** (Windows) or **Return** (Mac).

Naming layers keeps them recognizable and organized.

---

5 Select the **Brush** tool in the **Tools** panel. From the **Color** and **Options** sections of the **Tools** panel, select any brush size, shape, and color (other than white—you'll see why in Step 11).

The Brush tool paints only fills, not strokes, so you want to change the color in the Fill Color well.

In the next few steps, you'll write the word *xboard!* one letter at a time in a series of keyframes.

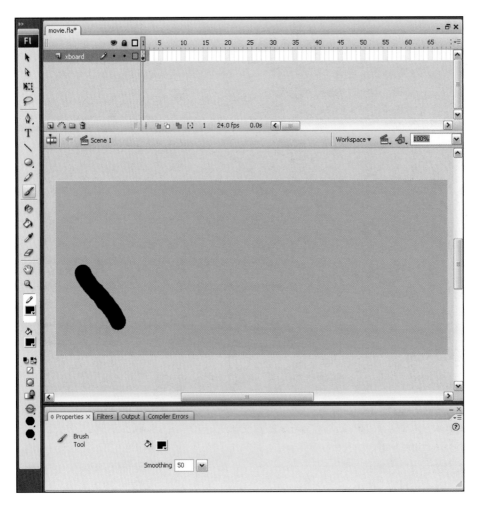

6 With the **Brush** tool selected in the **Tools** panel and with **Frame 1** selected on the **Timeline**, draw the first part of the letter *x* on the left side on the **Stage**, as shown in the illustration here.

Notice Frame 1 now contains a small black dot, indicating it contains artwork. Frame 1 is now referred to as a *keyframe*, rather than a blank keyframe, because it is no longer empty.

To make a change on the Timeline, you must place a keyframe where you want the change to occur. Adding a new keyframe will copy all the content from the previous keyframe to the new keyframe. Now that you have filled in the first keyframe of Layer 1, you'll add another keyframe at Frame 2 so you can draw the second frame of your animation.

---

7 On the **Timeline**, click **Frame 2** to select it, and choose **Insert > Timeline > Keyframe** or press **F6**.

This adds a new keyframe at Frame 2. Notice the contents of Frame 1 are the same as the contents of Frame 2. You'll add artwork to Frame 2 in the next step.

Tip: In Windows, remember the F6 keyboard shortcut, because you will be using it often to insert keyframes.

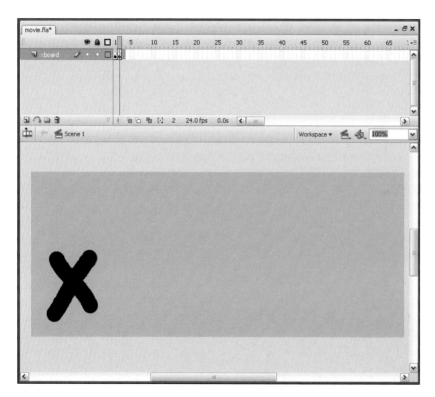

---

8 With the **Brush** tool still selected and with **Frame 2** selected on the **Timeline**, draw the second part of the x on the new keyframe.

---

9 Choose **Insert > Timeline > Keyframe** to add a new keyframe to the **Timeline** on **Frame 3**.

Notice Frame 3 has the same contents as Frame 2.

---

10 With the **Brush** tool still selected and with **Frame 3** selected on the **Timeline**, draw a *b* on the **Stage**. Drag (scrub) the **playhead** back and forth on the **Timeline** to quickly preview the animation. You'll see the *x* and *b* being drawn directly on the **Stage**.

---

11 Choose **Preview in Context** from the **Options** menu to display a thumbnail preview of the contents of each keyframe.

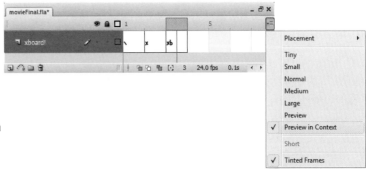

Viewing the Timeline with black dots representing keyframes with artwork might seem somewhat abstract to you. The Options menu has several options for displaying the contents of your individual frames on the Timeline.

You'll find the Preview in Context view helpful when creating frame-by-frame animations.

Note: Do you remember when you chose a color for the brush in Step 5, and you were asked to choose any color other than white? Now you can see why. If you had chosen white for the brush color, you would not see the artwork in the Preview in Context view because the Timeline frames are also white.

---

12 With **Frame 3** selected on the **Timeline**, choose **Insert > Timeline > Keyframe** to insert another keyframe on **Frame 4**.

---

13 With the **Brush** tool still selected, draw an *o* on the **Stage**. As you draw, you'll see the contents of **Frame 4** appear on the **Timeline** preview.

As you continue to draw the word *xboard!*, you don't have to draw the whole letter in each keyframe. Instead, you can draw part of the letter (just as you did with the *x*) in one keyframe, choose Insert > Timeline > Keyframe to insert the next keyframe, and draw the remaining parts of the letter in that keyframe to create a more realistic animation.

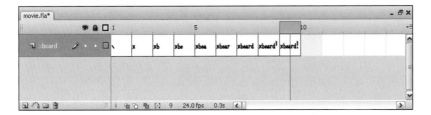

14 Using the techniques you learned in this exercise, use the **Brush** tool, and add new keyframes to finish drawing the word *xboard!*. When you are done, your **Timeline** should look like the one shown in the illustration here.

---

15 Scrub the playhead across the **Timeline** to preview the animation on the **Stage**.

16 Press **Enter** (Windows) or **Return** (Mac) to play the animation once.

Unlike scrubbing the playhead, when you press Enter (Windows) or Return (Mac) to preview the animation on the Stage, you see an accurate preview of the frame rate for the animation, which you set to 24 fps in Exercise 1.

17 Choose **Control > Loop Playback** and press **Enter** (Windows) or **Return** (Mac) to repeat the animation continuously. Looping repeats the animation until you choose to stop it.

Notice how fast the animation plays. Next, you'll learn how to slow down the animation by adjusting the frame rate, which defines how many frames your animation plays per second. Because of varying processor speeds, you have no guarantee your movie will always play back at the specified frame rate on every computer. Keep this in mind when you're designing and testing animations. If possible, always test your movies on a variety of computers with varying processor speeds so you can get an accurate idea of the range of results your viewers will see.

18 Press **Enter** (Windows) or **Return** (Mac) to stop the animation.

19 Choose **Normal** in the **Options** menu to change the **Timeline** to **Normal** view so you see keyframes on the **Timeline** instead of a preview of the artwork.

20 Make sure the **Property inspector** is visible. If it's not, choose **Window > Properties > Properties**.

21 Click the **Stage** to show the document properties in the **Property inspector**. In the **Frame rate** field, decrease the frame rate to **12**. As you learned in Exercise 1, 12 fps is the default frame rate when you create a new movie in Flash CS3.

22 Press **Enter** (Windows) or **Return** (Mac).

Notice the animation plays slower. The movie is taking twice as long to play the same number of frames. The lower the frame rate, the slower the animation plays (and vice versa). Go ahead and experiment with other frame rates. When you're finished experimenting, return the frame rate to its default setting of 12 frames per second so you're ready for the next exercise.

23 Save your **movie.fla** file by choosing **File > Save**. Close the file.

What Is the Frame Rate?

The **frame rate** determines the number of frames your movie plays per second. This rate corresponds directly to the length of time your animation takes to play.

Here's how to use the frame rate to calculate the playback time of your animation: Start with the total number of frames on the **Timeline** and divide it by the frame rate; the result is the number of seconds it will take to view your movie.

For example, if your **Timeline** has 36 frames and your frame rate is set to 12 fps, your animation will be 3 seconds. The following chart gives examples of how the frame rate affects the duration of the animation. Next, you will learn how to create more than one animation in the same movie and have them play at different speeds.

Frame Rate				
Number of Frames	÷	**Frame Rate**	=	**Duration**
24 frames	÷	12 fps	=	2 seconds
36 frames	÷	12 fps	=	3 seconds
48 frames	÷	24 fps	=	2 seconds

Recommended Frame Rates

When you set a frame rate in Flash CS3, you're setting the maximum frame rate for your movie, or how quickly the movie "tries" to play. The actual playback frame rate depends on several factors, including the download speed and processor speed of the computer used to view the movie. If the frame rate is set higher than the computer can display, the movie will play as fast as the computer's processor will allow. If you set the frame rate to 200 (which is really high), the average computer will not be able to display the movie at this rate. Also, frames with more objects,

colors, or transparency than others take more time for the computer to render. Thus, the actual frame rate can vary during playback because of the rendering requirements from one frame to another.

Based on these factors, use a frame rate of at least 12 fps and not more than 25 fps so the average computer can display your movie as you intended. A frame rate of 15 to 20 fps, which is similar to the 24 fps used in motion pictures, works well most of the time.

3 | Inserting and Deleting Frames

As you learn to create animations, you'll want to adjust the speed of your animations. In the previous exercise, you learned how to adjust the frame rate to increase and decrease the speed of an animation. But what do you do if you want only certain sections of your movie to play faster or slower than other sections? In this exercise, you will learn how to insert and remove frames on the **Timeline** so different sections of an animation play at different speeds, even though they all share the same frame rate.

---

1 Open **frames.fla** from the **chap_04** folder.

As you can see, the file contains one layer with a simple frame-by-frame animation using text. You'll get a chance to work with text in Chapter 13, *"Working with Text."*

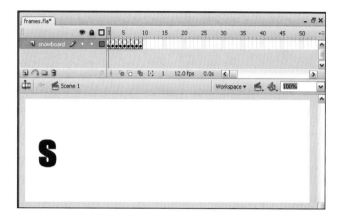

2 Press **Enter** (Windows) or **Return** (Mac) to preview the animation on the **Stage**.

As you can see, the animation plays so fast you almost lose the effect of the text appearing one letter at a time. Adjusting the frame rate to slow down this animation will affect the entire movie, which could be problematic because you may want other sections of your movie to play at a different speed. For example, in this project you may want the word *snow* to appear slowly and the word *board* to appear quickly. You can solve this problem easily by inserting duplicate frames at strategic points to lengthen parts of the animation.

---

3 On the **Timeline**, click **Frame 1** to select it. Choose **Insert > Timeline > Frame** (or press **F5**), which duplicates the contents of **Frame 1** and extends the **Timeline** by one frame.

When you add a new frame, Flash CS3 creates a duplicate of the previous frame. You aren't going to change this content; if you wanted to change the duplicate content, a keyframe would have been a better choice.

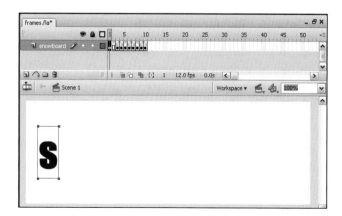

4 With **Frame 1** still selected on the **Timeline**, choose **Insert > Timeline > Frame** to insert another frame. Each time you choose **Insert > Timeline > Frame** or press **F5**, you will insert one frame to extend the **Timeline**.

What Do Those Dots Mean?

As you start adding content to your project, you'll notice different icons on the **Timeline**. The black dots indicate keyframes with content. The light gray frames without icons indicate frames (no change in content). For example, as shown in the illustration here, **Frame 2**, **Frame 3**, and **Frame 4** have the same content as **Keyframe 1**. The white rectangle indicates the last frame in a frame range, which means the next frame will be either a blank keyframe (empty) or a keyframe (with content). In this example, the empty circle icon indicates a blank keyframe.

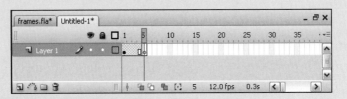

5 With **Frame 1** still selected on the **Timeline**, choose **Insert > Timeline > Frame**, or press **F5** nine more times (giving you a total of eleven additional frames between the first two keyframes).

By adding more frames, you are extending the distance between the first two keyframes on the Timeline. The additional frames slow down the speed of the animation because the content of Keyframe 1 will display for a longer period of time.

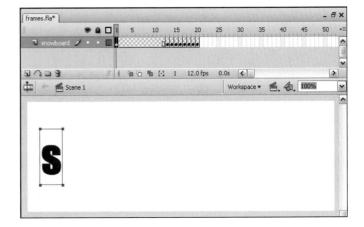

6 Press **Enter** (Windows) or **Return** (Mac) to preview the animation on the **Stage**.

Notice the significant delay between the letters *s* and *n*—about one second—because 12 frames divided by 12 fps equals 1 second. Even though you changed the delay between the letters *s* and *n*, you didn't affect the speed of the rest of the animation. As you can see, this is a great trick to use when you want to play different sections of an animation at different speeds.

7 On the **Timeline**, click **Frame 13** to select it.

Frame 13 is the new location of the second keyframe. It was originally on Frame 2 before you added more frames in Steps 3, 4, and 5.

---

8 Choose **Insert > Timeline > Frame** or press **F5** 11 times to insert 11 frames on the **Timeline**.

Each added frame contains the same content as Frame 13, creating another pause between the letters *n* and *o*.

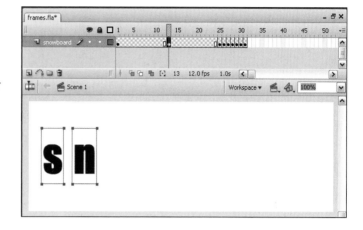

---

9 Using the techniques you learned in Steps 7 and 8, add frames between the letters *o* and *w* and between the letters *w* and *b*.

---

10 Press **Enter** (Windows) or **Return** (Mac) to preview the animation on the **Stage**.

Notice how much slower the word *snow* animates compared to the word *board*. As you can see from this exercise, you can control the timing of an animation without having to adjust the frame rate of the entire movie. Inserting frames slows down specific sections in the animation. The inverse is also true—you can speed up an animation by deleting frames. You'll learn how in the next few steps.

11 On the **Timeline**, click **Frame 2** to select it. **Right-click** (Windows) or **Ctrl-click** (Mac), and choose **Remove Frames** from the contextual menu or use the shortcut key **Shift+F5** to remove the currently selected frame.

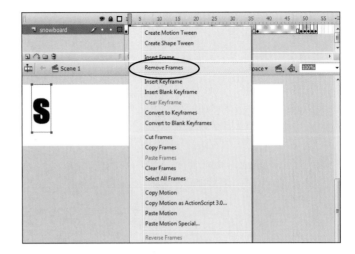

As you can see, you shortened the Timeline by one frame and decreased the amount of time between the letters *s* and *n* in your animation.

12 Click **Frame 7** and drag through **Frame 11** to multiple-select the frames.

13 With **Frame 7** through **Frame 11** selected, choose **Edit > Timeline > Remove Frames** (or use the shortcut key **Shift+F5**) to remove the selected frames and shorten your **Timeline** by five frames.

14 Using the techniques you learned in Steps 11, 12, and 13, reduce the number of frames so there are only five frames between the *s*, *n*, *o*, and *w* keyframes.

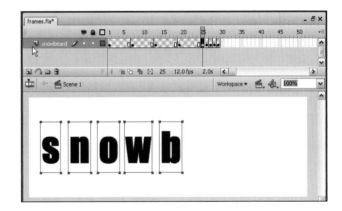

15 Press **Enter** (Windows) or **Return (Mac)** to preview your animation on the **Stage**.

As you can see, the word *snow* now plays faster than it did in Step 10 but still slower than the letters in the word *board*. The animation plays at two speeds because you have more frames between the keyframes in the word *snow* but fewer frames between the keyframes for the word *board*. Adding frames is a great technique for speeding up or slowing down the timing of animations without changing the frame rate of the entire movie.

16 Close **frames.fla**. You don't need to save your changes.

4 | Copying and Reversing Frames

Creating a looping animation (one that repeats indefinitely) can be a lot of work if you have to draw each frame over and over. In Flash CS3, you can copy, paste, and reverse a sequence of frames to create a looping animation. You will learn how in this exercise.

---

1 Open **loopingFinal.fla** from the **chap_04** folder.

---

2 Choose **Control > Loop Playback** to set the playback option to loop, which means it repeats indefinitely. Press **Enter** (Windows) or **Return** (Mac) to preview the animation on the **Stage**.

This is the completed version of the animation you'll create in this exercise. As you can see, the snowboarder cruises down and up the mountain slope over and over. You will create this same animation technique without having to draw all the frames again.

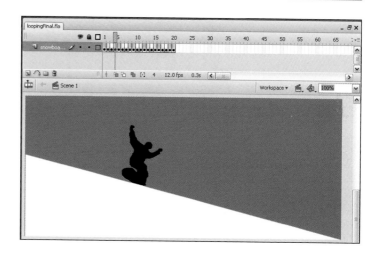

---

3 Choose **Control > Loop Playback** to stop the animation from looping. Press **Enter** (Windows) or **Return** (Mac) to stop previewing the animation on the **Stage**. Close **loopingFinal.fla**.

---

4 Open **looping.fla** from the **chap_04** folder.

The file contains a single layer named snowboarding, which contains a sequence of 10 keyframes. In each keyframe, the boarder is a little further down the slope, creating the illusion that the boarder is moving down the slope when the sequence plays back.

---

5 On the **Timeline**, click the **snowboarding** layer to select all the frames.

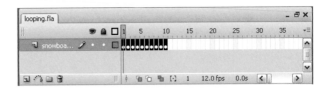

Selecting a layer on the Timeline is an easy way to multiple-select the frames on a layer. Next, you'll make a copy of the selected frames.

---

6 Position your cursor over the selected frames. Click and drag the frames to the right on the **Timeline**. Don't release the mouse just yet!

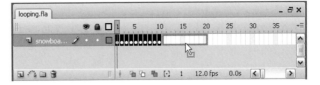

As you click and drag the frames, a light gray outline indicates the selected frames and where they'll be moved when you release the mouse.

---

7 Without releasing the mouse, hold down the **Alt** key (Windows) or the **Opt** key (Mac).

Notice the small plus sign appears to the right of the cursor indicating you will duplicate (or copy), not move (or cut), the frames when you release the mouse.

---

8 Release the mouse to create a copy of the selected frames on **Frame 11** through **Frame 20**.

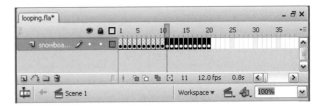

---

9 Press **Enter** (Windows) or **Return** (Mac) to preview the movie on the **Stage**.

Notice the animation does not look correct. The snowboarder reaches the bottom of the slope and jumps back up to the top, which is not the same as the single fluid motion you saw in the finished animation. In traditional animation, you'd have to redraw all the frames in reverse order to achieve this effect. Fortunately in Flash CS3, you can save yourself that manual process and simply duplicate and reverse the existing frames in the animation. You'll learn how in the next steps.

---

10 Click **Frame 11**, and then **Shift-click Frame 20** to select **Frame 11** through **Frame 20**. Choose **Modify > Timeline > Reverse Frames**.

You won't see a change on the Timeline, but you will notice the change on the Stage when you test the movie.

---

11 Press **Enter** (Windows) or **Return** (Mac) to preview your animation on the **Stage**. As you can see, the snowboarder races down the hill and goes back up the hill, as if you were rewinding the film to view an instant replay. Nice! If you choose **Control > Loop Playback**, you can watch the animation preview loop endlessly.

---

12 Close **looping.fla**. You don't need to save your changes.

---

5 | Using Onion Skinning

Now that you have created a couple of frame-by-frame animations, it's a good time to learn a few new tricks. First, you'll learn how to use the onion skinning feature, which lets you to see a ghost image of the previous frame so you can see where you want to place the artwork in relation to the previous frames. You will also learn to use the **Free Transform** tool, which allows you to scale, rotate, skew, and distort your artwork.

---

1 Open **onionFinal.fla** file from the **chap_04** folder.

---

2 Choose **Control > Loop Playback** to set the playback option to loop, which means it will repeat indefinitely. Press **Enter** (Windows) or **Return** (Mac) to preview the animation on the **Stage**.

This is the completed version of the animation you'll create in this exercise. In this animation, you'll see the snow-boarder catching some air! You will create this same animation technique without having to draw all the frames again.

---

3 Choose **Control > Loop Playback** to stop the looping. Press **Enter** (Windows) or **Return** (Mac) to stop previewing the animation on the **Stage**. When you're finished viewing the animation, close **onionFinal.fla**.

---

4 Open **onion.fla** from the **chap_04** folder.

This file contains one keyframe with the snowboarder beginning his jump on the top layer and one keyframe with the snow on the bottom layer. The snow layer has been locked so that you don't accidentally select something on it. You will be modifying the artwork and creating the frame-by-frame animation on the snowboarder layer in the next few steps.

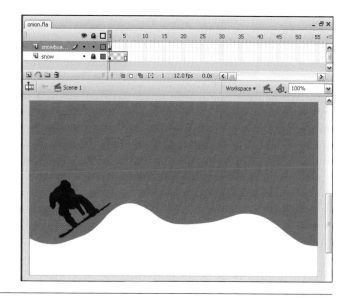

5 Click **Frame 2** of the **snowboarder** layer to select it, and choose **Insert > Timeline > Keyframe** to add a keyframe.

Frame 2 now contains a small black dot, indicating it contains content. As you know from Exercise 2, when you create a new keyframe, it copies the content from the previous keyframe—in this case, Frame 1.

Tip: If you try to add a keyframe without first selecting a frame, nothing happens. Why? When you have more than one layer in your document, you have to select the frame so Flash CS3 knows in which layer to insert the keyframe.

6 With the playhead on **Frame 2**, click the snowboarder artwork on the **Stage** to select it. You'll know it's selected when you see the dotted mesh. Drag the snowboarder up and to the right, as though he were advancing in his jump.

Dotted mesh

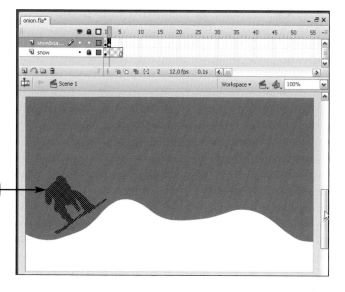

7 Click the **Onion Skin** button.

Notice the faint ghost image showing the content of Frame 1 on the Stage. Onion skinning lets you see the artwork in the previous keyframes and change the artwork relative to the ghost images.

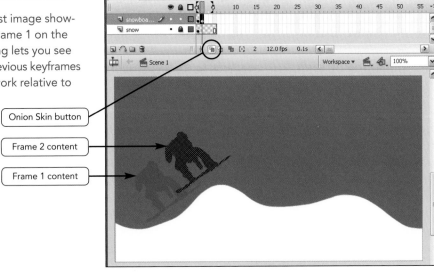

Onion Skin button

Frame 2 content

Frame 1 content

NOTE:

Onion Skin Markers

After you click the **Onion Skin** button, a gray bar with a draggable bracket on each end appears at the top of the **Timeline**. These are called **onion skin markers**. The start onion skin marker (the one on the left) is on **Frame 1** (the first frame of your animation), and the end onion skin marker (the one on the right) is on **Frame 5** (the last frame of your animation). If you click and drag your playhead to the right or left, the start onion skin marker will move along with it. You can also drag either of the onion skin markers to the left or right to include more frames if they are spanning fewer keyframes than you have on the **Timeline**.

Onion skin markers

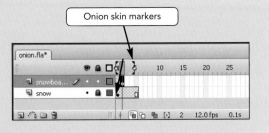

8 Select the **Free Transform** tool in the **Tools** panel.

The Free Transform tool lets you modify selected artwork by changing the size, rotation, skew, and distortion. To learn more about the Free Transform tool, check out the chart at the end of this exercise.

Free Transform Tool (Q,F)

9 Make sure the playhead is on **Frame 2**, and click the snowboarder on the **Stage** to select it.

Notice a bounding box appears around the artwork, indicating you can transform the artwork. If you position the cursor near or over the handles (the squares in the corners and on the edges of the bounding box), the cursor changes, indicating the transform options.

10 Position your cursor just outside the upper-right corner of the bounding box until it changes to the **rotate** icon (a round arrow). Click and drag to the right to rotate the snowboarder slightly to make the jump look more realistic.

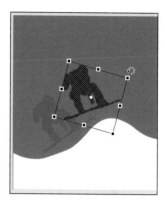

11 Click **Frame 3** to select it, and choose **Insert > Timeline > Keyframe** to insert another keyframe.

12 Click the snowboarder artwork with the **Free Transform** tool to select it. Click and drag the snowboarder to the right. Using the technique you learned in Step 9, click and drag to rotate the snowboarder.

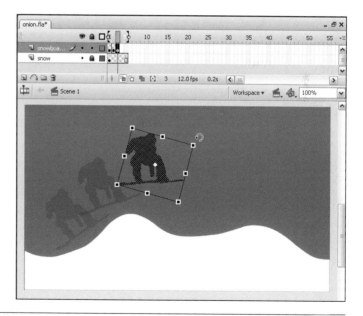

13 Repeat Steps 11 and 12 twice, adding keyframes to **Frame 4** and **Frame 5** and positioning and rotating the artwork in each keyframe. When you're finished, the artwork on the **Stage** should match the artwork shown in the illustration here.

14 Choose **Control > Loop Playback**. Press **Enter** (Windows) or **Return** (Mac) to preview the movie on the **Stage**. When you're finished, choose **Control > Loop Playback** to stop the movie from repeating, and press **Enter** (Windows) or **Return** (Mac) to stop the movie.

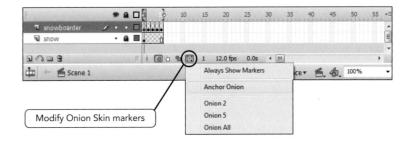

Modify Onion Skin markers

As you can see, the snowboarder is catching some air—just like in the final movie you looked at in Step 1!

If you do not want the onion skin markers to move when you move the playhead or click a frame on the Timeline, you can choose Anchor Onion in the Modify Onion Markers button pop-up menu to lock the onion skinning span where it is until you unlock it again or manually drag the start or end onion skin marker.

15 Experiment with the **Free Transform** tool to create more effects. Try resizing, rotating, and skewing using the editing nodes.

You'll get a chance to work with the Free Transform tool again in Chapter 6, *"Creating Symbols and Instances."*

16 When you are finished experimenting, close **onion.fla**. You don't need to save your changes.

VIDEO: | **onion.mov**

To learn more about onion skinning, check out **onion.mov** in the **videos** folder on the **Flash HOT CD-ROM**.

The Free Transform Tool

The **Free Transform** tool lets you modify objects in several ways. As you position the cursor over the bounding box of a selected object, it will change to indicate what type of transformation is available. As you click and drag, you will see a preview of the transformation you are about to make. The following chart lists how you can use the **Free Transform** tool to transform objects:

Free Transform Tool Features	
Example	**Description**
	Clicking and dragging up or down on a corner transform handle rotates the object. The cursor icon changes to a round arrow, indicating you can rotate the object.
	Clicking and dragging one of the corner transform handles diagonally modifies the scale of the object. The cursor changes to a diagonal double-pointed arrow when you can perform this transformation.
	Clicking and dragging one of the middle-side transform handles modifies the width or height of the object. The cursor changes to a horizontal (or vertical depending on which side you are on) double-pointed arrow when you can perform this transformation.
	Clicking and dragging between any two transform handles skews the object. The cursor changes, indicating you can skew the object.
	Clicking and dragging one of the middle-side transform handles to the other side of the object flips the object. The cursor changes to a horizontal or vertical double-pointed arrow depending on which side you are on.
	Clicking and dragging the center registration point modifies the center point of the object. After you alter the center point, all transformations will rotate or move in relation to the new center point location.

6 | Testing Movies

So far, you've been testing your movies by previewing them on the **Stage**. This is a great way to test the frame rate, but you can test your work in other ways. In this exercise, you will learn how to preview the movie file as a SWF file—the format you would use to publish the movie to the Web—with the **Test Movie** feature. You'll learn a really easy way to produce the HTML file required to view the SWF file in a browser. You'll also learn how to preview the movie in a browser with the **Preview in Browser** feature. This exercises covers the basics—you'll find more in-depth information about publishing Flash CS3 content in Chapter 17, *"Publishing and Exporting."*

---

1 Open **frames_Test.fla** from the **chap_04** folder.

It is important to know where your project file (FLA) has been saved before you use the Test Movie and Preview in Browser features because Flash CS3 generates new files and automatically saves them in the same location as your project file (FLA). If you saved your file in a different location, just make sure you know where it is. In this case, you're working with frames_Test.fla, which is included in the chap_04 folder.

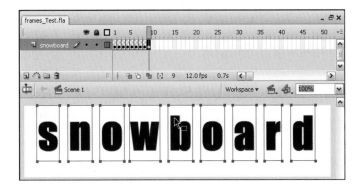

---

2 Choose **Control > Test Movie** or press **Ctrl+Enter** (Windows) or **Cmd+Return** (Mac) to preview the movie file in a new window as a SWF file.

When you test the movie, Flash CS3 automatically previews the movie as a SWF file, which is exactly what you'd see if you exported the file as a SWF.

Resize handle

Tip: You can click and drag the resize handle of the preview window to change its size. Although the size of the window changes, the snowboard letters stay the same size. You'll learn how to make content scalable using the publish settings in Chapter 17, *"Publishing and Exporting."*

Loop-de-Loop

At this point, you're probably wondering why your animation is looping (playing over and over). This is the default behavior of all movies in Flash CS3, although you don't see it when you simply press **Enter** (Windows) or **Return** (Mac) to preview your movie (unless you've turned on the **Loop Playback** option). If you uploaded this published file to the Web, it would loop. You will learn to control the looping in your final movie (SWF) file in Chapter 12, *"ActionScript Basics,"* when you learn how to add actions to frames. But if all this looping is making you dizzy, you can choose **Control > Loop** to turn this feature off in the SWF preview window.

3 With the preview window still open, choose **Window > Toolbars > Controller** to open the **Controller** toolbar.

This handy little gadget is especially useful with longer movies—it lets you easily stop, restart, or step back one frame at a time on the Timeline.

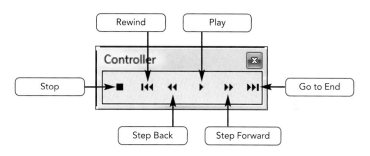

4 Click the **Stop** button on the **Controller** to stop your animation.

5 Click the **Play** button to play the animation. If you'd like, experiment with the other buttons on the **Controller**.

Although you didn't see it happen, when you tested the movie in Step 2, Flash CS3 automatically created the SWF for the movie and saved it in the same location as your project (FLA) file. You'll locate this file next.

6 Open the **chap_04** folder.

Notice the frames_Test.swf file inside this folder. Flash CS3 automatically generated this file. Also notice the SWF file has a different icon than the FLA files, which can be helpful visual feedback, especially if your file extensions are turned off. The SWF file is the file you'd use on a Web page in the same manner you would use a GIF or JPEG.

7 Return to Flash CS3, and close the preview window.

8 Choose **File > Publish Preview > Default – (HTML)** or press **F12** to launch your default browser with a preview of your movie file (SWF).

Previewing the SWF file in a browser is a quick and easy way to see what the movie looks like and how it plays back in a browser. Although this technique is great for previewing your movies, you'll learn better ways to publish the final SWF file in Chapter 17, *"Publishing and Exporting."*

NOTE:

Defining a Default Browser

If you have several browsers installed on your computer, you can specify which one Flash uses as the default browser. You can find a great explanation of how to define default browsers in Windows and on a Mac on Adobe's Web site:

www.adobe.com/cfusion/knowledgebase/index.cfm?id=tn_15133

---

9 Hide Flash CS3, and navigate to the **chap_04** folder.

Notice there is a frames_Test.html file inside the chap_04 folder. When you published a preview of the file in Step 8, Flash CS3 generated the HTML file automatically, which is what lets you view the SWF file in a browser.

At this point, all the files necessary to publish to the Web have been generated for you automatically. You'll find more thorough instructions and details about this process in Chapter 17, *"Publishing and Exporting."* The purpose of this exercise was to demonstrate a quick and easy way to preview your projects.

10 Return to Flash CS3. Close **frames_Test.fla**. You don't need to save your changes.

Congratulations—you just completed a long but essential part of your animation training! The next three chapters focus on more complex and specific animation topics, such as shape tweening, symbols and instances, and motion tweening. Now would be a great time for a break. You've worked through a lot of material, and you deserve one!

5

Shape Tweening

No doubt you've seen animations on the Web or on television showing an object transforming (or morphing) from one shape into another. You can create this effect in Adobe Flash CS3 Professional using a technique called *shape tweening*.

The exercises in this chapter offer a thorough introduction to shape tweening. By working through them, you will expand your Flash CS3 skill set to include shape tweening, shape hinting, and multiple shape tweening.

What Is Shape Tweening?

Shape tweening lets you gradually transform, or **morph**, a shape into another shape. For example, you can start with a circle and gradually transform it into a square by creating a series of shapes in between that slowly change from a circle to a square.

In traditional animation, a lead (or **key**) animator creates the **extremes**, which are the starting frame (in this case the circle) and the ending point (in this case the square). A second animator, the **in-betweener**, performs the tedious task of creating the transitional frames between the start and end points so the animation slowly morphs from the square to the circle.

In computer animation, the process is similar— you begin with a starting frame and an ending frame. Fortunately, the computer generates the in-between frames, saving you the time-consuming task of creating them. The process of generating the in-between frames is called **tweening**.

Before moving on to the hands-on exercises, take some time to familiarize yourself with some key terms—*shape, keyframes,* and *tweening*—which are described in the following chart:

Shape Tweening Terms and Definitions	
Terms	**Definition**
Shape	In Flash CS3, shapes are vector-based objects or a series of vector-based objects. You can create shapes in Flash CS3 using any of the drawing tools with either the Merge Drawing model or the Object Drawing model you learned about in Chapter 3, *"Using the Drawing and Color Tools."* Or you can import shapes into Flash CS3 from other vector-creation programs, such as Adobe Illustrator. For a shape to be suitable for shape tweening, it cannot be composed of grouped objects, bitmaps, or symbols. (You will learn about symbols in Chapter 6, *"Creating Symbols and Instances."*) You can shape tween with text if you first convert the text to a shape, which is called **breaking apart**. You will learn how to break text apart later in this chapter.
Keyframe 	In traditional animation, lead animators draw **extremes**, or the important frames that define motion or transition. In the example here, the key animator would create two keyframes—the first with a circle and the second with a square.
Tweening 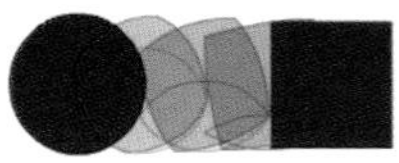	The term **tweening** is borrowed from traditional animation terminology and is slang for **in-betweening**. In traditional animation, a second animator, referred to as the **in-betweener**, takes the extremes created by the key animator and creates transitional frames between the starting point and the ending point to describe the motion. In this example, the in-betweener uses circle and square frames and draws a series of transitional shapes morphing from the circle to the square. As you can imagine, it requires a lot of precision and attention to detail to develop these frames. Fortunately, Flash CS3 creates the in-between frames for you.

Flash CS3 can also shape tween lines into shapes, or shapes into lines, regardless of differences in the colors or gradients between the starting and ending points, as shown in the illustration here.

The first step in creating a shape tween is to create two unique keyframes.

Next, apply a shape tween. Flash CS3 interpolates the difference between the keyframes and automatically generates all the in-between frames.

Shape tweening is the only process in Flash CS3 that lets you quickly animate from one distinct shape to another. You can also use shape tweening to animate from one gradient to another, from one color to another, or from one position on the **Stage** to another. The possibilities and limitations of shape tweening in Flash CS3 are as follows.

What shape tweening can do:

- Tween the shape of an object

- Tween the color of an object (including a color with transparency)

- Tween the position of an object

- Tween scale, rotation, and skew of an object

- Tween text that has been broken apart

- Tween gradients

What shape tweening can't do:

- Tween grouped objects

- Tween symbols

- Tween text that has not been broken apart

1 | Shape Tweening Basics

In this exercise, you'll learn the basics of shape tweening by creating an animation of a snowboard changing into the letter X.

---

1 Copy the **chap_05** folder from the **Flash HOT CD-ROM** to your desktop. Open **textTween_Final.fla** from the **chap_05** folder.

---

2 Press **Enter** (Windows) or **Return** (Mac) to preview the animation. When you're finished previewing the final animation, close **textTween_Final.fla**.

Notice the animation of the snowboard gradually morphs into the letter X. You'll learn how to create this animation with the shape tweening features in the following steps.

---

3 Open **textTween.fla** from the **chap_05** folder.

As you can see, the file contains two layers: one named boarding text with the word *boarding* on it and one named tween with the snowboard shape on it. You will be working on the tween layer.

4 With the **tween** layer selected, click **Frame 12** to select it, and press **F7** to add a blank keyframe.

By adding a blank keyframe rather than a keyframe, you can start with a blank slate, or Stage, on Frame 12. This is in contrast to copying the artwork from an existing keyframe by adding a keyframe, which you learned about in Chapter 4, *"Animating in Flash."*

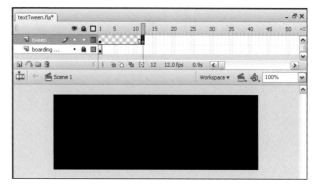

Notice Frame 12 is blank—it contains neither the snowboard nor the word *boarding*. Take a look at the Timeline closely. Notice the boarding text layer has only one frame, and the tween layer now has 12 frames. For the word *boarding* to appear throughout the entire animation, the boarding text layer must also contain 12 frames. You'll fix this in the next step.

5 On the **boarding text** layer, click **Frame 12**, and choose **Insert > Timeline > Frame** or press **F5** to add frames up to **Frame 12**.

Tip: Layers are not at all related to frames. **Layers** represent the relationship of objects in space (one object on top or below another object), whereas **frames** represent the relationship of objects in time (one object appearing after or before another object).

6 Select the **Text** tool in the **Tools** panel. On the **tween** layer, click **Frame 12** to select it. Position your cursor on the **Stage**, click once, and type the capital letter **X**.

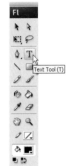

Note: The letter *X* I've typed here uses the following text options in the Property inspector: Arial font, size 86, white, and bold type, but you can use whatever options you'd like. You will learn more about the text options in Chapter 13, *"Working with Text."*

7 Select the **Selection** tool in the **Tools** panel. Click the *X* you created in the previous step to select it. Drag the *X* to position it as shown in the illustration here.

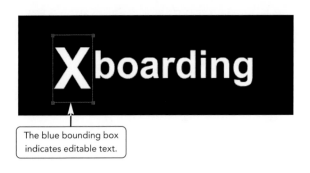

The blue bounding box indicates editable text.

When you create text using the Text tool, the text is still in an editable format, which means you can double-click it and change the letters to something else. If you deselect the text and use the Selection tool to select it again, you'll see a blue bounding box and no dotted mesh, indicating it is still editable text. To shape tween it, you have to convert it from editable text to an editable shape by breaking it apart; you cannot use editable text as the source of a shape tween. Although you may not think of type as a grouped object, you must break it to become a shape. You'll learn more about working with text in Chapter 13, *"Working with Text."*

8 With the *X* still selected, choose **Modify > Break Apart**, or press **Ctrl+B** (Windows) or **Cmd+B** (Mac), to break apart the text and convert it to a shape.

The dotted mesh indicates you're now working with a shape, which you can use to shape tween.

The dotted mesh indicates the selection is a shape.

9 Click anywhere between the two keyframes to select a frame. Any frame will work—just do not select a keyframe.

10 Make sure the **Property inspector** is open. If it is not, choose **Window > Properties > Properties**. In the **Property inspector**, choose **Shape** in the **Tween** pop-up menu to apply a shape tween between the keyframes.

You can also add a tween by right-clicking (Windows) or Ctrl-clicking (Mac) the selected frame on the Timeline and choosing Create Shape Tween. After you apply a shape tween between two keyframes, you'll see green shading between the keyframes on the Timeline, indicating the shape tween is active and working.

11 Hold down the **Shift** key and click **Frame 24** on both the **tween** and **boarding text** layers to multiple-select both frames. Choose **Insert > Timeline > Frame**, or press **F5**. Flash adds 12 more frames for you, extending the animation to **Frame 24**.

Adding these 12 frames adds 1 more second to the animation (provided the frame rate is set to the default setting of 12 frames per second) before it loops again, making the total length of the animation about 2 seconds.

12 Choose **Control > Test Movie** to view the movie in a preview window.

You'll see the snowboard morph into the letter X. If the animation does not morph the way you expected, don't worry—you'll learn how to control it more precisely with shape hints in the next exercise.

---

13 When you are finished testing, close the preview window, and return to Flash CS3. Save your changes, and leave **textTween.fla** open for the next exercise.

Fixing Broken Tweens

As you work more with shape and motion tweens, you'll sometimes encounter a broken (dashed) line in your **Timeline** instead of a solid arrow. The broken line indicates your tween is not working, making it easy to spot problems with your animations.

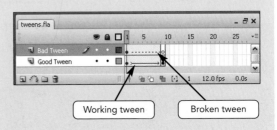

Working tween   Broken tween

Here are some tips for troubleshooting broken tweens:

- Make sure the objects in each keyframe are shapes and not grouped objects.

- Make sure the text has been broken apart.

Sometimes, you may even need to erase the tween and start over from the first keyframe. You'll learn more about the causes of broken shape tweens when you learn about symbols in future chapters.

2 | Using Shape Hints

When creating shape tweens, Flash CS3 automatically determines how one shape will change into the next shape. This process is automatic, so you don't have complete control over how the tween is constructed. Shape hinting helps you regain some control over a tween, and you'll use it primarily to fix a shape tween that doesn't tween quite to your liking. In this exercise, you'll use the animation you created in Exercise 1 and add shape hints to better control how the snowboard morphs into the X.

1 If you just completed Exercise 1, **textTween.fla** should still be open. If it's not, complete Exercise 1, and then return to this exercise. Press **Enter** (Windows) or **Return** (Mac) to preview the shape tween.

Notice as the shape tween progresses, the snowboard unnaturally appears to crumple up like a piece of paper and then all of a sudden pop into the letter X. In this exercise, you'll learn how to make the tween appear more fluid and natural.

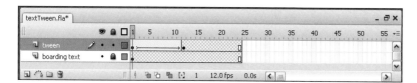

2 Click the **tween** layer to select it, and position the playhead on **Frame 1**.

When you add shape hints, you must start on the first frame of your animation.

3 Choose **Modify > Shape > Add Shape Hint**.

Notice the red circle with an *a* appears in the middle of the snowboard, indicating it is a shape hint.

4 Select the **Selection** tool in the **Tools** panel, and drag the shape hint to the upper-left corner of the snowboard.

5 Position the playhead on **Frame 12**, which is the last frame of the shape tween.

Just as in Step 3, you'll see a shape hint appear in the middle of the shape, in this case, the X. You'll position the shape hint in the next step.

---

6 Drag the shape hint to the upper-left inside corner of the X. Moving the shape hint ensures the upper-left corner of the snowboard ends up as the upper-left corner of the letter X.

When you release the mouse, the shape hint is supposed to change from red to green, but these color changes are not always reliable. This color change is Flash CS3's way of telling you the shape hint has been accepted. If your shape hint doesn't turn green on the final keyframe of the tween, you did not place it in the same (or in a similar) location as the first shape hint, and you'll need to make some adjustments. You may need to reposition shape hints to fine-tune a shape tween—sometimes just a small adjustment will help Flash CS3 get the hint (pun intended)!

According to the Flash CS3 documentation, shape hints should be yellow in the starting keyframe, green in the ending keyframe, and red when they are not on a curve (the edge of a shape), although this is not always the case. Again, since these color changes are not reliable, your best bet is to place shape hints in similar locations on each keyframe and pay more attention to how the tween animates than to the color of the shape hints.

---

7 Position the playhead on **Frame 1**, and press **Enter** (Windows) or **Return** (Mac) to preview the animation with the shape hint.

Notice the shape tween is already smoother and more natural. Next, you'll add more shape hints to improve it even more.

---

8 On the **Timeline**, make sure the playhead is on **Frame 1**. Choose **Modify > Shape > Add Shape Hint** to add another shape hint to the snowboard.

Notice the second shape hint icon has a small *b*, indicating it is the second shape hint.

---

9 Drag the second shape hint to the upper-right corner of the snowboard.

Multiple Shape Hints

After you add a second shape hint, it appears as a red circle with the letter *b*, rather than an *a*. If you create a third shape hint, it will be named *c*, and so on. When you get to *z*, that's it! You're all out of shape hints. You can use up to 26 shape hints per shape tween, which is more than enough for even the most complex shape tweens.

10 Position the playhead on **Frame 12** (the last keyframe of your shape tween). Drag the second shape hint (*b*) to the upper-right outside corner of the *X*.

11 Position the playhead on **Frame 1**, and press **Enter** (Windows) or **Return** (Mac) to preview your work.

As you can see, the transition is getting more and more natural looking!

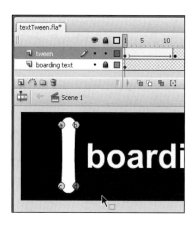

12 On the **Timeline**, make sure the playhead is on **Frame 1**. Repeat Steps 8, 9, and 10 two times to add two more shape hints, moving them to the remaining corners of the snowboard and the *X*. When you are finished, **Frame 1** and **Frame 12** should match the illustration shown here.

13 Press **Enter** (Windows) or **Return** (Mac) to test the shape tween.

Experiment with adjusting the positions of the shape hints. Moving them even slightly can give a completely different look to your shape tween.

Although adding hints helps smooth out a shape tween, sometimes you may want to remove shape hints. You'll learn how in the next few steps.

14 Position the playhead on **Frame 1**. **Right-click** (Windows) or **Ctrl-click** (Mac) the shape hint *d*. Choose **Remove Hint** in the contextual menu to remove the shape hint.

---

15 Press **Enter** (Windows) or **Return** (Mac) to see how removing the shape hint affects the animation. Remove another shape hint, and notice how it affects the animation.

---

16 When you are done experimenting, save your **textTween.fla** file by choosing **File > Save**. Close the file.

---

3 | Creating Multiple Shape Tweens

So far, you've learned how to create single shape tweens. In this exercise, you'll learn how to create multiple shape tweens by placing them on separate layers using the **Distribute to Layers** feature. Working with multiple layers is the only way to choreograph animations with multiple tweens. This exercise will also introduce the layer folder feature, which is a great way to organize and consolidate animations containing many different layers.

---

1 Open **mutplShpTwn_Final.fla** from the **chap_05** folder.

---

2 Press **Enter** (Windows) or **Return** (Mac) to preview the movie. If you can't see the entire **Stage**, choose **View > Magnification > Show All** so you can see the whole animation, complete with multiple shape tweens. When you're finished viewing the animation, close the file.

In this exercise, you'll re-create this animation by shape tweening the alpha channel, or transparency, and the size of multiple shapes. On the Timeline, notice the folder with all the layers inside. The folder icon represents a layer folder, which you'll learn about later in this exercise.

---

3 Open **mutplShpTwn.fla** from the **chap_05** folder.

You can tween one shape into many shapes using just a single layer, but as you can see, this file contains five different shapes. The tween you will create in the next few steps requires that each of the five shapes be on its own layer.

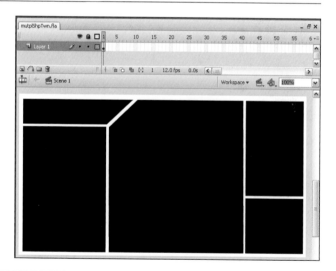

---

4 With **Layer 1** selected, click **Frame 1** to select all the shapes, and choose **Modify > Timeline > Distribute to Layers**.

The Distribute to Layers feature places each of the selected shapes on its own layer. If you click any of the shapes on the Stage, you'll see the corresponding layer highlighted on the Timeline.

5 Double-click **Layer 2**. When the bounding box appears, rename the layer to **Left bottom**, and press **Enter** (Windows) or **Return** (Mac). Rename **Layer 2** to **Left bottom**, **Layer 3** to **Left top**, **Layer 4** to **Middle**, **Layer 5** to **Right bottom**, and **Layer 6** to **Right top**.

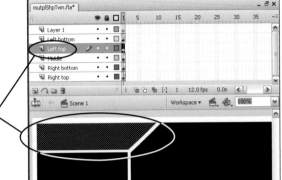

Giving layers descriptive names makes it easier to identify which shape is on each layer.

> When a layer is selected, the corresponding shape is selected on the Stage.

TIP:

Resizing the Timeline

Use the **edit bar** at the base of the **Timeline** to reveal more layers. Use the scroll bar to the right to extend the **Timeline** to reveal more of the layer names. You can also click and drag the **edit bar** to reduce or expand the height of the entire **Timeline**.

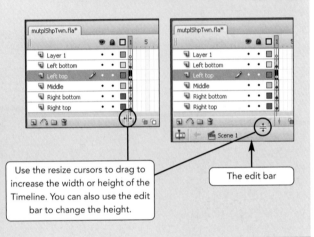

> Use the resize cursors to drag to increase the width or height of the Timeline. You can also use the edit bar to change the height.

> The edit bar

---

6 On the **Left bottom** layer, click **Frame 12** to select it. **Shift-click Frame 12** of the **Right top** layer to select **Frame 12** on all the layers.

---

7 Choose **Insert > Timeline > Keyframe** to add a keyframe to each layer.

Inserting a keyframe copies the artwork from Frame 1 of each layer, which will serve as the ending keyframe of your shape tween animation.

---

8 Position the playhead on **Frame 1**.

Next, you'll prepare the beginning point of the shape tween animation by altering the size of each shape on Frame 1.

---

9 On the **Timeline**, click the **Lock/Unlock All Layers** button, next to the **eye** icon, to lock all the currently selected layers. On the **Left bottom** layer, click the **lock** icon to unlock just that layer.

Locking layers makes it easier to work on just a single layer's shapes without affecting any of the other shapes.

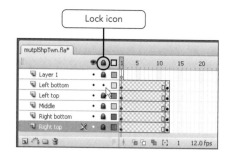

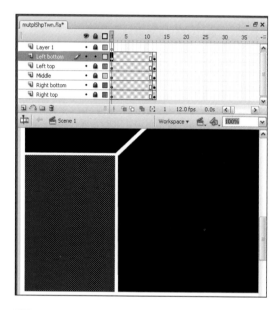

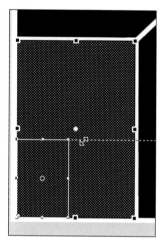

10 On the **Left bottom** layer, click **Frame 1** to select it. Select the **Free Transform** tool in the **Tools** panel. Position your cursor over the upper-right corner of the rectangle. When the resize cursor appears, drag toward the lower-left portion of the **Stage** to resize the shape, as shown in the illustration here. This will be the starting point of the animation for the **Left bottom** layer.

Tip: To scale the shape while keeping the same proportion (or aspect ratio), hold down the Shift key as you drag the resize cursor.

11 On the **Left bottom** layer, click the dot in the **lock** column to lock the layer. Click the **lock** icon for the **Middle** layer to unlock the layer.

Next, you'll resize the shape on the Middle layer.

12 On the **Middle** layer, click **Frame 1** to select it. With the **Free Transform** tool still selected in the **Tools panel**, hold down **Shift+Alt** (Windows) or **Shift+Opt** (Mac), and drag toward the lower left of the **Stage**, as shown in the illustration here.

Holding down Shift+Alt (Windows) or Shift+Opt (Mac) scales the shape down from its center, rather than one of the corners, creating the starting point for the animation in the center of the Middle layer.

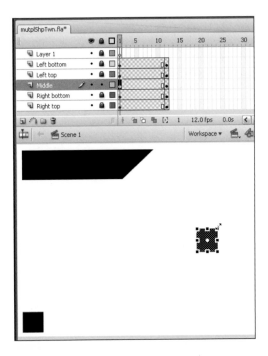

13 Repeat Steps 11 and 12 to select and resize the **Left top**, **Right bottom**, and **Right top** layers.

When you are finished, the shapes on the layers on Frame 1 should match the illustration shown here. If necessary, use the Selection tool to reposition the shape on the Middle layer near the center of the Stage.

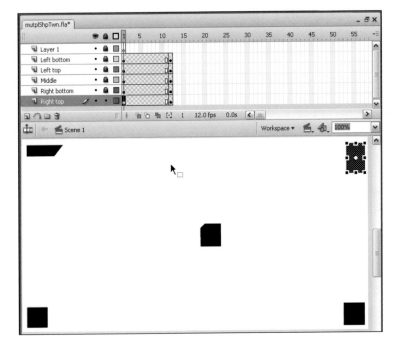

14 Click the **Lock/Unlock All Layers** button to unlock all the layers on the **Timeline**. Position the **playhead** on **Frame 1**. Make sure the **Color** panel is visible; if it's not, choose **Window > Color**.

Next, you'll use the Color panel to set all the keyframes to an alpha of 0%. The alpha setting lets you set the transparency of an object. In this case, you will set the transparency to 0% to make it invisible.

15 With the **Selection** tool, click the shape on the upper-left corner of the **Stage** to select it. You will change the alpha of this shape using the **Color** panel next.

16 Make sure the **Fill** color is selected in the **Color** panel. Type **0%** in the **Alpha** field, or drag the slider to **0%**. To see the changes to the shape on the **Stage**, deselect the shape by clicking a blank area on the **Stage**.

Since an Alpha setting of 0% means the object is completely transparent, the shape should now be invisible. Later, you will add a keyframe, change Alpha to 100% (completely visible), and create a tween to make the shape fade into view.

All shapes at 0 percent alpha

All shapes at 100 percent alpha

17 Hold down **Ctrl** (Windows) or **Cmd** (Mac), and click the remaining four shapes on the **Stage**—**Left bottom**, **Middle**, **Right top**, and **Right bottom**—to select them. In the **Color** panel, type **0%** in the **Alpha** field, and press **Enter** (Windows) or **Return** (Mac) to change the alpha for all four shapes at the same time. Click a blank area on the **Stage** to deselect all the shapes.

When you are finished, the Stage should appear as though it is blank. Don't worry, the shapes are still there—they are just completely transparent. Next, you'll add a shape tween to fade in the shapes from 0 to 100 percent alpha.

18 On the **Left bottom** layer, click **Frame 5** to select it. **Shift-click Frame 5** on the **Right top** layer to select **Frame 5** on all the layers.

---

19 Go to the **Property inspector**. If it is not open, choose **Window > Properties > Properties**. Choose **Shape** in the **Tween** pop-up menu to generate a shape tween

between each of the two keyframes on the currently selected layers.

Notice the solid arrow and the green tint between the keyframes, which signifies the tween is active and working.

---

20 Press **Enter** (Windows) or **Return** (Mac) to see the shape tween in action! Cool!

Notice the shapes fade in from invisible to visible while increasing in size at the same time. Next, you'll extend the last set of keyframes for 2 more seconds.

---

21 On the **Left bottom** layer, click **Frame 36** to select it. **Shift-click Frame 36** on the **Right top** layer to select **Frame 36** on all the layers.

---

22 Press **F5** to add 24 frames to the **Timeline**.

Provided the frame rate is set to the default of 12 frames per second, the final animation will be about 3 seconds long (2.9 to be exact, but 36 frames divided by 12 fps equals about 3 seconds). The shapes will tween from 0 to 100 percent alpha in the first second and remain on the Stage for another 2 seconds before looping again.

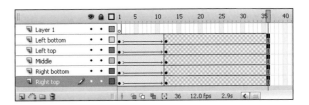

---

23 Choose **Control > Test Movie** to view the movie in a preview window and see the shape tweens in action again! When you're finished viewing the movie, close the preview window.

Notice the shapes in the animation fade in from 0 to 100 percent alpha and then remain on the Stage for about 2 more seconds before looping again. By using a multiple shape tween, you can have different animations on different layers all happening at the same time. In this case, each shape fading in and out is a separate animation.

What about that layer folder you saw in the finished version of this file? Next you'll learn how to put the shape tween layers into a layer folder.

24 Double-click the **Layer 1** icon to open the **Layer Properties** dialog box. Type **container** in the **Name** field, and select the **Folder** option. This changes **Layer 1** to a layer folder. Click **OK**.

For more information about the options in the Layer Properties dialog box, refer to the chart at the end of this exercise.

Layer icon

NOTE:

What Is a Layer Folder?

Layer folders let you store layers in an organized folder structure. Note that you cannot have artwork in a layer folder—the layer folder's sole purpose is to hold multiple layers so you can keep the **Timeline** compact and organized.

---

25 On the **Timeline**, hold down the **Shift** key and click the **Left bottom** and **Right top** layers to multiple-select the layers in-between but not the **container** layer folder. Drag the selected layers to the **container** layer folder to place the layers in the layer folder.

Layers outside folder

Layers inside folder

Notice the layers are all indented under the container layer folder, indicating they are part of the layer folder.

---

26 Click the triangle to the left of the **container** layer name to collapse the folder.

Now you see the layers, now you don't! Now this is organization! You will come to appreciate layer folders when you work on projects with dozens of layers.

Layers folder collapsed

---

27 Choose **Control > Test Movie** to view the movie file in a preview window. When you're finished viewing the movie, close the preview window.

Although you've moved the layers into a layer folder, the animation is left untouched. Layer folders are simply an organizational tool and do not alter the animation in any way.

---

28 Close **mutplShpTwn.fla**. You don't need to save your changes.

Understanding Layer Properties

The **Timeline** offers a number of ways of controlling layers, but other options are available in the **Layer Properties** dialog box. The following chart describes these additional options:

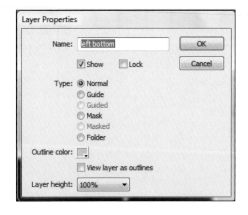

Layer Properties	
Option	**Description**
Guide	A **guide layer** lets you use the contents of a layer as a tracing image (or guide), which helps you create artwork on other layers. Guide layers are the only layers that are not exported with the movie.
Guided	A **guided layer** contains the objects that will animate by following the path defined on the guide layer. To create this animation, the guided layer is created first and then linked to the guide layer. Chapter 8, *"Motion Tweening and Timeline Effects,"* will give you hands-on experience working with guided layers.
Mask	A **mask layer** hides and reveals portions of artwork located in layers directly beneath the mask layer. You will learn more about mask layers in Chapter 9, *"Working with Bitmaps."*
Masked	**Masked layers** contain the artwork that is hidden or revealed by the mask layer above it. You will learn how to work with masked layers in Chapter 9, *"Working with Bitmaps."*
Folder	The **Folder** option lets you convert a regular layer into a layer folder. When converted, all content on the layer is automatically deleted. Layer folders contain one or more normal layers, making it easier to work with and organize projects with dozens of layers.
Outline color	When the **View layer as outlines** option is selected on the **Timeline**, Flash CS3 displays the contents of the layer as outlines on the **Stage**. The **Outline color** option lets you specify the color of these outlines. By default, each layer will use a different color; this option provides an additional degree of organizational control.
Layer height	This option lets you change the height at which a layer or folder is displayed on the **Timeline**. The default view is 100 percent, but Flash also provides two enlarged views (200 percent or 300 percent), which are especially useful for working with sounds.

With the exercises in this chapter, you've gained a solid foundation on the basics and subtle nuances of shape tweening. As you gain experience with Flash CS3, you'll find shape tweening a useful technique for accomplishing many types of effects. Next, you'll learn about symbols and instances.

6

Creating Symbols and Instances

Effective Adobe Flash CS3 Professional movies, even simple ones, often use symbols and instances. So, what are symbols and instances, and what can they do for you? **Symbols** let you create content once and use it over and over in your movies. This very powerful feature has several benefits. Symbols let you create complex movies from simpler components that are easier to create and update and that download faster. How? Symbols download only once, regardless of how many copies (called **instances**) you have in your movie. For example, if you have a symbol of a snowflake and you add 50 instances of that snowflake to the **Stage**, the file size would be not be significantly larger, because the snowflake has to download only once. If, instead, you were to draw 50 separate snowflakes, 50 snowflakes would have to download, which would increase the file size dramatically.

The concept of symbols and instances takes practice to fully comprehend. This chapter will give you that practice so you can better understand how to create and work with symbols and instances to create effective Flash CS3 projects.

Understanding the Symbol and Instance Structure

Think of a Flash symbol as a master object or stamp. You create a symbol once—it can be a simple shape or something complex—and use it multiple times throughout your movie. Each time you reuse a symbol in your project file, it is called an **instance**, which is a copy of a symbol.

The concept of symbols and instances is the key to reducing the file size and download time for your Flash CS3 documents. Symbols need to be downloaded, but instances are simply described in a small text file by their attributes (scale, color, transparency, animation, and so on), which is why they add so little to the final file size of your movie. The best way to reduce file sizes is to create symbols for any object you'll use more than

once in your movie. In addition to reducing file size and download time, symbols and instances also help you make quick updates to objects across your entire project file—a real time-saver! Later in the book, as you learn about more advanced animation techniques, you'll see symbols and instances play an important and dramatic role in animation, too!

Flash CS3 offers three types of symbols: graphic symbols, button symbols, and movie clip symbols. In this chapter, you'll be working only with graphic symbols (button and movie clip symbols are covered in later chapters).

Here's a handy chart defining some of the terms you'll encounter in this chapter:

Symbol Definitions	
Term	**Definition**
Symbol	A reusable object that serves as a master, which you can use to create copies (instances). When you create a symbol, it automatically becomes part of the project file's library.
Instance	A copy of the original symbol. You can alter the color, size, shape, and position of an instance without affecting the original symbol.
Button symbol	A symbol used for navigation within an animation or **Timeline**. Buttons, in combination with ActionScript, add interactivity to a movie via user clicks.
Graphic symbol	A symbol containing static artwork or animation. The graphic symbol **Timeline** is dependent on the main **Timeline**—graphic symbol animations play only while the main **Timeline** is playing. You'll learn more about this behavior as you work through the exercises in this book.
Movie clip symbol	A symbol containing one or more button or graphic symbols. A movie clip is like a Flash movie within a movie.

Symbol Naming Conventions

As you start creating symbols and instances, you'll need to name them. In more complex projects that include ActionScript, instance names become important, especially for movie clip symbols. For this reason, you need to adhere to some guidelines when naming symbols, instances, and document files in Flash CS3. Following these rules will keep you out of a lot of trouble.

Do Use

Do use the following in symbol names:

Lowercase letters (a–z) for the first character: Symbol names starting with numbers or uppercase letters can confuse ActionScript. For this reason, start symbol names with a lowercase letter. You can use numbers (1–9) for symbol names but not as the first character. Restricting your names to only lowercase letters makes them easier to remember.

Descriptive names: Try to use descriptive, easy-to-remember names. For example, use **gfxLogoBkgd** rather than **symbol6**. When using multiword names, capitalize the first letter of each word (except the first word) so you can read it easier. However, remember that when you refer to an object in ActionScript, you must reference the symbol with the same capitalization you used in its name.

Don't Use

Don't use the following in symbol names:

Special characters: Special characters such as !, @, #, &, $, and many others are forbidden. Many of these special characters have a specific meaning to Flash CS3 and can cause problems with ActionScript. To avoid accidentally using a special character, avoid everything but numbers and letters.

Spaces: Never use spaces in your names. Instead, string your words together, or use underscores. For example, instead of **my first symbol**, use **myFirstSymbol** or, even better, **my_first_symbol** (no uppercase letters to remember!).

Periods: Never put periods in your file or symbol names (other than the three-letter extension). For example, **snow.boarder.fla** will cause problems. Instead, use **snow_boarder.fla**.

Slashes: Slashes are misinterpreted as path locations on a hard drive. Never use them. For example, **my/new/symbol** would be interpreted as the object **symbol** located in the **new** folder located in the **my** folder.

Important Timeline Vocabulary Terms

This chapter reintroduces the **Timeline**; in the following exercises, you'll learn that symbols contain their own **Timelines** "nested" within the main **Timeline**. Therefore, you may have a single project with several different **Timelines**. The following chart will help you further understand the distinctions among the various types of **Timelines**:

Timeline Definitions	
Term	**Definition**
Main Timeline	When you open a Flash CS3 project file (FLA), it defaults to the main **Timeline**. The main **Timeline** is indicated by the **Scene 1** icon in the **edit bar** below the **Timeline**.
Symbol Timeline	Every symbol has its own **Timeline**. You can view a symbol **Timeline** by double-clicking an instance on the **Stage** or on the symbol icon in the **Library** panel. Graphic symbol **Timelines** are synchronized with the parent or main **Timeline**. Therefore, the **Timeline** for a graphic symbol and the scene in which the symbol is placed must have the same number of frames, or the symbol's animation will not play properly. This is a unique behavior of the graphic symbol; button and movie clip symbols do not behave the same way. They have their own **Timelines** that can be controlled independently. You'll learn about button and movie clip symbols in later chapters.
Scene Timeline	By default, every Flash project (FLA) starts with one scene, which is interchangeable with the main **Timeline**. However, you'll see in later chapters that Flash CS3 projects can have multiple scenes. The advantage to having multiple scenes is to be able to break out different sections of your animation without having separate project files. When the scenes are published, they are exported and compiled in a single SWF file. You'll learn more about scenes in Chapter 12, *"ActionScript Basics."*

1 | Creating Graphic Symbols

You can use symbols for many purposes in Flash CS3. Before you can learn the power and potential benefits of symbols, you'll need to know how to create them. This exercise shows you how to create a graphic symbol.

---

1 Copy the **chap_06** folder from the **Flash HOT CD-ROM** to your desktop. Open **graphicSymbol.fla** from the **chap_06** folder.

This file contains one layer with a snowflake on Frame 1. You'll convert this shape into a graphic symbol in the following steps.

2 Choose **Window > Library**, or press **Ctrl+L** (Windows) or **Cmd+L** (Mac), to open the **Library** panel.

Notice the project file name displayed at the top of the Library panel.

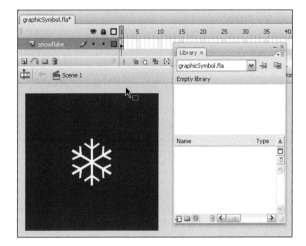

NOTE:

What Is the Library Panel?

The **Library** panel is a container where Flash CS3 stores and organizes symbols, bitmap graphics, sound clips, video clips, and fonts. Since each media has a different icon associated with it, it's easy to identify the different **Library** assets at a glance. For designers, it can be one of the most useful and frequently used interface elements in the program. The **Library** panel is attached to the movie on which you're working. If you give your project file (FLA) to someone else, that person will see the same **Library** panel you see when you have the file open.

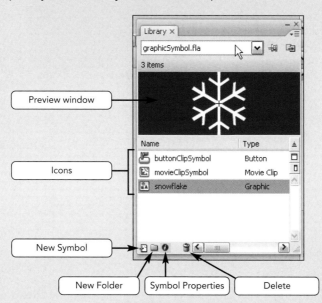

In the **Library** panel, you can sort the contents by name, kind, use count, and linkage. As your files become more complex, you can create folders within your **Library** panel to help separate your symbols into different categories. Since you will frequently work with the **Library** panel, learn the shortcut to open it: **Ctrl+L** (Windows) or **Cmd+L** (Mac). You will get an in-depth look at the **Library** panel and all its functions in later chapters.

3 Using the **Selection** tool, select the snowflake on the **Stage**. Notice the dotted mesh, indicating you have selected a shape. Drag the snowflake to the lower half of the **Library** panel to open the **Convert to Symbol** dialog box.

Note: Instead of dragging the shape to the Library panel, you can also select the shape and choose Modify > Convert to Symbol, or press F8, to open the Convert to Symbol dialog box.

4 Type **snowflake** in the **Name** field, select **Type: Graphic**, and make sure the middle box of the **Registration** square is selected. Click **OK**.

Note: In later chapters, you'll learn about movie clip and button symbols, which are more complex to explain and require an understanding of graphic symbols first. For this reason, this chapter focuses exclusively on graphic symbols.

Notice you now have two snowflakes in your project file: the snowflake symbol, which is located in the Library panel, and a snowflake instance (a copy of the original symbol) on the Stage. Instances are copies of symbols from the Library panel brought to the Stage. Congratulations! You just made your first graphic symbol!

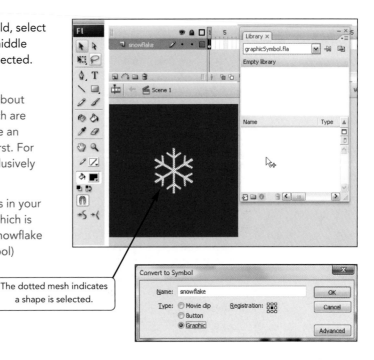

The dotted mesh indicates a shape is selected.

N O T E :

The Convert to Symbol Dialog Box

The **Convert to Symbol** dialog box offers two views: **Basic** (the default) and **Advanced**. To access the **Advanced** view, click the **Advanced** button. The **Advanced** view contains two extra sections: **Linkage** and **Source**. The **Source** section includes information and settings related to the source of the new symbol, such as its file location or whether it should always be updated before publishing. The **Linkage** settings will be covered in Chapter 14, *"Sound."* To return to **Basic** view, click the **Basic** button.

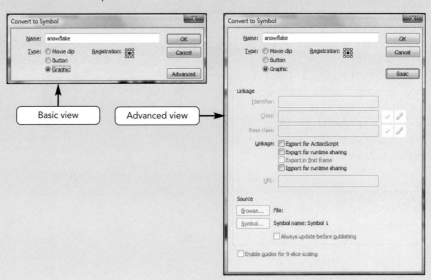

Basic view   Advanced view

What Is a Registration Point?

When you convert a shape into a symbol, Flash CS3 needs to know where you want the shape's center point to be located. Why? It becomes important when you create animation using rotation because the symbol will rotate around its registration point.

Selected snowflake before being converted to a symbol

Selected snowflake after being converted to a symbol

Registration point

Once converted to a symbol, the snowflake on the **Stage** changed slightly. Notice the bounding box and the circle with a crosshair in the middle of the snowflake. This provides visual feedback that your snowflake is now a graphic symbol. The circle and crosshair act as a marker, telling you where the center (or **registration point**) of the symbol is. This is an important indicator because it affects how all the instances of this symbol are rotated and scaled. You will learn how to rotate and scale instances later in this chapter.

5 With the **Selection** tool, click the **snowflake** instance on the **Stage** to select it.

6 Press the **Delete** key to delete the **snowflake** instance on the **Stage**.

Notice the snowflake is no longer on the Stage or on Frame 1 of the snowflake layer and the keyframe has been replaced by a blank keyframe. Notice also, however, the snowflake graphic symbol is still safely stored in the Library panel.

Note: Don't worry if you delete an instance from the Stage; you can still find it in the Library panel. However, if you delete a symbol from the Library panel, it may be gone forever. If you accidentally do this, quickly undo the deletion by choosing Edit > Undo Delete Library Item or pressing Ctrl+Z (Windows) or Cmd+Z (Mac). You can also choose File > Revert to return the project file to its state the last time you saved it.

7 In the **Library** panel, click the **snowflake** graphic symbol icon, and drag it to the **Stage** to add a **snowflake** instance on the **Stage**.

Notice a keyframe is placed on Frame 1 of the snowflake layer.

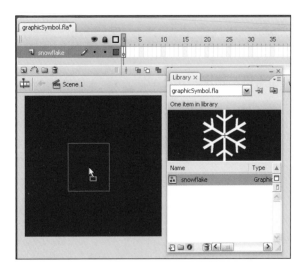

8 Save **graphicSymbol.fla** by choosing **File > Save**. Close the file.

In the next exercise, you will learn to work with symbol instances.

TIP:

Five Ways to Create a Symbol

You can create a symbol in five ways either by using artwork on the **Stage** or by creating a new symbol from scratch on a blank **Stage**:

- Select the artwork on the **Stage** and drag it to the **Library** panel to automatically turn the artwork you select into a symbol.

- Select the artwork on the **Stage** and choose **Modify > Convert to Symbol**, or press the shortcut key **F8**, to automatically turn the artwork you select into a symbol.

- Choose **Insert > New Symbol**, or press **Ctrl+F8** (Windows) or **Cmd+F8** (Mac), to open the **New Symbol** dialog box.

- Choose **New Symbol** in the **Library Options** menu (in the upper-right corner of the **Library**) to open the **New Symbol** dialog box.

- Click the **New Symbol** button (in the lower-left corner of the **Library** panel) to open the **New Symbol** dialog box.

2 | Creating Symbol Instances

In the previous exercise, you learned how to create a symbol. In this exercise, you will learn how to create and modify instances of a symbol. Since instances are just copies of the master symbol, you can modify them individually without affecting the master symbol in the **Library** panel. You will learn how in this exercise.

---

1 Open **instances.fla** from the **chap_06** folder.

This file contains two layers: a layer named background, which contains a bitmap image, and a layer named snowflake instances, where you will place instances of the snowflake graphic symbol you created in the previous exercise. The background layer has been locked so that you don't accidentally edit that layer.

---

2 Click the **snowflake instances** layer to select it.

---

3 Make sure the **Library** panel is visible. If it's not, choose **Window > Library**, or press **Ctrl+L** (Windows) or **Cmd+L** (Mac).

Notice the Library panel contains two items: the snowflake symbol and a bitmap image called backgroundPic.jpg. You might be wondering how those elements got there. The snowflake was converted to a symbol in this project file, after which it automatically appeared in the Library panel. The backgroundPic.jpg bitmap was imported into the Flash CS3 file for you. Anytime images are imported into Flash CS3, they automatically get added to the Library panel. As you know from the previous exercise, the Library panel stores more than just symbols; it also stores bitmaps, sounds, and video clips. You'll learn more about importing images and other content into Flash CS3 in Chapter 19, *"Integration."*

4 In the **Library** panel, click and drag the **snowflake** graphic symbol icon to the **Stage**.

When you release the mouse, you'll see an instance of the snowflake on the Stage. Notice a keyframe is placed on Frame 1 of the snowflake instances layer.

Note: Symbols are stored in the Library panel, and instances are located on the Stage. From every symbol, you can create as many instances as you want on the Stage.

5 Click and drag seven additional snowflakes from the **Library** panel to the **Stage**. When you're finished, you should have a total of eight **snowflake** instances on the **Stage**.

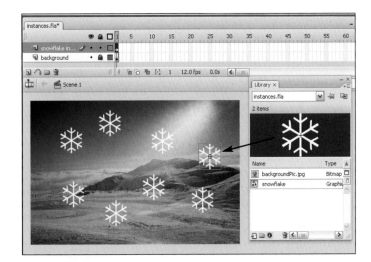

Tip: You can also insert instances by clicking in the Library panel's preview window and dragging an instance to the Stage.

Clicking and dragging from the Library is one way to create instances on your Stage, but you can also Alt-drag (Windows) or Opt-drag (Mac) an instance to the Stage to create a duplicate of it without dragging it from the Library panel.

6 Save your changes, and leave **instances.fla** open for the next exercise.

Next, you'll learn how to edit symbols.

3 | Editing Symbols

Instances on the **Stage** have a parent/child relationship with their corresponding symbols in the **Library** panel. One of the advantages of this special relationship is that if you change a symbol in the **Library** panel, all the instances on your **Stage** update. As you can imagine, this feature can save a lot of time when you're making large updates across an entire project. This ability to make quick—and sometimes large—updates is one of the most powerful advantages of symbols. In this exercise, you'll modify the appearance of the snowflake symbol to change all eight instances on the **Stage**.

1 If you just completed Exercise 2, **instances.fla** should still be open. If it's not, complete Exercise 2, and then return to this exercise.

2 Make sure the **Library** panel is visible. If it's not, press **Ctrl+L** (Windows) or **Cmd+L** (Mac) to open it.

3 In the **Library** panel, double-click the **graphic symbol** icon to the left of the **snowflake** symbol name.

Notice the Stage changes; you are now in symbol editing mode, which means you're no longer working in the main Timeline. Notice the gray Stage pasteboard is gone, as is the blue bounding box around the symbol. When you're in symbol editing mode (inside a symbol), you won't see the pasteboard area, unless you are using the Edit in Place feature, which you'll learn about later in this exercise. Also notice the edit bar above the Stage shows two names: Scene 1 and snowflake, which is another indicator you are no longer working on the main Timeline but instead are inside the snowflake graphic symbol Timeline.

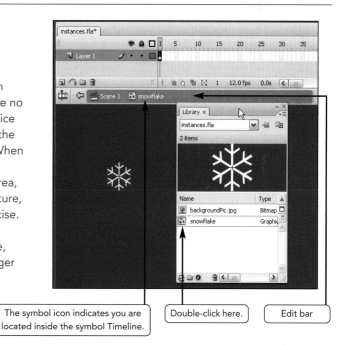

The symbol icon indicates you are located inside the symbol Timeline.

Double-click here.

Edit bar

TIP: **Frequently Check Your Location in the Edit Bar**

It's easy to get lost when moving in and out of symbol editing mode. You may not even be aware you have switched views. So, keep a watchful eye on the **edit bar**, which indicates where you are and on which **Timeline** you are working. Users of previous versions of Flash will notice that the **edit bar** has been moved from the top of the **Timeline** to the bottom.

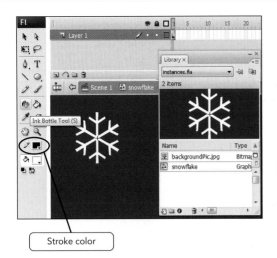
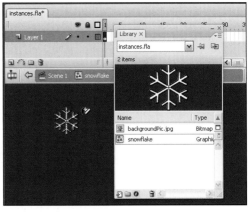

Stroke color

4 Select the **Ink Bottle** tool in the **Tools** panel, and select black from the **Stroke Color** palette. Click the **snowflake** to add a stroke to the shape.

The preview window in the Library panel updates instantly to reflect the change you made.

---

5 In the **edit bar**, click the **Scene 1** link to return to the main **Timeline**. You should see the bitmap with the snow and sky.

The gray Stage pasteboard appears again, and you see only the Scene 1 name, without the snowflake name next to it. Also notice how all the instances of the snowflake have a black stroke around them. Every time you modify a symbol, it affects all the instances you have in your project file. This can be a powerful way to make project-wide changes to your Flash files.

Stage pasteboard

---

6 With the **Selection** tool, double-click a **snowflake** instance on the **Stage**.

Double-clicking an instance lets you edit the symbol in place, which means in the context of the other instances on the Stage. When you edit a symbol in place, the other objects on the Stage dim to differentiate them from the symbol you are editing. You can also edit the symbol in place by selecting an instance and choosing Edit > Edit in Place.

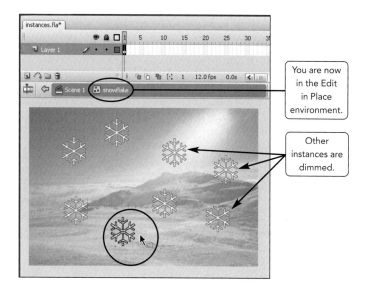

You are now in the Edit in Place environment.

Other instances are dimmed.

TIP:

Techniques for Editing Symbols

Editing an instance in place (double-clicking the instance on the **Stage**) produces the same end result as editing the symbol in the **Library** panel (double-clicking the graphic symbol icon to the left of the symbol name in the **Library** panel). Both techniques change the appearance of the master symbol as well as all of its instances. The difference between the two techniques is that when you edit the symbol in the **Library** panel, you cannot see the main **Timeline**. When you edit an instance in place, you see a dimmed version of the **Stage**, and you can preview your changes in context with the rest of the objects on the **Stage**.

Stroke selected

Stroke deleted from all snowflake instances

7 Select the **Selection** tool in the **Tools** panel, and double-click the stroke around the **snowflake** to select it. Press the **Delete** key to remove the stroke.

Notice the strokes on all the other snowflake instances have been deleted as well. Again, each time you edit a symbol, all the other instances of that symbol update as well. Next, you'll make a change to the fill of the snowflake symbol.

8 With the **Selection** tool, click to select the **snowflake** instance on the **Stage**.

9 In the **Property inspector**, click the **Fill Color** box, and choose a shade of blue.

Because the snowflake was already selected, the fill color of the snowflake updated as soon as you selected a color. Again, all the other instances of the snowflake change color as well.

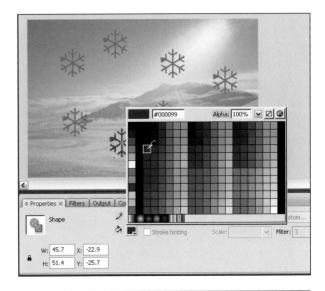

10 In the **edit bar**, click the **Scene 1** link to return to the main **Timeline**. You now see the **background** bitmap and the **snowflake instances** in full color.

11 Save your changes, and leave **instances.fla** open for the next exercise.

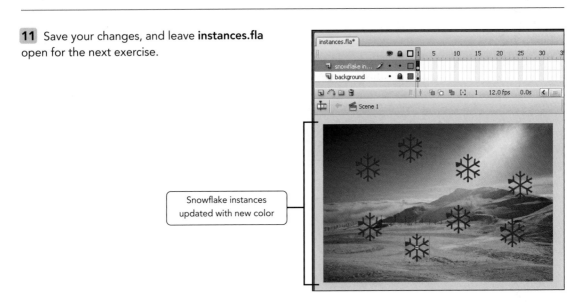

Snowflake instances updated with new color

4 | Editing Symbol Instances

In the previous exercise, you learned how to modify a symbol to make changes to all the instances on the **Stage**. What do you do if you want to change the color of one instance or change the color of each instance individually? Not to worry, you select an instance on the **Stage** in the main **Timeline** and modify the color in the **Property inspector**. The **Property inspector** lets you change the tint, brightness, and alpha settings of symbol instances. This is the only way to change the color values of an instance because the **Paint Bucket** and **Brush** tools work only on shapes, not on symbol instances. In this exercise, you will use the **Property inspector** and the **Free Transform** tool to change the appearance of instances—in this case, individual snowflakes.

1 If you just completed Exercise 3, **instances.fla** should still be open. If it's not, complete Exercise 3, and then return to this exercise.

2 Select the **Selection** tool in the **Tools** panel. Click the **snowflake** instance in the upper-left corner of the **Stage** to select it.

Make sure you click the snowflake instance just once. If you double-click it accidentally, you'll enter symbol editing mode, which means you'll be editing the symbol, not the instance. If this happens, return to the main Timeline by clicking the Scene 1 link in the edit bar.

Click once to
select a snowflake
instance.

3 Make sure the **Property inspector** is visible. If it's not, choose **Window > Properties > Properties**, or use the shortcut **Ctrl+F3** (Windows) or **Cmd+F3** (Mac) to open it.

4 Choose **Brightness** in the **Color** pop-up menu in the **Property inspector**. Click the slider to the right of the pop-up menu, and drag it up to **100%** to increase the brightness level of the selected instance.

Note: The Brightness option controls the brightness value of the instance and has a range of -100% (completely black) to 100% (completely white).

Instance updated to a brightness of 100 percent

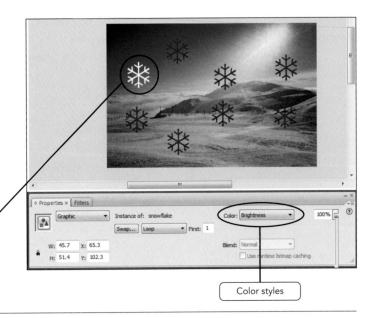

Color styles

---

5 With the **Selection** tool, click to select a different **snowflake** instance on the **Stage**. Select any snowflake you want.

---

6 Choose **Tint** in the **Color** pop-up menu in the **Property inspector** to apply a tint to the base color of your instance. Click the **Tint Color** box, and select a shade of yellow in the pop-up color palette.

---

7 Click and drag the **Tint** slider to **75%**.

As you drag the slider, notice how the color becomes brighter. The Tint option has a range of 0% (no tint) to 100% (fully saturated). Tinting changes the amount of color applied to the instance. It also changes the RGB values in the Property inspector.

Note: You control the color of the instance by modifying the percentage of the tint being applied and the individual RGB (**R**ed, **G**reen, and **B**lue) values. The Tint option is the only way you can change the color of an instance, other than setting the RGB values directly in

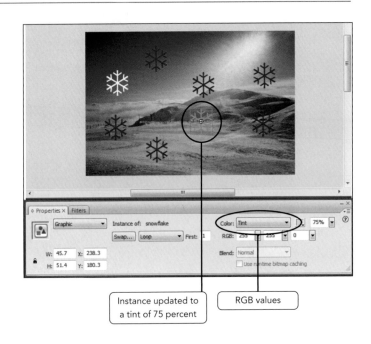

Instance updated to a tint of 75 percent

RGB values

the Advanced Effect dialog box, which you will do later in this exercise. This option also changes both the Fill and Stroke settings to the value you specify. You cannot change these settings separately when editing the instance; you can edit Fill and Stroke settings only when you are editing the symbol.

8 With the **Selection** tool, click to select another **snowflake** instance on the **Stage**. Select one that has not been modified yet.

9 Choose **Alpha** in the **Color** pop-up menu in the **Property inspector**.

The Alpha setting, which has a range of 100% (opaque) to 0% (transparent), lets you control the transparency value of the selected instance.

10 Click and drag the **Alpha** slider to **0%** to decrease the transparency. Watch the selected snowflake disappear as you drag the slider. Return the **Alpha** slider to **30%**.

In the next few steps, you'll learn about the Advanced option in the Color pop-up menu, which lets you modify multiple settings for a selected object. For example, you can use this option to adjust both the Tint and Alpha settings of the selected instance. The best way to learn about the Color pop-up menu is to use it, so you'll do that next.

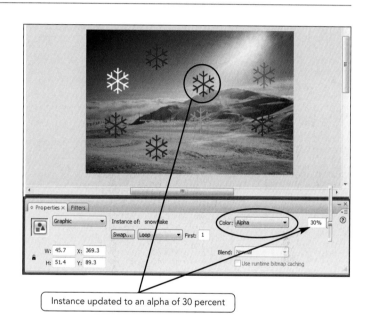

Instance updated to an alpha of 30 percent

11 With the **Selection** tool, click to select another unmodified **snowflake** instance on the **Stage**.

12 Choose **Advanced** in the **Color** pop-up menu in the **Property inspector**. Click the **Settings** button.

13 In the **Advanced Effect** dialog box, click the **arrow**, and drag the **Red** slider to **60%**, the **Blue** slider to **10%**, and the **Alpha** slider to **50%**.

The left column of fields in the Advanced Effect dialog box lets you manipulate the colors using percentages, and the right column of fields lets you manipulate the colors using numbers corresponding with color values.

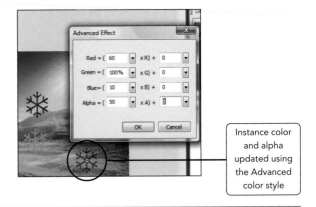

Instance color and alpha updated using the Advanced color style

---

14 For the remaining snowflakes, practice changing the brightness, tint, alpha, or a combination of these, using the **Advanced** feature.

It never hurts to practice! If you'd like to learn more about the controls in the Color pop-up menu, check out the chart at the end of this exercise.

NOTE:

Removing Color Styles

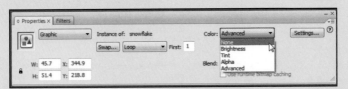

Up to this point in the exercise, you have added many different color styles to the instances on the **Stage**. If you want to remove the styles you applied to an instance, you can simply select the instance and choose **None** in the **Color** pop-up menu to restore the instance to its original condition.

So far, you've changed symbol instances by modifying their brightness, tint, and alpha. However, you can also rotate, scale, and skew instances. In the following steps, you'll learn how using the Free Transform tool.

---

15 With the **Selection** tool, click to select any unmodified snowflake on the **Stage**.

---

16 Select the **Free Transform** tool in the **Tools** panel.

When you select the Free Transform tool, notice a bounding box appears around the selected snowflake.

---

17 Position the cursor over the bottom-middle handle of the bounding box. When the cursor changes to the **scale** cursor, click and drag to increase the height of the snowflake.

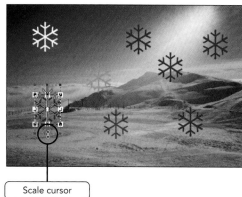

Free Transform Tool (Q,F)

Scale cursor

18 Position the cursor between the bottom-left and middle handles (slightly above the handles) until you see the **skew** cursor. Then click and drag to the left to skew the selected snowflake.

Skew cursor

19 With the **Free Transform** tool, click to select another unmodified snowflake on the **Stage**.

20 Position the cursor over the bottom-left handle. When the cursor changes to the scale cursor, click and drag diagonally to scale the snowflake to a larger size.

Tip: If you hold down the Shift key while you drag one of the handles, the snowflake will scale proportionally on all sides.

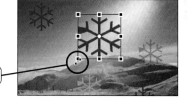

Scale cursor

21 With the **Free Transform** tool, click to select another unmodified snowflake on the **Stage**.

22 Position the cursor over a corner handle until the **rotate** cursor appears. Click and drag to rotate the selected snowflake.

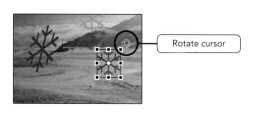

Rotate cursor

Changing the Registration Point

When using the **Free Transform** tool, you'll notice each selected object has the circle in the center, which serves as an anchor from which position, rotation, and scale originate. You can move the center point (registration point) if you want.

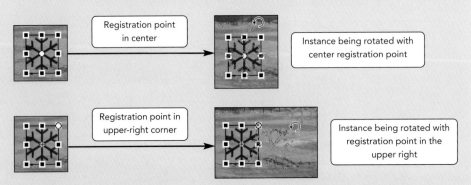

Registration point in center

Instance being rotated with center registration point

Registration point in upper-right corner

Instance being rotated with registration point in the upper right

Here's how: To change the registration point, select the instance with the **Free Transform** tool, and click and drag the center circle to a new location. From then on, any transformations you make will originate from this new position. Use this technique when you want to rotate from a corner; you can even move the registration point off the image to rotate on a distant axis.

23 Using the **Free Transform** tool, click to select the last snowflake on the **Stage**. Apply any transformation you like.

Remember, practice makes perfect, so have some fun creating your own transformation to the last unchanged snowflake instance.

24 When you are done experimenting, close **instances.fla**. You don't need to save your changes.

Using Color Styles

The following chart explains the options available in the **Color** pop-up menu in the **Property inspector**. As you learned in Exercise 4, you can use the color style options to change the color and alpha of an instance.

Color Style Options	
Option	**Description**
Brightness	Controls the brightness (lightness or darkness) of the selected symbol. The percentage slider goes from **-100%** (black) to **100%** (white).
Tint	Tints a selected symbol with a specific RGB color. You can choose a color from the **Tint** color palette and use the slider to modify the percentage of that specific color. You can set the range from **100%** (fully saturated at the specified color) to **0%** (contains none of the specified color). You can also choose a color by moving the **R**, **G**, and **B** color sliders up and down.
Alpha	Changes the transparency of a selected instance. Using the slider, you can make instances completely opaque (**100%**), completely transparent (**0%**), or any value in between.
Advanced	Adjusts both the tint and alpha of an instance. Experiment with the different settings to get the appearance you want.

5 | Animating Graphic Symbols

Until now, you have been working with static graphic symbols. In this exercise, you'll learn how to create a graphic symbol containing an animation. When you use animated graphic symbols in Flash CS3, the number of frames inside the symbol must be the same as the number of frames on the main **Timeline**. In this exercise, you will modify the **snowflake** graphic symbol and add a simple shape tween animation to its **Timeline** to convert it to an animated graphic symbol. The end result will be a snowflake that turns into a small snowball and then fades away.

---

1 Open **animSymbol_Final.fla** from the **chap_06** folder.

---

2 Choose **Control > Test Movie** to preview the animation. When you're finished, close the preview window, and close **animSymbol_Final.fla**.

It's snowing! In this exercise, you'll play Mother Nature and create this snowing animation.

---

3 Open **animSymbol.fla** from the **chap_06** folder.

This file contains two layers: one named background, which contains a bitmap background image, and one named animSymbol, where you will place the animated graphic symbol you are about to create. The background layer has been locked so you don't modify it accidentally.

---

4 Make sure the **Library** panel is visible. If it's not, press **Ctrl+L** (Windows) or **Cmd+L** (Mac) to open it.

The Library panel contains two items: backgroundPic.jpg, which is the background image, and a snowflake graphic symbol, which you will animate in the next steps.

---

5 In the **Library** panel, double-click the **graphic symbol** icon to the left of the **snowflake** symbol name to enter symbol editing mode.

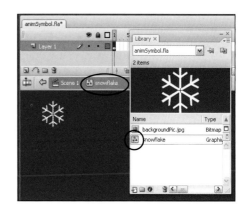

Notice that the contents of the Stage have changed and that the snowflake graphic symbol icon appears in the edit bar. These two clues indicate you are in symbol editing mode.

In the following steps, you will create a shape tween animation to make the snowflake look like it is falling as it changes into a small snowball and then fades away. Keep in mind you are creating this animation of your snowflake on the graphic symbol Timeline, which is different from the main Timeline in Scene 1. As a result, the animation will affect all the instances of this symbol on the main Timeline because you are editing the master symbol.

---

6 In the **Timeline**, double-click **Layer 1**. When the bounding box appears, type **snowflake**, and press **Enter** (Windows) or **Return** (Mac) to rename the layer. Press **F7** on **Frame 12** to add a blank keyframe.

Remember, a blank keyframe copies no artwork from the previous keyframe.

---

7 At the bottom of the **Timeline**, click the **Onion Skin** button. Drag the start onion skin marker to **Frame 1** and the end onion skin marker to **Frame 12**. Click the **Modify Onion Skins** button, and choose **Anchor Onion** in the pop-up menu.

By turning on onion skinning, you will be able to see a faint ghost image of the artwork on Frame 1 and add artwork relative to it.

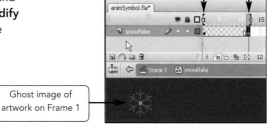

Onion skin markers

Ghost image of artwork on Frame 1

---

8 Select the **Oval** tool in the **Tools** panel, and set **Stroke** to **none** and **Fill** to **white**.

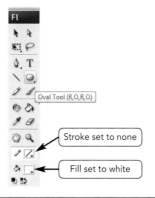

Oval Tool (R,O,R,O)

Stroke set to none

Fill set to white

9 Make sure the playhead is on **Frame 12**. With the **Oval** tool, draw a small **snowball** just below the ghost image of the snowflake.

Notice the new keyframe on Frame 12. You will create the tween between the two keyframes in the following steps.

---

10 Make sure you are still on the **snowflake** graphic symbol **Timeline** (check the edit bar), and click anywhere between **Frame 1** and **Frame 12** to select one of the frames.

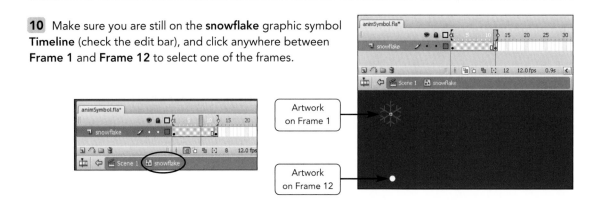

Artwork on Frame 1

Artwork on Frame 12

---

11 Make sure the **Property inspector** is visible. If it is not, press **Ctrl+F3** (Windows) or **Cmd+F3** (Mac). Since the snowflake and the snowball are both shapes, choose **Shape** in the **Tween** pop-up menu.

---

12 Press **Enter** (Windows) or **Return** (Mac) to get a quick preview of what your animation will look like. Notice the snowflake turns into a snowball in about 1 second, provided your frame rate is set to the default setting of 12 frames per second (12 frames divided by 12 fps equals 1 second).

---

13 Press **F6** on **Frame 24** to add a keyframe. Select the **Selection** tool in the **Tools panel**. Click and drag the snowball circle on **Frame 24** down, as shown in the illustration here.

Remember, a keyframe identifies a change in the Timeline and copies the artwork of the previous keyframe. In this case, you copied the artwork of the snowball on Frame 12 to Frame 24 and then moved the artwork down. Next, you'll make the snowball disappear.

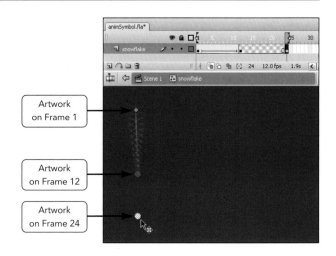

Artwork on Frame 1

Artwork on Frame 12

Artwork on Frame 24

14 Make sure the **Color** panel is visible. If it's not, choose **Window > Color**, or press **Shift+F9** (Windows only). With the snowball still selected on **Frame 24**, make sure the **Fill** color is selected in the **Color panel**, and set **Alpha** to **0%** to make the snowball on **Frame 24** transparent. Watch it disappear! Click anywhere other than the snowball to deselect it and get the full effect.

You'll add a second tween in the next steps.

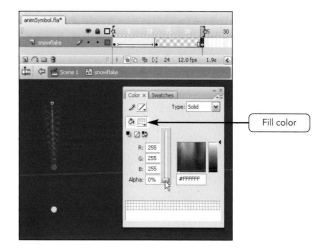

Fill color

15 In the **snowflake** graphic symbol **Timeline**, click anywhere between **Frame 12** and **Frame 24** to select one of the frames.

16 In the **Property inspector**, choose **Shape** from the **Tween** pop-up menu to add a second tween, showing the snowball falling and disappearing.

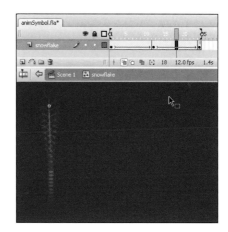

17 At the bottom of the **Timeline**, click the **Onion Skin** button to turn off onion skinning.

Notice the onion skin markers have disappeared.

18 Position the playhead on **Frame 1**, and press **Enter** (Windows) or **Return** (Mac) to preview the entire animation. As the snowflake falls, it should turn into a snowball, and then the snowball should fade away, all in about 2 seconds (24 frames divided by 12 fps equals 2 seconds). Not bad!

TIP:

Where Do You Change the Alpha Transparency?

Use the **Property inspector** to set the alpha transparency of an instance (bounding box).

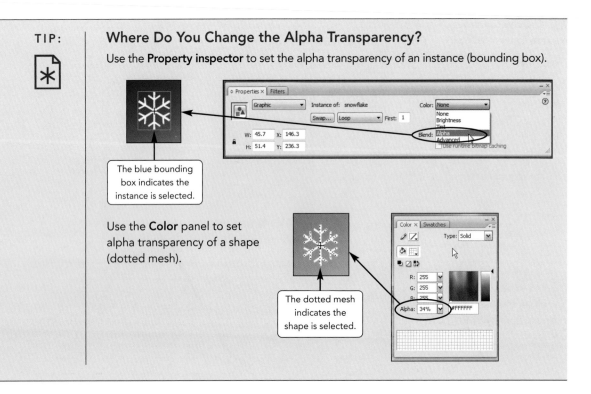

The blue bounding box indicates the instance is selected.

Use the **Color** panel to set alpha transparency of a shape (dotted mesh).

The dotted mesh indicates the shape is selected.

19 When you are happy with the animation, click the **Scene 1** link in the **edit bar** to return to the main **Timeline**.

You'll add the snowflake animated graphic symbol to the main Timeline next.

20 Select **Frame 1** on the **animSymbol** layer. Click and drag the **snowflake** graphic symbol from the **Library** panel to the **Stage** to add an instance of the animated **snowflake** graphic symbol to the main **Timeline**, **Scene 1**.

Notice there is now a keyframe on Frame 1 of the animSymbol layer.

Instance of the snowflake graphic symbol

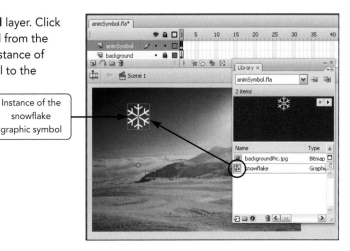

21 Choose **Control > Test Movie** to preview your movie. But wait, the snowflake is not animating! Why? You will learn how to fix this next. Close the preview window to return to the main **Timeline**.

The Timeline of the animated graphic symbol is directly related to the main Timeline (the current scene—in this case, Scene 1) of the project. If the animated graphic symbol is 24 frames long, the main Timeline also needs to be at least 24 frames long. Currently, the main Timeline is one frame long; therefore, only one frame is displayed. To fix this animation, you need to extend the main Timeline to at least 24 frames.

---

22 Click **Frame 24** on the **animSymbol** layer and **Shift-click Frame 24** of the **background** layer to select both frames.

---

23 Press **F5** to insert frames and extend the **Timeline** of both layers to 24 frames.

Frames 2 through 24 in both layers are now shaded gray because you added frames. The main Timeline is now at least as long as the graphic symbol Timeline, and you'll see the entire animation play. Your snowflake is about to animate!

Note: You just extended both layers so that the content of these layers is displayed for the same length of time. For example, extending just the animSymbol layer would cause the background layer to disappear when the playhead reached Frame 2. Extending both layers to Frame 24 ensures that all layers are displayed for the same length of time.

---

24 Choose **Control > Test Movie** to preview your movie.

Cool—this time your snowflake is animating! Notice the animation starts as a snowflake, turns into a snowball, and disappears as it falls toward the ground. Next, you'll add more instances of the snowflake graphic symbol to the Stage to create the effect of falling snow.

---

25 Close the preview window.

---

26 On the main **Timeline**, select **Frame 1**, and drag ten more instances of the animated **snowflake** symbol to the **Stage** to make a total of eleven.

The dotted mesh indicates the shape is selected.

27 Choose **Control > Test Movie** to open a new window with a preview of your movie.

Notice the snowflakes are all falling in unison, which doesn't look very natural. In the next few steps, you'll learn how to change the starting frames of each animated graphic symbol to create more realistic-looking snowfall.

---

28 Close the preview window.

---

29 Click to select a **snowflake** instance on the **Stage**.

30 Type a value between **1** and **24** in the **First** field of the **Property inspector** to set the frame where you'd like the animation to begin. Since the snowflake animated graphic symbol has a total of 24 frames, you can type any number from 1 to 24. Setting the animation to start playing partway through will give the effect of the snowflakes falling at different times, rather than in perfect unison.

---

31 Repeat this process for all the snowflakes on the **Stage**, typing a different value in the **First** field of the **Property inspector**.

Changing the starting frame of each animation changes the starting point of each animation, yielding a more realistic snowfall effect.

32 Choose **Control > Test Movie** to preview your movie. It's snowing! When you are done previewing your movie, close the preview window.

In Flash CS3, you can often produce the same effect in a number of ways. However, some methods are more efficient than others. The exercise you just completed outlines an efficient way of using one symbol to create several instances that look and behave differently. You could have created and animated each of the snowflakes separately to produce the same effect, but that would have required much more work.

---

33 Save your **animSymbol.fla** file by choosing **File > Save**. Close the file.

N O T E :

Looping

You might have noticed the 24-frame animation of the falling snowflakes played over and over again when you tested the movie. This type of behavior is called a **loop**, which is an animation sequence that repeats endlessly. Flash CS3 defaults to looping whatever is on the **Stage**, unless you use ActionScript to tell it not to do so. You will learn about ActionScript in Chapter 12, *"ActionScript Basics."*

Great job! You've made it this far; by now you should feel a lot more comfortable working with symbols and instances and understand the role they can play in your projects. But you aren't finished yet. Future chapters on buttons and movie clips will continue this learning process. So, don't stop now—you are just getting to the good stuff.

7

Filters and Blend Modes

Adobe Flash CS3 Professional offers image-compositing effects called *blend modes* and image special effects called *filters*, which you can use to create sophisticated, eye-catching graphic effects. In the past, you would have created this content in an image-editing program, such as Adobe Photoshop or Adobe Illustrator, and imported it into Flash, dramatically increasing the size of the project. What's more, once you imported it into Flash, the artwork was no longer fully editable. In Flash CS3, layers and effects such as filters and blend modes are completely editable in all three of these applications: Flash, Illustrator, and Photoshop. However, blend modes and filters are included in Flash CS3, so you can create this content natively, giving you more flexibility and control with much smaller file sizes.

This chapter introduces you to the blend modes and filters in Flash CS3; however, this will by no means be a comprehensive treatment. The various ways to use and combine these visual effects is limited only by your imagination and your time. Experiment on your own beyond the material presented in this chapter to transform your Flash images.

What Are Blend Modes?

Blend modes mix the color information of a graphic object with the color information of the graphic object(s) beneath it. You can use blend modes to change the appearance of an image on the **Stage** by combining it in interesting ways with the content of objects beneath it. For example, with the **Lighten** blend mode, you can make areas of an object appear lighter in color based on the colors of the objects beneath it.

Flash CS3 has a variety of blend modes to help you achieve the look you want. If you've worked with Photoshop or Illustrator, you may already be familiar with the concept of blend modes and how to use them to achieve interesting visual effects. Fortunately, blend modes work much the same way in Flash. For example, you can create highlights or shadows, colorize a grayscale image, change the color of a symbol, and do much more.

To use blend modes, you must have at least two objects on the **Stage**, and you must convert the objects to either buttons or movie clip symbols. Blend modes do not work with graphic symbols. You'll learn more about buttons and movie clip symbols, including the benefits of working with them, in later chapters. For now, just remember you can use blend modes only with buttons and movie clip symbols, not with graphic symbols.

Blend modes let you alter how a current image or object blends with the images or objects underneath to create interesting effects.

The example shown on the left shows two images stacked on top of each other with no blending—a mountain scene and an orange opaque star. The example on the right shows the same two images with the **Overlay** blend mode applied. As you can see, the orange star on top is blending with the landscape below to produce an interesting visual effect. The orange star has turned from fully opaque to partially transparent, allowing the landscape below to come through with some of the color of the original orange star.

When you use blend modes, four important factors come into play:

- **Base object and color:** The object below the object you want to blend. In the illustration shown here, the base object consists of shades of blues and gray in the mountain scene photograph.
- **Blend object and color:** The object you are blending or applying the blend mode to. In the illustration, shown here, the blend object is the orange star.

- **Result object or color:** The result of the blend mode on the base object or color. In the illustration, shown here, the **Overlay** blend mode kept the base color of the blend object the same but adjusted the opacity, which is what makes the photographic content from the base object and color visible through the orange.

- **Opacity:** The degree of transparency applied to the blend mode. Depending on the color of the blending object and the blend mode you choose, you'll get different levels of transparency. In the illustration, shown here, the combination of the orange blend object and the **Overlay** blend mode yields a high degree of transparency.

Blend Mode Basics

If you've worked with blend modes in image-editing applications, you've probably done some experimenting to get the desired result. In some cases, experimentation can be frustrating because the results can vary widely, depending on the color(s) of the base object and the color(s) of the blend object. This section helps you understand the different blend modes and, I hope, eliminates some of the guesswork.

The blend modes in Flash CS3 are divided into categories, just like in Photoshop. Understanding how these categories work will help you understand the results you'll get when using blend modes. This section provides detailed information about the most common blend modes you'll use in Flash CS3 and how they work.

Normal and Layer Blend Modes

The **Normal** and **Layer** blend modes do not blend the objects. They maintain the original appearance of the objects stacked on top of each other. Using the **Layer** blend mode lets you stack multiple movie clips on top of each other without affecting the appearance.

Normal blend mode

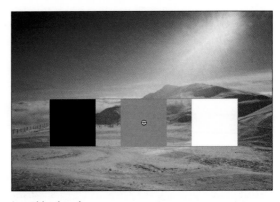

Layer blend mode

In the illustrations shown here, you can see three squares—one black, one gray, and one white—on top of a photograph of a mountain scene. On the left is the **Normal** blend mode, which does not blend the black, gray, and white squares with the photograph below. On the right is the **Layer** blend mode. Like the **Normal** blend mode, the **Layer** blend mode does not blend the objects—it simply lets you stack multiple movie clips on top of each other without affecting the appearance of the movie clips.

Darken and Multiply Blend Modes

The **Darken** and **Multiply** blend modes ignore white, making objects darker.

Darken

Multiply

In the above illustration, the **Darken** blend mode (on the left) eliminated the white square because the pixels are lighter than the photograph below. However, it kept the black square intact because the pixels are darker than the photograph below. The gray square was eliminated in the areas that are darker in the photograph below but maintained in the areas that are lighter. As you can see, a small corner of the gray square is still intact because the pixels below the square in that small area are lighter than the photograph below.

In the above illustration, the **Multiply** blend mode (on the right) also eliminated the white square because the pixels are lighter than the photograph below but kept the black square intact because the pixels are darker than the photograph below. Where you can see the difference between the **Darken** and **Multiply** blend modes is in the gray square. The **Multiply** blend mode darkened the gray and made the square transparent. Unlike the **Darken** blend mode, which simply cancels out pixels that are lighter, the **Multiply** blend mode multiplies the base color by the blend color, which results in darker, richer colors.

Darken

Multiply

When the blend object has a hue other than black, white, or gray, you can see the difference between **Darken** and **Multiply**. As shown in the above illustration, because the **Darken** blend mode (on the left) replaces only areas that are lighter than the blend color, it produces a greenish tinge over the darker areas. Because the **Multiply** blend mode (on the right) multiplies the base color by the blend color, it produces a darker, richer result.

Lighten and Screen Blend Modes

The **Lighten** and **Screen** blend modes yield the opposite result of the **Darken** and **Multiply** blend modes—they ignore black, making objects lighter.

Lighten

Screen

In the above illustration, the **Lighten** blend mode (on the left) eliminated the black square because the pixels are darker than the photograph below. It kept the white square intact because the pixels are lighter than the photograph below. The gray square was eliminated in the areas darker than the photograph below but was maintained in the areas that are lighter. As you can see, the lower-left corner of the gray square was eliminated because the pixels in that small area are darker than the photograph below.

In the above illustration, the **Screen** blend mode (on the right) also eliminated the black square because the pixels are darker than the photograph below but kept the white square because the pixels are lighter than the photograph below. Where you can see the difference between the **Lighten** and **Screen** blend modes is in the gray square. The **Screen** blend mode lightened the gray and made the square transparent. Unlike the **Lighten** blend mode, which simply cancels out pixels that are darker, the **Screen** blend mode multiplies the base color by the inverse of the blend color, which results in lighter colors that appear bleached out.

Lighten

Screen

When the blend object has a hue other than black, white, or gray, it is easy to see the difference between **Lighten** and **Screen**. As shown in the above illustration, because the **Lighten** blend mode (on the left) replaces only areas that are darker than the blend color, it produces a pinkish tinge over the high-contrast areas, specifically in the shadows on the mountain. Because the **Screen** blend mode (on the right) multiplies the inverse of the blend color with the base color, it produces a bleaching effect that is truer to the blend color.

Overlay and Hard Light Blend Modes

Where the **Darken** and **Multiply** blend modes ignore white and the **Lighten** and **Screen** blend modes ignore black, the **Overlay** and **Hard Light** blend modes ignore gray, which results in greater contrast and increased saturation.

Overlay

Hard Light

In the above illustration, the **Overlay** blend mode (on the left) multiplies the blend color, thus eliminating the gray square and increasing the contrast and saturation over the areas where the black and white squares blend with the photograph. With the black square, the **Overlay** blend mode increased the contrast saturation, yielding a darker result than the photograph. With the white square, the **Overlay** blend mode decreased the contrast and saturation, yielding a lighter result than the photograph.

In the above illustration, the **Hard Light** blend mode (on the right) also eliminated the gray square but had no effect on the black and white squares. Whereas the **Overlay** blend mode multiplies the colors depending on the *base* color, the **Hard Light** blend mode multiplies the colors depending on the *blend* color, which in this case results in no blending.

Overlay

Hard Light

When the blend object has a hue other than black, white, or gray, you can easily see the different results of the **Overlay** and **Hard Light** blend modes. As shown in the above illustration, the **Overlay** blend mode (on the left) produces a more subtle effect because it uses the base color, whereas the **Hard Light** blend mode (on the right) produces a more saturated result.

1 | Working with Blend Modes

When you work with blend modes in Flash CS3, you can apply them only to buttons and movie clip symbols—you cannot apply them to graphic symbols. This exercise shows you how to convert objects to movie clip symbols and shows you how to apply blend modes. After completing this exercise, you'll have no trouble experimenting on your own!

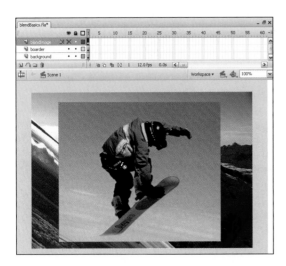 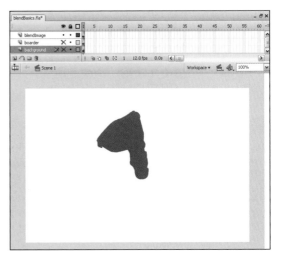

1 Copy the **chap_07** folder from the **Flash HOT CD-ROM** to your desktop. Open the **blendBasics.fla** file from the **chap_07** folder.

This file consists of three layers—the background image, a photograph of a snowboarder, and a graphic that mimics the shape of the snowboarder's jacket. In this exercise, you'll apply blend modes to this colored shape to see how it interacts or blends with the original colors in the jacket below.

2 Select the **Selection** tool in the **Tools** panel. Click the burgundy graphic (the blend image) to select it.

Before you can apply blend modes to an object, you must convert it to either a button or a movie clip symbol, which you'll do next.

Wondering what button and movie clip symbols are? Not to worry, you'll learn more about both in later chapters—they are more complex than the graphic symbols you have learned about up to this point. For now, just remember you can apply blend modes only to buttons and movie clip symbols.

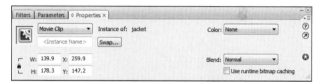

3 Press **F8** to open the **Convert to Symbol** dialog box. Type **jacket** in the **Name** field. Make sure **Type: Movie clip** is selected. Click **OK** to convert the shape to a movie clip so you can start applying blend modes to it.

Take a look at the Property inspector. Notice the Blend pop-up menu. Next, you'll apply a blend mode to the jacket.

4 Choose **Multiply** in the **Blend** pop-up menu.

Notice the snowboarder's jacket is now shades of burgundy and purple. By applying the Multiply blend mode, you darkened the jacket using the shades of the burgundy shape. Next, you'll experiment with the Screen blend mode.

5 Choose **Screen** in the **Blend** pop-up menu.

Notice the snowboarder's jacket now has a bleached effect. Because the colors of the blend object are darker than the screen, applying the Screen blend mode created a very different result than working with the Multiply blend mode. Next, you'll experiment with the Overlay blend mode.

6 Choose **Overlay** in the **Blend** pop-up menu.

Notice the result is different yet again! This time, the snowboarder's jacket is shades of burgundy and white.

Which result is best? It depends on the result you want.

7 Experiment with the other blend modes in the **Blend** pop-up menu so you can see the wide range of results that are possible.

Note: You can also apply multiple overlapping blends by converting the snowboarder graphic to a movie clip and applying blends to it (which will blend colors with the underlying background image). Experiment with the other blends to achieve some interesting results. You can also experiment with the movie clip color and transparency settings, which can also have an effect on the blending results.

8 When you are done experimenting, close **blendBasics.fla**. You don't need to save your changes.

What Are Filters?

Filters process the content of a graphic object to produce a special effect. For example, you can apply a **Bevel** filter to an object to make its edges appear rounded, apply a **Blur** filter to make edges of an object appear softer, or apply a **Drop Shadow** filter to cast a shadow behind an object.

Using filters, you can make objects appear to glow, cast a shadow, make objects blurry, and more. In the past, the only way to add this type of look was by importing content from an image-editing application such as Photoshop.

In Flash CS3, you can apply filters to text, buttons, and movie clips to create a variety of interesting visual effects. You can also animate filters using motion and shape tweens. For example, if you add a drop shadow to an object, you can simulate the look of the light source moving from one side of the object to another by changing the position of the drop shadow from its beginning and ending frames on the **Timeline**.

You can work with filters from a dedicated tab in the **Property inspector**. From here you turn on, turn off, or delete filters. After you apply a filter, you can change its options anytime or rearrange the order of filters to experiment with combined effects. When you remove a filter, the object returns to its previous appearance. View filters are applied to an object by selecting it, which automatically updates the filter list in the **Property inspector** for the selected object.

The following chart summarizes the seven filters available in Flash CS3:

Flash CS3 Filters	
Filter	**Description**
Drop Shadow 	The **Drop Shadow** filter simulates the look of an object casting a shadow onto a surface or cutting a hole in the background in the shape of the object. In the illustration shown here, you can see the **Drop Shadow** filter is simulating a light source shining from the upper left, casting a shadow on the lower-right areas of the snowflake.
Blur  	The **Blur** filter softens the edges and details of objects. In some cases, blur can make an object appear as if it is further in the background or can make an object appear to be in motion. In the illustrations shown here, the top image shows the original, and the bottom image shows the same image with a blur.

continues on next page

Filter	Description
Glow 	The **Glow** filter applies a selected color around all the edges of an object, casting a soft glow. In the illustration shown here, you can see an orange glow behind the snowflake.
Gradient Glow 	The **Gradient Glow** filter creates a glow using a gradient rather than just a single color. This filter requires one color at the start of the gradient with an **Alpha** value of **0**. You can choose any color, but you cannot move the position of this color. In the illustration shown here, you can see the **Gradient Glow** filter casts a glow behind the snowflake. Unlike the **Glow** filter, the **Gradient Glow** filter uses a gradient and can have multiple colors that fade from one to the next. In this example, the gradient glow fades from white to black to red.
Bevel	The **Bevel** filter applies a highlight effect along the edges of an object, making it appear to be curved up above the background surface. Options include inner bevels, outer bevels, and full bevels. In the illustration shown here, you can see the green oval has a bevel, giving it a three-dimensional appearance.
Gradient Bevel 	The **Gradient Bevel** filter produces a raised look with a gradient color across the surface of the bevel that makes an object appear to be raised above the background. The gradient bevel requires one color in the middle of the gradient with an **Alpha** value of **0**. You cannot move the position of this color, but you can change its color. In the illustration shown here, you can see the bevel is constructed using a gradient. Unlike the bevel you saw in the previous example, the **Gradient Bevel** filter uses multiple colors that fade from one to the next. In this example, the gradient glow fades between shades of blue and black.
Adjust Color 	The **Adjust Color** filter adjusts the brightness, contrast, hue, and saturation of the selected button, movie clip, or text object. In the illustration shown here, the colors have been adjusted to shades of green.

2 | Working with Filters

When you apply filters, you use a dedicated **Filter** tab in the **Property inspector** to apply, disable, rearrange, and delete a sampling of filters. You can also apply multiple filters to an object, as you'll see in this exercise. Each time you add a new filter, it is added to the list of applied filters for that object in the **Property inspector**, where you can modify the settings for each applied filter at any time.

---

1 Open the **filterBasics.fla** file from the **chap_07** folder.

This file consists of two layers: a text layer containing a text label and a buttons layer containing a simple button shape. In this exercise, you'll experiment with a variety of filter effects by applying them to both the text and the button graphic. To start, you'll convert the button shape to a symbol.

---

2 Click the button shape with the **Selection** tool to select it. Press **F8** to open the **Convert to Symbol** dialog box. Name the symbol **master_btn**, and set **Type** to **Button**. Click **OK**.

You'll learn more about button symbols in Chapter 10, "*Buttons.*" They are more complex than the graphic symbols I have covered up to this point, but for now, just know you can apply filters only to button symbols, movie clip symbols, or text.

---

3 Choose **Window > Properties > Properties** to open the **Property inspector**, if it is not already open. Make sure the button instance is still selected on the **Stage**. Click the **Filters** tab. Click the **Add filter** button, and choose **Bevel** in the pop-up menu.

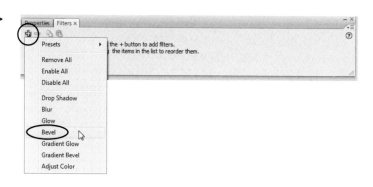

4 Set the **Strength** property of the **Bevel** filter to **50%**. Leave the rest of the settings at the default values.

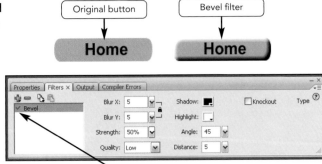

Take a look at the button; you have just applied your first filter effect! Next, you'll make some copies of the button so you can practice applying more filters.

Tip: To temporarily turn off the filter so you can compare it to the original image, click the green check mark next to the filter name in the filter list. (A red *X* then replaces the green check mark.) To turn the filter back on, click the red *X*.

Turn the filter off with this icon.

---

5 Click **Frame 2** in the **button** layer, and drag up to select **Frame 2** in the **text** layer. Press **F6** to add a keyframe to both layers.

This copies not only the button artwork and the text but also the filter you added to the button in Step 3.

---

6 Click any blank area on the **Stage** to deselect the two frames. Click the button text label with the **Selection** tool to select it. On the **Filters** tab, click the **Add Filter** button. Choose **Glow** in the pop-up menu, and set the values as shown in the illustration here. Choose any red color in the color palette to produce a soft red glow around the letters of the text.

---

7 Click the button instance with the **Selection** tool to select it. On the **Filters** tab, click the **Add Filter** button. (Notice the **Bevel** filter you added in Step 3 is also present in the filter list.) Choose **Drop Shadow** in the pop-up menu. Set **Strength** to **70%**. Leave the other settings at their default values.

Move the playhead back and forth between Frame 1 and Frame 2 to simulate this animation. It's not a bad animation for the small effort you expended!

---

8 On the **buttons** layer, click **Frame 2**, and select the button on the **Stage**. Click the **Filters** tab. Notice the **Drop Shadow** filter assumes the second position in the filter list. Click and drag the **Drop Shadow** filter above the **Bevel** filter in the list.

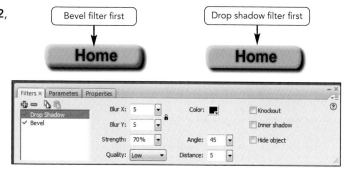

Bevel filter first

Drop shadow filter first

You can move filters up and down in the list to change their order, resulting in subtle to major changes in the appearance of the object. In this case, rearranging the order does yield a small difference, as shown in the illustration here.

In addition to temporarily disabling or rearranging the filters, you can also erase them, which you'll do next.

---

9 With **Frame 2** still selected on the **buttons** layer, select the **Bevel** filter in the filter list. Click the **Remove filter** button to remove the filter from the button, changing its appearance on the **Stage**.

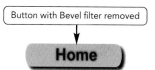

Button with Bevel filter removed

---

10 Click **Frame 3** on the **button** layer, and drag up to select **Frame 3** on the **text** layer. Press **F6** to add a keyframe to both layers, which provides you with another button (without the **Bevel** filter but still containing the **Drop Shadow** filter) to explore the remaining filters. Experiment by adding some filters to the button and text.

After working a bit with filters, you'll probably develop some favorites. Luckily, you can save filter settings as preset libraries, which you can easily apply to additional buttons, movie clips, and text objects. You'll do this next.

---

11 On the **Filters** tab, select a filter in the filter list. Click the **Add Filter** button, and choose **Presets > Save As** in the pop-up menu.

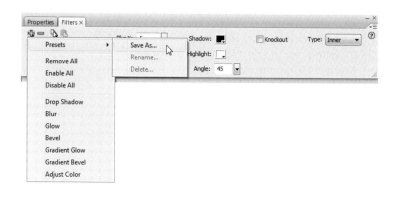

12 In the **Save Preset As** dialog box, type a descriptive name for your filter preset in the **Preset name** field, and click **OK**.

You may start to accumulate quite a few filter presets, so give them descriptive names.

Note: You cannot use spaces or special characters in preset names.

---

13 To use the saved preset, select a button, movie clip, or text on the **Stage**. Click the **Add Filter** button, and choose **Presets** in the pop-up menu. Your saved presets appear at the base of the submenu.

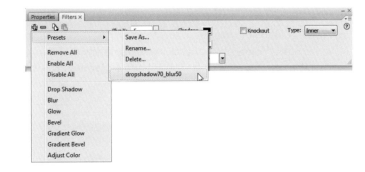

---

14 To delete a filter preset, click the **Add Filter** button, and choose **Presets > Delete** in the pop-up menu to open the **Delete Preset** dialog box. Select the preset you want to remove, and click **Delete**.

---

15 Close **filterBasics.fla**. You don't need to save your changes.

TIP:

Creating Preset Filter Libraries

You can also share your filter presets with other users by providing them with the filter configuration file. The filter configuration files are XML (eXtensible Markup Language) files saved in the Flash configuration filters folder, which is in the following location:

Windows:

C:\Documents and Settings\username\AppData\Local\Adobe\Flash CS3\en\ Configuration\Filters\

Mac:

Macintosh HD/Users/username/Library/Application Support/Adobe/Flash CS3/en/ Configuration/Filters/

Note: This folder will be present in this location only once you save a filter preset.

3 | Colorizing a Grayscale Image

In this exercise, you'll apply both a blend and a filter to colorize a grayscale image. You'll also learn how to resize and precisely position **Stage** elements and get an introduction to the **Info** panel, which contains the size and position information of an object on the **Stage**.

---

1 Open **colorizing.fla** from the **chap_07** folder.

As you can see, colorizing.fla has a single frame and two layers: overlay on the top and bw pic on the bottom. The overlay layer is empty. The bw pic layer contains a grayscale image of a snowboarder. You'll be working on the overlay layer; the bw pic layer is locked.

---

2 Press **Ctrl+L** (Windows) or **Cmd+L** (Mac) to open the **Library** panel.

The Library panel contains two bitmap images: a grayscale photo and a stylized colored rendering of this photo labeled theOverlay.

Shortly, you'll add an Overlay blend to an instance of the colored rendering to accomplish a coloring effect on the underlying grayscale photo. But first, you need to position the image on the Stage. Then you'll convert it to a movie clip symbol.

---

3 On the **overlay** layer, select **Frame 1**. Drag a copy of **theOverlay** to the **Stage**.

Notice that the image is too big and extends beyond the edges of the Stage. You'll fix this by resizing the image next.

---

4 Choose **Window > Info** to open the **Info** panel.

This handy panel contains the current information of a selected object, including object dimensions and location. You'll use this panel to resize and position the overlay image.

5 Make sure that **theOverlay** is still selected on the **Stage**. In the **Info** panel, set **W** (the width) to **225**, and set **H** (the height) to **300**. Set both the **X** and **Y** values to **0.0**. Press **Enter** (Windows) or **Return** (Mac) to accept the settings.

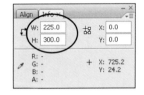

These settings resize the overlay image to the same size and location as the photograph underneath it. You're almost ready to add a blend and a filter to the overlay. First, you must convert the bitmap to a movie clip symbol, which you'll do next.

6 Make sure **theOverlay** is still selected. Press **F8** to open the **Convert to Symbol** dialog box. Enter **overlay_mc** in the **Name** field, set **Type** to **Movie clip**, and click **OK**.

7 In the **Property inspector**, click the **Properties** tab, and then choose **Overlay** in the **Blend** pop-up menu.

The photo is instantly colorized! Flash is blending color information of the colored overlay onto the grayscale image underneath. Next, you'll add a filter to the overlay.

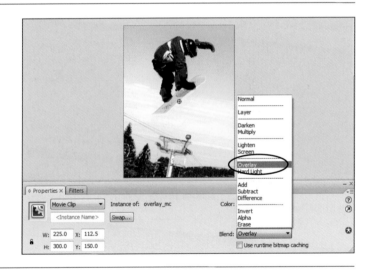

8 In the **Property inspector**, click the **Filters** tab. Click the **Add filter** button, and choose **Blur** in the pop-up menu.

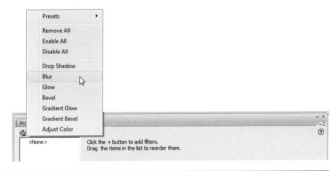

9 Set both the **Blur X** and **Blur Y** properties to **20**. Leave the **Quality** setting at its default.

The colorized image now has a Blur effect superimposed on top of it. This is a great example of combining blends and filters to quickly and easily produce an interesting image.

10 Save your **colorizing.fla** file by choosing **File > Save**. Close the file.

You'll work with a similar file in the next chapter, when you learn how to animate this Blur filter!

NOTE:

Filters and Flash Player Performance

Many aspects of filters can affect the performance of Flash Shockwave (SWF) files during playback. Specifically, the type, number, and quality of the filters you apply to objects will all have a direct impact on playback performance. The simple rule is that the more filters you apply to an object, the greater the number of calculations the Flash Player must process to correctly display the visual effects, and the slower the playback performance will be. For this reason, apply only the minimum number of filters necessary to achieve the visual effect desired.

In addition, each filter includes settings that let you control the strength and quality of the applied filter. Use lower settings to improve performance on slower computers or for projects requiring a lot of filter processing.

You've now completed this chapter, which provided an introduction to blend modes and filter effects in Flash CS3. These image tools will let you create a broad range of interesting visual imagery by adding effects to text, buttons, and movie clips. A unique feature of Flash is that you can animate the filters you apply using motion and shape tweens, which are the topics of the next chapter.

8

Motion Tweening and Timeline Effects

Similar to shape tweening, **motion tweening** is a method of animation that takes the position and attributes of an object in a start keyframe, takes the position and attributes of an object in an end keyframe, and calculates the animation that will occur between the two objects. However, unlike shape tweening, motion tweening requires you to use symbols, groups, and text blocks, rather than shapes, to create animation. In addition to position, motion tweens can animate scale, tint, transparency, rotation, and distortion. In this chapter, you will learn much more than simple motion tweening. You will learn how to edit multiple frames, how to use motion guides, how to use **Timeline** effects, and how to animate filters, which is new to Adobe Flash CS3 Professional.

Adobe Flash CS3 Professional ships with eight **Timeline** effects grouped into three categories: **Assistants**, **Effects**, and **Transform/Transition**. These **Timeline** effects automate routine **Timeline** tasks, making your work easier and faster. Flash CS3 also provides capabilities for animating its new graphic filters. You will get a chance to work with both effects and filters later in the chapter, but first it's important to gain an understanding of the nuances of motion tweening so you can quickly start creating your own animations.

Shape Tweening vs. Motion Tweening

When you start working in Flash CS3, you might be confused about which type of tween to choose: motion or shape. You might waste time trying to figure out why your animation isn't working when in fact you simply selected the wrong type of tween. The basic distinction between the two types of tweening is that **shape tweens** use shapes to morph one shape into another (turning a red square into a blue circle), whereas **motion tweens** use groups, text, or symbols to animate the position or attributes of an object. Use the following chart to help you decide which type of tween to use:

Tween Types Simplified		
Element	Shape Tween	Motion Tween
Merge shape	Yes	No
Object shape	Yes	Yes
Group	No	Yes
Symbol	No	Yes
Text blocks	No	Yes
Broken-apart text	Yes	No

1 | Understanding Basic Motion Tweening

This exercise demonstrates how to create a basic motion tween using a graphic symbol. Motion tweens work only with symbols, grouped objects, and editable text. They are quite simple, especially once you've learned shape tweening. The big difference is not in the technique but in understanding when to use which of the five tween object types: shapes, groups, symbols, text blocks, and broken-apart text. You may find yourself often referring to the previous "Tween Types Simplified" chart, because remembering the rules of objects and tweening is harder than the process itself.

---

1 Copy the **chap_08** folder from the **Flash HOT CD-ROM** to your desktop. Open **motionTween_Final.fla** from the **chap_08** folder.

---

2 Choose **Control > Test Movie** to preview the motion tween animation you are about to create.

The snowboarder begins on the left side of the Stage, travels up to the peak of the slope, completes a jump off the lip of the peak, and flips counterclockwise down to the right side of the Stage. Also notice the snowboarder changes in size and color. In the next two exercises, you will tween the snowboarder's position, size, and color.

---

3 When you are finished previewing the animation, close the preview window as well as **motionTween_Final.fla**. Open **motionTween.fla** from the **chap_08** folder.

This file contains two layers: a layer named snowboarder, which will contain the motion tween, and a layer named background, which contains a bitmap image of the snow slope. The background layer is locked to prevent you from editing it. The Library panel contains only a bitmap image of the slope called jump.jpg. Next, you'll convert the snowboarder shape to a graphic symbol.

---

4 Select the **Selection** tool in the **Tools** panel. Click the snowboarder to select it. Notice the dotted mesh, which indicates you selected the shape successfully. Drag the snowboard shape to the bottom half of the **Library** panel to open the **Convert to Symbol** dialog box.

The dotted mesh indicates the shape is selected.

5 In the **Convert to Symbol** dialog box, type **snowboarder** in the **Name** field. Select **Type: Graphic**. For the registration point, make sure the middle square is selected. Click **OK**.

After you convert the shape of the snowboarder to a symbol, a blue bounding box around the snowboarder replaces the dotted mesh. Also, the Library panel now contains a new graphic symbol called snowboarder. You are now ready to create your first motion tween.

The blue bounding box indicates the symbol is selected.

6 With the **Selection** tool still selected in the **Tools** panel, click and drag the **snowboarder** instance from the **Stage** to the lower-left corner of the **pasteboard** (the gray area surrounding the **Stage**).

Dragging the snowboarder from the Stage will make the snowboarder enter the Stage from the left.

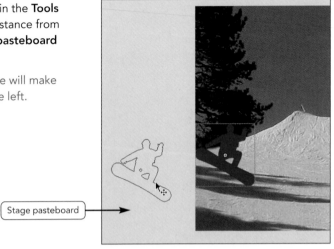

Stage pasteboard

7 On the **Timeline**, select **Frame 12** on the **snowboarder** layer, and press **F6** to add a keyframe to copy the contents of **Frame 1** to **Frame 12**. On the **background** layer, select **Frame 12**, and press **F5** to add frames up to **Frame 12**.

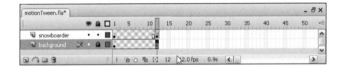

You will move the position of the snowboarder instance on Frame 12 next.

8 On the **Timeline**, select the keyframe on **Frame 12** on the **snowboarder** layer. Move the instance of the snowboarder from the **pasteboard** to just above the slope peak on the **Stage**.

You will add the motion tween in the following steps.

9 On the **Timeline**, click anywhere between **Frame 1** and **Frame 12** to select a frame.

10 Make sure the **Property inspector** is open. If it's not, choose **Window > Properties > Properties**, or press **Ctrl+F3** (Windows) or **Cmd+F3** (Mac). Choose **Motion** in the **Tween** pop-up menu to set a motion tween for the range of frames between **Frame 1** and **Frame 12** of the **snowboarder** layer.

Notice the blue tint and the solid arrow between those frames, indicating a motion tween is active.

The arrow means the motion tween is active.

11 Move the playhead to **Frame 1**, and press **Enter** (Windows) or **Return** (Mac) to view the motion tween.

The snowboarder enters from the left of the Stage and animates up to the peak of the slope. All you did was set up the beginning and ending keyframes and turn on motion tweening—Flash CS3 did all the rest!

Note: You can also scrub (move) the playhead back and forth to view the motion tween. On Windows, you can press the less-than (**<**) or greater-than (**>**) keys to advance the playhead forward or backward one frame at a time.

12 On the **Timeline**, select **Frame 36** on the **snowboarder** layer, and press **F6** to add a keyframe and to copy the contents of **Frame 12** to **Frame 36**. On the **background** layer, select **Frame 36**, and press **F5** to add frames up to **Frame 36**.

Next, you will move the position of the snowboarder instance on Frame 36.

13 On the **Timeline**, select the keyframe on **Frame 36** on the **snowboarder** layer. Click and drag to move the instance of the snowboarder from the slope peak to the lower-right corner of the pasteboard.

You will add the last motion tween in the following steps.

14 On the **Timeline**, click anywhere between **Frame 12** and **Frame 36** to select a frame.

15 In the **Property inspector**, choose **Motion** in the **Tween** pop-up menu to set another motion tween on the **snowboard** layer for the range of frames between **Frame 12** and **Frame 36**.

Again, notice the blue tint and the solid arrow between those frames, indicating a motion tween is active.

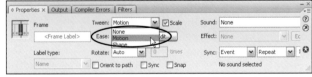

16 Move the playhead to **Frame 1**, and press **Enter** (Windows) or **Return** (Mac) to view the motion tween.

The snowboarder enters from the bottom left of the Stage, animates up to the slope peak, and then slides down the slope to the lower-right corner of the Stage pasteboard.

Congratulations, you have created your first motion tween—two motion tweens to be exact!

---

17 Save your changes, and leave **motionTween.fla** open for the next exercise.

---

2 | Using Tweening Effects

Surprisingly, despite its name, a motion tween isn't used solely for tweening motion. You can also tween the alpha, tint, brightness, size, position, and skew of a symbol. This exercise shows you how to do just that, which opens the door for you to create a wide range of animated effects—far beyond simply moving an object from one location to another.

1 If you just completed Exercise 1, **motionTween.fla** should still be open. If it's not, complete Exercise 1, and then return to this exercise.

2 Make sure the playhead is on **Frame 1** on the **Timeline**.

To make this animation a bit more realistic, you will rotate and scale the instance of the snowboarder in the following steps.

3 Select the **Free Transform** tool in the **Tools** panel. On the **Stage**, click the **snowboarder** instance to select it.

You will scale the snowboarder instance next.

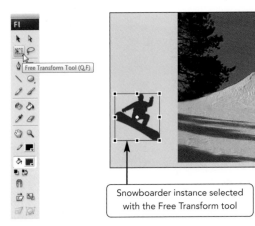

Snowboarder instance selected with the Free Transform tool

4 Move the cursor over the upper-right corner handle until the scale icon appears. Click and drag diagonally to scale the snowboarder to a smaller size.

Next you'll rotate the snowboarder instance.

Tip: If you hold down the Shift key while you drag one of the handles, the snowboarder will scale proportionally on all sides.

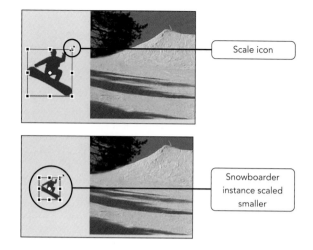

Scale icon

Snowboarder instance scaled smaller

5 Move the cursor over the upper-left corner handle of the **snowboarder** instance until the rotate icon appears. Click and drag down until the board in the **snowboarder** instance is pointing upward.

You will rotate the snowboarder instance on Frame 12 next.

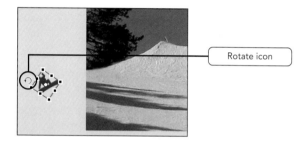

Rotate icon

6 On the **Timeline**, select the keyframe on **Frame 12** on the **snowboarder** layer. With the **Free Transform** tool still selected in the **Tools panel**, move the cursor over the upper-left corner handle of the **snowboarder** instance until the rotate icon appears. Click and drag down until the board in the **snowboarder** instance is pointing upward.

You will make the snowboarder instance do a jump in the following steps.

Snowboarder instance rotated

7 On the **Timeline**, select any frame between **Frame 12** and **Frame 36** on the **snowboarder** layer to select the second motion tween. In the **Property inspector**, choose **CCW** in the **Rotate** pop-up to make the snowboarder rotate counterclockwise one time during the last motion tween.

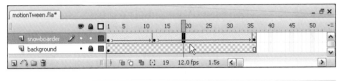

8 Press **Enter** (Windows) or **Return** (Mac) to preview the animation.

Now that's a jump! You're almost done—you will scale and change the tint of the snowboarder instance on the last keyframe in the following steps.

9 On the **Timeline**, select the keyframe on **Frame 36**. With the **Free Transform** tool still selected in the **Tools** panel, move the cursor over the upper-right corner handle until the scale icon appears. Click and drag diagonally to scale the snowboarder to a smaller size.

Remember, holding down the Shift key while you drag will maintain the original aspect ratio of the image. You'll change the tint color of the snowboard instance next.

10 Make sure the playhead is on **Frame 36**. Select the **Selection** tool in the **Tools** panel. On the **Stage**, click the **snowboarder** instance.

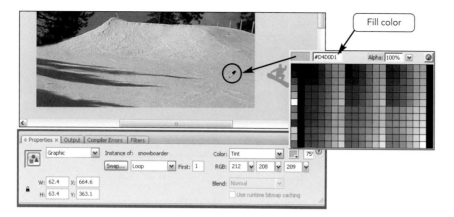

Fill color

11 In the **Property inspector**, set **Color** to **Tint**. Click the **Fill Color** box, and notice the cursor changes to an eyedropper. Move the eyedropper to the background image, and click to sample a color from the snow.

You'll see the snowboarder update to the color you have sampled—in this case a shade of gray.

12 Choose **Control > Test Movie** to preview your animation. When you are finished, close the preview window.

The snowboarder enters the Stage from the left side, starts off small, and gets larger as he moves toward the peak of the slope. When he reaches the peak, the snowboarder jumps the lip and rotates counter-clockwise once until he reaches the bottom of the slope. At the same time the size is tweening, the tint of the snowboarder is also changing as he moves! You are now tweening the tint and scale (not to mention the position) in a motion tween!

13 Experiment by making changes to the keyframes in the motion tween with the **Free Transform** tool or by modifying the color in the **Property inspector**.

14 When you are done experimenting, close **motionTween.fla**. You don't need to save your changes.

3 | Editing Multiple Frames

Suppose you create a motion tween but then decide you would rather have the animation occur in a different position on the **Stage**. Can you imagine repositioning the items one frame at a time? With the **Edit Multiple Frames** feature, you can bypass this tedious chore. This exercise shows you a method to move the entire animation with ease.

---

1 Open **editMultipleFrames.fla** from the **chap_08** folder.

This file contains one layer with a background image. The background layer is locked so you don't accidentally edit it.

Tip: If you can't see the whole background image, choose View > Magnification > Show All.

---

2 On the **Timeline**, click the **Insert Layer** button to add a new layer on the **Timeline**. Double-click **Layer 2**, rename the layer **tween**, and press **Enter** (Windows) or **Return** (Mac).

---

3 Press **Ctrl+L** (Windows) or **Cmd+L** (Mac) to open the **Library** panel. Click the **boarder** graphic symbol in the **Library** panel, and drag it to the **tween** layer in the upper-left corner of the sky in the background image.

This is where the snowboarder will start the animation.

4 On the **tween** layer, select **Frame 12**, and press **F6** to add a keyframe. This copies the contents of **Frame 1** to **Frame 12**. On the **background** layer, select **Frame 12**, and press **F5** to add frames to that layer as well. This makes the background image visible throughout the motion tween.

5 With the playhead on **Frame 12** and the **Selection** tool selected in the **Tools** panel, drag the snowboarder to the right side of the **Stage** in the sky.

This spot will serve as the end point for your animation.

6 On the **Timeline**, click anywhere between the two keyframes on the **tween** layer to select a frame between **Frame 1** and **Frame 12**.

7 In the **Property inspector**, choose **Motion** in the **Tween** pop-up menu. Choose **CCW** in the **Rotate** pop-up menu, which will make the snowboarder rotate counterclockwise one time during the motion tween.

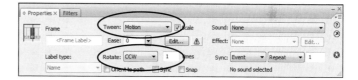

8 Press **Enter** (Windows) or **Return** (Mac) to preview the motion tween.

Notice this looks good, but for a more realistic look, the animation should occur in the snow rather than in the sky. You will change this next.

9 At the bottom of the **Timeline**, click the **Edit Multiple Frames** button.

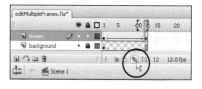

Note: When you click the Edit Multiple Frames button, you'll see two markers—which look similar to the onion skinning markers you learned about in Chapter 4, "Animating in Flash"—at the top of the Timeline. However, don't be fooled by the similarities. Editing multiple frames is quite different from onion skinning. The Onion Skinning bar represents the range of frames visible at the same time on your Stage. The Edit Multiple Frames markers represent the range of keyframes you can edit at the same time.

10 Position the starting point and ending point of the markers (representing your **Edit Multiple Frames** range) to span from **Frame 1** to **Frame 12**. If either the starting point or the ending point is not on the correct frame, click and drag the bar to the correct frame. By doing this, you are defining which keyframes to edit simultaneously.

Next, you will move your entire animation to the bottom part of the Stage, so you want to make sure the Edit Multiple Frames bar covers all the frames. Since your animation is composed of two keyframes (Frame 1 and Frame 12), these are the frames you need the bar to cover.

---

11 Click the **tween** layer name to select the entire layer.

Notice you can see the snowboarder on the first keyframe and the snowboarder on the last keyframe. Unlike with onion skinning, you won't see ghosted representations of all the frames between the two keyframes. Also, notice both snowboarders are selected (they have borders around them), which means you can move both at the same time.

---

12 With the **Selection** tool, click either one of the snowboarders on the **Stage**, and drag downward. Notice both snowboarders move as you drag.

---

13 Turn off the **Edit Multiple Frames** feature by clicking the **Edit Multiple Frames** button.

It's important to turn off Edit Multiple Frames after you have completed your task. If you leave Edit Multiple Frames turned on and continue to work in your movie, Flash CS3 will become confused as to which frame you're working in, and your movie will produce unexpected results. If you do make this mistake, remember that by default you can undo up to the previous 100 steps.

---

14 Press **Enter** (Windows) or **Return** (Mac) to preview the animation.

Now the whole animation has been moved to the bottom of the Stage, and the snowboarder is moving across the snow rather than in the air.

Note: The Edit Multiple Frames feature is a great technique to use when you need to move the contents of many frames all at once. It is also the only way to move an entire animation together at one time.

15 Close **editMultipleFrames.fla**. You don't need to save your changes.

4 | Using a Motion Guide

This exercise shows you how to create a motion tween using a motion guide. A **motion guide** is a special layer on which you can draw a path, allowing a symbol to animate along the path, rather than traveling a straight line between two keyframes. In Flash CS3, this is the only way to make a motion tween follow a curved path, so it is an important technique.

---

1 Open **motionGuide_Final.fla** from the **chap_08** folder.

---

2 Choose **Control > Test Movie** to view the movie (SWF) file.

This file is a finished version of the file you are about to create. Notice how the snowflake moves from side to side in a downward direction before reaching the bottom of the screen. Using a motion guide, you will create this same effect next.

---

3 When you are finished previewing the animation, close the preview window, and close the project file **motionGuide_Final.fla**. Open **motionGuide.fla** from the **chap_08** folder.

Notice the file contains one layer with the background image. The background layer is locked to prevent you from editing that layer. You'll be adding the falling snowflake in the following steps.

---

4 On the **Timeline**, click the **Insert Layer** button to add a new layer to the **Timeline**. Double-click **Layer 2**, rename the layer **snowflake**, and press **Enter** (Windows) or **Return** (Mac).

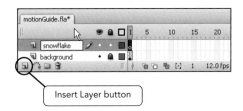

Insert Layer button

---

5 In the **Library** panel, drag an instance of the **snowflake** graphic symbol to the upper-left corner of the **Stage**. Close the **Library** by pressing **Ctrl+L** (Windows) or **Cmd+L** (Mac) to make your workspace less cluttered.

This spot will be the starting position of the animation—notice the keyframe in Frame 1 of the snowflake layer.

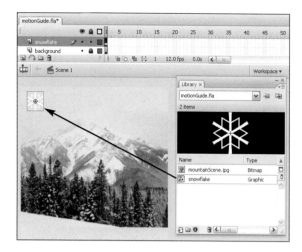

---

6 On the **Timeline**, click **Frame 48** of the **background** layer, and press **F5** to add frames to **Frame 48**.

This step will make sure the background shows throughout the snowflake animation, which you will create next.

---

7 On the **snowflake** layer, click **Frame 48** and press **F6** to add a new keyframe and to copy the contents of **Frame 1** to **Frame 48**. With the playhead on **Frame 48**, click the **snowflake** instance, and drag it to the lower-right corner of the screen.

This spot will be the ending position of the animation.

---

8 On the **Timeline**, click anywhere between **Frame 1** and **Frame 40** to select a frame between the two keyframes.

9 In the **Property inspector**, choose **Motion** in the **Tween** pop-up menu.

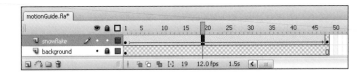

Notice the blue tint and the solid arrow between Frame 1 and Frame 48 of the snowflake layer, indicating a motion tween is active.

10 Move the playhead to **Frame 1**. Press **Enter** (Windows) or **Return** (Mac) to test the motion tween animation.

Notice the snowflake move from the upper-left corner of the Stage down to the lower-right corner of the Stage in a linear motion. Next you'll make the snowflake follow a motion guide so that it moves across the Stage from right to left in a side-to-side fashion before reaching the ground. But first, you will add the motion guide.

11 Click the **snowflake** layer to select it. At the bottom of the **Timeline**, click the **Add Motion Guide** button to add a motion guide layer to the **snowflake** layer.

Notice this new layer has automatically been named Guide: snowflake. Also, notice the icon in front of the motion guide layer. This icon provides visual feedback that this layer is now a guide layer. The snowflake layer is also indented below the guide layer. This means the snowflake layer is taking instructions from the guide layer. The snowflake layer contains the motion tween, and the guide layer contains the path for the tween to follow. Before it can follow the path, however, you'll have to draw one, which you'll do soon, so keep following along.

12 Lock the **snowflake** layer to avoid editing it, and click the **Guide: snowflake** layer to select it.

13 Select the **Pencil** tool in the **Tools** panel. Choose **Smooth** in the **Pencil Mode** pop-up menu. Make sure **Object Drawing** is deselected in the **Tools** panel.

This option smoothes out irregularities as you draw the path for the snowflake to follow.

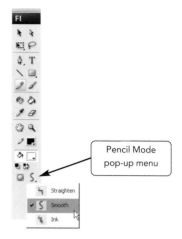

Pencil Mode pop-up menu

14 On the **Stage**, draw a curved line, similar to the one shown in the illustration here.

This line will serve as the path the snowflake will follow. It doesn't matter what color or stroke width you choose, because this line will not show in the final animation. Flash CS3 is concerned only with the path of the line.

15 Unlock the **snowflake** layer. Lock the **Guide: snowflake** layer because you're done with it and want to avoid accidentally moving or editing it.

16 Position the playhead on **Frame 1**. Select the **Selection** tool in the **Tools** panel, and click the **snowflake** instance to select it. Click the registration point in the center, and drag the snowflake to the beginning of the path you drew on the guide layer. When you get close to the path, the snowflake will "snap" to it, and the registration point will turn into a small open circle. This is where the snowflake will start following the path.

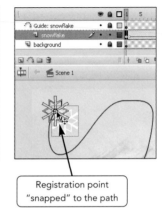

Registration point

Registration point "snapped" to the path

Note: To get the motion guide working properly, it's important to grab the snowflake symbol instance from the registration point. You'll know you have done this correctly when the registration point turns into an open circle, as shown in the illustration here.

---

17 Move the playhead to **Frame 48**, the last keyframe of the animation. Click and drag the registration point of the nowflake instance to the bottom of the path you drew on the guide layer.

This is where the snowflake will stop following the path. That's it! Your animation is ready!

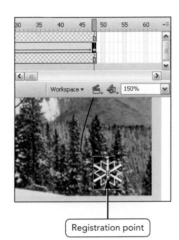

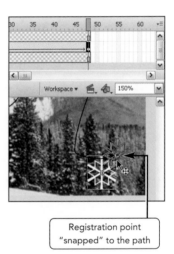

Registration point

Registration point "snapped" to the path

---

18 Press **Enter** (Windows) or **Return** (Mac) to preview the snowflake animation.

Notice the snowflake now follows the path you drew on the guide layer.

---

19 Choose **Control > Test Movie**.

You don't see the line at all because the contents of your motion guide layer are never displayed in the final movie (SWF) file. However, your snowflake will still continue to follow the path.

Wouldn't it be nice if the snowflake rotated in the direction of its movement, instead of always facing in the same direction? In other words, if the snowflake is moving down, it should be pointing down, don't you think? In the next exercise, you'll learn about the new custom ease controls in Flash CS3 to do just that!

---

20 Close the preview window.

---

21 Save your changes, and leave **motionGuide.fla** open for the next exercise.

---

5 | Using the Custom Ease Controls

Flash CS3 has new custom ease controls that give you greater control over the speed and pacing of your tween animations. Before, Flash's ease controls gave you control over just the starting and ending speeds. With this new functionality, you now have control over the starting, ending, and middle parts of your animations.

---

1 If you just completed Exercise 4, **motionGuide.fla** should still be open. If it's not, complete Exercise 4, and then return to this exercise.

In this exercise, you will use the visual Custom Ease In / Ease Out graph to achieve a high level of control over the speed of all parts of your tween animations.

---

2 Click the motion tween of the **snowflake** layer anywhere. In the **Property inspector**, select the **Orient to path** option.

With this option selected, Flash CS3 will do its best to face the snowflake in the direction it's moving.

---

3 Choose **Control > Test Movie** to view the snowflake animation.

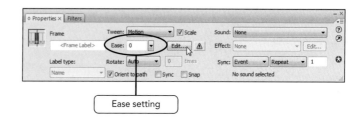

Ease setting

As the snowflake falls, it faces the direction of the path. Nice!

To make this animation a bit more realistic, you'll use the new custom ease controls in Flash CS3 to vary the snowflake's speed as it falls toward the ground, simulating a gust of wind.

---

4 Close the preview window. Click the tween of the **snowflake** layer anywhere to select the motion tween. In the **Property inspector**, click the **Edit** button to open the **Custom Ease In / Ease Out** dialog box.

The Custom Ease In / Ease Out dialog box displays a graph representing the degree of motion over time. The horizontal axis represents frames, and the vertical axis represents the percentage of change (in this case, the percentage of the entire animation).

The Ease setting in Flash CS3 lets you control the speed at the start and end of a tween. The custom easing graph also lets you set up easing in the middle of a tween! In the next steps, you'll use the controls in this window to add more realism to your falling snowflake by altering its speed during its descent.

Understanding Ease In and Ease Out

Ease In and **Ease Out** relate to the speed of an animation. The term **easing** is used because when an animation begins slowly and then speeds up, it is considered to have been "eased in" to its motion. When slowing an animation at the end, it is said to be "eased out." Leaving the **Ease** setting at its default of **None** will produce animations with a linear motion, meaning all frames move at the same speed. With the new custom ease controls in Flash CS3, you can speed up and slow down portions of the animation.

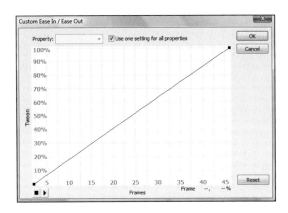

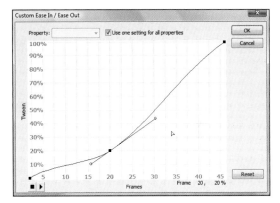

5 In the **Custom Ease In / Ease Out** dialog box, **Ctrl-click** (Windows) or **Cmd-click** (Mac) the diagonal line where it crosses **Frame 15** in the horizontal axis and approximately **30%** in the vertical axis to add a new control point to the line. Click and drag the line down to the **20% Tween** point on the vertical axis, while keeping it at **Frame 15** or **Frame 20** on the horizontal axis. (You don't need to be exact.)

The line is now a complex curve.

---

6 Test your work clicking the **Play** and **Stop** buttons in the **Custom Ease In / Ease Out** dialog box. Make sure to move the window so you can see the **Stage**.

---

7 In the **Custom Ease In / Ease Out** dialog box, **Ctrl-click** (Windows) or **Cmd-click** (Mac) the diagonal line where it crosses **Frame 37** in the horizontal axis and **70%** in the vertical axis to add a second control point to the line. Click and drag the line up to about the **90% Tween** point on the vertical axis, while keeping it at **Frame 30** or **Frame 35** on the horizontal axis.

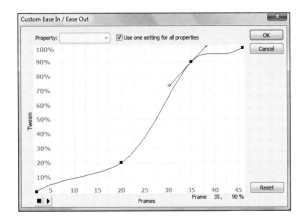

8 Test your work again by clicking the **Play** and **Stop** buttons.

You've created a more complex easing curve than the straight line with which you started. This change will cause the tween to start slow, speed up in the middle, and then slow again at the end. Next, you'll test the movie to preview your work.

---

9 Click **OK** to close the **Custom Ease In / Ease Out** dialog box. Choose **Control > Test Movie** to preview your work.

The custom easing curve you defined in Steps 4 and 5 creates an animation that simulates your snowflake getting caught in a gust of wind as it descends to the ground. Experiment by adding more control points and using them to modify the shape of the graph.

Altering the ease speed of the snowflake in the Custom Ease In / Ease Out dialog box gave a more realistic look to the snowflake's movement. The motion guide, Orient to path, and Ease settings, when used in combination, are a terrific (and easy) way to create tween animations involving complex movements well beyond the linear visual effects you have used up to this point.

---

10 Close the preview window.

---

11 Close **motionGuide.fla**. You don't need to save your changes.

VIDEO: | **customEase.mov**

To learn more about the new custom ease controls in Flash CS3, check out **customEase.mov** in the **videos** folder on the **Flash HOT CD-ROM**.

6 | Animating Text

In this exercise, you'll create the effect of a word exploding on the screen. In the process, you'll get a chance to practice creating a symbol from text, breaking apart the letters, and distributing them to layers.

---

1 Open **explode_Final.fla** from the **chap_08** folder.

---

2 Choose **Control > Test Movie** to test the animation.

The words explode before your eyes! When you are finished previewing, close the file. You will create this animation next.

---

3 Open **explode.fla** from the **chap_08** folder.

This file has a blue background with a frame rate of 20 frames per second.

---

4 On the **Timeline**, double-click **Layer 1**, and rename it **big air**. Press **Enter** (Windows) or **Return** (Mac).

You will add the text to this layer in the following steps.

---

5 Select the **Text** tool in the **Tools** panel. In the **Property inspector**, choose **Verdana** in the **Font** pop-up menu, choose **96** in the **Font Size** pop-up menu, click the **Fill Color** box to choose a dark blue color, choose **Align Left**, and click the **Bold** button.

---

6 Click **Stage** anywhere, and type **big air**.

Notice there is now a keyframe on Frame 1 on the big air layer.

---

7 Choose **Modify > Break Apart** to break the text box into six individual text boxes, one box for each letter.

Text box before being broken apart   *Text box after being broken apart*

NOTE:

Motion Tweening Text

You don't have to convert a regular text block to a symbol to use it as the artwork for a motion tween. However, you are limited in the effects you can apply to text boxes. With a text block, you can animate the position and scale, rotation, skew, and flip. However, with a graphic symbol with text inside, you can animate color styles, such as color, brightness, alpha, and tint. With a symbol, you have more options for creating effects in your motion tween than you have using a regular text block.

8 With all six text boxes still selected, choose **Modify > Timeline > Distribute to Layers**.

This technique places each letter on a separate layer. This step is important because in order to create several motion tweens occurring at once, each tween must reside on its own layer. Likewise, each symbol (which you will create next) must reside on a separate layer.

9 Select the **Selection** tool in the **Tools** panel, and click anywhere off the **Stage** to deselect all six letters. Select the letter *b*, and press **F8** to convert it to a symbol. In the **Convert to Symbol** dialog box, type **letter_b** in the **Name** field, and select **Type: Graphic**. Make sure the registration point is in the center. Click **OK**.

10 Select the letter *i*. Press **F8** to convert it to a symbol. In the **Convert to Symbol** dialog box, type **letter_i** in the **Name** field, and select **Type: Graphic**. Make sure the registration point is in the center. Click **OK**.

11 Repeat Step 10 to convert the letters *g*, *a*, and *r* to symbols. In the **Convert to Symbol** dialog box, name the symbols **letter_g**, **letter_a**, and **letter_r**, respectively. Do not convert the letter *i* in the word *air*.

Note: You might be wondering why you didn't convert the letter *i* in the word *air* to a symbol. Since you already created a letter_i graphic symbol in Step 10, you will use that graphic symbol to create another instance of the letter_i. This is the beauty of symbols: create just one symbol, and use it to produce multiple instances on the Stage, without increasing the file size or download time.

12 Choose **Window > Info** to open the **Info** panel. Make sure the registration/transformation point (the button by the X and Y coordinates) is set to the lower-right corner. With the **Selection** tool still selected in the **Tools** panel, click the letter *i* in the word *air* on the **Stage** to select it.

Take note of the X and Y coordinates in the Info panel. In the example here, the coordinates are set to 376.6 and 103.8, respectively. Yours may be different if the text is located at a different location on the Stage, but don't worry—you can still follow along with the exercise. With 0,0 being the coordinates for the upper-left corner of the Stage, X as 367.6 means the letter *i* is 367.6 pixels from the left side of the Stage; Y as 103.8 means *i* is 103.8 pixels down from the top of the Stage.

Note: You can also get the X and Y positions of an element in the Property inspector. However, with the Info panel, you can access additional information, such as the registration point, the RGB values, and the alpha transparency values.

13 Delete the letter *i* in the word *air* from the **Stage**.

Notice the keyframe in Frame 1 of the second i layer is now a blank keyframe. Next, you will place an instance of the letter_i graphic symbol in this blank keyframe.

14 Press **Ctrl+L** (Windows) or **Cmd+L** (Mac) to open the **Library** panel. Click and drag an instance of the **letter_i** graphic symbol to the **Stage**.

Notice Frame 1 of the second i layer now has a keyframe. Don't worry about positioning it precisely. You will use the Info panel to do that next.

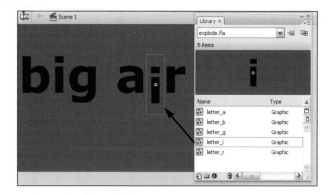

15 Make sure the letter *i* in the word *air* is still selected. In the **Info** panel, change the **X** and **Y** values to the values you noted in Step 12.

Notice the letter *i* in the word *air* is now in its original position. You now have two instances of the letter_i graphic symbol instead of one. If you'd like, you can close the Info and Library panels.

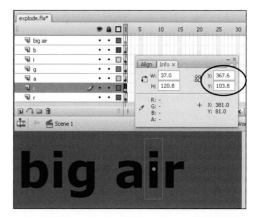

16 On the **Timeline**, click **Frame 20**, and **Shift-click** each of the six layers containing a symbol to select the frames. Press **F6** to add a keyframe on **Frame 20** to all six layers. Using the same technique, add a keyframe on **Frame 40** to all six layers.

Frame 40 is where the letters are going to finish their animation.

17 Click anywhere off the **Stage** to deselect all the symbols. Position the playhead on **Frame 40**, and click and drag the **letter_b** instance from the left side of the **Stage** to the pasteboard.

The letter *b* will end up in this position.

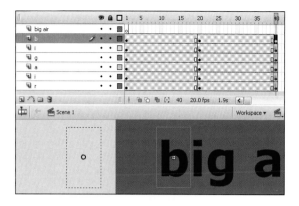

18 Select the **Free Transform** tool in the **Tools** panel. Use this tool to rotate and scale the **letter_b** instance. You can use any degree of rotation and scale you like, or you can match what's shown in the illustration here.

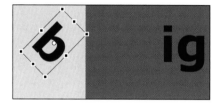

19 In the **Property inspector**, choose **Alpha** in the **Color** pop-up menu, and set the amount to **0%**.

This step makes the letter *b* fade out completely by the end of the animation.

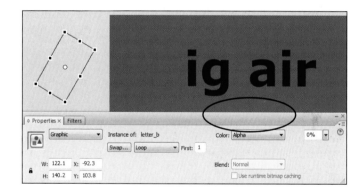

20 Repeat Steps 17, 18, and 19 to modify the positions of the other graphic symbols on **Frame 40**, scaling, rotating, and adding an alpha effect to each one. You may want to change the view magnification to be able to see more of the artboard. Feel free to move, scale, rotate, or even flip and skew each letter in any way you want, but make sure to keep the **Alpha** setting at **0%** to ensure all the letters disappear at the same time.

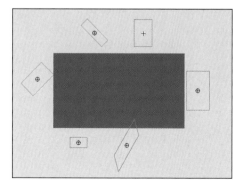

21 Click anywhere between **Frame 20** and **Frame 40** on the **b** layer. **Shift-click** the same frame in the **r** layer to select all the layers of that frame. In the **Property inspector**, choose **Motion** in the **Tween** pop-up menu, and use the slider to increase **Ease** to **80 Out**, which will add a motion tween to all the layers at once and make the motion tween start off fast and then slow down toward the end. This is a handy workflow shortcut.

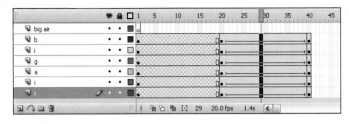

In the previous exercise, you used the custom tween settings, accessible via the Edit button in the Property inspector, to set up more complex speed changes in your motion tween animation. The basic Ease setting you used here is a quick, easy way to add a simple ease at the start or end of the tween.

---

22 Choose **Control > Test Movie**, or press **Ctrl+Enter** (Windows) or **Cmd+Return** (Mac), to preview the animation.

Notice that the animation is a total of about 2 seconds and that the words *big air* stay on the Stage for about 1 second before exploding and fading away.

You currently have a large number of layers on the Timeline. If you find it difficult to work with so many layers, group the layers into a folder using the techniques you learned in Exercise 3 of Chapter 5, *"Shape Tweening."*

---

23 Close the preview window.

---

24 Close **explode.fla**. You don't need to save your changes.

In the next exercise, you will learn to use Timeline effects to automate the creation of specific kinds of motion tween animations.

NOTE:

Motion Tweening Options and Limitations

Here are a few tasks that motion tweening can and cannot do.

For symbol instances, motion tweening can do the following:

- Tween position
- Tween brightness
- Tween tint
- Tween alpha
- Tween scaling
- Tween rotation
- Tween skew
- Tween filters

For symbol instances, motion tweening can't do the following:

- Tween merge drawing model shapes
- Tween broken-apart text
- Tween multiple items on same layer

For grouped objects, text blocks, and object drawing model shapes, motion tweening can do the following:

- Tween position
- Tween scaling
- Tween rotation
- Tween skew
- Tween filters (text blocks only)

NOTE:

What Are Timeline Effects?

Flash CS3 includes prebuilt **Timeline** effects that can create common **Timeline** animations with just one step, reducing the need for excessive keyframing. You can modify **Timeline** effects repeatedly or undo them. Effects include **Copy to Grid**, **Distributed Duplicate**, **Blur**, **Drop Shadow**, **Expand**, **Explode**, **Transition**, and **Transform**. You can apply **Timeline** effects to text and graphics, including shapes, groups, graphic symbols, bitmap images (which you will learn about in Chapter 9, *"Working with Bitmaps"*), button symbols (which you will learn about in Chapter 10, *"Buttons"*), and movie clips (which you will learn about in Chapter 11, *"Movie Clips"*).

7 | Using Timeline Effect Assistants

This exercise shows you how to use **Timeline** effects to create animations that would otherwise require a lot of planning and time to create. You will learn how to use the **Timeline** effect assistants, **Distributed Duplicate** and **Copy to Grid**, to duplicate and distribute an object multiple times on the **Stage**, as well as how to create a grid of lines painlessly and in little time.

---

1 Open **assistants_Final.fla** from the **chap_08** folder.

This file is the finished version of the project you'll be building in this exercise.

---

2 Choose **Control > Test Movie** to preview the movie.

Although nothing plays in the movie, notice the vertical and horizontal lines and the snowboard outlines. In the following steps, you will draw each line once and learn how to use Timeline effect assistants to quickly duplicate the lines and distribute them across the Stage effortlessly.

---

3 When you are finished previewing the movie, close the preview window and the **assistants_Final.fla** file. Open **assistants.fla** from the **chap_08** folder.

Notice there are five layers, and the text and bkgd layers are locked so you won't accidentally edit them. You will learn how to duplicate and distribute the snowboard outline using the Timeline effect called Distributed Duplicate in the following steps.

---

4 Select the **Selection** tool in the **Tools** panel. On the **Stage**, click to select the snowboard outline, and choose **Insert > Timeline Effects > Assistants > Distributed Duplicate** to open the **Distributed Duplicate** dialog box.

You will configure the settings here next.

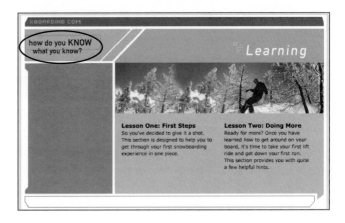

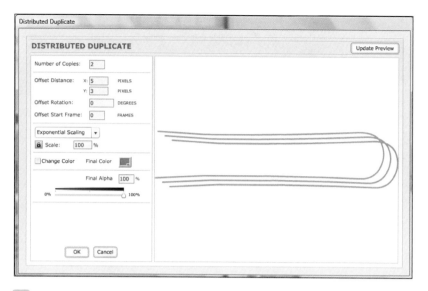

5 In the **Distributed Duplicate** dialog box, type **2** in the **Number of Copies** field to duplicate the snowboard outline two more times for a total of three snowboard outlines on the **Stage**. For **Offset Distance X**, type **5**, and for **Y**, type **3**. Leave **Offset Rotation** and **Offset Start Frame** at **0**, and make sure the **Change Color** option is deselected. The other settings should match those shown in the illustration here. When you are done configuring your settings, click the **Update Preview** button to update the preview screen with the settings you applied. When you are satisfied with the results, click **OK**.

Distributed Duplicate allows you to quickly duplicate an object on the Stage, as well as change the scale, color, rotation, and alpha transparency while animating it over a specified number of frames. In this example, each copy of the snowboard outline is offset 5 pixels horizontally (X) and 3 pixels vertically (Y) from the previous snowboard outline. Offset Start Frame specifies the number of frames to play before the next object appears.

Notice that the Stage now contains three snowboard out-lines. Also, notice that the snowboard layer was renamed Distributed Duplicate 1, reflecting the name of the effect you applied to it. That's all there is to it! Next, you will examine what Flash CS3 actually did to the shape.

Note: The number 1 in the Distributed Duplicate layer may be different in your project file. This number represents the order in which the effect is applied out of all effects in your document. What's important to note is that it was renamed with the effect you applied, in this case Distributed Duplicate.

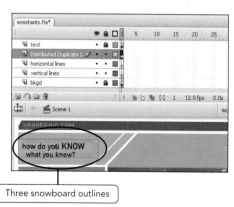

Three snowboard outlines

6 Make sure the **Property inspector** is open; if it's not, press **Ctrl+F3** (Windows) or **Cmd+F3** (Mac). Select the snowboard outlines on the **Stage**.

Notice it has been converted to a graphic symbol. The Property inspector also displays the name of the Timeline effect you applied and an Edit button. Clicking the Edit button lets you open the Distributed Duplicate dialog box again with your settings intact so you can change them if you'd like.

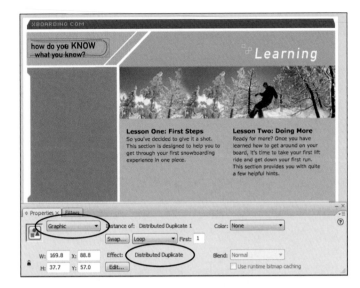

NOTE:

What Happens When You Add a Timeline Effect?

When you add a **Timeline** effect to an object, Flash CS3 creates a layer and transfers the object to the new layer. The object is placed in the effect graphic symbol, and all tweens and transformations required for the effect reside in the graphic symbol on the newly created layer.

This new layer automatically receives the same name as the effect, appended with a number representing the order in which the effect is applied, out of all effects in your document.

When you add a **Timeline** effect, a folder with the effect's name is added to the **Library** panel, containing the elements used in creating the effect.

7 Notice the **Library** panel contains an **Effects Folder** folder. In that folder is the original shape. You'll also see another symbol, **Distributed Duplicate 1**, containing the snowboard outline with the settings you applied in the **Distributed Duplicate** dialog box.

Now that you have an understanding of how Timeline effects work, you'll learn to use the Timeline effect called Copy to Grid in the following steps. You can use this effect to copy the selected item in a matrix formation based on the settings you specify. This tool is useful for creating repeating patterns.

Editing Timeline Effects

If a symbol on the **Stage** has a **Timeline** effect applied to it, you cannot double-click to edit it. You can modify a symbol with a **Timeline** effect in one of three ways:

- **Property inspector:** Select the symbol on the **Stage**, and click the **Edit** button in the **Property inspector**.

- **Menu:** Select the symbol on the **Stage**, and choose **Modify > Timeline Effects > Edit Effect**.

- **Contextual menu:** Select the symbol on the **Stage**, **right-click** (Windows) or **Ctrl-click** (Mac), and choose **Timeline Effects > Edit Effect** from the contextual menu.

Whichever method you use will open the **Edit Effect** dialog box of the **Timeline** effect.

Editing Symbols That Have Timeline Effects

As noted earlier, when you use a **Timeline** effect, Flash CS3 creates a layer and transfers the object to the new layer. The object is placed in the effect graphic symbol, and all tweens and transformations required for the effect reside in the graphic symbol on the newly created layer.

When you double-click a symbol with a **Timeline** effect applied to it, such as the **Distributed Duplicate 1** symbol shown here, you will be presented with an **Effect Settings Warning**. Basically, the warning lets you know that if you proceed to edit the symbol, you will lose the ability to adjust the effect you applied earlier.

8 On the **Timeline**, lock the **Distributed Duplicate 1** layer to avoid accidentally changing it. Click the **horizontal lines** layer to select it.

You will draw a horizontal line on the Stage with the Line tool in the following steps.

9 Choose **Window > Color** to open the **Color** panel. Select the **Line** tool in the **Tools** panel, and select white in the **Stroke Color** palette in the **Color** panel. Set **Alpha** to **50%**, and press **Enter** (Windows) or **Return** (Mac).

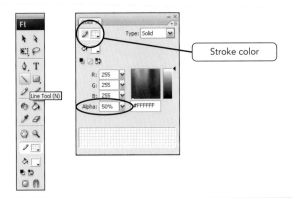

Stroke color

---

10 On the **Stage**, hold down the **Shift** key to draw a straight horizontal line where the photo meets the solid gray area. After you've drawn the line, select the **Selection** tool in the **Tools** panel, and click the line to select it. In the **Property inspector**, set **Stroke height** to **0.25**.

You will add Copy to Grid next.

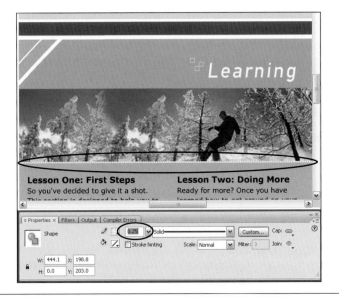

---

11 With the line still selected on the Stage, **right-click** (Windows) or **Ctrl-click** (Mac) and choose **Timeline Effects > Assistants > Copy to Grid** in the contextual menu to open the **Copy To Grid** dialog box.

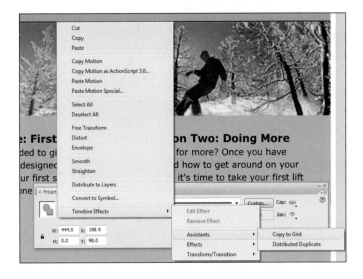

---

12 In the **Copy To Grid** dialog box, type **24** in the **Grid Size: Rows** field, type **1** in the **Grid Size: Columns** field, type **5** in the **Grid Spacing: Rows** field, and type **1** in the **Grid Spacing: Columns** field. These settings create a grid of 24 lines with 1 column. The spacing between each line will be 5 pixels above and below. Click the **Update Preview** button.

When you click the Update Preview button, you can't see anything in the preview window. That's because the lines you are drawing are white. You will learn how to get around this next.

---

13 Move the **Copy To Grid** dialog box so you can see the **Stage**. Notice the **Stage** has been updated with rows of horizontal lines. In the **Copy To Grid** dialog box, click **OK** to accept these settings.

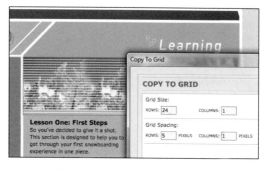

Notice the changes on the Timeline and in the Library panel. On the Timeline, the layer named horizontal lines was renamed Copy to Grid 1. This layer contains the grid of horizontal lines you just created. In the Effects Folder folder in the Library panel, notice that there are now two graphic symbols, the original snowboard outline and the original horizontal line. Also in the Library panel is the Copy to Grid 1 graphic symbol, which contains the setting you applied to the horizontal line in the Copy To Grid dialog box in Step 12.

Note: The numbers appended to the symbols in the Library panel may be different in your project file.

14 On the **Timeline**, lock the **Copy to Grid 1** layer, and click the **vertical lines** layer to select it.

15 Select the **Line** tool in the **Tools** panel. On the **Stage**, draw a vertical line where the photo meets the solid dark gray area. Hold down the **Shift** key, and click and drag to draw a straight line.

You will add Copy to Grid next.

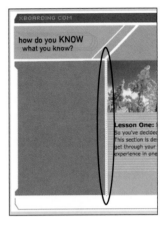

16 With the line still selected on the **Stage**, **right-click** (Windows) or **Ctrl-click** (Mac), and choose **Timeline Effects > Assistants > Copy to Grid** from the contextual menu.

17 In the **Copy To Grid** dialog box, match the settings to the ones shown in the illustration here. These settings will create a grid of 30 vertical lines. The spacing between each line will be 5 pixels on both sides of the line. Click the **Update Preview** button, and slide the **Copy To Grid** dialog box out of the way for a moment so you can view the changes on the **Stage**.

18 When you are satisfied with your settings, click **OK** in the **Copy To Grid** dialog box to accept the settings.

Notice the changes on the Timeline and in the Library panel. On the Timeline, the vertical lines layer was renamed Copy to Grid 2. This layer contains the grid of vertical lines you just created. In the Effects Folder folder in the Library panel, notice there are now three graphic symbols, one for each original shape (snowboard outline, horizontal line, and vertical line). Also in the Library panel is the Copy to Grid 2 graphic symbol, which contains the setting you applied to the vertical line in the Copy To Grid dialog box in Step 17.

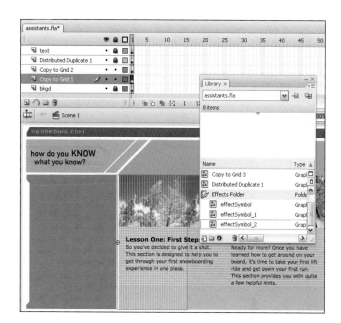

Note: The numbers appended to the layer names on the Timeline and to the symbol names in the Library panel may be different in your project.

___

19 Choose **Control > Test Movie** to check out your new interface design.

Nice! Instead of doing all the work creating the shape, turning it into a graphic symbol, and laying out all the instances on the Stage in a repeating pattern, you used the Copy to Grid and Distributed Duplicate Timeline effect assistants, which saved you the time and energy of doing it all yourself!

Note: If you want to change the stroke color of the lines, double-click the graphic symbol's icon in the Effects Folder folder in the Library panel to open it in symbol editing mode.

___

20 When you are done previewing the interface design, close the preview window.

___

21 Close **assistants.fla**. You don't need to save your changes.

In the next exercise, you will learn how to animate the new Flash CS3 filter effects.

___

8 | Animating with the Blur Filter

In this exercise, you will combine animation techniques you learned in this chapter with the filter techniques you learned in Chapter 7, *"Filters and Blend Modes."* As you will see in this exercise, animating filters is an easy way to create interesting visual effects for your Flash movies.

---

1 Open **blurAnimation.fla** from the **chap_08** folder.

If you followed Exercise 3 in Chapter 7, *"Filters and Blend Modes,"* this file will look familiar! This file has an overlay object with a blending mode and Blur filter applied to produce a colorizing effect. The first animation in this exercise involves changing the properties of the Blur filter over three keyframes and animating these changes over twelve frames.

2 In the **Property inspector**, click the **Filters** tab. Select **Frame 1** on the **overlay** layer, and select the image on the **Stage**. On the **Filters** tab, click the small lock/unlock icon to unlock the **Blur X** and **Blur Y** settings. Type **0** in the **Blur X** field, but leave the **Blur Y** field set to **20**.

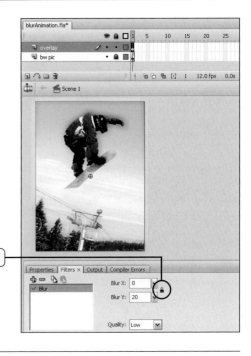

Lock/unlock icon

3 On the **overlay** layer, select **Frame 6**, and press **F6** to add a keyframe. This will copy the contents of **Frame 1**, including the **Blur** filter, to **Frame 6**. Select **Frame 12** on the **bw pic** layer, and press **F5** to add frames.

4 On the **overlay** layer, select **Frame 6**. Click the **Stage** with the **Selection** tool to select the overlay image. On the **Filters** tab in the **Property inspector**, match the **Blur** settings to the ones shown in the illustration here.

Now that you have two keyframes with different filter settings, you can set up the first tween, which you'll do next.

5 On the **overlay** layer, click anywhere between **Frame 1** and **Frame 6** to select a frame. In the **Property inspector**, select the **Properties** tab, and choose **Motion** in the **Tween** pop-up menu. This will create the first motion tween of the animation. To see the results of the tween, scrub the playhead back and forth between **Frame 1** and **Frame 6**. The blur around the snowboarder shrinks.

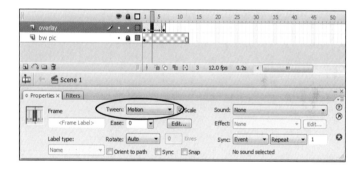

Next, you will set up the third keyframe and create the second tween animation.

6 Click **Frame 12** on the **overlay** layer, and press **F6** to add a keyframe. This adds a copy of the **overlay** image from **Frame 6** to **Frame 12**. Click the **Stage** with the **Selection** tool to select the **overlay** image. On the **Filters** tab in the **Property inspector**, match the **Blur** settings to the ones shown in the illustration here.

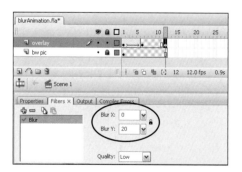

7 On the **Timeline**, click anywhere between **Frame 6** and **Frame 12** in the **overlay** layer to select a frame. In the **Property inspector**, select the **Properties** tab, and choose **Motion** in the **Tween** pop-up menu to add the second filter tween.

8 Move the playhead to **Frame 1**, and press **Enter** (Windows) or **Return** (Mac) to view the motion tween.

The blur around the snowboarder shrinks and grows from the center. Tweening the filter settings of two or more keyframes is a simple, yet effective, way to add visual interest and polish to Flash projects.

Next, you'll work through another example to get a better appreciation for the potential and power of animating with the new filters in Flash CS3.

9 Close **blurAnimation.fla**. You don't need to save your changes.

9 | Animating with the Drop Shadow Filter

In this exercise, you'll learn how to animate the **Drop Shadow** filter, continuing to combine animation techniques you learned in this chapter with the filter techniques you learned in Chapter 7, *"Filters and Blend Modes."*

---

1 Open **jumpShadow_final.fla** from the **chap_08** folder.

---

2 Choose **Control > Test Movie** to preview the final animation.

Notice the snowboarder's shadow changes in strength and location depending on the position of the snowboarder image. The Drop Shadow filter is perhaps the most important and popular filter; you will learn how to work with its various properties and settings as you re-create this animation.

---

3 When you are finished previewing the animation, close the preview window and **jumpShadow_final.fla**. Open **jumpShadow.fla** from the **chap_08** folder. Scrub the playhead back and forth between **Frame 1** and **Frame 48**.

Notice the Timeline animation sequence is composed of seven keyframes and six motion tweens. To create the drop shadow animation, you will add a Drop Shadow filter and modify its settings in each of the first six keyframes.

---

4 Position the playhead at **Frame 1**. Select the **Selection** tool in the **Tools** panel, and click the snowboarder image on the **Stage**. In the **Property inspector**, click the **Filters** tab, and click the **Add Filter** button (**+**). Choose **Drop Shadow** from the list of filters.

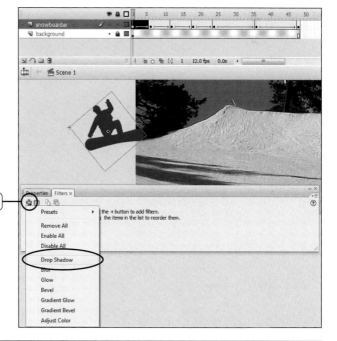

5 Match the settings in the **Filters** tab to the ones shown in the illustration here. Make sure the color is set to black and the **Knockout**, **Inner shadow**, and **Hide object** options are all deselected.

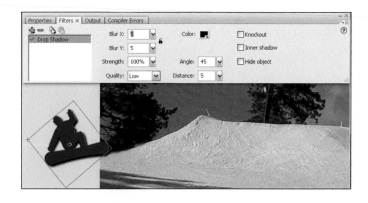

The Distance and Angle settings establish how far and at what angle the shadow will be positioned from the object. The Blur settings establish how diffuse or sharp the edges of the shadow will be.

The Drop Shadow filter offers a number of different options that let you carefully customize your drop shadows. For more information about the options for customizing drop shadows, refer to the note at the end of this exercise.

---

6 Move the playhead to **Frame 6**. On the **Stage**, click the snowboarder to select it.

Flash CS3 has already added a Drop Shadow filter to this keyframe because of the tween animation on the Timeline on Frame 1. If you apply a filter and motion tween to one frame, the ending keyframe of the tween will automatically receive the same filter treatment (although the filter settings may be different, as is the case here).

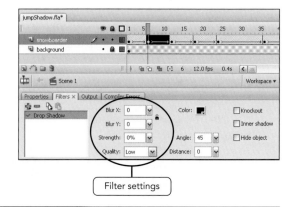

Filter settings

---

7 Match the settings in the **Filters** tab to the ones shown in the illustration here.

Notice the drop shadow is now much farther from the snowboarder graphic and is much blurrier. This is a result of the larger Distance and Blur settings.

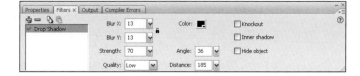

---

8 Move the playhead to **Frame 12**, and select the snowboarder on the **Stage**. Match the settings in the **Filters** tab to the ones shown in the illustration here.

Notice the Drop Shadow is farther away and even blurrier. The higher Blur settings and the lower Strength setting create this effect.

9 Change the **Drop Shadow** settings for the keyframes on **Frames 18**, **24**, and **36**. The keyframe on **Frame 48** is off the **Stage**, so it does not need a drop shadow. Use the information in the following chart for the filter settings for each keyframe:

Frame 18	Frame 24	Frame 36
Blur X/Y: 18	**Blur X/Y:** 12	**Blur X/Y:** 5
Strength: 70%	**Strength:** 80%	**Strength:** 90%
Quality: Low	**Quality:** Low	**Quality:** Low
Angle: 68	**Angle:** 39	**Angle:** 38

10 After you set the properties for each of the keyframes, move the playhead to **Frame 1**, and press **Enter** (Windows) or **Return** (Mac) to preview your work. You can also scrub the playhead back and forth along the **Timeline** to see the results.

Notice the drop shadow moving along with, but also changing shape and distance from, the snowboarder. This is a great way to add more interest and visual appeal to a simple motion tween animation. Experiment with the various Drop Shadow filter settings to refine and change the animation.

11 When you are done experimenting, close **jumpshadow.fla**. You don't need to save your changes.

Animating filters, as demonstrated in the exercises in this chapter, is a fast and easy way to add more interest, polish, and realism to your standard motion tweens. Once you become adept at creating motion tween animations and are familiar with the new filter effects in Flash, you can then combine the two techniques to create more effective and impressive animations.

VIDEO: | **jumpShdow.mov**

To make this animation more realistic, you could create a secondary movie clip that is flipped horizontally and use the **Hide Object** feature to create a more realistic shadow for your original movie clip. To learn how to do this, check out **jumpShdow.mov** in the **videos** folder on the **Flash HOT CD-ROM**.

Understanding the Drop Shadow Settings

Drop Shadow Settings	
Blur X and Y	Sets the width and height of the drop shadow.
Distance	Sets the distance of the shadow from the object.
Color	Sets the shadow color.
Strength	Sets the darkness of the shadow. The higher the numerical value, the darker the shadow.
Angle	Sets the angle of the shadow.
Quality	Sets the quality level of the drop shadow. A high setting approximates a Gaussian blur. A low setting maximizes play-back performance.
Knockout	Knocks out (or visually hides) the source object and displays only the drop shadow on the knockout image.
Inner shadow	Applies the shadow within the boundaries of the object.
Hide object	Hides the object and displays only its shadow, creating a more realistic shadow.

Congratulations! You have finished a very important chapter. In this chapter, you learned how to create motion tween animations with symbols, how to use Timeline effects to automate certain animation tasks, and how to use the new copy motion feature in Flash CS3. The knowledge you gained will give you an excellent starting point for experimenting with your own animations. When you are ready, turn the page to learn how to work with bitmap images.

Working with Bitmaps

So far, even though you have used bitmaps as background images in several of the exercise files, you've mostly worked with vector-based graphics. Although many people think of Adobe Flash CS3 Professional as simply a vector-editing and animation program, you will soon learn it has some pretty impressive bitmap-editing features as well. This chapter concentrates on editing bitmap images, specifically examining how Flash CS3 treats them differently from vectors-based graphics. You will learn how to import and optimize bitmaps, how to create a static and animated mask of a bitmap, and how to create interesting animation effects after converting bitmap images to vector-based graphics.

Understanding the Benefits of Bitmaps

Vector graphics are best known for their crisp appearance, small file size, and flexibility in scaling. Their efficient file size helps movies download and play faster. However, vector graphics have a few negative aspects. Complex vector artwork made up of many individual vector objects can generate large files, making them harder for the computer to process and play back. Also, a photographic look is hard to achieve with vector graphics. As a result, a common complaint is that many Flash projects look very similar.

Bitmap images (also known as **raster graphics**) are stored in the computer as a series of pixel values, with each pixel taking a set amount of memory. Because each pixel is defined individually, this format is great for photographic images with complex details. However, bitmaps lose their image sharpness when you drastically increase or decrease their size.

To counter this problem, Flash CS3 includes a feature called **bitmap smoothing** that improves the image quality at these severely enlarged or reduced sizes, as shown in the illustration below.

To apply bitmap smoothing, double-click the bitmap image in the **Library** panel to open the **Bitmap Properties** dialog box, and then select the **Allow smoothing** option.

In addition, the appearance of bitmaps in the Flash CS3 authoring program and in the Adobe Flash Player is now more consistent. Conveniently, Flash CS3 lets you import bitmap graphics in many different formats, including JPEG, GIF, and TIFF. If you have Apple QuickTime 4 or newer installed on your machine, the list of files available for import increases even further. The chart on the following page lists the bitmap file formats you can import into Flash CS3. For a chart describing the vector file types supported by Flash CS3, see Chapter 19, *"Integration."*

Bitmap smoothing turned on

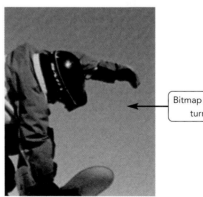

Bitmap smoothing turned off

Bitmap File Types

File Type	Extension	Windows	Mac	QuickTime 4 or Later Needed?
Bitmap	.bmp	X	X	Windows: No; Mac: Yes
GIF and animated GIF	.gif	X	X	No
JPEG	.jpg	X	X	No
PICT	.pct, .pict, .pic	X	X	Windows: No; Mac: Yes
PNG	.png	X	X	No
MacPaint	.pntg	X	X	Yes
Photoshop	.psd	X	X	Yes
QuickTime images	.qtf	X	X	Yes
Silicon Graphics	.sai	X	X	Yes
TGA	.tgf	X	X	Yes
TIFF	.tif, .tiff	X	X	Yes

Note: Flash CS3 honors the transparency settings of graphic file formats that support transparency, such as GIF, PNG, and PICT files.

Understanding Compression in Flash CS3

When you export a movie, Flash CS3 automatically applies its own compression settings to bitmaps. You can change the graphics compression settings in two ways. You can set a single compression method and amount for every graphic in the project using the global **Publish** settings, which you'll learn about in Chapter 17, *"Publishing and Exporting,"* or you can use the **Bitmap Properties** dialog box to set and preview compression settings for each individual file. Any changes you make in the **Bitmap Properties** dialog box will affect the image in the **Library** panel and all the instances of it in the project file.

Lossy (JPEG) compression

Lossless (PNG/GIF) compression

In the following exercise, you will learn how to compress bitmap images by changing the compression settings in the **Bitmap Properties** dialog box. You have two choices for compression: **Photo (JPEG)**, also known as **lossy**, and **Lossless (PNG/GIF)**. Generally, a photographic image will compress better with lossy (JPEG) compression, and images with a lot of solid colors will compress better as lossless (PNG/GIF). What's nice is that you'll be able to see a preview within this dialog box to determine which choice produces images that look better.

When Flash CS3 outputs your finished movie, it takes this individual image compression into account and overrides the default compression settings.

1 | Importing and Compressing Bitmaps

This exercise demonstrates how to import a bitmap and adjust its compression settings.

---

1 Copy the **chap_09** folder from the **Flash HOT CD-ROM** to your desktop. Open a new ActionScript 3.0 document in Flash CS3 by choosing **File > New > Flash File (ActionScript 3.0)**. Save the file (by choosing **File > Save As**) in the **chap_09** folder as **import.fla**.

---

2 Choose **File > Import > Import to Stage**, or press **Ctrl+R** (Windows) or **Cmd+R** (Mac) to open the **Import** dialog box. Browse to the **import1.jpg** file in the **chap_09** folder. Select the file, and click **Open** (Windows) or **Import** (Mac).

When you import a file using the Import to Stage command, you might wonder where the file goes. Flash CS3 automatically places the file in three locations: on the Stage, in the Library panel, and in the Bitmap Fill section of the Color panel.

Note: The import1.jpg file may or may not have the .jpg extension, depending on which platform you are using (Windows or Mac) and whether you have the extensions turned on or off. Either way is fine, since the file name, import1, is what's required to locate this file. For more information about hiding and revealing file extensions, refer to the introduction of this book.

---

3 Press **Ctrl+L** (Windows) or **Cmd+L** (Mac) to open the **Library** panel.

---

4 In the **Library** panel, select the **import1** image. Click the **Properties** button to open the **Bitmap Properties** dialog box.

Properties

TIP: Additional Ways to Access the Bitmap Properties

In addition to clicking the **Properties** button in the **Library** panel, you can access the **Bitmap Properties** dialog box in three other ways:

1. Double-click the thumbnail preview in the **Library** panel.

2. Double-click the icon next to the image name in the **Library** panel.

3. In the upper-right corner of the **Library** panel, click the panel **Options** button, and choose **Properties** in the contextual menu.

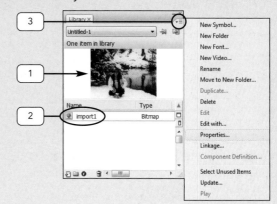

5 In the **Bitmap Properties** dialog box, position the cursor over the preview window. Notice the cursor changes to a hand. Click and drag the image in the preview window until you see the girl.

Since the girl is the focus of the image, you want to make sure the preview window will give you a much better view of the compression changes you are about to make.

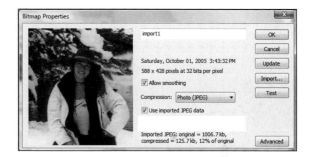

6 Choose **Lossless (PNG/GIF)** in the **Compression** pop-up menu, and click **Test** to update the preview image and the compression information at the base of the window.

Notice the new compression information appears in the dialog box. You just changed the compression settings for the import1 image. The new compressed image size is 580.4 KB, 57 percent of the original, which was 1006.7 KB. If you click OK, this setting will alter the bitmap in the Library panel and the instance on the Stage. Don't click OK just yet—you're going to make a couple more changes.

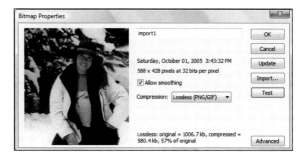

Why Is File Size Important?

As you build project files in Flash CS3, you may have to keep your total SWF file size less than a certain threshold to make playback optimal for all users viewing the Web site, including those using dial-up connections. With this in mind, you need to find a good balance between image quality (check the preview window after you click the **Test** button) and file size. You may have to experiment with several settings, but the file size savings will be well worth the time spent!

7 In the **Bitmap Properties** dialog box, choose **Photo (JPEG)** in the **Compression** pop-up menu. Deselect the **Use imported JPEG data** check box, and add your own quality setting by typing **80** (100 is best; 0 is worst) in the **Quality** box. Click the **Test** button again.

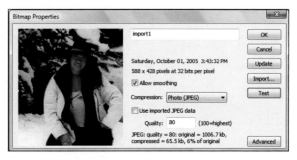

Notice the new compression information appears in the dialog box. The new compressed image size is 65.5 KB, significantly smaller than the size obtained using lossless PNG/GIF compression, which at 580 KB was more than 10 times the size. Additionally, the image still looks great in the preview window. A good rule of thumb is that most photographic content compresses best with the Photo (JPEG) setting, and graphical content with solid colors, graphic shapes, text, and so on, compresses best with the Lossless (PNG/GIF) setting.

8 Click **OK**. When the Flash file is published, this bitmap will be compressed using the last settings you applied.

9 Close **import.fla**. You don't need to save your changes.

Understanding the Bitmap Properties Dialog Box

The **Bitmap Properties** dialog box contains a number of options. This handy chart will help you understand the options:

Bitmap Properties Dialog Box	
Option	**Description**
Preview window	Shows the current bitmap properties so you can see how the settings you choose affect the image.
File Name	Displays the bitmap's **Library** item name. Clicking in the **File Name** field and typing a new name will change the bitmap's name in the **Library** panel as well.

continues on next page

Bitmap Properties Dialog Box *continued*

Option	Description
Image path	Displays the file path for the image.
File information	Shows the date the bitmap was last modified, the file's dimensions, and the color depth.
Allow smoothing	Smoothes or dithers the image when selected. If this box is deselected, the image will appear aliased or jagged.
Compression	Lets you choose between **Photo (JPEG)** or **Lossless (PNG/GIF)** compression. Photo compression (JPEG) is best for complex bitmaps with many colors or gradations. Lossless compression (PNG/GIF) is best for bitmaps with fewer colors and simple shapes filled with single colors.
Use imported JPEG data	Lets you use the original compression settings and avoid double compression when selected. If this box is deselected, you can type your own values—from 1 to 100—for the quality of the image.
Update button	Lets you update the bitmap image if it has been changed outside of Flash CS3. It uses the image path to track the original image's location and updates the image selected in the **Library** panel with the file located in the original location.
Import button	Lets you change the bitmap in the **Library** panel by specifying the path to another image. If a new path is specified, a new image will appear in the **Library** panel, and all instances in the project file automatically update with the new bitmap.
Test button	Lets you see the changes you make to the settings of the **Bitmap Properties** dialog box in the preview window and displays the new compression information at the bottom of the dialog box.
Advanced/Basic	Opens and closes the **Linkage** properties options.
Linkage	Allows you to add bitmaps to a document at runtime or to share them with other Flash projects. To do this, specify a name for the bitmap in the linkage identifier field and then choose the **Export** options desired.

2 | Importing Bitmap Sequences

One way to create a "mock" video effect in Flash CS3 is to use a sequence of photographs in which each image is just slightly different from the previous image. When these images are placed in keyframes, one right after another, and you test the movie, it will appear as if the camera is rolling! This exercise demonstrates how to create frame-by-frame animations (or mock video) by importing a series of bitmap graphics all at once.

---

1 Open **bitmapSequence_Final.fla** from the **chap_09** folder.

You'll see a series of images on Frames 1 through 14.

---

2 Press **Enter** (Windows) or **Return** (Mac) to preview the movie.

Although it's just a series of still photographs, it appears as though you are watching a video of a snowboarder making a jump. As you can see, you can effectively simulate video footage by using still images in Flash CS3. You'll learn how to create this animation sequence next.

---

3 Close **bitmapSequence_Final.fla**.

---

4 Open **bitmapSequence.fla** from the **chap_09** folder.

This is a blank file with a black background. Next, you'll import the series of images you want to use.

---

5 Choose **File > Import > Import to Stage**, or press **Ctrl+R** (Windows) or **Cmd+R** (Mac). Open the **sequence** folder in the **chap_09** folder.

Notice there are 14 numbered files named bigair--xx in the sequence folder.

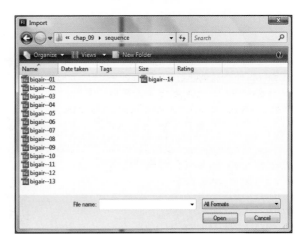

---

6 Select the **bigair--01.png** file, and click **Open** (Windows) or **Import** (Mac). Flash CS3 automatically detects the image you are trying to import as part of a sequence of images. In the warning message that appears, click **Yes** to import the whole series of images.

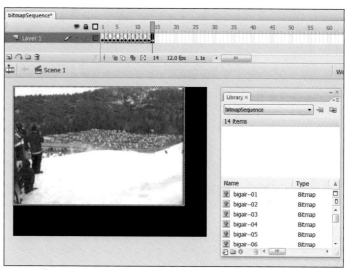

If you ever want to import a sequence of images as successive frames and have Flash recognize it as a sequence, be sure to number the images in the order you want the sequence to appear, such as image01, image02, and so on. Whenever Flash CS3 sees sequentially numbered images in the same folder, it will ask you whether the images should all be imported as a sequence.

When you click Yes in this step, Flash CS3 imports all 14 files in the sequence, places them on the Stage, and creates a new keyframe for each one on the Timeline. Notice the imported images are not centered on the Stage. Why? By default, Flash CS3 places the imported sequence in the upper-left corner of the Stage. You'll change this in the next steps.

---

7 In the status bar on the **Timeline**, click the **Edit Multiple Frames** button. Make sure the **Edit Multiple Frames** markers span all 14 frames. If they don't, drag the handles so they cover all 14 frames. Click the layer name to select all the frames on the layer. Click and drag the bitmap image to the center of the **Stage**. When finished, turn off **Edit Multiple Frames** by clicking the button again.

Although it may seem complicated, using the Edit Multiple Frames feature lets you reposition all the frames at once.

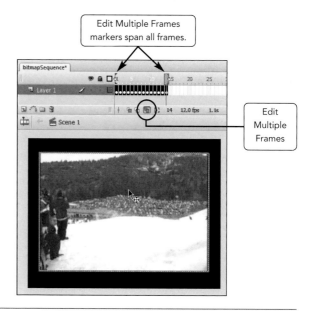

8 Choose **Control > Test Movie** to test the movie. When you are finished, close the preview window.

Even though each frame contains a separate image, when you test the movie, it appears as if you're watching video footage!

Note: Next, you'll change the movie frame rate to make it look more realistic.

9 Select the **Selection** tool in the **Tools** panel. Click anywhere outside the image on the **Stage** to deselect it. In the **Property inspector**, type **16** in the **Frame rate** field to speed up the movie and make the bitmap sequence animation appear more realistic. Choose **Control > Test Movie** to preview the movie.

The bitmap images will be displayed on the Stage much quicker, better simulating video playback, which usually displays 15 to 30 pictures, or frames, per second.

10 When you're finished previewing the movie, close the preview window. Type **6** in the **Frame rate** field in the **Property inspector**. Choose **Control > Test Movie** to preview the movie.

Depending on the effect you're looking for, you may need a few tries to determine the perfect frame rate.

11 When you're done experimenting, close the preview window.

12 Save your changes, and leave **bitmapSequence.fla** open for the next exercise.

3 | Converting Bitmaps to Vectors

When you import bitmaps, you are not limited to using the files as they exist in their original forms. You can convert imported bitmap images to vector graphics using the **Trace Bitmap** feature in Flash CS3. This feature traces the shapes of a bitmap graphic and creates a new set of vector shapes simulating the appearance of the original bitmap image. Using the **Trace Bitmap** feature is not an exact science; it requires a little experimentation to get the best results. This exercise demonstrates how to use the **Trace Bitmap** feature to turn a bitmap image into a vector graphic.

1 If you just completed Exercise 2, **bitmapSequence.fla** file should still be open. If it's not, complete Exercise 2, and then return to this exercise. Turn off the **Edit Multiple Frames** button.

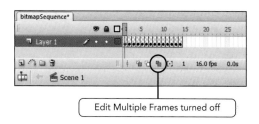

Edit Multiple Frames turned off

2 With **Frame 1** selected on the **Timeline** and the **Selection** tool selected in the **Tools** panel, select the image on the **Stage**, and choose **Modify > Bitmap > Trace Bitmap** to open the **Trace Bitmap** dialog box.

Using the settings in the Trace Bitmap dialog box, you'll transform the bitmap on the Stage into a vector graphic.

NOTE:

What Is Trace Bitmap?

The **Trace Bitmap** feature lets you convert imported bitmaps into vector art. You might want to do this to create an interesting animation effect, reduce the file size of a photographic image, or zoom into a photographic image during an animation. The **Trace Bitmap** feature traces the outlines and internal shapes of a bitmap graphic and simulates the appearance of the bitmap file by creating a new set of vector shapes. You can use the settings in the **Trace Bitmap** dialog box to control how closely the new vector shapes match the original image.

3 In the **Trace Bitmap** dialog box, type **80** in the **Color threshold** field, and type **5** in the **Minimum area** field. Choose **Very Tight** in the **Curve fit** pop-up menu, and choose **Many corners** in the **Corner Threshold** pop-up menu to create a vector shape with sharp edges that more closely matches the original bitmap. Click **OK**.

This combination of settings will produce a vector graphic that closely resembles the original bitmap because it will reproduce more detail from the original bitmap. Be aware that the more detail a bitmap contains and the lower your settings in the Trace Bitmap dialog box, the longer it will take to convert the bitmap to a vector and the larger your movie's file size will be. A reference chart describing all the settings in the Trace Bitmap dialog box is provided at the end of this exercise.

Original bitmap

Vector image after using Trace Bitmap

4 When the conversion process completes, click anywhere outside the image to deselect it.

Notice the traced bitmap closely resembles the original.

Note: When you use the Trace Bitmap function, the changes will affect only the selected image on the Stage. The bitmap in the Library panel will remain unchanged. When you publish your movie, the new vector image will appear instead of the original image.

5 Move the playhead to **Frame 14**. On the **Stage**, select the bitmap on **Frame 14**, and choose **Modify > Bitmap > Trace Bitmap** to open the **Trace Bitmap** dialog box.

You will modify the last image in the sequence next.

6 In the **Trace Bitmap** dialog box, type **200** in the **Color threshold** field, and type **10** in the **Minimum area** field. Choose **Very Smooth** in the **Curve fit** pop-up menu, and choose **Few Corners** in the **Corner threshold** pop-up menu. Click **OK**.

As you can see, this combination of settings creates a vector graphic that is more abstract and does not resemble the original image as closely as the settings you used on the Frame 1 image. Fewer corners, as well as corners that are smoother and less defined, were reproduced from the original bitmap, resulting in a vector image with a lot less detail and definition.

---

7 Repeat Steps 5 and 6 to convert the remaining 12 bitmap images on the **Stage** to vector graphics. Experiment with different settings for each image to see how the original image changes.

Tip: If you don't like how the new image turned out, undo it—Ctrl+Z (Windows) or Cmd+Z (Mac). You can always return the vector art to the original bitmap version and try it again.

---

8 Choose **Control > Test Movie** to preview the animation.

You have produced a stylized version of the video containing vector graphics. This technique is often used for aesthetic reasons. If you scale vector graphics, they keep crisp edges, whereas if you scale bitmap graphics, they become blurry and jagged.

Note: Tracing works best on bitmaps with few colors and gradients. Tracing a bitmap with many colors will not only tax the computer's resources but can also result in a vector graphic that is larger in file size than the original bitmap. To achieve the best results, experiment with different settings, and take note of the file sizes.

---

9 Close the preview window, and close **bitmapSequence.fla**. You don't need to save your changes.

Understanding the Trace Bitmap Options

The **Trace Bitmap** dialog box has a number of options. This handy chart will help you understand them:

Trace Bitmap Dialog Box	
Option	**Description**
Color threshold	Sets the amount by which the color of each pixel can vary before it is considered a different color. As the threshold value increases, the number of colors in the image decreases, and the resulting traced bitmap image will have fewer colors than the original. The color threshold range is 1 to 500.
Minimum area	Determines the number of surrounding pixels to consider when determining the color of a pixel. The lower the number, the more the pixel color will resemble the pixels nearby. The higher the number, the less the color will resemble adjacent pixels. The area range is 1 to 1000.
Curve fit	Determines how smooth (**Smooth** or **Very Smooth**) the outlines in the traced shape are drawn or how closely they match the original image (**Tight** or **Very Tight**).
Corner threshold	Determines whether to use sharp edges (**Many Corners**) or smoother edges (**Few Corners**).

Choosing the appropriate options in the **Trace Bitmap** dialog box can be confusing. Here are two tips: If you want to conserve file size or create a more abstract image, choose a higher color threshold, a higher minimum area, a smooth curve fit, and few corners. If you want to match the original image as closely as possible, choose a lower color threshold, a lower minimum area, a very smooth curve fit, and many corners.

4 | Using Basic Masking

Masking is a technique that lets you hide and reveal areas of a layer. The **mask layer** is a special layer that defines what is visible on the layer beneath it. Only layers that are beneath the shapes in the mask layer will be visible. This technique is useful when you want to fill text with a photograph or hide (mask) a portion of the background of a photo. In this exercise, you will create a mask with text so the image on the layer below appears inside the text.

---

1 Open **mask.fla** from the **chap_09** folder. Make sure the **Library** panel is visible. If it's not, choose **Window > Library**.

This file has a blue background and contains one symbol in the Library panel.

---

2 Choose **File > Import > Import to Stage**. In the **chap_09** folder, double-click the **sideMountain.jpg** file to open and automatically place the bitmap on the **Stage**.

---

3 On the **Timeline**, double-click **Layer 1**, and rename it **mountain**. Press **Enter** (Windows) or **Return** (Mac).

In the next few steps, you'll mask this layer.

---

4 Lock the **mountain** layer by clicking the dot under the **Lock** icon for the layer.

Locking layers prevents you from accidentally moving or selecting the bitmap on the mountain layer.

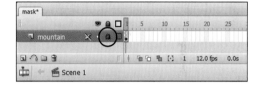

---

5 Click the **Insert Layer** button to add a new layer. Double-click the newly created layer, rename it **xboarding**, and press **Enter** (Windows) or **Return** (Mac). Make sure the stacking order of the layers matches the order shown in the illustration here. If it doesn't, click and drag to reposition the layers so the **xboarding** layer is above the **mountain** layer.

Insert Layer

---

6 Take a look at the contents in the **Library** panel. Notice the **siteName** symbol. I've included this graphic symbol in the **mask.fla** file to help you with this exercise. Drag an instance of the **siteName** symbol to the **Stage**, and position the **X** over the snowboarder in the bitmap image.

The symbol instance of the xboarding.com name is going to end up as the mask for the bitmap. You can think of the text inside the symbol instance as a cookie cutter that will let you see only what you cut out of the mountain image.

Tip: To better see where the snow-boarder is in relation to the xboarding graphic, click the **View Outlines** icon for the **xboarding** layer.

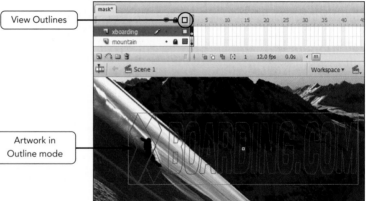

View Outlines

Artwork in Outline mode

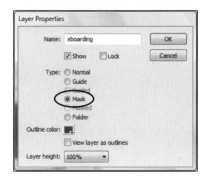

7 With the **xboarding** layer selected, choose **Modify > Timeline > Layer Properties** to open the **Layer Properties** dialog box. Select **Mask** for **Type**, and click **OK** to convert the **xboarding** layer to a mask layer.

Tip: When converting a layer to a mask layer, you can choose to bypass the Layer Properties dialog box by right-clicking (Windows) or Ctrl-clicking (Mac) the layer name and choosing Mask in the contextual menu.

In this step, you created a mask layer (the xboarding layer), which has a defined mask area based on the siteName symbol. Next, you need to create the masked layer—the layer beneath that will show through the mask layer.

228   **Adobe Flash CS3 Professional** : H·O·T

8 To make the **mountain** layer become masked by the **xboarding** mask layer, double-click the **mountain** layer icon to open the **Layer Properties** dialog box. Select **Masked** for **Type**, and click **OK**.

Notice that the icon and position of the mountain layer has changed.

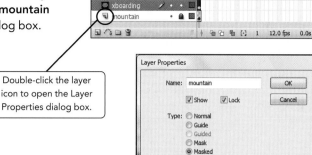

Double-click the layer icon to open the Layer Properties dialog box.

9 Click the dot under the **Lock** icon for the **xboarding** layer so both layers are locked.

The bitmap now shows through the text shapes!

Tip: To see the mask, you must have both the mask layer and the masked layer locked. To lock the layer, you can either click the Lock column in the layers or right-click (Windows) or Ctrl-click (Mac) the layer's name and choose Show Masking in the contextual menu.

You have just created your first mask! As you can see, you can create some really interesting effects using mask and masked layers in Flash CS3. Next, you will animate the mask.

Mask layer   Masked layer

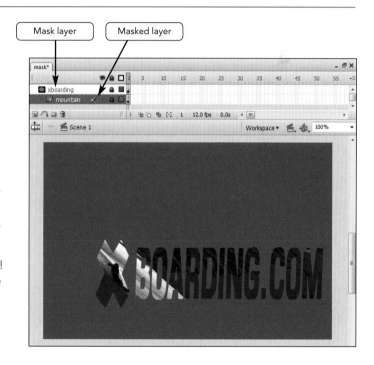

10 Save your changes, and leave **mask.fla** open for the next exercise.

5 | Using Animated Masks

In the previous exercise, you learned how to create a basic mask using text. But masks don't have to be static! This exercise demonstrates how to create a text mask that moves over a bitmap background.

---

1 If you just completed Exercise 4, **mask.fla** should still be open. If it's not, complete Exercise 4, and then return to this exercise.

Make sure that View Outlines is turned off.

---

2 On the **xboarding** layer, click **Frame 20** to select it, and choose **Insert > Timeline > Keyframe** to add a keyframe.

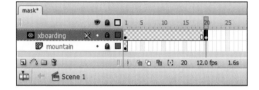

---

3 On the **mountain** layer, click **Frame 20** to select it, and press **F5** to add frames.

---

4 Unlock the **xboarding** layer by clicking the **Lock** icon. Select **Frame 1**, and click and drag to move the **xboarding** instance off the **Stage** to the left.

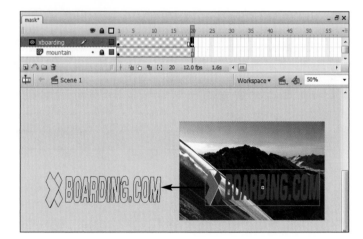

5 With the **xboarding** instance still selected on **Frame 1**, choose **Modify > Transform > Flip Vertical** to flip the **xboarding** instance upside down.

This position will serve as the beginning of the animation.

6 On the **Timeline**, select one of the frames on the **xboarding** layer between **Frame 1** and **Frame 20**. In the **Property inspector**, choose **Motion** in the **Tween** pop-up menu to add a motion tween to the mask.

7 Click the dot under the **Lock** icon to lock the **xboarding** layer.

Notice you can immediately see the masked image on the Stage.

8 Move the playhead to **Frame 1** and press **Enter** (Windows) or **Return** (Mac) to test the animation. The **xboarding** text flips and rotates with the mountain picture peeking through the letters.

Great job! In just a few steps, you changed the basic mask from the previous exercise to an animated mask.

9 Close **mask.fla**. You don't need to save your changes.

6 | Animating Bitmaps

When you are working with bitmaps, you can make them fade in from invisible to visible, or vice versa. You can accomplish this handy technique by converting the bitmap to a symbol and creating a motion tween of the symbol's **Alpha** setting. You will learn how to do this in the following steps.

1 Open **effectsFinal.fla** from the **chap_09** folder.

This is a finished version of the project you will complete in this exercise.

2 Choose **Control > Test Movie** to preview the SWF file.

You will see a pencil outline being drawn, the outline being filled with a bitmap that fades into view, and then a background image fading into view. In this exercise, you will complete the last part of the animation—fading the bitmaps from invisible to visible.

3 Close the preview window, and close **effectsFinal.fla**.

4 Open **bitmapEffects.fla** from the **chap_09** folder.

This file contains the first part of the animation demonstrated in the effectsFinal.fla file. The file contains two layers: the boarder layer contains a bitmap of a jumping snowboarder, and the stroke layer contains a pencil outline animation around the snowboarder and is locked so you don't accidentally modify it. You'll be working with the boarder layer in this exercise.

The first thing you'll do is create a motion tween of the snowboarder changing from invisible to visible.

5 On the **boarder** layer, click the keyframe on **Frame 1** to select it. Click and drag the keyframe from **Frame 1** to **Frame 6** to move the keyframe.

As you can see, you can easily move keyframes on the Timeline by clicking and dragging.

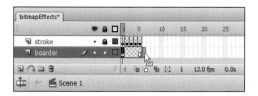

6 With the **Selection** tool selected in the **Tools** panel, click the snowboarder on the **Stage** to select it, and press **F8** to open the **Convert to Symbol** dialog box. Type **boarder** in the **Name** field, and select **Graphic** for **Type**. Click **OK**.

This will be the starting point of the tween animation.

Wondering why you converted the snowboarder to a symbol? In the next few steps, you will be using alpha to create the fade effect, and you can't apply an alpha effect to an object that is not a graphic symbol or movie clip symbol.

7 On the **boarder** layer, select **Frame 20**, and choose **Insert > Timeline > Keyframe** to add a keyframe to **Frame 20**.

This will be the end of the tween animation.

8 Move the playhead to **Frame 6**, and click to select the **boarder** symbol instance on the **Stage**. (Be careful to select the instance on the **Stage** and not just the frame it's on, or the **Property inspector** won't show you the correct attributes.) In the **Property inspector**, choose **Alpha** in the **Color** pop-up menu, and set the value to **0%**.

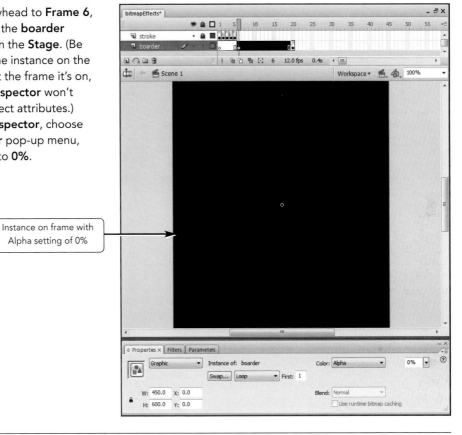

Instance on frame with Alpha setting of 0%

9 Click anywhere between **Frames 6** and **20** to select one of the frames. In the **Property inspector**, choose **Motion** in the **Tween** pop-up menu.

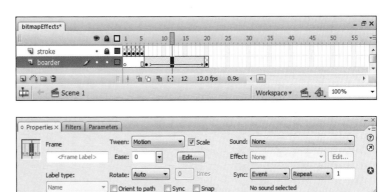

10 On the **stroke** layer, select **Frame 20**, and press **F5** to add frames to match the number of frames on the **boarder** layer.

Once the outline animates around the snowboarder, this step keeps the outline visible on the Stage during the following tween animation.

---

11 Press **Enter** (Windows) or **Return** (Mac) to preview the animation. The outline will draw itself, and then the **boarder** layer will fade from invisible to full color.

You have one more tween animation to create.

---

12 On the **Timeline**, lock the **boarder** layer, and click the **Insert Layer** button to add a new layer. Rename the new layer **background**. Click and drag to position it below the **boarder** layer so it is the bottom layer on the **Timeline**.

---

13 Select **Frame 20**, and press **F7** to add a blank keyframe to **Frame 20** of the **background** layer. Hide the **stroke** and **boarder** layers so you can see only the **background** layer for the next few steps.

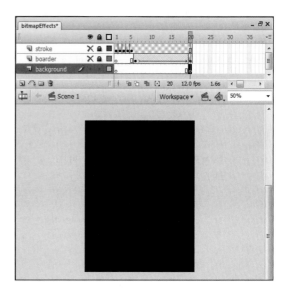

14 Press **Ctrl+L** (Windows) or **Cmd+L** (Mac) to open the **Library** panel. Drag an instance of the **boarderCloseUp** bitmap graphic to the **Stage**.

15 Press **Ctrl+K** (Windows) or **Cmd+K** (Mac) to display the **Align** panel. Click the **To stage** button, and then click the **Align vertical center** and **Align horizontal center** buttons to center the image.

Note: The Align panel lets you position selected objects relative to the Stage (if the To Stage button is selected) or relative to one another (if several objects are selected).

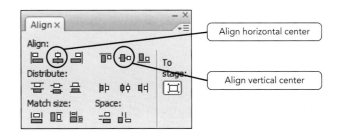

16 With the snowboarder bitmap still selected on the **Stage**, press **F8** to convert the bitmap to a symbol. In the **Convert to Symbol** dialog box, type **origImage** in the **Name** field, and select **Graphic** for **Type** to convert the bitmap to a symbol so you can create a motion tween in the following steps. Click **OK**.

17 Select **Frame 35** on the **background** layer, and choose **Insert > Timeline > Keyframe** to add a keyframe to **Frame 35**.

This will be the end of the tween animation.

18 Move the playhead to **Frame 20**, and select the **origImage** symbol instance on the **Stage**. (Be careful to select the instance on the **Stage** and not the frame so the **Property inspector** shows you the right attributes.) In the **Property inspector**, choose **Alpha** in the **Color** pop-up menu, and set the value to **0%**.

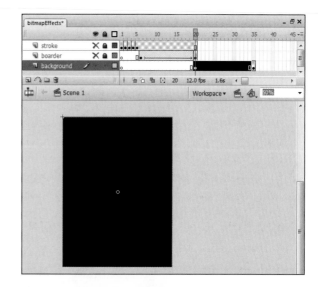

This will be the beginning of the animation on the background layer.

19 Click anywhere between **Frames 20** and **35** of the **background** layer to select one of the frames. In the **Property inspector**, choose **Motion** in the **Tween** pop-up menu.

20 On the **boarder** layer, click **Frame 35** to select it, and press **F5** to add frames to match the number of frames on the **background** layer.

This will make the boarder layer remain visible on the Stage during the background tween animation.

21 Click **Frame 45** of the **boarder** layer and then **Shift-click Frame 45** of the **background** layer to select both frames. Choose **Insert > Timeline > Frame** to add frames up to **Frame 45**.

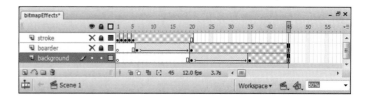

This will add frames so once the background fades in, it will remain for 10 more frames before the animation starts over again.

22 Choose **Control > Test Movie** to preview the final animation. The outline will draw itself, the **boarder** layer will fade from invisible to full color, and then the background will fade in. Great work!

Note: When you press Enter (Windows) or Return (Mac), you see only a preview of the animation inside the editing environment, which may not play exactly as the SWF file will in the Flash Player. To see a more realistic test of the animation, choose Control > Test Movie, which will play back the actual SWF in the Flash Player. In Chapter 17, *"Publishing and Exporting,"* you will learn an even more reliable way to see how the file will look in a browser: using the Publish command.

---

23 When you are done experimenting, close the preview window.

---

24 Close **bitmapEffects.fla**. You don't need to save your changes.

That's it—you've finished another chapter! Get ready to learn about buttons next.

10

Buttons

Adobe Flash CS3 Professional has three types of symbols: graphic symbols, button symbols, and movie clip symbols. You learned about graphic symbols in Chapter 6, *"Creating Symbols and Instances,"* and you'll learn about movie clip symbols in Chapter 11, *"Movie Clips."* You'll learn about button symbols in this chapter.

Buttons are a useful type of symbol. They can contain rollover states and animated rollover states or even be made invisible. What you might not realize is that there's more to making buttons than creating the artwork for them. You can also program buttons to accept code written in ActionScript (covered in Chapter 12, *"ActionScript Basics"*). Through ActionScript, you can make buttons play, stop, rewind, and fast-forward, as well as change artwork and do numerous other things in your Flash movies! Before programming your buttons, however, you need to learn how to create them. Learning Flash CS3 involves putting a lot of puzzle pieces together, and button symbols are an extremely important part of the puzzle. You will find a use for them in all your Flash projects. In this chapter, you will build a solid foundation for working with buttons, including how to create, add sound to, test, and preview them.

Understanding Button States

Just as with graphic and movie clip symbols, button symbols have their own **Timeline** panels. The difference with a button symbol's **Timeline** is that it displays four prelabeled, premade frames: **Up**, **Over**, **Down**, and **Hit**. The first three frames of the button **Timeline** determine the appearance of the button during three different kinds of cursor interactions. The fourth frame, **Hit**, determines the clickable area of the button. The terms **Up**, **Over**, **Down**, and **Hit** are also called **states**, which are described in the following chart. As you know from previous chapters, the **Timeline** must contain keyframes in order to contain changing content. Button **Timeline** panels have slots for the **Up**,

Over, **Down**, and **Hit** states, but they start out empty. You must insert keyframes in these slots, where you can then place content that constitutes the button in the various states of interaction.

When you create a button symbol, Flash CS3 automatically adds a blank keyframe in the first frame—the **Up** state—of the button.

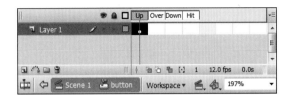

Button States	
State	**Description**
Up	The **Up** keyframe contains artwork defining the button appearance before the user's cursor interacts with the button.
Over	The **Over** keyframe defines the button appearance when the user moves the cursor over the **Hit** area of the button. This is also referred to as the **rollover state** of the button.
Down	The **Down** keyframe defines the button appearance when it's clicked. The user sees this state for only a split second (or longer if holding down the mouse).
Hit	The **Hit** keyframe defines the actual, active area of the button. It is also referred to as the **hot area** of the button. The contents of the **Hit** frame are always invisible to the user.

Understanding Button Types

Fundamentally, all button symbols are constructed alike. However, you can significantly change their appearance and type by altering the frames you use and the content of the four keyframes. The possibilities are nearly endless, but they generally fall into the following four categories:

Button Types	
Type	**Description**
Basic	A basic button has the same content in the **Up**, **Over**, and **Down** states. Users can click it, and it can contain actions; however, it does not change appearance or provide visual feedback during the user's interaction with it.
Rollover	A rollover button changes appearance when the user moves the cursor over it, providing visual feedback about the user's cursor position. You can accomplish this by inserting different content in the **Over** state than in the **Up** state.
Animated	An animated rollover button is similar to a rollover button, but one or more of its keyframes (usually the **Over** state) contains an animation within a movie clip instance. Whenever that keyframe is displayed, a movie clip animates. You will learn how to make animated rollover buttons and movie clips in the next chapter.
Invisible	Invisible buttons contain a blank keyframe in the **Up** state and a keyframe in the **Hit** state. They can also contain artwork in the **Over** or **Down** state, although they never contain artwork in the **Up** state. Because there is no artwork in the **Up** state, the button is invisible to users until they move their cursors over it. You will learn how to make an invisible button in Exercise 5 later in this chapter.

1 | Creating Rollover Buttons

This exercise teaches you how to create, test, and preview a basic rollover button. You will learn how a button's **Timeline** is different from the main **Timeline** and about the four different states of buttons.

---

1 Copy the **chap_10** folder from the **Flash HOT CD-ROM** to your desktop. Open **rollOverButton.fla** from the **chap_10** folder.

This is a blank file with a gray background. You'll use this file to create buttons.

---

2 Choose **Insert > New Symbol** to create a new button symbol and to open the **Create New Symbol** dialog box. Type **btnRollo** in the **Name** field, and select **Button** for **Type**. Click **OK**.

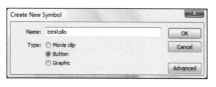

As soon as you click OK, you will enter the button's Timeline. Each button symbol has its own independent Timeline. Note the four frames of the button Timeline: Up, Over, Down, and Hit. Even though the button contains multiple button states, it will occupy only one frame on the main Timeline. Buttons do not automatically "play" as the main Timeline does or as animated graphic symbols do. Rather, the button's Timeline remains paused on the Up state keyframe, displaying only the content in this keyframe, until the movie is

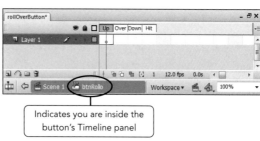

Indicates you are inside the button's Timeline panel

published and the user's cursor has a chance to come into contact with the button. The other keyframes in the button symbol (Over and Down) are shown only in reaction to the cursor position.

NOTE: | **Button Naming Conventions**

When developing Flash content, use symbol names that include an abbreviation indicating which type of symbol it is. For example, use **btnRollo** or **rollo_btn**. If you start the name with the symbol abbreviation, you can sort symbols alphabetically in the **Library** panel with the buttons grouped together, all the graphic symbols grouped together, and all the movie clip symbols grouped together.

---

3 Choose **View > Grid > Show Grid** to cover the **Stage** with a grid.

The grid is visible only in the Flash CS3 editing environment and will not be exported with your movie.

---

4 Select the **Line** tool in the **Tools** panel. Make sure the stroke color is set to **black** and **Object Drawing** is deselected. Draw a small triangle that spans about two grid boxes in height. The right point of the triangle should be on the center crosshair on the **Stage** (which is actually the **registration point** of the button), as shown in the illustration here.

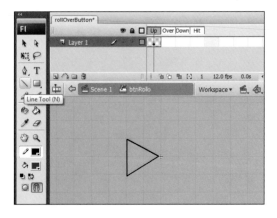

Placing the triangle on the center crosshair ensures the triangle is set to pivot on this point. If you choose to rotate, scale, transform, or position the triangle button, it will always pivot from the registration point, as you learned to do in Chapter 4.

The triangle you created in this step will serve as the Up state for the button, which is the default button image the user sees before interacting with it.

Tip: To make it easier to draw the triangle, change the view to 200% by using the View pop-up menu in the edit bar.

---

5 Select the **Paint Bucket** tool in the **Tools** panel. Set the fill color to the fourth color down in the first column of the **Fill Color** palette (value **#999999**). Click once the triangle once to fill the triangle with gray.

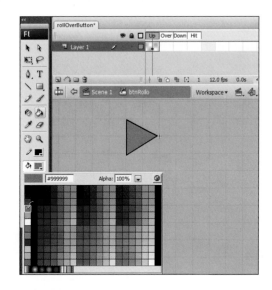

Why do you have to choose that specific gray? The next three exercises will build on one another, and it is important to use the right color in this first exercise so that by the time you get to Exercise 3, the colors will match the interface you will be using.

---

6 Select the **Selection** tool in the **Tools** panel, and move the cursor over the black stroke of the triangle. Double-click it to select all three line segments. (You can also **Shift-click** each line segment if double-clicking does not select all three segments.) Press **Delete** on the keyboard to delete the black stroke.

You now have a solid gray triangle without a stroke around it.

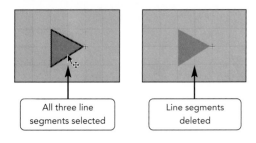

All three line segments selected

Line segments deleted

7 Select the **Over** frame and press **F6** to add a keyframe and copy the content—the triangle—from the last keyframe to the **Over** frame.

8 Select the **Paint Bucket** tool in the **Tools** panel, and choose **white** for the fill color. Click the triangle once to fill the triangle with white.

9 Press **F6** to add a keyframe to the **Down** state of the button. Set the fill color to the same color you used in Step 5: **#999999**. Click the triangle once to fill it with gray.

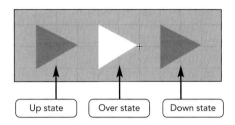

Up state   Over state   Down state

10 Scrub the playhead to see the different states of the button. The **Up** state triangle should be gray, the **Over** state triangle should be white, and the **Down** state triangle should be gray again.

To complete the button symbol, you need to define the Hit state of the button, which you'll do next.

11 Select the **Hit** frame and press **F6** to add a keyframe.

The Hit frame defines the hot area of the button, or the area that will react to the cursor interaction. In this case, this area will be the same shape as the button.

The Hit state is invisible to the user, so it does not matter what color the content in the Hit keyframe is. The Hit state defines the Stage area that will be used to activate the button rollover.

NOTE:

Hit Me!

The **Hit** state of the button has one objective: to define the area that is active when the cursor comes into contact with it. Because the **Hit** keyframe defines the area of the button that is reactive to the cursor, the **Hit** area must cover the entire active area of the button. If the button is tiny and the **Hit** area is small or smaller, users may have difficulty interacting with the button at all. If you leave the **Hit** keyframe blank, its content will default to the graphic content in the last filled keyframe. For tiny buttons or text-only buttons, add a solid shape to the **Hit** keyframe that is slightly larger than the button's **Up** or **Over** states.

12 In the **edit bar**, click **Scene 1** to return to the main **Timeline**.

Where's the Button?

When you choose create a new symbol, such as a button (as you did in Step 2), Flash CS3 automatically places the symbol in the **Library** panel, but it does not automatically place an instance on the **Stage**. If you want to use the new button in your movie, you must drag an instance to the **Stage**. However, to test the button, you actually have three options: You can test it using the **Library** panel, using the **Stage**, or using **Control > Test Movie**. You will try each option next.

13 Press **Ctrl+L** (Windows) or **Cmd+L** (Mac) to open the **Library** panel. Click the **btnRollo** symbol in the **Library** panel. In the preview window, click the **Play** button to preview the button in the **Library** panel.

The button will play one frame right after the next (Up, Over, Down, and Hit). This quick preview, however, may not be very realistic. The following steps show you how to preview the button on the Stage.

14 Choose **View > Grid > Show Grid** to hide the grid on the **Stage**. Drag an instance of the button you created to the **Stage**.

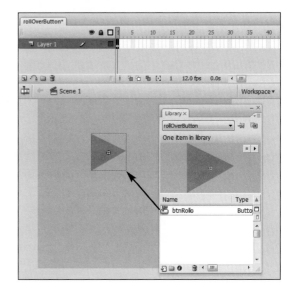

15 Choose **Control > Enable Simple Buttons**, which will let you test the button right on the **Stage**.

16 Move your cursor over the button to see the **Over** state. Click the button to see the **Down** state.

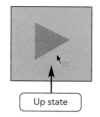 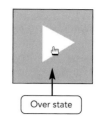 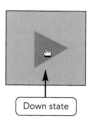

Up state   Over state   Down state

---

17 Choose **Control > Enable Simple Buttons** to deselect this option. The button will no longer be active on the **Stage**.

---

18 Choose **Control > Test Movie** to produce a SWF file (you'll learn more about this in Chapter 17, *"Publishing and Exporting"*), which lets you test buttons in yet another way.

This method of testing will yield the same visual results as choosing Enable Simple Buttons; it's just another way to accomplish the same thing.

---

19 Move the cursor over the button to trigger the **Over** state. When you are finished, close the SWF file to return to the editing environment.

---

20 Save **rollOverButton.fla**, and leave it open for the next exercise.

2 | Creating Rollover Buttons with Text

In the previous exercise, you learned how to create and test a button. This exercise shows you how to alter that button by altering its **Hit** state and adding text.

---

1 If you just completed Exercise 1, **rollOverButton.fla** should still be open. If it's not, complete Exercise 1, and then return to this exercise.

---

2 In the **Library** panel, double-click the symbol icon next to **btnRollo** to open the button's **Timeline**.

---

3 On the button symbol's **Timeline**, double-click **Layer 1**, and rename it **triangle**.

---

4 Click the **Insert Layer** button to add a new layer to the button's **Timeline**. Rename the layer **text**.

---

5 Select the **Text** tool in the **Tools** panel. In the **Property inspector**, choose **Static Text** as the **Text type**, **Verdana** in the **Font** pop-up menu, and **16** in the **Font Size** pop-up menu. Choose **white** in the **Text Color** box. Click the **Bold** button and the **Align Left** button.

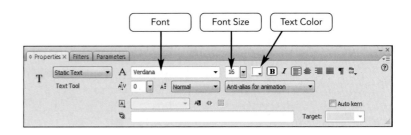

---

6 On the **Stage**, click to the right of the triangle, and type the word **BACKGROUND** in capital letters.

When you add the text, it automatically adds frames to the Timeline so the word *BACKGROUND* appears across each of the Up, Over, Down, and Hit states.

---

7 Select the **Selection** tool in the **Tools** panel. On the **Timeline**, select the **Over** state of the button on the **text** layer. Press **F6** to add a keyframe to the **Over** frame.

8 With the **Selection** tool, click the text block on the **Stage** in the **Over** frame. In the **Property inspector**, click the **Text Color** box, and choose a **dark gray** color, **#666666**, to change the text color for the text in the **Over** frame.

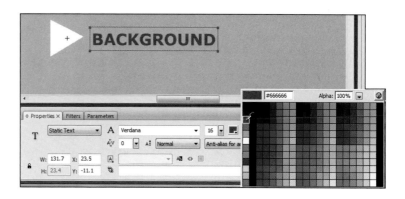

9 Choose **Control > Test Movie** to test the button.

NOTE:

Using Text in the Hit State

You may have noticed the button might not work depending on where you click. Because you used text in the **Hit** state, the button will not be active until the cursor passes directly over the actual text itself (not in between the characters), which can be confusing. The button will not work unless the user moves the cursor directly over a solid part of a letter. A hole in an O or even the space between letters can cause the button to flicker on and off, which is a good reason not to use text to define the **Hit** state of your buttons. You will learn how to use a solid shape to define the **Hit** state next.

Button activated

Button not activated

10 When you test a movie, it opens the results in a separate preview window. Close the preview window to return to the editing environment. Move the playhead to the **Hit** frame.

To trigger the button, the cursor must move over the area defined as the Hit state. In this case, the Hit frame is defined by the content inside it, which consists of the triangle and the text, BACKGROUND. The current Hit state causes the button to be triggered only when the cursor rolls exactly over the text or the arrow. This is not the correct way to create a Hit state, so you need to modify it.

11 On the button's **Timeline, Shift-click** both layers in the **Hit** frame to select both layers. **Right-click** (Windows) or **Ctrl-click** (Mac) the selected layers, and choose **Remove Frames** in the contextual menu to remove both keyframes in the **Hit** state.

You will be adding new content to define the Hit area in the next few steps.

12 Lock the **text** and **triangle** layers, and click the **Insert Layer** button to add a new layer to the button's **Timeline**. Position the new layer below the **triangle** layer, and rename it **hit**.

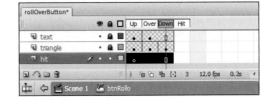

13 On the **hit** layer, click the **Hit** frame, and press **F7** to add a blank keyframe to the **Hit** button state.

14 Click the **Onion Skin** button. Make sure the onion skin markers span all four states of the button.

You will be creating the new Hit state next, and you need to be able to see the artwork in the other frames.

15 Select the **Rectangle** tool in the **Tools** panel. On the **Stage**, draw a rectangle covering both the triangle and the text.

When you create the Hit area this way, the cursor will need to move over the rectangle only in order for the button to be triggered.

16 Click the **Onion Skin** button to turn off onion skinning.

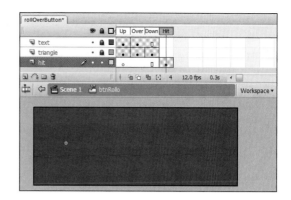

After you draw the rectangle, you end up with a solid shape that will define the new Hit area of the button. It doesn't matter what color the Hit state is or if it contains a stroke and a fill. Just make sure it covers the appropriate area.

17 In the **edit bar**, click **Scene 1** to leave the button symbol's **Timeline** and return to the main **Timeline**.

Notice the button instance you placed on the Stage in the previous exercise. Since you modified the actual symbol in this exercise, the button instance on the Stage will automatically be updated with the text and the new Hit state.

18 Choose **Control > Enable Simple Buttons** to test the button on the **Stage**. Move your cursor over the button to see the **Over** state. Click the button to preview the **Down** state.

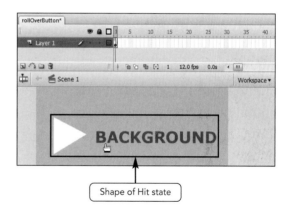

Shape of Hit state

Now that you've defined the Hit state as a solid shape covering the entire Up state of the button (the arrow and the text), it's much easier to interact with. As soon as the cursor reaches the edge of the invisible rectangle shape (the Hit state), the Over state is triggered and the image in the Over keyframe is displayed.

19 Choose **Control > Enable Simple Buttons** to deselect this option. The button will not be active on the **Stage** anymore.

20 Save your **rollOverButton.fla** as **textButton.fla** files by choosing **File > Save**. Close the file.

Understanding the Hit State

If there is no frame or keyframe in the specified **Hit** state, the **Hit** shape of the button is set by the currently displayed keyframe. Therefore, if the **Up** and **Over** keyframes contain different shapes, the Hit state will change when the user moves the cursor over the button. This is not an ideal way to create buttons.

If a frame is specified in the **Hit** state, it will use the contents of the last set keyframe.

Setting a blank keyframe in the **Hit** state will disable the rollover—a **Hit** state is required to trigger the **Over** and **Down** states. If the shape for the button is large enough for the **Hit** state, you don't have to create a keyframe or new artwork in that frame. In this exercise, however, the text was not an adequate shape or size for the user to trigger the rollover consistently. The best method is to test your rollovers first to ensure that the **Hit** state is an adequate shape for the job.

Remember, the **Hit** state should cover the entire area you want to designate as reactive to the cursor.

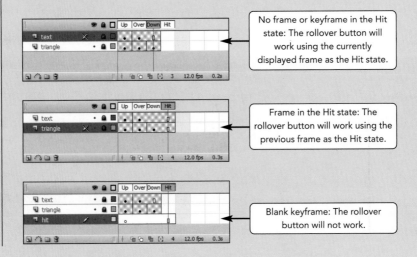

No frame or keyframe in the Hit state: The rollover button will work using the currently displayed frame as the Hit state.

Frame in the Hit state: The rollover button will work using the previous frame as the Hit state.

Blank keyframe: The rollover button will not work.

3 | Duplicating and Aligning Buttons

In the previous two exercises, you learned how to create buttons and preview the results, and you learned why the **Hit** state is important. Another handy skill is making duplicate copies of buttons. For example, you can quickly create a navigation bar for a Web site by copying buttons and changing the text in each copy. This exercise shows you how to duplicate buttons in the **Library** panel and how to align them on the **Stage**. You'll also learn how to use **Library** panel items from other movie projects. This exercise demonstrates a practical workflow for reusing and modifying an existing button design.

---

1 Open **duplicateAlign.fla** from the **chap_10** folder.

This file contains one layer with a background image.

---

2 Press **Ctrl+L** (Windows) or **Cmd+L** (Mac) to open the **Library** panel.

Notice there are three items in the Library panel: the interface graphic symbol and two bitmaps.

---

3 Choose **File > Import > Open External Library**, and select **textButton.fla** from the **chap_10** folder. This will open just the **Library** panel, including the button symbol you created in the exercise, of the **textButton.fla** file.

You will be using the button from the textButton.fla library in the following steps.

Notice there are now two Library panels open. One is the Library panel from the duplicateAlign movie you are currently working on; the other is the Library panel from the textButton movie.

The Open External Library technique comes in handy when you need to use assets from another project without having to open up the project file (FLA). This technique will save you time, keep your computer screen less cluttered, and help you avoid the headache of managing several open projects at the same time.

---

4 On the main **Timeline**, insert a new layer, and rename it **buttons**. Make sure the **buttons** layer is positioned above the **background** layer.

---

5 In the **textButton Library** panel, drag an instance of the **btnRollo** symbol to the **Stage**, and place it over the gray box on the left side of the **Stage**.

Notice after you place the instance on the Stage, the btnRollo symbol is included in both libraries. You added the symbol from the textButton movie to the duplicateAlign movie, and Flash CS3 automatically adds the symbol to the Library panel for you.

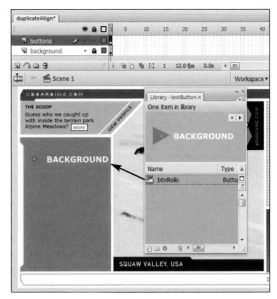

6 In the **duplicateAlign Library**, right-click (Windows) or **Ctrl-click** (Mac) the **btnRollo** symbol, and choose **Duplicate** in the contextual menu to make a copy of the button symbol and to open the **Duplicate Symbol** dialog box.

7 In the **Duplicate Symbol** dialog box, type **btnSafety** in the **Name** field, and make sure **Button** is selected for **Type**. Click OK.

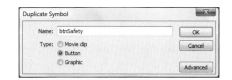

You have just made an exact duplicate of the button you created in Exercise 2. Notice the new btnSafety symbol immediately appears in the duplicateAlign Library panel.

---

8 In the **Library** panel, double-click the **btnSafety** button icon to open its **Timeline**. Lock the **hit** layer so you don't accidentally edit anything on that layer and then unlock the **text** layer.

Notice the Timeline looks identical to the original button you created. You'll be changing the text of this button next.

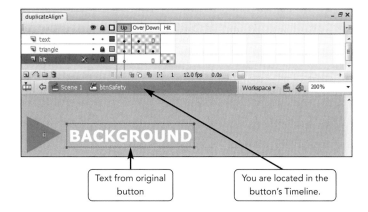

Text from original button

You are located in the button's Timeline.

---

9 On the **text** layer, click **Frame 1** (the **Up** state of the button). Choose the **Selection** tool in the **Tools** panel, and double-click the text block on the **Stage** to highlight the text. Type the word **SAFETY** to replace the existing text.

---

10 On the **text** layer, click **Frame 2** (the **Over** state of the button). Double-click the text block on the **Stage**, and type the word **SAFETY** in capital letters.

---

11 In the **edit bar**, click **Scene 1** to return to the main **Timeline**.

---

12 Drag an instance of the new button, **btnSafety**, from the **Library** panel to the **Stage**, just below the **background** button. Choose **Control > Enable Simple Buttons** to test the button. When you are finished testing, choose **Control > Enable Simple Buttons**.

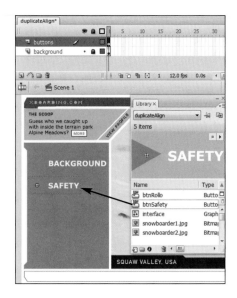

13 Repeat Steps 6 through 10 to create three more duplicate buttons. Name them **btnLearning**, **btnGear**, and **btnWhatsNew**, respectively. In each button, type the text **LEARNING, GEAR**, and **WHAT'S NEW**.

14 In the **edit bar**, click **Scene 1** to return to the main **Timeline**.

15 Drag the right corner of the **duplicateAlign Library** panel down diagonally to resize the entire panel so you can see all the buttons you created. If your **textButton Library** is still open, close this **Library** first by clicking the **Close** button.

16 Drag the **btnLearning, btnGear**, and **btnWhatsNew** buttons to the **Stage** below the other two buttons.

17 Press **Ctrl+A** (Windows) or **Cmd+A** (Mac) to select all five buttons on the **Stage**. Choose **Window > Align** to open the **Align** panel. Make sure the **To Stage** button is deselected. Click the **Align left edge** and **Distribute vertical center** buttons to align all the buttons on the **Stage** to the left and to space them apart equally.

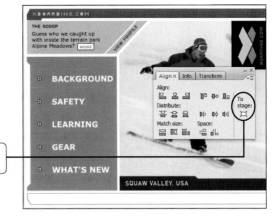

To Stage: button not pressed

---

18 Make sure the buttons are still selected. Using the **arrow** keys on the keyboard, nudge the buttons to the left or right so that the left side of each button is parallel with the white border. To aid in this placement, choose **Control > Enable Simple Buttons** and move your cursor over the buttons. The white triangle in the button **Over** state should line up with the white interface border. When you are finished, choose **Control > Enable Buttons** to turn off this feature.

---

19 Choose **Control > Test Movie** to test the rollover buttons.

You streamlined the creation of this navigation system by creating the artwork for only one button, duplicating it four times, and changing only the text in each button.

---

20 Close the preview window. Save **duplicateAlign.fla**, and leave it open for the next exercise.

NOTE:

Duplicate vs. Instance

In the previous exercise, you could not have just dragged the button from the **Library** panel to the **Stage** and then changed the text because the text is embedded in the symbol. To change the text, you would have to go into the symbol **Timeline** to modify it. You can change the shape, size, rotation, skew, and color of any instance but cannot change actual artwork or text without changing the original symbol, which would change all the instances on the **Stage**. To get around this problem, you duplicated the symbol first and then changed the text before placing an instance of the duplicate on the **Stage**.

4 | Adding Sound to Buttons

Each button state can hold a different sound to give feedback to the user. This exercise shows you how to add a simple sound to a button.

---

1 If you just completed Exercise 3, **duplicateAlign.fla** should still be open. If it's not, complete Exercise 3, and then return to this exercise.

---

2 Choose **File > Import > Open External Library**, and select the **buttonSounds.fla** file from the **chap_10** folder.

This command opens only the Library panel of the buttonSounds.fla file. In this exercise, you will be using the sound files in this Library panel.

---

3 In the **duplicateAlign Library**, double-click the **btnGear** button icon to open its **Timeline**. Click the **Insert Layer** button to add a new layer. Rename the layer **sound**, and make sure it is the topmost layer.

---

4 Select the **Selection** tool in the **Tools** panel. On the **sound** layer, click the **Over** frame, and press **F7** to add a blank keyframe.

You will be adding a sound to this frame next.

---

5 In the **buttonSounds Library** panel, select any of the sound files, and click the **Play** button in the **Library** preview window to preview the sound.

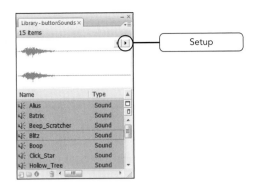

Setup

6 With the **Over** frame selected in the **sound** layer, drag an instance of the **Intruder_Alert** sound from the **buttonSounds Library** panel to anywhere on the **Stage**.

That's all there is to it! You have just added a sound to the button.

Note: You will not see a visual representation of the sound on the Stage. Instead, you will see a waveform in the Over frame of the Timeline. It's OK if the sound extends into the Hit frame on the button's Timeline. Having a sound in the Hit frame will have no effect on the button because the Hit state is determined by artwork on the Stage, not sound on the Timeline.

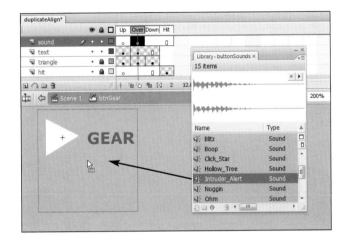

7 In the **edit bar**, click **Scene 1** to return to the main **Timeline**.

Since you modified the button in the Library, the btnGear instance on the Stage will be updated. You will test this next.

8 Choose **Control > Enable Simple Buttons** to test the button on the **Stage**. When you are finished testing it, choose **Control > Enable Simple Buttons**.

You should hear the sound play when you move the cursor over the btnGear button, because you added the sound to the Over state of that button. You will add a sound to the Down state of the What's New button next.

Tip: This is a brief introduction to working with sound. You'll learn more about Flash's sound capabilities, including which sound formats Flash CS3 supports, in Chapter 14, *"Sound."*

9 In the **duplicateAlign Library** panel, double-click the **btnWhatsNew** icon to open its **Timeline**.

10 Lock the **text** layer. Click the **Insert Layer** button to add a new layer. Rename this layer **sound**, and make sure it's the topmost layer.

11 With the **Selection** tool selected in the **Tools** panel, click the **Down** frame in the **sound** layer, and press **F7** to add a blank keyframe.

12 With the **Down** frame selected in the **sound** layer, drag an instance of the **Blitz** sound from the **buttonSounds Library** panel to the **Stage**.

Notice the sound wave appears in the Down and Hit frames of the Timeline.

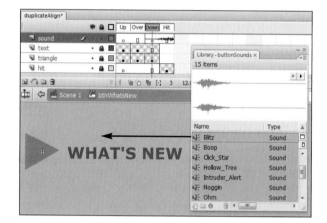

13 Choose **Control > Test Movie** to test your buttons.

Notice the sound in the Gear button plays when the cursor move over the button and the sound in the What's New button plays when you click the button (because you placed the sound in the Down state instead of the Over state).

Tip: You can also choose Control > Enable Simple Buttons in the editing environment to hear the button sounds on the Stage.

Notice the sounds you added to the Gear and What's New buttons are now in the duplicateAlign Library panel.

14 Repeat Steps 9 through 12 to add sounds of your choice to the remaining buttons: **btnSafety**, **btnLearning**, and **btnRollo** (the **Background** button).

15 Close **duplicateAlign.fla**. You don't need to save your changes.

5 | Creating Invisible Buttons

You learned about the importance of the **Hit** state for rollover buttons in previous exercises. You can also use the **Hit** state to create invisible buttons. This kind of button comes as an unexpected surprise to users, because there's no visible display of the button object until the user moves the cursor over an invisible region. In this exercise, you will learn how to change regular buttons into invisible buttons.

1 Open **invisButton_Final.fla** in the **chap_10** folder.

This is the finished version of the movie you are going to create in this exercise.

2 Choose **Control > Test Movie** to preview this movie. Move your cursor over the buildings, or lodges, in the picture.

Notice how the descriptions pop up from the image. You will be creating this same effect next.

3 When you are finished looking at this movie, close the preview window and the file.

4 Open **invisible.fla** in the **chap_10** folder. I've already created the buttons in this file so you can jump right into making the buttons invisible.

Notice the file contains two layers—one with a background image on it and the other with three buttons on it.

5 Choose **Control >Test Movie** to preview the buttons. Move your cursor over the buttons, and notice they are not invisible.

They behave just like normal rollover buttons, with the text changing color when you move your cursor over them. You will turn them into invisible buttons to create a surprise rollover effect next.

6 Close the preview window. Back in the project file, open the **Library** panel. Double-click the **alpine** button's icon to open its **Timeline**. Notice the button has three layers. Scrub the **playhead** to preview the **Up**, **Over**, **Down**, and **Hit** states of the button.

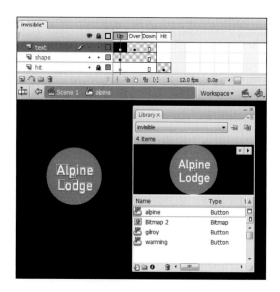

7 Click a blank area of the **Stage** to make sure you have nothing selected. In one motion, click and drag to select the first two frames in the **text** and **shape** layers. Drag the four selected frames one frame to the right, and release the mouse.

Why did you move the frames out of the Up state? When you create an invisible button, the Up state must be empty so users won't know that a button even exists until the cursor moves over the area defined in the Hit frame. You will test the button next.

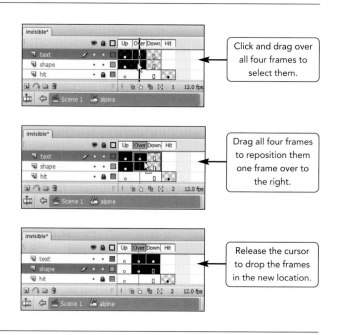

Click and drag over all four frames to select them.

Drag all four frames to reposition them one frame over to the right.

Release the cursor to drop the frames in the new location.

8 In the **edit bar**, click **Scene 1** to return to the main Timeline.

Notice the alpine button already looks different. Because you modified the button in the Library, any instances on the Stage will be automatically updated. Now that the button has no Up state, Flash CS3 displays the shape of the Hit frame in a transparent blue color, providing a visual hint to the button's location.

Why not just use a shape with a transparent fill for the Up state when you create a button? That would certainly work as an invisible button, but you would have a difficult time seeing the instances of the button while you work on the project file. When you create an invisible button, Flash senses this and turns the Hit state a translucent blue, and then you don't have to guess the button's location.

Alpine button

Up state = Invisible

Over state = White text

Down state = Black text

9 Choose **Control > Test Movie** to test the invisible button you just created.

Notice the three different states of the button. Since you moved the frames to the right by one frame in Step 7, the old Up state of the button (white text, graphic background) is now the Over state, and the old Over state (black text, graphic background) is now the Down state. Test the gilroy button and the warming button to see the difference between the invisible button and the regular buttons.

10 Repeat Step 7 for the other two buttons in the **Library**: the **gilroy** and **warming** buttons.

---

11 Choose **Control > Test Movie** to test all three buttons. Neat!

---

12 When you are finished, close the preview window, and close **invisible.fla**. You do not need to save the changes.

VIDEO: **buttonFilters.mov**

You can transform even plain and simple buttons with the application of one or more of the new filter effects in Flash CS3. You can use the **Drop Shadow**, **Blur**, **Glow**, and **Bevel** filters individually or in various combinations to produce interesting and attractive Flash buttons. Here are some examples:

The first **Home** button here uses the **Bevel** and **Drop Shadow** filters to make the button look more three-dimensional. The second button uses a drop shadow applied to the inside of the text label to give it quite a different three-dimensional look.

To learn more about applying filter effects to buttons, check out **buttonFilters.mov** in the **videos** folder on the **Flash HOT CD-ROM**.

That's it! This chapter gave you a solid foundation for working with and understanding Flash button symbols. You learned about the different button states and the different kinds of buttons you can create in Flash, how to add sound to your buttons, and even how to duplicate and align buttons to quickly create menus. The next chapter will introduce you to movie clips—another important topic in your Flash education.

11

Movie Clips

Understanding movie clip symbols is key to producing interactive Adobe Flash CS3 Professional movies. This understanding is the last step in building a foundation that will prepare you for Chapter 12, *"ActionScript Basics."* As you will see, ActionScripting often requires a movie clip symbol, so don't underestimate the importance of the information contained in this chapter.

Up to this point in the book, you've learned how to create both graphic and button symbols. At last, you will be introduced to movie clip symbols and gain a solid understanding of how to create and use them effectively.

What Is a Movie Clip?

Movie clips are the most versatile, powerful, and useful symbols in Flash CS3. However, they are also the most difficult to understand and use. Before you get started with the hands-on exercises, take some time to learn some of the key terms and concepts:

Movie Clip Vocabulary	
Term	**Definition**
Main Timeline	The main **Timeline**, introduced in Chapter 6, *"Creating Symbols and Instances,"* is the **Timeline** of the scene (or scenes) in your project file. If you have more than one scene, Flash CS3 will consider them part of the same main **Timeline** and will add together the number of frames in each scene to make up one main **Timeline**. For example, if **Scene 1** contains 35 frames and **Scene 2** contains 20 frames, Flash will consider the main **Timeline** to span 55 frames. You will learn more about managing and naming scenes in Chapter 12, *"ActionScript Basics."* Graphic symbols are also closely related to the main **Timeline**. For example, if your graphic symbol contains 10 frames of animation, the main **Timeline** must also contain 10 frames for the graphic symbol to play.
Movie clips	Movie clip symbols can contain multiple layers, graphic symbols, button symbols, and even other movie clip symbols, as well as animations, sounds, and ActionScript. Movie clips operate independently of the main **Timeline**. They can continue to play even if the main **Timeline** has stopped, and they require only a single keyframe on the main **Timeline** to play, regardless of how long the movie clip's **Timeline** is. This is an important concept when you start to work with ActionScript.
Timeline independent	Unlike graphic symbols, button and movie clip symbols do not have a direct relationship to the main **Timeline**. They are "timeline independent" since they can function (play animation, sounds, and so on) regardless of how many frames the main **Timeline** contains. For example, if you have a movie clip that contains a 10-frame animation of a chairlift moving up a hill and you place this on the **Stage** on the main **Timeline**, the chairlift will continue to move up the hill even if the **Timeline** contains only a single frame. This ability to have different animations and actions occur independently of the main **Timeline** is what makes movie clips so useful and powerful.

Although movie clips are extremely powerful and flexible, you can't preview them by pressing **Enter** (Windows) or **Return** (Mac), as you can with button and graphic symbol instances. Preview movie clips in the **Library** panel (out of context of the main movie) by choosing **Control > Test Movie** or by publishing the final movie. (You'll learn about this in Chapter 17, *"Publishing and Exporting."*)

1 | Creating a Movie Clip

This exercise starts you off by showing how to make a movie clip.

---

1 Copy the **chap_11** folder from the **Flash HOT CD-ROM** to your desktop. Open **movieClip_Final.fla** from the **chap_11** folder.

Notice there is only one keyframe on the main Timeline.

---

2 Choose **Control > Test Movie** to preview the movie clip. When you are finished previewing this movie, close the preview window and the file.

The fill of the movie clip fades in and out repeatedly. This is the xboarding logo you are going to animate and convert to a movie clip in the following steps.

---

3 Open **movieClip.fla** from the **chap_11** folder.

I've created this file to help you get started. It has two layers: one named *outline*, which contains the outline of the X, and the other named *text*, which contains the *boarding.com* letters. You are going to create a simple motion tween next.

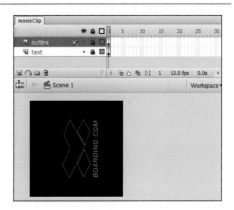

---

4 Click the **Insert Layer** button to add a new layer on the **Timeline**. Double-click the layer. When the bounding box appears, type **fillTween**, and press **Enter** (Windows) or **Return** (Mac) to rename the layer.

---

5 Press **Ctrl+L** (Windows) or **Cmd+L** (Mac) to open the **Library** panel. Drag an instance of the **gfxFill** graphic symbol to the **Stage** on the **fillTween** layer. Using the arrow keys on the keyboard, position the **gfxFill** instance so it covers the X outline exactly.

In the next few steps, you will be creating an animation of this outline and filling in with color, so make sure the gfxFill symbol is positioned directly on top of the outline artwork on the Stage.

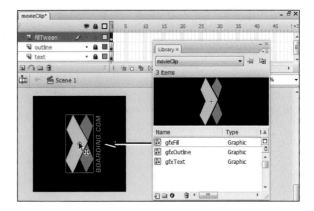

Tip: You may want to change the magnification in the edit bar to 200% so you can better see the placement of your artwork.

6 On the **fillTween** layer, add keyframes to **Frame 20** and **Frame 40** by selecting each frame and choosing **Insert > Timeline > Keyframe**.

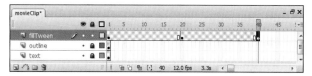

In the following steps, you will be creating a motion tween in which the gfxFill instance starts off invisible in Frame 1, becomes completely visible in Frame 20, and fades to invisible again in Frame 40.

7 Move the playhead to **Frame 40**, and select the instance on the **Stage**. In the **Property inspector**, choose **Alpha** in the **Color** pop-up menu, and change the percentage to **0**.

8 Move the playhead to **Frame 1**, and select the instance on the **Stage**. In the **Property inspector**, choose **Alpha** in the **Color** pop-up menu, and change the percentage to **0**.

9 Click the **fillTween** layer to select all the frames on the layer. In the **Property inspector**, choose **Motion** in the **Tween** pop-up menu to add a motion tween across all the frames.

10 On the **outline** layer, click **Frame 40**, and **Shift-click Frame 40** on the **text** layer to select **Frame 40** in both layers. Press **F5** to add frames up to **Frame 40**.

The artwork on the outline and text layers will now be visible throughout the motion tween on the fillTween layer.

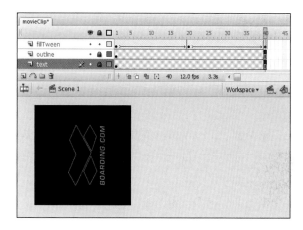

11 Move the playhead to **Frame 1** and press **Enter** (Windows) or **Return** (Mac) to test the animation.

The *X* outline fills in with color, and then the fill fades away.

Next you will create a movie clip using this animation.

---

12 Click the **text** layer to select all the frames on that layer. **Shift-click** the **outline** and **fillTween** layers to select all the frames on both of those layers as well. Choose **Edit > Timeline > Cut Frames** to cut the selected frames from the main **Timeline**.

Note: Make sure you choose Cut Frames and not Cut. Cut Frames lets you cut multiple frames on multiple layers, but a simple Cut command doesn't.

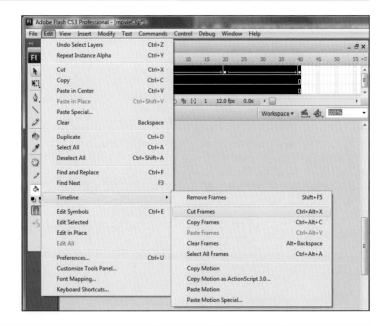

---

13 Choose **Insert > New Symbol**, and type **mcOutlineFill** in the **Name** field. Make sure **Movie clip** is selected for **Type**. Click **OK** to create a movie clip symbol, and open the movie clip symbol's **Timeline**.

---

14 Select the first keyframe, and choose **Edit > Timeline > Paste Frames**, which will paste all the frames and all the layers right in the movie clip, maintaining the layers and layer names just as they were on the main **Timeline**.

You just created your first movie clip! You will be able to test it in the next steps.

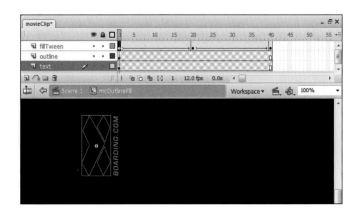

---

15 In the **edit bar**, click the **Scene 1** button to return to the main **Timeline**.

On the main Timeline, the three layers you originally had are still there, although they have no content on them because you cut the frames and pasted them into the movie clip symbol.

---

16 You no longer need the **text** or **outline** layer, so select each one, and click the **Delete Layer** button to delete them.

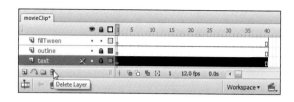

You may be thinking, "What's with all this cutting, pasting, and copying? Wouldn't it be easier to just create the content in the movie clip in the first place?" Although it would be easier, it may not always be the workflow you actually use. Often, you create artwork on the main Timeline first and later decide to turn it into a movie clip. Because creating artwork in a movie clip is the easier of the two workflows, practice the harder method, which is to copy and paste artwork from the main Timeline into a movie clip symbol's Timeline.

---

17 Double-click the **fillTween** layer name, and rename it **movieClip**. On the **Timeline**, click **Frame 42**, and drag backward to **Frame 2** to select **Frame 2** through **Frame 40**.

Because there are no frames on Frame 41 or Frame 42, only the frames up to Frame 40 will be selected. However, this method of "overselecting" ensures you don't miss any.

---

18 **Right-click** (Windows) or **Ctrl-click** (Mac) the selected frames. Choose **Remove Frames** in the contextual menu to remove all the selected frames.

Note: The Cut Frames command cuts the content of the layers and frames, but the Timeline still contains the frames. The only way to remove the frames is to use the Remove Frames command.

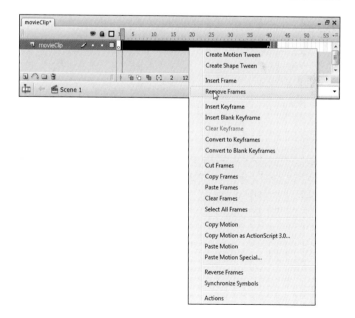

19 Press **Ctrl+L** (Windows) or **Cmd+L** (Mac) to open the **Library** panel, and drag an instance of the **mcOutlineFill** movie clip symbol to the **Stage**.

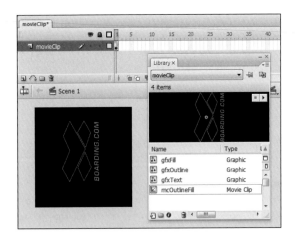

20 Choose **Control > Test Movie** to preview the movie clip you just made.

Note the movie clip plays even though there is only one frame in the main Timeline—the movie clip's Timeline is truly independent from the main Timeline.

21 Close the preview window. Save your changes, and leave **movieClip.fla** open for the next exercise.

TIP:

Modifying Movie Clip Instances

Not only do movie clips have a **Timeline** that is independent from the main movie, but, as you've learned in previous chapters, you can apply **Timeline** effects, filters, and blend modes to movie clip instances as well. Create the movie clip just once, and then change the attributes (such as scale, alpha, skew, and rotation) of each instance on the **Stage** to achieve different visual effects. By adding transformations, filters, or blends to the instances on the **Stage**, you can change the appearance of the movie clip with just a few clicks. The original movie clip, however, will remain unchanged in the **Library** panel.

Using Animated Graphic Symbols vs. Using Movie Clip Symbols

In this exercise, you'll learn the differences between animated graphic symbols and movie clip symbols. As you'll see, the animated graphic symbol requires multiple frames on the main **Timeline** whereas a movie clip does not. You'll learn firsthand why there's so much emphasis placed on the **Timeline** independence of movie clips.

1 If you just completed Exercise 1, **movieClip.fla** should still be open. If it's not, complete Exercise 1, and then return to this exercise. Choose **File > Save As** to save another version of this file. Name the new file **mcVsGfx.fla**, and save it in the **chap_11** folder.

2 Click the **Stage**. In the **Property inspector**, click the **Size** button to open the **Document Properties** dialog box. Type **400 px** in the **Dimensions** field for the width, and click **OK** to change the width of the **Stage** to 400 pixels, which will give you a little more room to work.

The best way to learn the difference between an animated graphic symbol and a movie clip symbol is to have one of each symbol type in your project file. You created a movie clip symbol in the previous exercise, so in the following steps, you will duplicate this symbol and convert the copy to an animated graphic symbol.

3 Press **Ctrl+L** (Windows) or **Cmd+L** (Mac) to open the **Library** panel if it isn't already open. **Right-click** (Windows) or **Ctrl-click** (Mac) the **mcOutlineFill** movie clip symbol in the **Library** panel. Choose **Duplicate** in the contextual menu to make a copy of the symbol and to open the **Duplicate Symbol** dialog box.

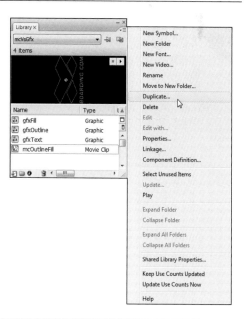

4 Type **gfxOutlineFill** in the **Name** field, and select **Graphic** for **Type**. Click **OK** to make an exact copy of the movie clip symbol.

Setting the Type option to Graphic changes the way the new symbol functions. Because it contains animation (the fill tween), this kind of symbol is referred to as an *animated* graphic symbol.

---

5 In the **Library** panel, select the **gfxOutlineFill** symbol, and click the **Play** button in the preview window to test the graphic symbol. In the **Library** panel, select the **mcOutlineFill** symbol, and click the **Play** button to test this movie clip symbol.

Both animations appear to be the same.

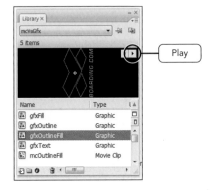

---

6 On the main **Timeline**, add a new layer by clicking the **Insert Layer** button. Rename the new layer **animGfx**.

This layer will hold the animated graphic symbol.

---

7 Drag an instance of the **gfxOutlineFill** symbol to the **Stage**, and position it to the right of the **mcOutlineFill** movie clip symbol to add the animated graphic symbol to the main **Timeline**.

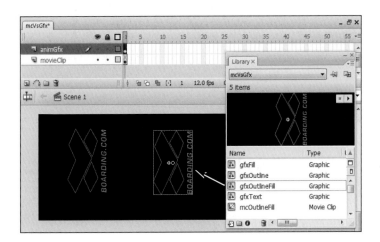

---

8 Select the **Text** tool in the **Tools** panel. In the **Property inspector**, make sure the **Text type** is **Static**, the stroke color is set to **white** and the font is **Arial** and the font size is set to **16**. Below the **gfxOutlineFill** instance, click the **Stage**, and type the text label **Animated Graphic Symbol**. Click the **Stage**, and type the text label **Movie Clip Symbol** below the **mcOutlineFill** instance.

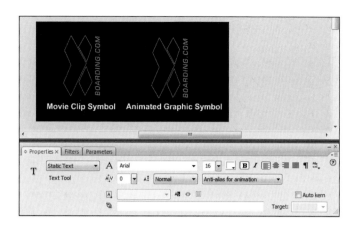

As you test the movie in the following steps, the text labels will help you remember which instance is which.

---

9 Select the **Selection** tool, and press **Enter** (Windows) or **Return** (Mac) to preview the movie.

Nothing happens, because pressing Enter (Windows) or Return (Mac) moves the playhead across all the frames on the main Timeline of the movie. But in this movie, you have only one frame, so the playhead has nowhere to go. Therefore, you will see both symbols in their static states only.

---

10 Choose **Control > Test Movie** to test the movie.

Notice the movie clip symbol plays and the animated graphic symbol does not. Why?

The main difference between an animated graphic symbol and a movie clip symbol is that the movie clip's Timeline is completely independent of the main movie's Timeline. A movie clip's Timeline can play regardless of how many frames the main Timeline contains. On the other hand, the Timeline of an animated graphic symbol is tied to the main Timeline.

In actuality, the graphic symbol Timeline plays in sync with the main Timeline. Therefore, at least the same number of frames on the graphic symbol's Timeline must exist on the main Timeline in order for the graphic symbol to play to the end of its animation.

---

11 Close the preview window, and return to the project file. Back on the main **Timeline**, **Shift-click Frame 40** on both layers, and press **F5** to add frames up to **Frame 40**.

Why 40 frames? This is the same number of frames that exist in both the graphic symbol's Timeline and the movie clip's Timeline.

12 Press **Enter** (Windows) or **Return** (Mac) to test the movie.

This time, the animated graphic symbol plays, but the movie clip does not. Now you have enough frames on the main Timeline so that the animated graphic symbol can play. However, as you learned in Exercise 1, you cannot preview movie clips on the Stage. You must view them either by using the Library panel or by choosing Control > Test Movie. This is one of the "rules" of movie clips. They don't preview in the editing environment.

13 Choose **Control > Test Movie**.

Now, both symbols animate. To summarize, the animated graphic symbol will play if there are enough frames on the main Timeline, but the movie clip will play in the preview window regardless of how many frames are on the Timeline.

NOTE:

Why Is Timeline Independence Important?

The **Timeline** independence of movie clips is extremely important when programming interactive presentations. You can use ActionScript, which you'll learn about in the next chapter, with movie clips because they have the capacity to be "named" and referenced in scripts, whereas graphic symbols do not.

14 Close the preview window. Save your changes, and leave **mcVsGfx.fla** open for the next exercise.

3 | Creating an Animated Rollover Button

This exercise demonstrates how to turn a normal rollover button into an animated rollover button by nesting a movie clip in the **Over** state of a button symbol. If you've been wondering why **Timeline** independence is important, this example will drive the point home.

1 If you just completed Exercise 2, **mcVsGfx.fla** should still be open. If it's not, complete Exercise 2, and then return to this exercise. Choose **File > Save As**, and save a copy of the file as **animRolloBtn.fla** in the **chap_11** folder.

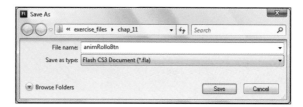

2 Click anywhere on the **Stage** with the **Selection** tool. In the **Property inspector**, click the **Size** button to open the **Document Properties** dialog box. Type **600 px** in the **Dimensions** field for the width, and click **OK** to change the width of the **Stage** to 600 pixels, which will give you more room to work with in this exercise.

After changing the document dimensions, your Stage should match the illustration shown here.

3 In the **Library** panel, click the **New Symbol** button to open the **Create New Symbol** dialog box.

You will be creating an animated button symbol in the following steps.

4 In the **Create New Symbol** dialog box, type **btnAnim** in the **Name** field, and select **Button** for **Type**. Click **OK**.

You are now in the editing environment for the button symbol's Timeline.

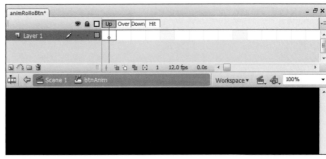

5 Drag an instance of the **gfxOutline** symbol to the **Stage**.

This symbol is static and contains only the outline of the X.

6 With the **gfxOutline** instance still selected on the **Stage**, choose **Window > Align** to open the **Align** panel. Click the **To stage** button, and then click the **Align vertical center** and **Align horizontal center** buttons to perfectly align the instance in the center of the **Stage**.

7 In the **Library** panel, drag an instance of the **gxfText** symbol to the **Stage**, just to the right of the X outline. This symbol is static and contains **boarding.com** on only one frame.

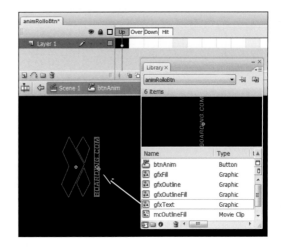

8 The **Align** panel should still be open. If it is not, press **Ctrl+K** (Windows) or **Cmd+K** (Mac). Make sure the **To Stage** button is selected, and click **Align vertical center** in the **Align** panel. You have now created the **Up** state of the button.

---

9 In the **Down** frame, press **F5** to add frames in both the **Over** and **Down** states of the button. You will be adding a movie clip symbol to the button in the following steps.

---

10 Click the **Insert Layer** button to add a new layer. Rename it **movieClip**. Change the name of **Layer 1** to **outline**.

---

11 In the **Library** panel, **right-click** (Windows) or **Ctrl-click** (Mac) the **mcOutlineFill** movie clip symbol. Choose **Duplicate** in the contextual menu to make a copy of the symbol and to open the **Duplicate Symbol** dialog box.

---

12 Type **mcOverAnim** in the **Name** field, and select **Movie clip** for **Type**. Click **OK** to make an exact copy of the symbol.

This movie clip will be used for the Over state of the button, but first you have to make a few modifications, which you'll do next.

---

13 In the **Library** panel, double-click the **mcOverAnim** movie clip icon, which will take you into the movie clip's **Timeline**.

Notice that it looks exactly like the Timeline for the mcOutlineFill movie clip symbol you created in Exercise 1. You will modify this movie clip next.

Double-click here to view the movie clip's Timeline.

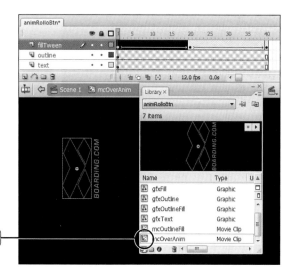

14 Select the **text** layer, and click the **Delete Layer** button to delete the **text** layer. Repeat this step to delete the **outline** layer.

The Timeline for the mcOverAnim movie clip should now have only one layer with the fill tween on it.

You deleted these extra layers because you need only the X artwork for the animated Over state you are creating for the button.

---

15 Scrub the playhead to see the motion tween animation. This movie clip will serve as the **Over** state of the button (once you add it to the button's **Timeline**).

Tip: You can also preview the motion tween inside the movie clip by pressing Enter (Windows) or Return (Mac) or by selecting mcOverAnim in the Library panel and clicking the Play button in the Library panel's preview window.

---

16 In the **Library** panel, double-click the **btnAnim** icon to open the button symbol's **Timeline**. On the **movieClip** layer, select the **Over** and **Down** frames, and choose **Insert > Timeline > Blank Keyframe** to add blank keyframes to both the **Over** and **Down** states of the button.

---

17 In the **movieClip** layer, select the **Over** frame, and drag an instance of the **mcOverAnim** movie clip onto the **Stage**. Use the **Align** panel to center the movie clip in the middle of the **Stage**, over the **gfxOutline** graphic, just as you did in Step 6.

You have just added the movie clip to the Over state of the button. You will add the Hit state to the button next to complete the exercise.

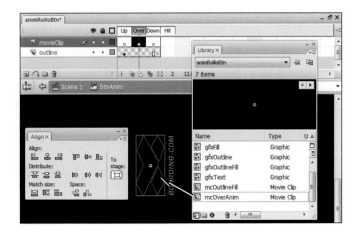

---

18 Click the **Insert Layer** button to add a new layer to the button symbol's **Timeline**. Rename the new layer **hit**, and place it at the bottom of the **Timeline**.

---

19 In the **Hit** frame of the **hit** layer, choose **Insert >
Timeline > Keyframe** to add a blank keyframe. In
the **Tools** panel, select the **Rectangle** tool, and
draw a rectangle that covers the *X* outline and the
boarding.com text. You may want to unlock the
outline layer and click the **Onion Skin Outlines**
button to turn on onion skinning outlines to make
sure the rectangle covers the *X* outline and the
boarding.com text. Turn the onion skin outlines
off when you are done positioning these elements.

The rectangle will serve as the Hit state of the
button, so when the user's cursor touches any part
of the rectangle, the Over state will be triggered.

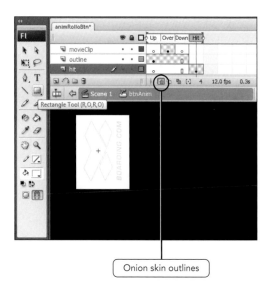

Onion skin outlines

---

20 You are finished with the button. Click **Scene 1** to return to the main **Timeline**.

---

21 On the main **Timeline**, lock both
the **animGfx** and **movieClip** layers.
Click the **Insert Layer** button to add
a new layer, and rename the layer
animBtn. Move **animBtn** to the top
of the layer stack. You will be placing
the button you just created on this
layer next.

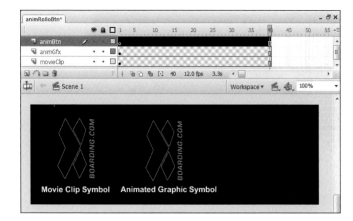

22 Select the **Selection** tool in the **Tools** panel, and drag an instance of the **btnAnim** button symbol to the **Stage**, to the right of the animated graphic symbol. In the **Tools** panel, select the **Text** tool. Below the **btnAnim** instance, click the **Stage**, and type the text label **Animated Button Symbol**.

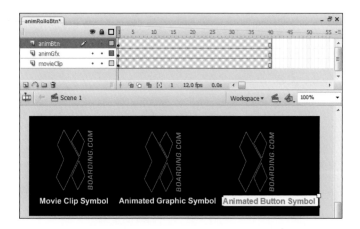

23 Choose **Control > Test Movie** to preview and test all the symbols.

The movie clip and animated graphic symbol continue to animate, while the button symbol animates only when you move the cursor over it.

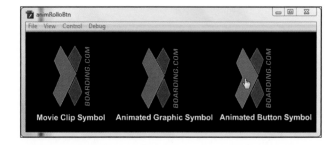

24 Close the preview window. Save your changes, and leave **animRolloBtn.fla** open for the next exercise.

Putting an Animated Rollover Button into Action

In the previous exercise, you learned how to use a movie clip in a button's **Over** state to create an animated rollover button. In this exercise, you'll learn how to use that same button in a different project file and place it in a Web page interface.

1 If you just completed Exercise 3, **animRolloBtn.fla** should still be open. If it's not, complete Exercise 3, and then return to this exercise. Press **Ctrl+L** (Windows) or **Cmd+L** (Mac) to open the **Library** panel if it is not already open.

Notice the Library Selection pop-up menu at the top of the panel reads animRolloBtn.fla. Next, you will be taking the animated button symbol you made in the previous exercise and using it in another file.

2 Open the **animBtnLive.fla** from the **chap_11** folder.

This file is similar to one you worked on in the previous chapter, but in this file, the logo is missing from the interface. You will add the logo in a few steps. Notice the Library Selection pop-up menu has changed to animBtnLive.fla. By default, the Library panel displays the currently active project file.

Logo is missing

3 Choose **animRolloBtn** in the **Library Selection** pop-up menu. Click the **New library panel** button to open an additional **Library** panel. Choose **animBtnLive** in the **Library Selection** pop-up menu in the new panel.

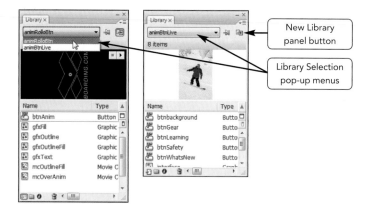

Now, libraries from both open project files are visible at the same time, and you will be able to share assets from one project to the other. In addition to the File > Import > Open External Library workflow you learned in Chapter 10, *"Buttons,"* this is another way you can use assets such as symbols from one project in another project. You will add the movie clip symbol from the animRolloBtn movie to the animBtnLive movie next.

---

4 On the main **Timeline** of **animBtnLive.fla**, insert a new layer, and rename it **logo**. Move the **logo** layer to the top of the layer stack.

---

5 In the **animRolloBtn Library**, drag an instance of **btnAnim** to the **Stage**, and place it over the black box, as shown in the illustration here.

After you place the instance on the Stage, btnAnim appears in the animBtnLive Library. When you add a symbol from one movie to another movie, Flash CS3 automatically copies the symbol to the movie's Library panel for you.

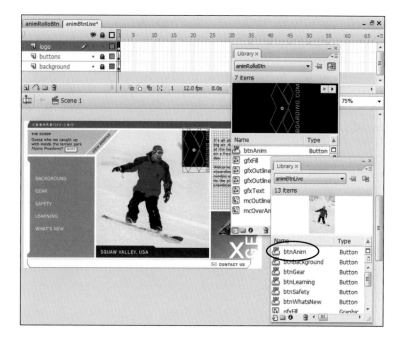

6 Close the **Library** panels. Choose **Window > Transform** to open the **Transform** panel. Select the **btnAnim** instance, make sure the **Constrain** box is selected, type **75.0%** in either the **width** or **height** field, and press **Enter** (Windows) or **Return** (Mac) to change the size of the instance so it fits in the box in the interface. If needed, use the arrow keys on your keyboard to move the instance over the center of the black background.

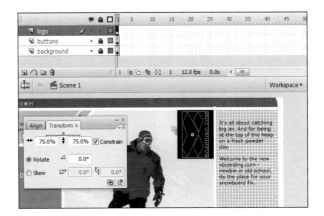

7 Choose **Control > Test Movie**, and move your cursor over the logo to test the animation.

8 When you are finished, close the preview window, and close **animRolloBtn.fla** and **animBtnLive.fla**. You don't need to save your changes.

Congratulations! You have made it through an essential chapter. You have learned how to create, modify, and nest movie clips inside buttons. In the next chapter—one of the most challenging chapters in the book—you will use movie clips in more advanced ways. When you're ready, turn the page and get started.

12

ActionScript Basics

You've learned how to draw, mask, animate, and create symbols. Creating fully interactive presentations, however, requires ActionScript 3.0, the internal programming language in Adobe Flash CS3 Professional. It's similar, but not identical, to Java. Previous versions of ActionScript were more similar to JavaScript. However, you do not have to know Java or JavaScript or be a programmer to include ActionScript in your movies. Though it is a little more difficult to learn than ActionScript 2.0, ActionScript 3.0 runs faster (in many cases), is more consistent, and is overall more powerful than ActionScript 2.0.

ActionScript is important because you can't accomplish many basic Flash activities—such as controlling audio volume—without it. ActionScript also extends the power and flexibility of your project by letting you navigate the main **Timeline**, control movie clips, link to other Web pages, and load other movies into a Flash CS3 movie. By the time you are finished with this chapter, you will have a solid understanding of how to add ActionScript to your movies.

Working with ActionScript code is one of the most technically challenging aspects of Flash CS3. This chapter will not teach you everything there is to know about ActionScript but will cover the basics and give you a solid foundation on which to build.

Where Can I Place ActionScript?

ActionScript 3.0 can be placed on keyframes in the **Timeline** or in external text files with an extension of **.as**. Using ActionScript in external files is beyond the scope of this book.

Using the Actions Panel

In Flash CS3, you use the **Actions** panel to build ActionScript that can control your movie. The **Actions** panel is where you create and edit actions, which you'll learn about in great detail later in this chapter.

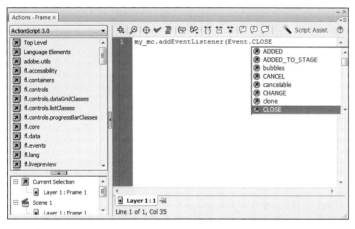

Normal mode

The **Actions** panel works in two modes, displaying a slightly different interface for each mode. **Normal** mode, the topmost view, lets you create ActionScript by choosing from the list of code in the **Actions** pane, by clicking the **Add New Item** (+) button, or by typing code in the **Script** pane. The **Actions** panel requires that you write the correct syntax and any additional parameters required by the action statements.

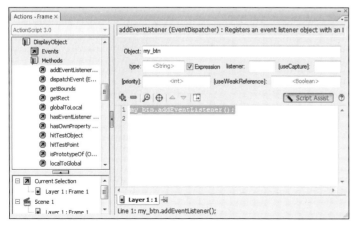

Script Assist mode

Script Assist mode, at the bottom of the previous page, lets you build scripts the same way but assists with syntax and action parameters by letting you choose from options available in text boxes and pop-up menus above the **Script** pane. In Flash 8, **Script Assist** mode was a useful tool to write ActionScript. In Flash CS3, because of the complexity of ActionScript 3.0, **Script Assist** mode is more of an aid that helps you remember what to type in a block of code.

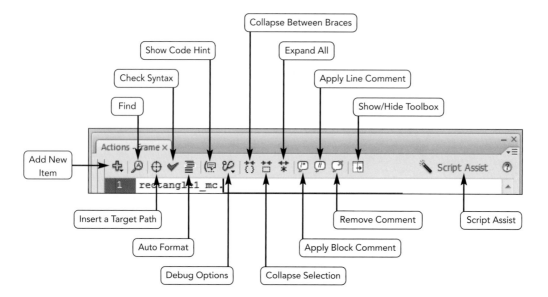

The following chart contains list of the buttons in the **Actions** panel, along with what they do:

Actions Panel Buttons	
Button	**Description**
Add New Item	The **Add New Item** (+) button is a tool used mostly in **Script Assist** mode to help you find ActionScript to use.
Find	The **Find** button allows you to find and replace parts of your code.
Insert a Target Path	The **Insert a Target Path** button helps you find an instance in your Flash file.
Check Syntax	The **Check Syntax** button checks for errors in your code.
Auto Format	The **Auto Format** button formats your code according to the settings you specify in Flash CS3 **Preferences**.
Show Code Hint	The **Show Code Hint** button gives you tips of the parameters to send into functions and pop-up menus that help you write code more quickly.
Debug Options	The **Debug Options** button gives you options for debugging your code.
Collapse Between Braces	The **Collapse Between Braces** button collapses a block of code from the open curly brace you select to the closed curly brace, or vice versa.
Collapse selection	The **Collapse Selection** button collapses your selected code.
Expand All	The **Expand All** button expands all your collapsed code.
Apply Block Comment	The **Apply Block Comment** button disables the code you select by turning it into a comment.
Apply Line Comment	The **Apply Line Comment** button converts a line of code into a comment, thus disabling it.
Remove Comment	The **Remove Comment** button removes comments from any code you have selected.
Show/Hide Toolbox	The **Show/Hide Toolbox** button shows or hides the **Toolbox**, which is mostly used with **Script Assist** mode.

Because this book is targeted at beginners, the code you write will be kept relatively simple. Once you're finished with this book, you'll have a solid understanding of ActionScript basics and will be better prepared to go deeper into ActionScript 3.0.

Introducing ActionScript 3.0 Elements

In this chapter, you will learn about several core ActionScript 3.0 elements, including the following:

- Variables
- Instances
- Properties
- Functions and methods
- Events, event handlers, and event listeners
- Classes
- Conditional statements

These are not *all* the elements of ActionScript 3.0, but knowing how to use these elements will allow you to do most of the common ActionScript tasks. The following sections can act a reference for you to understand each of the ActionScript 3.0 elements used in this book. If you get to a section in a later chapter that seems difficult or confusing, return to this chapter and review these terms.

Variables

Variables are containers that hold data. To understand variables, think of a game where the player has a score. The information (or **data**) about how many points the player has is contained in a variable. When the player gets more points, the number in the score variable increases. Thus, the score acts as a container (or variable) for a number (or data).

The data in a variable is not limited to numbers only. Variables can hold many types of data. Variables can hold text values, such as a user name, password, or text in a text field. They can also hold **true** or **false** values, such as whether or a user logged into a Web site has administrator status. The type of data a variable holds is called its **data type**.

In ActionScript 3.0, you create variables using the keyword, **var**. The code to create a variable called **score** is **var score**.

Whenever you create a variable in ActionScript 3.0, you must give the variable a data type. To tell

Flash CS3 the type of data a variable will hold, type a colon and then the data type. Most data types begin with a capital letter. The code to tell Flash CS3 that the **score** variable will hold a **Number** data type is **var score:Number**.

The name of the data type that holds text is **String**, and the name of the data type that holds **true** or **false** values is **Boolean**.

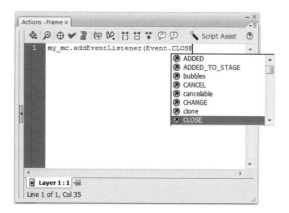

Note: If you typed the code shown in the illustration here in the **Script** pane in the **Actions** panel, you may have noticed that after you typed the colon, a small menu appeared. This menu is called the **Code Hint** menu and is a useful tool in writing ActionScript 3.0.

You give a value to a variable using an equals sign. You can do this on the same line as you create your variable. The code used to assign a value of **0** to a variable called **score** is **var score:Number = 0;**. The code to create a variable called **text** with a value of **"This is my text"** is **var text:String = "This is my text";**.

Note: Notice the quotation marks around the text variable's value. Anytime you use the String data type, the value must be in quotation marks, or Flash CS3 will think you are referencing a variable. All other data types do not use quotation marks.

Also notice the semicolon after the number value in **var score:Number = 0;**. A semicolon in ActionScript 3.0 is similar to a period in a sentence. Both denote the end of a statement.

Many variables do not contain the same value forever. Consider a player's score again—it may start at 0, but as the player gets more points, the value can change to 100; 500; or 1,948,762. To assign a new value to a variable that has already been created, do not use the **var** keyword. Instead, on a different line of code, type the variable name, an equals sign, and then the new value (followed by a semicolon, of course). The code to assign a value of **100** to a variable called **score** that was initially created on a previous line of code with a value of **0** is **score = 100;**.

Instances and Instance Names

You are already familiar with instances. When you drag a symbol from the **Library** panel in Flash CS3, you are creating an **instance** of that symbol. One symbol can have many instances, but each instance is linked to only one symbol.

In Flash CS3, you must name instances if you want to communicate with them via ActionScript. For example, if you want your Flash movie to stop playing when you click a button, you must give that button an instance name. You can give instance names to movie clips, buttons, and text fields, but not to graphic symbols. To give an instance name to an instance, select the instance, and type an instance name in the **Instance Name** field in the **Property inspector**.

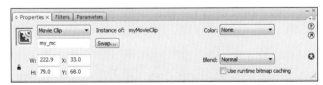

In ActionScript, you refer to individual instances by their instance names, not by the symbol names in the **Library** panel. The name you give your instances is important and is similar to how you must name your symbols. Always start with a lowercase letter, and do not use spaces or special characters other than underscores. It is a best practice to pick a naming convention and use it consistently. Instance names should also be descriptive but brief (so you don't have to type more than necessary). Some examples of good instance names are **contact_btn** , **nav_mc**, and **body_txt**.

Note: If you end your instance names with **_mc** for movie clips, **_btn** for buttons, and **_txt** for text fields, Flash CS3 will give you access to code hinting in the **Actions** panel. This makes writing code much easier and faster.

Properties

Believe it or not, you are already familiar with properties by this point. Properties are simply variables that are attached to an instance of a symbol. If that sounds a little cryptic, think of properties as attributes you can modify in the **Property inspector**. Specifically, the x and y positioning and the width and height of an instance are some of its properties. Working with movie clips or buttons, some other properties include alpha, blend mode, and even filters. You can modify properties in ActionScript using **dot syntax**, which means you type the instance name, a dot, the property you want to modify, and then the value you want to give that property using an equals sign (just like setting the value of a variable). The code to modify the x position of a movie clip with an instance name of **my_mc** and set it to **100** is **my_mc.x = 100;**.

Functions and Methods

When using ActionScript 3.0, you will often write large blocks of code that you reuse many times. Copying the same code several times can be frustrating and tedious. Fortunately, you can write a block of code one time and recycle it using functions and methods. **Functions** and **methods** are essentially the same—both are reusable blocks of code.

Many functions already exist in Flash CS3. If you want to stop a movie from looping continuously, you can use a prebuilt function, or method, called a **stop()** method. To use a function, type the name of the function, and then type a pair of parentheses. The code to run the **stop()** method is **stop();**. Another common prebuilt function in Flash CS3 is **gotoAndPlay()**. The **gotoAndPlay()** function plays the Flash movie starting at a particular frame. When you run the **gotoAndPlay()** function, you tell Flash CS3 the frame you want to play in the parentheses. For example, the code to play a movie from the fifth frame is `gotoAndPlay(5);`.

Note: The parentheses are what make the function run, and they differentiate a function from a variable. If you just typed **stop** with no parentheses, Flash CS3 would think you were referring to a variable called **stop.**

Some functions do not already exist in Flash CS3, so you will have to create them. Writing custom functions requires a few steps. First, you must tell Flash CS3 you are creating a function by using the **function** keyword. Next, you tell Flash CS3 the name of your function. If you wanted to create a function called **myFirstFunction**, you would type **function myFirstFunction**. The next step is to type a pair of parentheses. You will learn more about what the parentheses are used for when you learn about events. After the parentheses, you need to tell Flash CS3 the return data type using a colon (similar to how you set a data type for a variable). The return data type for all functions used in this book will be **void**. Last, you put all the code block that you will reuse inside curly braces. For example, the code to create a complete function called **myFirstFunction** is as follows:

```
function myFirstFunction():void
{
    (Block of code goes here)
}
```

Running a custom function is similar to running a prebuilt function. Simply type the name of the function and then the pair of parentheses. The code to run a function called **myFirstFunction** is **myFirstFunction();**.

Events, Event Handlers, and Event Listeners

Events are things that happen while a Flash movie is playing. Many types of events exist, such as when a visitor to your Web site clicks a button, presses a key on the keyboard, or starts downloading a file. You can utilize events by running functions when events happen. The special functions that run when events happen are called **event handlers**.

To write an event handler, simply create a basic function. The only difference with an event handler function is that it receives information about the event that made the function run. The code to create an event handler function called **playMovie()** that reacts to a button click is as follows:

```
function playMovie(event:MouseEvent):void
{
}
```

Note: The **event:MouseEvent** code in the parentheses is significant. This is how you capture information about what caused the function to run. The word **event** represents the event that happened, and the colon specifies the data type of this event, which is **MouseEvent**. Before this function will run when you click a button, you need to attach the event handler function to the event (the button click).

To attach an event to an event handler, you need to use something called an **event listener**. Event listeners wait for events to happen, and when the events happen, the appropriate event handler function runs. To understand event listeners, think of a radio station broadcasting music as an event. It broadcasts whether or not you listen to it. Tuning your radio to a station is like listening for an event. When you hear the music, you choose how to react to it (that is, sing along, change the station, or turn the volume up). In the same way your selection of a radio station connects you to the signal being broadcast, event listeners connect event handlers to events.

To have a button or any object in Flash CS3 listen for an event, use the **addEventListener** method (again, **method** being synonymous with **function**) of any object. You do this by typing the instance name, a dot, and then **addEventListener**. Then in parentheses, tell Flash CS3 the event the instance is listening for, type a comma, and then type the name of the function that will run when the event happens. For example, if you had a button with an instance name of **play_btn** and you wanted to run a function called **playMovie()** when you clicked it, you would type the following:

```
play_btn.addEventListener(MouseEvent.CLICK,
playMovie);
```

Note: In Flash CS3, events start with the data type of the event (in this case **MouseEvent**), then have a dot, and then have the specific event name in all caps.

Also note that anytime you send in multiple values to a function, you separate the values with commas.

Classes

Classes might be somewhat familiar to you already. A **class** is a blueprint, or concept, of something. Think of movie clip symbols and button symbols. What are some differences between the two? Movie clips have nearly an unlimited number of frames, and they play when your Flash movie is running unless you use ActionScript to tell them otherwise. Buttons have a timeline with only four frames and do not play unless you roll over or click them. The **MovieClip** class is the blueprint for all movie clips. Though each movie clip symbol may look different, all movie clips have certain similarities. Classes all begin with a capital letter, and all classes are also data types. Number, String, and Boolean are all classes.

When you drag instances of movie clip or button symbols out of your **Library** panel and put them on the **Stage**, you are creating instances of the **MovieClip** or **Button** class. Many classes are not visual, so you must create instances of those classes with ActionScript using the **new** keyword. After the **new** keyword, type the class name and a pair of parentheses. One nonvisual class is called **Loader** and is used to load external content. To create a new instance of the **Loader** class called **myLoader**, you would type the following:

```
var myLoader:Loader = new Loader();
```

Note: This code creates a new instance of the **Loader** class and is similar to creating instances of many other nonvisual classes. After the **new** keyword, notice the name of the class and the pair of parentheses. This looks similar to the syntax used to run a function—because it *is* a function. It's a special function called a **constructor function** that creates a new instance of that particular class.

Conditional Statements

Conditional statements allow you to run a block of code based on a condition being true or false. Picture yourself getting dressed in the morning (or whatever time of the day you prefer to get dressed). Assuming you are planning to wear both shoes and socks that day, you put your shoes on only if you are already wearing socks. If you don't have socks on, then you put socks on and then shoes.

In ActionScript 3.0, conditions are computed in a similar way. Consider a variable called **socksOn** with a **true** or **false** data type (Boolean). To write a conditional statement, you first use the keyword **if**, then you place the expression that is evaluated as **true** or **false** in parentheses, and finally you place the code that executes in curly braces. In code, a conditional statement that would put shoes on if socks were already on would look like this:

```
if(socksOn)
{
    (Put shoes on)
}
```

Note: If the **socksOn** variable had a value of **true**, the code that says **(Put shoes on)** would run. Everything in the parentheses after the keyword **if** is evaluated as **true** or **false**.

You can also run a block of code if a condition is not true. To do that, use the keyword **else**, and place the code you want to run in curly braces. Using the previous code, if you wanted to put shoes on if **socksOn** were true and put socks on if **socksOn** were false, you would type the following:

```
if(socksOn)
{
    (Put shoes on)
}
else
{
    (Put socks on)
}
```

Note: You don't need any parentheses after the **else** keyword.

1 | Controlling the Timeline

In Flash CS3, once a movie starts, it plays in its entirety (or it reaches the last frame of the **Timeline**) unless instructed otherwise. Fortunately, you can control how Flash CS3 plays movies by adding code in the **Actions** panel. This exercise teaches you how to add a **stop()** method to a frame in order to control an animation on the main **Timeline**.

---

1 Copy the **chap_12** folder from the **Flash HOT CD-ROM** to your desktop. Open **stopAndPlay_Final.fla** from the **chap_12** folder.

This is the finished version of the project you'll be building in this exercise.

---

2 Choose **Control > Test Movie** to preview the movie. In the SWF file, click the **PLAY** button to set the snowboarder in motion, moving down the mountain. Click the **STOP** button to stop the snowboarder. When you are finished stopping and playing this movie, close the preview window, and then close **stopandPlay_Final.fla**.

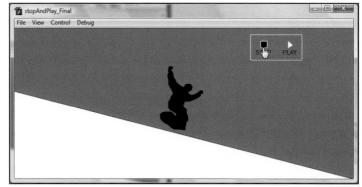

You will learn how to add the same functionality to this movie in the following steps.

---

3 Open the **stopAndPlay.fla** file from the **chap_12** folder. Choose **Control > Test Movie** to preview the movie. Click the **STOP** and **PLAY** buttons.

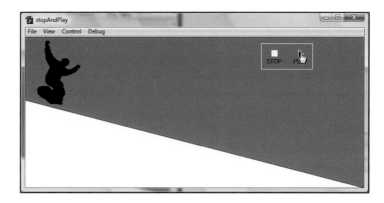

This is an unfinished version of the movie you just previewed. It contains everything except the ActionScript, which you will add in this exercise. Notice how nothing happens when you click the STOP button—the movie continues to play. Why? Well, no actions have been added to this file yet, and therefore the buttons do not control the movie. You will learn to do this next.

---

4 Close the preview window, and return to the project file. In the **Timeline**, select the **buttons** layer, and click the **Insert Layer** button. Name the new layer **actions**.

NOTE:

Adding a Layer for ActionScript

Throughout the rest of this book, I model good practice by having you create a separate layer to hold actions. It will always be located on top of all the other layers and be labeled **actions**. As the movies you create become more and more complex, troubleshooting and debugging a movie will be significantly easier if you know you can always find your ActionScript in the same place: on the first layer of the movie and on the layer named **actions**.

5 Select the first keyframe of the **actions** layer, and choose **Window > Actions** or press **F9** (Windows) or **Opt+F9** (Mac) to open the **Actions** panel.

Notice the top of the Actions panel reads *Actions – Frame*. Because you have selected a keyframe, Flash CS3 knows you will be adding actions to the keyframe you selected. If the Actions panel reads *Current selection cannot have actions applied to it*, make sure to click the keyframe where you want to apply ActionScript.

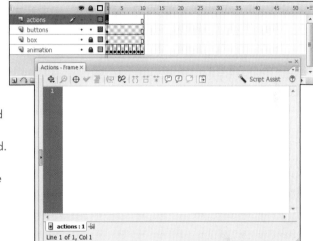

6 In the **Actions** panel, make sure **Script Assist** is turned off.

7 In the **Script** pane, type **stop();**.

This line of script instructs Flash CS3 to run the **stop()** method, which will stop the movie from playing when you preview the movie. Next, you will see that code in action!

8 Choose **Control > Test Movie** to preview the movie. Notice the movie does not play.

You have just added your first action to the project. Sweet! Next, you'll add interactivity to the buttons on the Stage and use them to control the playback of your movie.

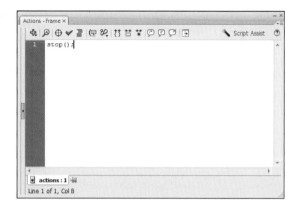

9 Close the preview window, and return to Flash. Close the **Actions** panel. Click the **PLAY** button on the **Stage**, click the **Instance Name** field in the **Property inspector**, and type **play_btn**. Then click the **STOP** button on the **Stage**, and type **stop_btn** in the **Instance Name** field in the **Property inspector**.

Remember when you learned about instance names previously in this chapter? Instance names are necessary in order to use these buttons to control the playback of the movie.

10 Select the first keyframe of the **actions** layer, and choose **Window > Actions** or press **F9** (Windows) or **Opt+F9** (Mac) to open the **Actions** panel.

11 In the **Script** pane, after the code you wrote in Step 7, type the following:

```
function playMovie(event:MouseEvent):void
{
}
```

This ActionScript tells Flash CS3 to create a function called `playMovie()` that receives a `MouseEvent` (within the parentheses) and has no return data type (`void`). So far, this function does nothing because there is no ActionScript between the

curly braces. This is called a **skeleton** of a function. You will get a lot of practice writing functions as you go through the rest of the exercises in this book.

---

12 Click in the curly braces of the code you wrote in the previous step, and type **play();**. When this function runs, the movie will play.

Notice the syntax for the **play()** method is similar to the **stop()** method. In the next step, you will add an event listener to **play_btn** to connect the button to the event and the event handler function.

---

13 After all your code, type the following:

```
play_btn.addEventListener(MouseEvent.CLICK,
playMovie);
```

This ActionScript links **play_btn** to the event (**MouseEvent.CLICK**) and the event handler (the **playMovie()** function). Now that you have attached an event listener to the button, the button will listen for and be able to react to a mouse click.

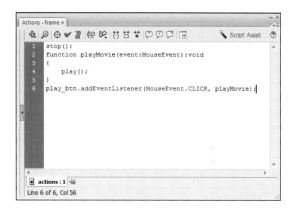

---

14 Choose **Control > Test Movie** to preview the movie. Click the **PLAY** button, and watch the movie play. Yes!

Notice the movie plays through once and stops at the first frame. That is because of the **stop()** method you put on the first frame of the movie. In the next step, you will make the movie loop after you click the PLAY button.

---

15 Close the preview window. In the main **Timeline**, select **Frame 10** on the **actions** layer, and press **F6** to add a keyframe. In the **Actions** panel, type **gotoAndPlay(2);**.

This script tells Flash CS3 to send the playhead to Frame 2 and play the movie when the playhead reaches Frame 10, creating a small loop. Each time the playhead reaches Frame 10, it will go to Frame 2, play the rest of the frames, and then return to Frame 2, bypassing Frame 1 and its **stop()** method. Nice!

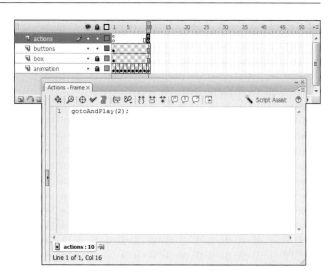

16 Close the **Actions** panel. Choose **Control > Test Movie** to test the movie again.

The movie begins in a stopped state. As soon as you click the PLAY button, the movie plays and continues to play over and over, without stopping. In the next steps, you will make the STOP button stop the movie from looping.

---

17 Select **Frame 1** on the **actions** layer, and open the **Actions** panel by choosing **Window > Actions**. Select all the code after the **stop()** method, and press **Ctrl+C** (Windows) or **Cmd+C** (Mac) to copy the code. Then, after the last line of code, paste the code you just copied by pressing **Ctrl+V** (Windows) or **Cmd+V** (Mac).

The code to stop the movie is similar to the code to play the movie. In the next step, you will modify the code you pasted to stop the movie.

Copying and pasting code is a great way to save time in the code-writing process. As you learn more ActionScript, you will learn when it is most effective to copy and paste code.

---

18 In the pasted code, change the word **play**, everywhere it appears, to **stop**.

Tip: The word *play* appears four times:
playMovie() is the name of the function,
play() runs in the function and plays the movie,
play_btn is the instance name of the button, and
playMovie is called out again in the event listener.

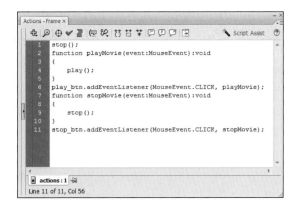

---

19 Choose **Control > Test Movie** to test the movie again. Click the **PLAY** button, and watch the movie play indefinitely. Then click the **STOP** button, and watch the movie stop. You are in control!

---

20 You are now finished, so close the preview window, and then close **stopAndPlay.fla**. You don't need to save your changes.

---

2 | Controlling Movie Clips

In the previous exercise, you attached the **stop()** and **play()** methods to button instances to control an animation on the main **Timeline**. You can also use the **stop()** and **play()** methods to control the **Timeline** of any movie clip. To control a movie clip, you must give it an instance name, and it must be present on the **Timeline**. This exercise shows you how.

---

1 Open **stopAndPlayMC.fla** from the **chap_12** folder.

This project file looks similar to the original project file from Exercise 1, with two exceptions: In the stopAndPlayMC.fla project file, there is a movie clip rather than an animation layer in the main Timeline, and there is only one frame in the main Timeline. The ActionScript you wrote for the first frame on the actions layer in the previous exercise is in this exercise. With a few small changes to your code, you will be able to control the playback of a movie clip.

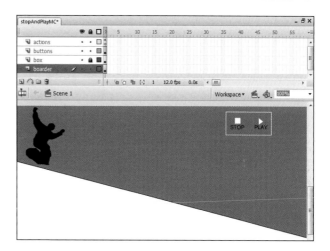

---

2 Choose **Control > Test Movie** to preview the movie. Click the **STOP** and **PLAY** buttons. When you are finished previewing the movie, close the preview window.

Notice nothing happens, and the movie continues to play. Because the ActionScript of these buttons is telling the main Timeline to play and stop, the buttons do not control the movie clip. You will add actions to control the movie clip in the steps that follow.

---

3 On the **Stage**, click the snow to select the movie clip instance. In the **Property inspector**, type **boarder_mc** in the **Instance Name** field to assign an instance name to the movie clip on the **Stage**.

In Exercise 1, the **stop()** and **play()** methods you added automatically controlled the main Timeline. Conversely, to control a movie clip, you have to refer to the movie clip by its instance name when you apply actions to the buttons in the next steps.

The Power of Movie Clip Symbols

Many exercises in this chapter use movie clip symbols. Movie clip symbols are addressed differently in ActionScript than other kinds of symbols. As you learned in Chapter 11, *"Movie Clips,"* movie clip symbols are the most powerful and flexible of all symbols since they can contain multiple layers, graphic symbols, button symbols, and even other movie clip symbols, as well as animations, sounds, and ActionScript. Because movie clip symbols can contain all of these things and can be represented on the **Timeline** in just one keyframe, your **Timeline** will be more organized and less cluttered. And, don't forget that movie clip symbols are **Timeline**-independent, meaning that the movie clip will continue to play even though the playhead in the main **Timeline** has stopped.

Although movie clip symbols are more complex to learn, with practice you will find that they actually make creating your Flash projects easier! In the following steps, you will learn how to control a movie clip symbol by giving it an instance name so that you can refer to it in ActionScript.

4 Select the first keyframe on the **actions** layer, and open the **Actions** panel. Notice the code is the same as you typed in the previous exercise.

In the next step, you will see how little the code needs to be changed in order to control a movie clip.

```
Actions - Frame ×
  1   stop();
  2   function playMovie(event:MouseEvent):void
  3   {
  4       play();
  5   }
  6   play_btn.addEventListener(MouseEvent.CLICK, playMovie);
  7   function stopMovie(event:MouseEvent):void
  8   {
  9       stop();
 10   }
 11   stop_btn.addEventListener(MouseEvent.CLICK, stopMovie);

actions : 1
Line 11 of 11, Col 56
```

5 To control the playback of a movie clip instead of the main **Timeline**, click before the **play()** method in the code and type **boarder_mc.** (don't forget the dot!). Do the same thing for the **stop()** method.

This ActionScript tells Flash CS3 to make the snowboarder movie clip stop or play when you click the appropriate button. To control any object using ActionScript, type its instance name and a dot. Then type the name of the function you want to run (**stop()**, **play()**, or **gotoAndPlay()**). This method of controlling objects is referred to as dot syntax.

```
Actions - Frame ×
  1   stop();
  2   function playMovie(event:MouseEvent):void
  3   {
  4       boarder_mc.play();
  5   }
  6   play_btn.addEventListener(MouseEvent.CLICK, playMovie);
  7   function stopMovie(event:MouseEvent):void
  8   {
  9       boarder_mc.stop();
 10   }
 11   stop_btn.addEventListener(MouseEvent.CLICK, stopMovie);

actions : 1
Line 11 of 11, Col 56
```

6 Choose **Control > Test Movie** to try the buttons. Notice the **boarder_mc** movie clip is being controlled using buttons on the main **Timeline**. Great!

Placing animations in movie clips is a great practice and will keep the main Timeline uncluttered.

---

7 When you are finished, close the preview window, and close **stopAndPlayMC.fla**. You don't need to save your changes.

What Is Dot Syntax?

In the previous exercise, you added a period, or dot (.), between the instance name and the **stop()** and **play()** methods, like so: **boarder_mc.stop();**. In ActionScript, the period indicates functions or methods that relate to a movie clip or other objects. This is part of the ActionScript syntax, also referred to as dot syntax.

In Flash CS3, dot syntax simply refers to the formatting convention used to create ActionScript. Dot syntax is used to construct statements that consist of objects, properties, methods, and variables. Each dot syntax statement begins with the name of the object followed by a period (.) and

ends with the property, method, or variable you want to identify. For example, in the statement **boarder_mc.play();**, the object is the movie clip named **boarder_mc**, and the method or function is **play**. The parentheses hold the parameters (also called **arguments**) that apply to an action; in this case, no parameters are required. With the action **gotoAndPlay();**, the argument or parameter would go between the parentheses and would be the frame number you want to go to. The semicolon (;) marks the end of a statement (just as a period marks the end of a sentence).

3 | Using Conditional Statements

In addition to the **stop()** and **play()** methods, Flash also has more specific actions that tell the playhead exactly where to start and stop on the **Timeline**. This exercise demonstrates how you can use ActionScript to create a Flash CS3 movie you can navigate one frame at a time, similar to a slideshow. Using conditional statements and the **gotoAndStop()** function, you will write code that will navigate to a different frame depending on what frame the playhead is currently on.

1 Open **slideShow_Final.fla** from the **chap_12** folder. This is the finished version of the slideshow you are going to create. Choose **Control > Test Movie** to preview the movie. Click the **NEXT** button to advance the slideshow forward. Click the **BACK** button to display the previous slide. When you are finished, close the preview window.

2 Select the first keyframe of the **actions** layer, and choose **Window > Actions** to open the **Actions** panel. Examine the code, and try to determine how this movie works. When you are done, close the **slideShow_Final.fla** file.

```
1   stop();
2   function goBack(event:MouseEvent):void
3   {
4       if(currentFrame == 1)
5       {
6           gotoAndStop(totalFrames);
7       }
8       else
9       {
10          prevFrame();
11      }
12  }
13  function goForward(event:MouseEvent):void
14  {
15      if(currentFrame == totalFrames)
16      {
17          gotoAndStop(1);
18      }
19      else
20      {
21          nextFrame();
22      }
23  }
24
25  back_btn.addEventListener(MouseEvent.CLICK, goBack);
26  next_btn.addEventListener(MouseEvent.CLICK, goForward);
```

actions : 1

Line 26 of 26, Col 56

3 Open the **slideShow.fla** file from the **chap_12** folder. Click the **BACK** button and then the **NEXT** button. Notice they both already have instance names. Select the first keyframe of the **actions** layer, and choose **Window > Actions** to open the **Actions** panel. Take a look at the code written already. At the top, the **stop()** method prevents the movie from playing when it starts. The rest of the code has two functions and event listeners for those functions. Notice that the **back_btn** button is attached to the **goBack()** function, and the **next_btn** button is connected to the **goForward()** function.

```
Actions - Frame
1   stop();
2   function goBack(event:MouseEvent):void
3   {
4
5   }
6   function goForward(event:MouseEvent):void
7   {
8
9   }
10
11  back_btn.addEventListener(MouseEvent.CLICK, goBack);
12  next_btn.addEventListener(MouseEvent.CLICK, goForward);

   actions : 1
Line 12 of 12, Col 56
```

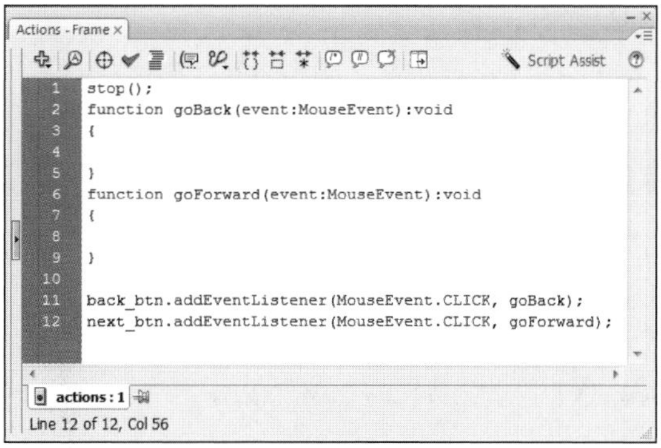

This is an unfinished version of the movie you just previewed, containing only the slideshow images, the buttons, and some ActionScript. You will add to the ActionScript of this file to make it work properly.

---

4 Click in the curly braces of the **goBack()** function, and type **prevFrame();**. Then, click in the curly braces of the **goForward()** function, and type **nextFrame();**.

The **prevFrame()** function tells Flash CS3 to go back one frame and stop (if you click the Back button). The **nextFrame()** function tells Flash CS3 to go forward one frame and stop (if you click the NEXT button).

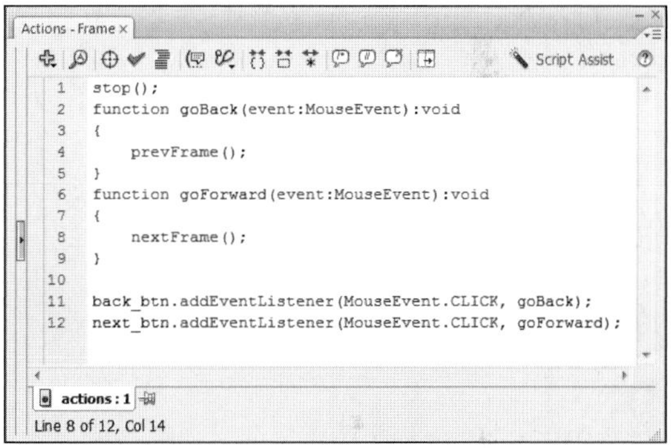

```
Actions - Frame
1   stop();
2   function goBack(event:MouseEvent):void
3   {
4       prevFrame();
5   }
6   function goForward(event:MouseEvent):void
7   {
8       nextFrame();
9   }
10
11  back_btn.addEventListener(MouseEvent.CLICK, goBack);
12  next_btn.addEventListener(MouseEvent.CLICK, goForward);

   actions : 1
Line 8 of 12, Col 14
```

---

5 Choose **Control > Test Movie** to preview the movie. Click the NEXT button a few times to go to the next picture, and click the BACK button a few times to go to the previous picture. What happens if you try to go beyond **Frame 5**? Or go before **Frame 1**?

This ActionScript is great for a simple slideshow, but you will need to use conditional statements if you want the slides to loop around if you try to go past the last frame or before the first frame. You will learn how to do that in the next steps.

---

6 Close the preview window, and return to the **Actions** panel. In the `goBack()` function, select the `prevFrame` line of code, and delete it. Don't worry, you will write it again later. Replace that code by typing the following:

```
if(currentFrame == 1)
{
}
```

This ActionScript is a skeleton of a conditional statement. The code in the curly braces (which you will write in the next step) will run if the expression in parentheses is true. The `currentFrame` property is prebuilt in Flash CS3 and represents the frame the playhead is currently on.

```
1  stop();
2  function goBack(event:MouseEvent):void
3  {
4      if(currentFrame == 1)
5      {
6
7      }
8  }
9  function goForward(event:MouseEvent):void
10 {
11     nextFrame();
12 }
13
14 back_btn.addEventListener(MouseEvent.CLICK, goBack);
15 next_btn.addEventListener(MouseEvent.CLICK, goForward);
```

Notice the two equals signs. Two equals signs mean *is equal to*, which is different from one equals sign. One equals sign sets the value of something, and two equals signs are used to compare values in conditional statements. In this conditional statement, the code you put in the curly braces (in the next step) will execute if the current frame *is equal to* 1. If the current frame *is equal to* 1 when you click the BACK button, you will have the movie go to its last frame. You will do that in the next step.

---

7 Click between the curly braces of the code you just wrote, and type the following:

```
gotoAndStop(totalFrames);
```

This ActionScript tells Flash CS3 to go to and stop on the last frame of the movie, indicated by the prebuilt property `totalFrames`. The `totalFrames` property represents the total number of frames in a particular Timeline. Because this code is on the main Timeline, it represents the total number of frames on the main Timeline, which is five.

```
1  stop();
2  function goBack(event:MouseEvent):void
3  {
4      if(currentFrame == 1)
5      {
6          gotoAndStop(totalFrames);
7      }
8  }
9  function goForward(event:MouseEvent):void
10 {
11     nextFrame();
12 }
13
14 back_btn.addEventListener(MouseEvent.CLICK, goBack);
15 next_btn.addEventListener(MouseEvent.CLICK, goForward);
```

There is a significant advantage to using the `totalFrames` property over a number. Consider this—what if you decided to add more pictures to your slideshow? If you used **5**, you would have to add them as keyframes and then update your code. You would also have to update the code if you took frames out of the slideshow. The `totalFrames` property knows how many frames are in your movie, so adding or subtracting frames does not require a change to your code. It is always a best practice to write code in a way that will not require you to change it should you decide to change the art in your movie.

---

8 Choose **Control > Test Movie** to preview the movie. Click the BACK button, and watch the movie go to the last frame. Nice! Click the button again, and notice that nothing happens. In the next step, you will learn how to control the playback of your movie if the `currentFrame` property *is not equal* to 1.

---

9 Close the preview window, and return to the **Actions** panel. After the closed curly brace of the conditional statement (not after the closed curly brace of the **goBack()** function), type the following:

```
else
{
    prevFrame();
}
```

Remember the **else** keyword from when you read about conditional statements previously in this chapter? The **else** keyword defines what happens if its matching **if** statement is not true. **Else** statements must always be placed immediately after an **if** statement. The code that is executed in an **else** statement is placed within curly braces.

```
1  stop();
2  function goBack(event:MouseEvent):void
3  {
4      if(currentFrame == 1)
5      {
6          gotoAndStop(totalFrames);
7      }
8      else
9      {
10          prevFrame();
11      }
12  }
13  function goForward(event:MouseEvent):void
14  {
15      nextFrame();
16  }
17
18  back_btn.addEventListener(MouseEvent.CLICK, goBack);
19  next_btn.addEventListener(MouseEvent.CLICK, goForward);
```

actions : 1
Line 11 of 19, Col 3

This code will move the movie to the previous frame (set by the **prevFrame()** function), if the **currentFrame** property is *not equal to* 1. Now, clicking the **BACK** button will cause the movie to move backward unless it is on the first frame, in which case it will move to the last frame. Sweet!

---

10 Choose **Control > Test Movie** to preview the movie. Click the BACK button. Click it again…and again…and again as many times as you want! Notice the movie steps backward, unless it is on the first frame. If the movie is on the first frame, the movie jumps to the last frame. Cool!

In the next steps, you will use similar code in the **goForward()** function to step the movie forward unless it is on the last frame.

---

11 Close the preview window, and return to the **Actions** panel. Select the **nextFrame()** code in the **goForward()** function, and delete it by pressing **Delete** on your keyboard.

---

12 Select all the code within the **goBack()** function (both the **if** and **else** statements, along with opened and closed curly braces for each one), and press **Ctrl+C** (Windows) or **Cmd+C** (Mac) on your keyboard to copy the code.

---

13 Click in the **goForward()** function, between the opened and closed curly braces, and press **Ctrl+V** (Windows) or **Cmd+V** (Mac) on your keyboard to paste the code.

Now that you have copied and pasted the code from the conditional statements in the **goBack()** function, you will modify the code to make it work for the **goForward()** function. Before moving to the next step, think about what you would have to change in the pasted code to make it work properly.

14 In the parentheses after the **if** keyword, in the code you just pasted, select **1** and change it to **totalFrames**. That line of code should read as follows:

if(currentFrame == totalFrames)

With the NEXT button, you want the movie to loop back to the first frame if the movie is on the last frame. This code tells Flash CS3 to check whether the movie is on the last frame (using the same **totalFrames** property you used in Step 7). In the next step, you will tell Flash CS3 to return to Frame 1 if the movie is on the last frame.

```
    Actions - Frame ×
    ⊕ ₽ ⊕ ✔ ⌘ ⏚ ⏛ ⏜ ⏝ ⏞ ⏟ ⏠ ⏡ ⏢ ⏣          🔧 Script Assist  ⑦
 1  stop();
 2  function goBack(event:MouseEvent):void
 3  {
 4      if(currentFrame == 1)
 5      {
 6          gotoAndStop(totalFrames);
 7      }
 8      else
 9      {
10          prevFrame();
11      }
12  }
13  function goForward(event:MouseEvent):void
14  {
15      if(currentFrame == totalFrames)
16      {
17          gotoAndStop(totalFrames);
18      }
19      else
20      {
21          prevFrame();
22      }
23  }
24
25  back_btn.addEventListener(MouseEvent.CLICK, goBack);
26  next_btn.addEventListener(MouseEvent.CLICK, goForward);
```

```
    ▪ actions : 1
    Line 15 of 26, Col 32
```

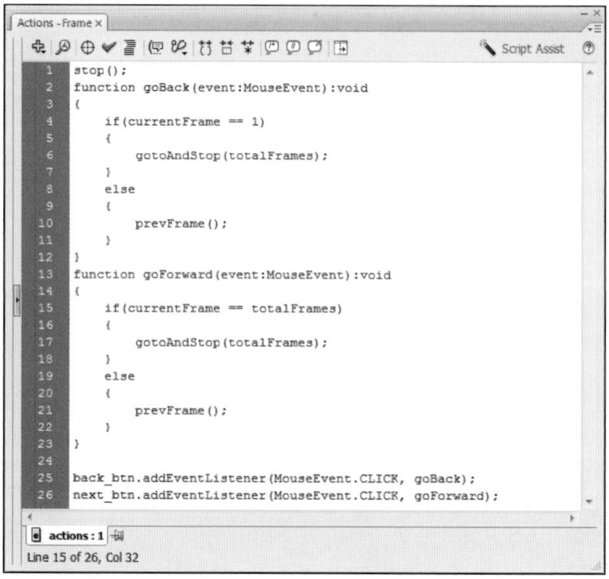

15 In the **gotoAndStop()** function (still within the **if** statement of the **goForward()** function), change **totalFrames** to **1**.

Now when you click the NEXT button, if the movie is on the last frame, it will go to the first frame. Notice the absolute number here instead of a property name. Why is that? It is unnecessary to use a property here, because you want the movie to loop back to the first frame. If you wanted the movie to loop back to a different frame, you could put that frame number here instead. Next, you will make a simple change to the **else** statement, and the button code will be complete!

---

16 In the **goForward()** function, inside the **else** statement, change **prevFrame()** to **nextFrame()**.

This simple change makes the movie advance to the next slide when you click the NEXT button, unless the movie is on the last frame. In that case, the movie will loop to the first frame (because you specified that in the previous step). Your code typing is done! Now it's time to see this movie in action!

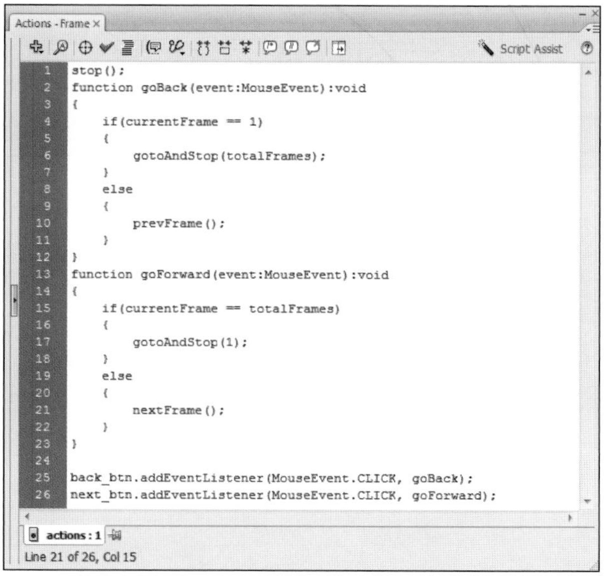

```
    Actions - Frame ×
    ⊕ ₽ ⊕ ✔ ⌘ ⏚ ⏛ ⏜ ⏝ ⏞ ⏟ ⏠ ⏡ ⏢ ⏣          🔧 Script Assist  ⑦
 1  stop();
 2  function goBack(event:MouseEvent):void
 3  {
 4      if(currentFrame == 1)
 5      {
 6          gotoAndStop(totalFrames);
 7      }
 8      else
 9      {
10          prevFrame();
11      }
12  }
13  function goForward(event:MouseEvent):void
14  {
15      if(currentFrame == totalFrames)
16      {
17          gotoAndStop(1);
18      }
19      else
20      {
21          nextFrame();
22      }
23  }
24
25  back_btn.addEventListener(MouseEvent.CLICK, goBack);
26  next_btn.addEventListener(MouseEvent.CLICK, goForward);
```

```
    ▪ actions : 1
    Line 21 of 26, Col 15
```

---

17 Choose **Control > Test Movie** to preview the movie. Click the NEXT button five or six times, and watch the playhead loop back to the first frame! Click the BACK button, and watch the movie step back and loop to the last frame.

Great job! Using this ActionScript, you can add or remove as many slides as you want and never worry about changing the code.

---

18 When you are finished testing the movie, close the preview window, and close **slideShow.fla**. You don't need to save your changes.

What Is the URLRequest Class?

In the next exercise, you'll write code using the **URLRequest** class. The **URLRequest** class is used whenever you are using a URL (**U**niform **R**esource **L**ocator) for something, including linking to a Web site, generating an e-mail message, and loading external files. The **URLRequest** class is fairly simple and can be created on one line of code. One difference between the **URLRequest** class and most other classes you will learn in this book is that you

pass in a value through parentheses when you create an instance of the class. The value you pass in is the URL you will be using, in the form of a String (so the URL will be surrounded with quotation marks). If you wanted to create an instance of the **URLRequest** class called **lynda_req** that held a URL of the Lynda.com Web site, you would type

```
var lynda_url:URLRequest = new
URLRequest("http://www.lynda.com");
```

4 | Using the navigateToURL Function

You can open other Web sites from within a Flash CS3 movie. This exercise introduces the **URLRequest** class and the `navigateToURL()` function, which are used to create links to other documents on the Web. The following steps demonstrate how to use the **URLRequest** class and the `navigateToURL()` function to link to an external Web site and to generate a preaddressed e-mail message.

---

1 Open **navigateToUrl.fla** from the **chap_12** folder.

I created this file to get you started.

You'll see two button instances on the Stage: MORE and CONTACT US. You will add ActionScript to link the MORE button to a Web page, and you will have the CONTACT US button open a site visitor's e-mail program to send an e-mail.

---

2 On the **Stage**, click the **MORE** button. In the **Property inspector**, notice the button has an instance name of **scoop_btn**. Click the **CONTACT US** button. In the **Property inspector**, notice the button has an instance name of **contact_btn**.

---

3 Select the first keyframe on the **actions** layer, and open the **Actions** panel by pressing **F9** (Windows) or **Option+F9** (Mac). Examine the code.

The code in the file already is just two skeletons of functions that have event listeners. In the next few steps, you will define what these functions do.

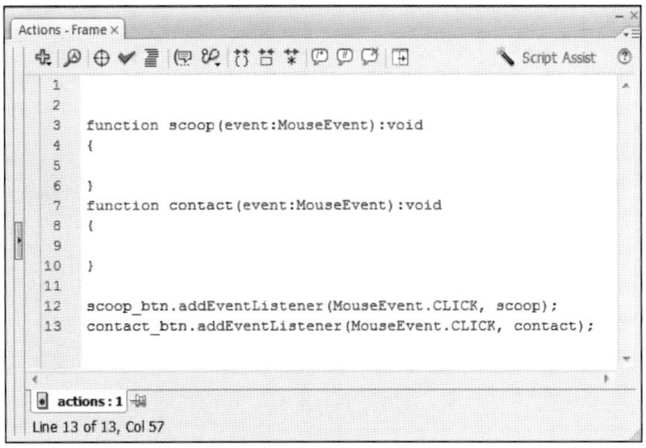

4 Click in the **Script** pane on line 1 of the code (before the **scoop()** function), and type the following:

```
var scoop_req:URLRequest = new URLRequest("theScoop.html");
```

This code creates a variable called **scoop_req** that has a data type of URLRequest and is a new instance of the **URLRequest** class. Inside the parentheses the **Scoop.html** file refers to an .html file in the chap_12 folder.

5 Click in the curly braces of the **scoop()** function, and type the following:

```
navigateToURL(scoop_req, "_blank");
```

This code runs the built-in **navigateToURL()** function.

Note: The theScoop.html file is located in the chap_12 folder. If you want to keep your HTML files in another directory, separate from the project file, simply define the directory it is in followed by a slash (/), like so: newdirectory/thescoop.html.

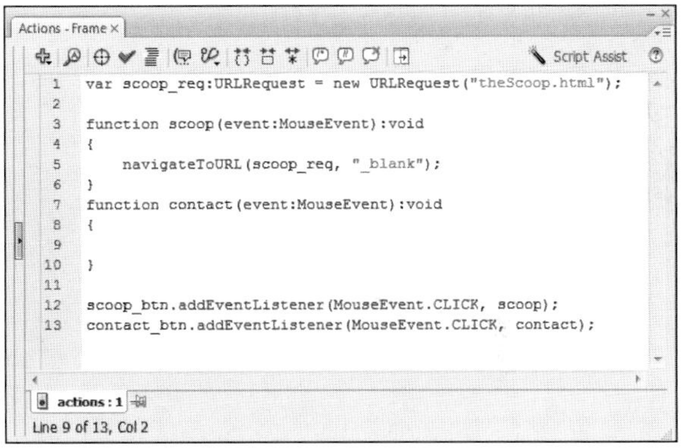

The **navigateToURL()** function is used to link to Web pages and create preaddressed e-mail messages. When you run the **navigateToURL()** function, you must pass in two parameters (values you send into a function), separated with commas. The first parameter is required: the URL you want to open in the form of a **URLRequest**. You created the **URLRequest**, **scoop_req**, in the previous step. The second parameter is optional and is used to tell Flash CS3 how the link will work. There are four options, all of which are explained in the following chart. The **_blank** option tells Flash CS3 to open the link in a new, blank browser window (instead of using the same window as the Flash movie). This will either open a new window or a new tab, depending on the browser you are using.

navigateToURL() Window Parameter Options	
Option	**Description**
_blank	Opens the link in a new browser window or tab, depending on the browser you are using
_self	Opens the link in the same browser window that is occupied by the current Flash CS3 movie
_parent	Opens the link in the parent window of the current window
_top	Opens the link in the same browser window and removes any existing framesets

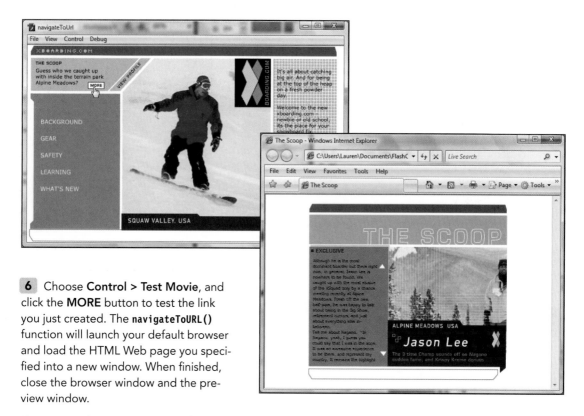

6 Choose **Control > Test Movie**, and click the **MORE** button to test the link you just created. The `navigateToURL()` function will launch your default browser and load the HTML Web page you specified into a new window. When finished, close the browser window and the preview window.

You can use the `navigateToURL()` function as an e-mail link by adding `mailto` to an e-mail address (like you can with an `HREF` tag in HTML). In the steps that follow, you will add the `navigateToURL()` function to the second button to create an e-mail link that will produce a preaddressed e-mail message: mailto:flcs3hot@lynda.com.

7 Return to the **Actions** panel. Select the first line of code, and press **Ctrl+C** (Windows) or **Cmd+C** (Mac) to copy the code. On the next line, paste the code by pressing **Ctrl+V** (Windows) or **Cmd+V** (Mac). In the pasted code, make the following changes: Change **scoop_req** to **contact_req**, and change **theScoop.html** to **mailto:flcs3hot@lynda.com** (make sure the quotation marks are still there).

```
1  var scoop_req:URLRequest = new URLRequest("theScoop.html");
2  var contact_req:URLRequest = new URLRequest("mailto:flcs3hot@lynda.com");
3
4  function scoop(event:MouseEvent):void
5  {
6      navigateToURL(scoop_req, "_blank");
7  }
8  function contact(event:MouseEvent):void
9  {
10
11 }
12
13 scoop_btn.addEventListener(MouseEvent.CLICK, scoop);
14 contact_btn.addEventListener(MouseEvent.CLICK, contact);
```

This ActionScript creates a variable called **contact_req** that has a data type of URLRequest and is a new instance of the **URLRequest** class. Inside the parentheses, mailto:flcs3hot@lynda.com refers to the address that will be displayed in a site visitor's e-mail program when it opens. In the next step, you will use the **navigateToURL()** function again to open a site visitor's e-mail program.

---

8 In the **scoop** function, select the **navigateToURL(scoop_req, "_blank");** code, and copy it by pressing **Ctrl+C** (Windows) or **Cmd+C** (Mac). Paste the code inside the **contact()** function (within the curly braces) by pressing **Ctrl+V** (Windows) or **Cmd+V** (Mac). In the pasted code, change **scoop_req** to **contact_req**.

```
1  var scoop_req:URLRequest = new URLRequest("theScoop.html");
2  var contact_req:URLRequest = new URLRequest("mailto:flcs3hot@lynda.com");
3
4  function scoop(event:MouseEvent):void
5  {
6      navigateToURL(scoop_req, "_blank");
7  }
8  function contact(event:MouseEvent):void
9  {
10     navigateToURL(contact_req, "_blank");
11 }
12
13 scoop_btn.addEventListener(MouseEvent.CLICK, scoop);
14 contact_btn.addEventListener(MouseEvent.CLICK, contact);
```

This ActionScript uses the same **navigateToURL()** function you used in Step 5 to open a site visitor's e-mail program, preaddressed to the URL held in the **contact_req** variable. The only difference between the two URLs used in this exercise is that the e-mail address begins with **mailto:**. To create a link to any e-mail address, make sure the URL for the **URLRequest** instance you create begins with **mailto:** and is followed by the e-mail address to which you want to link.

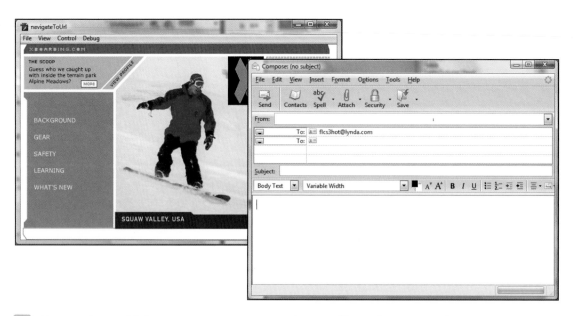

9 Choose **File > Publish Preview > HTML** to open the SWF file in a browser window so you can test the e-mail link. When the browser window opens, click the **CONTACT US** button to test the link.

A new e-mail message window should open in your default mail client when you click the button!

10 When you are finished testing the movie, close your browser window and **navigateToUrl.fla**. You don't need to save your changes.

What Are Frame Labels, and Why Use Them?

Frame labels identify a frame by a name rather than by a number. When you add and delete frames in the movie, the frame numbers change, causing problems in ActionScript where it refers to frame numbers. At the same time, frame labels do not change when frames are added or deleted, keeping your ActionScript viable and working.

In the next exercise, rather than break up the navigation into separate scenes, you will keep all the work in a movie clip and use frame labels to divide the movie clip's **Timeline** into sections.

Plus, you'll use ActionScript to direct the playhead to the appropriate frame label within the **Timeline**. Although you'll be working with frame labels within movie clip **Timelines**, you can include frame labels in the main **Timeline** as well.

Creating a Pop-Up Menu Using Frame Labels

You can create interactive menus in Flash CS3 in many ways. From scrolling menus to animated menus to draggable menus, all you need is a little creativity and a few bits of ActionScript to develop a rich variety of navigation systems. This exercise gives you additional practice with ActionScript and buttons and starts you on your way to creating interactive navigation schemes by teaching you how to develop a basic pop-up menu using frame labels.

---

1 Open **menu_Final.fla** from the **chap_12** folder. This is the finished version of the menu you are going to create. Choose **Control > Test Movie** to preview the movie. Click the different navigation buttons, and notice some of them will reveal a pop-up menu. When you are finished, close the preview window, and close **menu_Final.fla**.

---

2 Open **menu.fla** file from the **chap_12** folder.

This is an unfinished version of the movie you just previewed. Notice there is one layer named **btns**, which contains some navigational buttons.

In this exercise, you will expand the navigation to include a pop-up menu, using frame labels and ActionScript to make this pop-up menu work. In the next exercise, you will build upon what you have learned and take your project a step further by using the same movie clip symbol and adding functionality to the buttons on the menu to load different SWF files into the interface by using the **Loader** class.

As you may have guessed by now, this movie clip contains buttons symbols and graphic symbols, as well as ActionScript, and it will be used over and over throughout the completed project in this book, which is why you're going to use a movie clip symbol over a button symbol or graphic symbol.

---

3 Double-click the menu on the **Stage** to open the movie clip's **Timeline**, and examine how the **mcMenu** movie clip is set up. Choose **Control > Test Movie** to preview the menu. When you are finished previewing the menu, close the preview window.

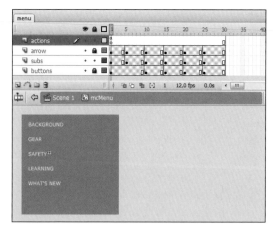

As you click each button, you will see that there are no pop-up menus. You will be creating them next.

Notice there are four layers. The actions layer has a `stop()` method, so the movie will not play. You will control the playback later using ActionScript. The arrow layer has an arrow icon that will be next to the button that the site visitor clicked last. If you move to the different frames in the Timeline, you will see the arrow beside the buttons. The subs layer holds all the submenu buttons. They are already placed for you. Move the playhead to different frames to see them. Note that they are on every keyframe, but on some keyframes they are off the Stage and have an alpha of 0. Keeping them on the Stage makes it easier for you to control them using ActionScript. The bottom layer is the buttons layer. Unlock the layer, and then click each of the buttons and note their instance names. Notice their instance names do not end with **_btn**. This will be more significant when you use frame labels in a later step.

---

4 In the project file, in the **mcMenu** movie clip, click the **Insert Layer** button to add a new layer to the **Timeline**. Rename this layer **labels**. Make sure this layer is above the **arrow** layer.

---

5 In the **Timeline**, select **Frame 1** in the **labels** layer. This is the point when the menu is in the starting position. In the **Property inspector**, type **begin** in the **Frame Label** field.

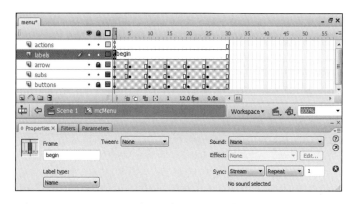

As soon as you add the label name, notice the hollow circle and the flag on the Timeline—visual cues showing you a label exists on this frame.

Tip: Using frame labels is an effective way to organize your Flash movies.

Using frame labels, you can use the `goto...()` functions to navigate through your Timeline using label names instead of numbers. One advantage to using labels is that it is easier for you to find sections of your Flash file that require changes. Another advantage (and an extremely significant one at that) is that if you move frames around along with their labels, you do not have to change your ActionScript. This can save you an unbelievable amount of time (and stress…and maybe even money!).

---

6 Select **Frame 5** on the **labels** layer, and press **F7** to insert a new blank keyframe. In the **Property inspector**, type the name **bkgd** in the **Frame Label** field. Repeat for **Frames 10, 15, 20,** and **25,** adding the names **gear, safety, learning,** and **whatsNew,** respectively. When you are finished, your **Timeline** should match the illustration shown here.

Tip: For a frame label to be visible on the Timeline, there must be enough frames to display the entire name, so by pressing F5, you can add frames and see the name.

Note: Even if you can't see the whole name, the label is still there; you can always tell that by looking for the flag on the frame or by looking at the frame label in the Property inspector.

---

7 Select **Frame 1** in the **actions** layer. Press **F9** (Windows) or **Opt+F9** (Mac) to open the **Actions** panel. In the **Script** pane, after the **stop()** method, create a skeleton for a function called **buttonClick** that you will use to control clicks of the main navigational buttons by typing this:

```
function buttonClick(event:MouseEvent):void
{
}
```

This action creates a skeleton of a function that receives a mouse event. You will write what this function does in the next step.

---

8 Click in the curly braces of the function, and type **gotoAndStop("bkgd");**.

All it takes to navigate to a frame label is to type the label name (in quotation marks, because it is a String) inside a **goto** function, in this case, **gotoAndStop**. This ActionScript tells Flash CS3 to navigate to the **bkgd** frame label. You will attach this function to the BKGD button in the next step.

---

9 After the **buttonClick** function, add an event listener to attach the **buttonClick** function to the BKGD button when a site visitor clicks it by typing this:

```
bkgd.addEventListener(MouseEvent.CLICK,
buttonClick);
```

This ActionScript connects the BKGD button (using **addEventListener**) to the **buttonClick** function. The function will run when a site visitor clicks the button (specified by **MouseEvent.CLICK**).

10 Choose **Control > Test Movie** to preview the movie. Click the **BACKGROUND** button, and watch the arrow on its left side appear. Sweet! Close the preview window when you are done.

Now that your button is working properly with its frame label, you can control the interactivity of the rest of the buttons. One option is to create individual functions for each button. Though this way will work, there is a more effective way. Notice the frame label names, and compare them to the instance names of the navigational buttons. They are the same. If there were a way to get the name of each button when you clicked it, you could create one function that would work for every button! You will learn how to do that in the next step.

---

11 In the `buttonClick` function, replace **"bkgd"** with `event.target.name` (make sure to remove the quotation marks).

This ActionScript does something amazing. It represents the instance name of the button you clicked. Here's how it works: When the `buttonClick` function runs, it receives information about the event that made it run. This information is received in the `buttonClick` function as a variable called **event**. You specified this when you created the function and typed `event:MouseEvent` in parentheses. In the code

you wrote in this step, **event** represents the event that triggered the function—a mouse click. **target** represents the target object that caused the event. **name** is a property of a button that holds its instance name in the form of a String (which is why you do not need to use quotation marks).

---

12 Choose **Control > Test Movie** to preview the movie. Click the **BACKGROUND** button.

Notice the same thing happens as the last time you tested the movie. Now that the code is working properly, you can use this function for all the buttons. You will do that in the next step.

---

13 Close the preview window, and return to the **Actions** panel. After the code you wrote in Step 9, type `gear.addEventListener(MouseEvent.CLICK, buttonClick);`.

14 Repeat Step 13 for the remaining buttons, changing the instance name each time.

Tip: The code should look like `safety.addEventListener(MouseEvent.CLICK, buttonClick);` for each button.

---

15 Choose **Control > Test Movie** to preview the movie. Click the **BACKGROUND** button, and click the rest of the buttons to watch the movie navigate through its **Timeline**. Sweet!

Because you used frame labels and the `event.target.name` code from Step 11, the `buttonClick` function works for every button. Nice! The next task is to disable the button you clicked last, so you cannot click it again. You will do this in the next few steps.

---

16 Close the preview window, and return to the **Actions** panel. In the `buttonClick` function, after the `gotoAndStop` function, type `bkgd.enabled = true;`.

The **enabled** property controls the appearance of buttons. With **enabled** equal to **true**, the user sees a hand icon when they roll over the button. With **enabled** set to **false**, the user sees the arrow-shaped cursor. The next steps are to turn on all the buttons and to turn off the last button clicked. That way, every button will show a hand icon, except the selected button.

---

17 Repeat Step 16 for the remaining buttons, making sure to change the instance name each time.

Tip: The code should look like `gear.enabled = true;`, and so on.

---

18 After the code you wrote in Steps 16 and 17, set the **enabled** property of the button the user clicked to **false** by typing `event.target.enabled = false;`.

This ActionScript turns off the hand icon for the last button the user clicks.

```
1    stop();
2    function buttonClick(event:MouseEvent):void
3    {
4        gotoAndStop(event.target.name);
5        bkgd.enabled = true;
6        gear.enabled = true;
7        safety.enabled = true;
8        learning.enabled = true;
9        whatsNew.enabled = true;
10       event.target.enabled = false;
11   }
12   bkgd.addEventListener(MouseEvent.CLICK, buttonClick);
13   gear.addEventListener(MouseEvent.CLICK, buttonClick);
14   safety.addEventListener(MouseEvent.CLICK, buttonClick);
15   learning.addEventListener(MouseEvent.CLICK, buttonClick);
16   whatsNew.addEventListener(MouseEvent.CLICK, buttonClick);
```

actions : 1

Line 10 of 16, Col 31

---

19 Choose **Control > Test Movie** to preview the movie. Click a button. Roll over the button after you click it, and notice you do not see a hand icon. Great! Close the preview window when you are finished.

Now that you have a nice finishing touch to your button, you are ready to make the buttons load external SWF files using the **Loader** class. You will learn how to do that in the next exercise.

---

20 Close **menu.fla**. You don't need to save your changes.

What Is the Loader Class?

In previous chapters, you learned the differences between the project file (FLA) and the movie file (SWF). In this chapter, you will learn how a SWF file can load other SWF files into itself. This idea is similar to links on an HTML page that replace content with other HTML pages when clicked.

Why would you want to do this in Flash CS3? Large projects can take a long time to download. You can structure your projects so many smaller movies are loaded on demand, which creates a better user experience. You usually create this process by using an ActionScript class called **Loader**.

The **Loader** class can load several different types of external files into Flash movies. The **Loader** class works in conjunction with the **URLRequest** class to access external files. Once you use the **Loader** class to get an external SWF file, you need to place it on the **Stage** using a function called **addChild()**.

What Is addChild?

Many visual objects have something called a **display list**, which is a list of visual objects in a display object container. This is a lot of fancy language for something you already know how to use.

Think of the main **Timeline** of a Flash movie. To create almost any Flash movie, you place artwork on the **Stage**. The elements on the **Stage** of the main **Timeline** or a movie clip make up its display list. The main **Timeline** and movie clips are examples of display object containers, because they can display visual objects.

When you create an object using ActionScript or load one externally using the **Loader** class, you must place that object in a display object container using the **addChild()** function. If you neglect to use the **addChild()** function, you will not see the object you created. This is a common error among people using ActionScript 3.0 and is one of the first things you want to check if you cannot see something you created with ActionScript or loaded externally.

6 | Loading Movies Using the Loader Class

Loading multiple SWFs into a main SWF using the **Loader** class is an efficient way of presenting large Flash CS3 documents. The **Loader** class can load individual SWF files on demand, eliminating the need to load a large file all at once. This exercise shows you how.

1 Open the **Loader** folder in the **chap_12** folder. In it you will see many SWF files and one FLA file. Double-click any of the SWF files to open and preview the artwork in them. These are the SWF files you will be loading into the main FLA file in the steps that follow. When you are finished, close the SWF files.

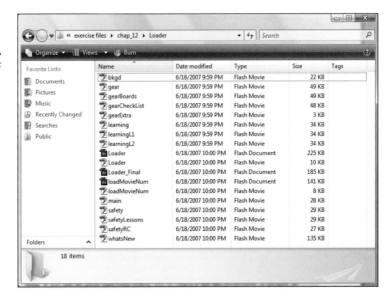

2 Open **Loader.fla** from the **Loader** folder. I created this file to get you started. Choose **Control > Test Movie** to preview the movie. When you are finished previewing the movie, close the preview window.

Notice all you see is an empty interface with the navigation menu. This will serve as the main movie file. In the steps that follow, you will use the **Loader** class to load the external movies you previewed in Step 1 into the main movie.

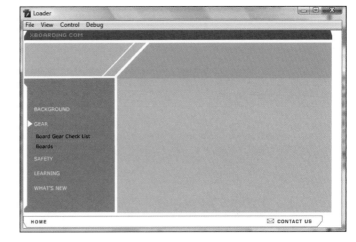

Note: If you get an error message telling you to check whether the file destination is locked or to check whether the file name is not too long, try removing the Read-only option for both chap_12 and its subfolder, Loader.

3 In the project file, select the first keyframe on the **actions** layer, and open the **Actions** panel by choosing **Window > Actions**.

4 In the **Script** pane, type the following:

```
var myLoader:Loader = new Loader();
```

This ActionScript creates a new variable called **myLoader** that has a data type of **Loader** and is a new instance of the **Loader** class. You will use the **load()** method of this **Loader** instance to load an external file in the next step.

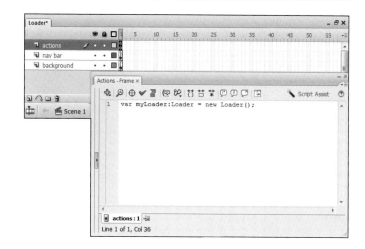

5 On the next line in your code, type the following:

```
myLoader.load(new URLRequest("main.swf"));
```

In this ActionScript, the **load()** function of the **Loader** class is used to load an external SWF file. When you use the **load()** function, you need to tell Flash CS3 the URL or location of the file you want to load, in the form of a **URLRequest** class. Previously in this chapter, you used the **URLRequest** class to link to an HTML page. When you did that, you created the **URLRequest** class on a separate line of code. This ActionScript creates a new instance of the **URLRequest** class with a URL of main.swf and loads that file, all in the same line of code. This is also an acceptable practice.

If you were to test the movie at this point, it would seem like the file is not loading properly. To see the loaded content, you will need to use the **addChild()** function to place the content in the main Timeline's display list. You learned about display lists previously in this chapter.

6 After the code you typed in the previous step, type **addChild(myLoader);**.

This ActionScript adds the **myLoader** instance to the display list of the main Timeline, which will now make the loaded content visible. Because this code is not in a function attached to a button, it will run automatically when the movie plays. You will see the file main.swf over the rest of the content when you preview the movie.

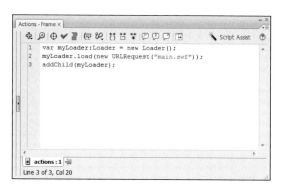

7 Choose **Control > Test Movie** to preview the movie, and watch the file **main.swf** load in over the main content of the movie. Nice! Close the preview window when you are done viewing the movie.

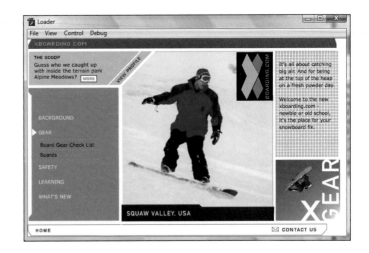

In the next few steps, you will make the `myLoader` instance load files from the navigation menu you made in the previous exercise.

8 Close the **Actions** panel. Choose **Window > Library** to open the **Library** panel, and double-click the **mcMenu** movie clip in the **Library** to enter its **Timeline**. Move the playhead to different keyframes, and click the active buttons on the **Stage**. Also note the names of the frame labels from the previous exercise.

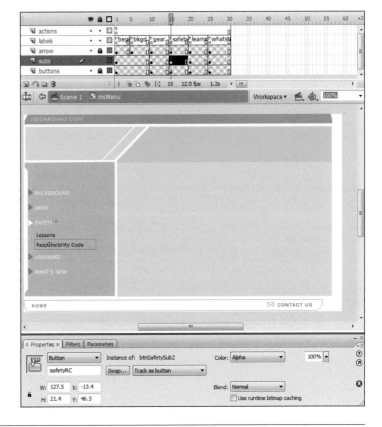

9 Select the first keyframe of the **actions** layer, and open the **Actions** panel by choosing **Window > Actions**. Examine the code. It is the same code you wrote in the previous exercise, with a few additions. Look at lines 21–31. These lines of code create a function called **subClick**, which is connected to all the submenu buttons.

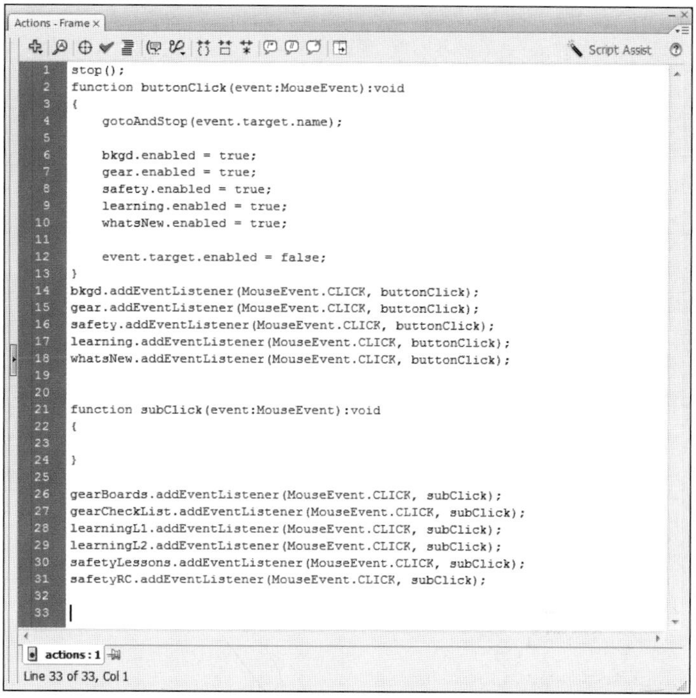

Similar to the previous exercise, you will use the same function for all the submenu buttons.

```
 1  stop();
 2  function buttonClick(event:MouseEvent):void
 3  {
 4      gotoAndStop(event.target.name);
 5
 6      bkgd.enabled = true;
 7      gear.enabled = true;
 8      safety.enabled = true;
 9      learning.enabled = true;
10      whatsNew.enabled = true;
11
12      event.target.enabled = false;
13  }
14  bkgd.addEventListener(MouseEvent.CLICK, buttonClick);
15  gear.addEventListener(MouseEvent.CLICK, buttonClick);
16  safety.addEventListener(MouseEvent.CLICK, buttonClick);
17  learning.addEventListener(MouseEvent.CLICK, buttonClick);
18  whatsNew.addEventListener(MouseEvent.CLICK, buttonClick);
19
20
21  function subClick(event:MouseEvent):void
22  {
23
24  }
25
26  gearBoards.addEventListener(MouseEvent.CLICK, subClick);
27  gearCheckList.addEventListener(MouseEvent.CLICK, subClick);
28  learningL1.addEventListener(MouseEvent.CLICK, subClick);
29  learningL2.addEventListener(MouseEvent.CLICK, subClick);
30  safetyLessons.addEventListener(MouseEvent.CLICK, subClick);
31  safetyRC.addEventListener(MouseEvent.CLICK, subClick);
32
33
```

Line 33 of 33, Col 1

10 Click in the **buttonClick** function, and after all the code in the function, type the following:

this.parent.myLoader.load(new URLRequest(event.target.name + ".swf"));

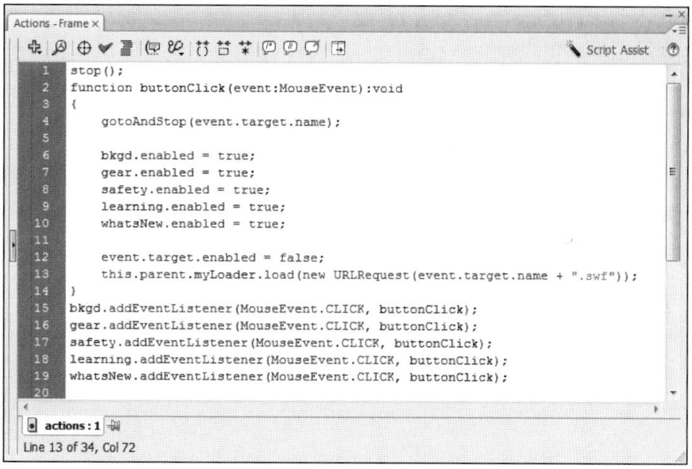

This ActionScript tells Flash CS3 to make the **myLoader** instance on the main Timeline load a file with the same name as the instance name of the button the user clicks, with an extension of .swf.

The **this** keyword represents the object or instance in which the

```
 1  stop();
 2  function buttonClick(event:MouseEvent):void
 3  {
 4      gotoAndStop(event.target.name);
 5
 6      bkgd.enabled = true;
 7      gear.enabled = true;
 8      safety.enabled = true;
 9      learning.enabled = true;
10      whatsNew.enabled = true;
11
12      event.target.enabled = false;
13      this.parent.myLoader.load(new URLRequest(event.target.name + ".swf"));
14  }
15  bkgd.addEventListener(MouseEvent.CLICK, buttonClick);
16  gear.addEventListener(MouseEvent.CLICK, buttonClick);
17  safety.addEventListener(MouseEvent.CLICK, buttonClick);
18  learning.addEventListener(MouseEvent.CLICK, buttonClick);
19  whatsNew.addEventListener(MouseEvent.CLICK, buttonClick);
20
```

Line 13 of 34, Col 72

keyword resides. In this example, this means **mcMenu**. If the **this** keyword were in code on the main Timeline, it would be referring to the main Timeline.

The **parent** keyword tells Flash CS3 to navigate backward one level. Because the **mcMenu** movie clip resides on the main Timeline, it is considered a child of the main Timeline. The main Timeline is considered the parent of the **mcMenu** movie clip. Because the **myLoader** instance resides on the code of the main Timeline, this is the only way to access it.

The URL of the file comes from **event.target.name**, which is the instance name of the button that was clicked and the extension, .swf. The plus sign is used both in Math and with Strings. With Strings, a plus sign is used for something called **concatenation**. This means the string after the plus sign is appended to the string before the plus sign. So the URLs would be bkgd.swf, learning.swf, and so on. Not only do the button instances have the same names as the frame labels, they also have the same names as the files they are supposed to load. This technique allows you to continue to use one function for all your buttons.

11 Choose **Control > Test Movie**. Click each of the top-level navigation buttons to test the movie. When you are finished, close the preview window. You will add ActionScript to the subnavigation buttons in the steps that follow.

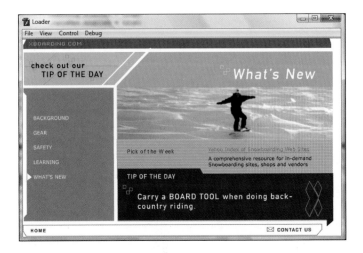

12 In the **Actions** panel, copy the code you wrote in Step 10 by selecting it and pressing **Ctrl+C** (Windows) or **Cmd+C** (Mac). Paste the code in the **subClick** function (on line 24) by pressing **Ctrl+V** (Windows) or **Cmd+V** (Mac).

Because the submenu buttons also have the same instance names as the files they are supposed to load (minus the .swf extension), the same code will work. Nice!

```
10        whatsNew.enabled = true;
11
12        event.target.enabled = false;
13        this.parent.myLoader.load(new URLRequest(event.target.name + ".swf"));
14    }
15  bkgd.addEventListener(MouseEvent.CLICK, buttonClick);
16  gear.addEventListener(MouseEvent.CLICK, buttonClick);
17  safety.addEventListener(MouseEvent.CLICK, buttonClick);
18  learning.addEventListener(MouseEvent.CLICK, buttonClick);
19  whatsNew.addEventListener(MouseEvent.CLICK, buttonClick);
20
21
22  function subClick(event:MouseEvent):void
23  {
24      this.parent.myLoader.load(new URLRequest(event.target.name + ".swf"));
25  }
26
27  gearBoards.addEventListener(MouseEvent.CLICK, subClick);
28  gearCheckList.addEventListener(MouseEvent.CLICK, subClick);
29  learningL1.addEventListener(MouseEvent.CLICK, subClick);
30  learningL2.addEventListener(MouseEvent.CLICK, subClick);
31  safetyLessons.addEventListener(MouseEvent.CLICK, subClick);
```

13 Close the **Actions** panel, and choose **Control > Test Movie**. Click each of the top-level navigation buttons to test the movie. Then click each of the submenu buttons, and watch all the movies load. Sweet!

The last step is to make the HOME button have the main.swf file load, which you will do next.

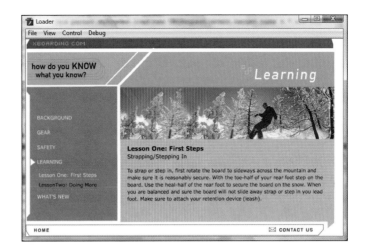

14 Close the preview window, and return to Flash. In the **Timeline**, return to the main **Timeline** by clicking **Scene 1**. Double-click the **HOME** button on the **Stage** to enter its **Timeline**. Select the button, and note the instance name of the button in the **Property inspector**. Select the first keyframe on the **actions** layer, and open the **Actions** panel by choosing **Window > Actions**.

Take a look at the code already written for you. This code is a skeleton of a function for the HOME button. All you have to do is add similar code to Step 10 to make the button work. You will do that in the next step.

15 Click in the `home()` function, and press **Ctrl+V** (Windows) or **Cmd+V** (Mac) to paste the code. Then, in the pasted code, change `event.target.name + ".swf"` to `"main.swf"` (be sure to include the quotation marks).

This will make the `myLoader` instance on the main Timeline load main.swf. If choosing Edit > Paste did not paste any code, type *this.parent.myLoader.load(new URLRequest("main.swf"));*.

```
function home(event:MouseEvent):void
{
    this.parent.myLoader.load(new URLRequest("main.swf"));
}

home_btn.addEventListener(MouseEvent.CLICK, home);
```

Notice this code is still using `this.parent`, even though it is inside a different movie clip than mcMenu. Because the Home movie clip is also on the main Timeline, the main Timeline is also its parent.

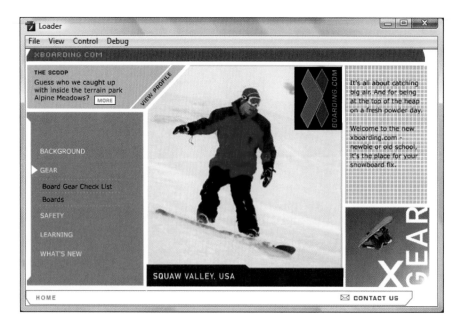

16 Choose **Control > Test Movie** to preview the movie. Click a navigational button, and then click the **HOME** button to return to the **main.swf** file. Nice!

---

17 When you are finished, close the preview window, and close **Loader.fla**. You don't need to save your changes.

That's a wrap on this chapter. A lot of information was covered in the exercises, and if anything isn't crystal clear, you can always go back and review it. Take a well-deserved break, and then get ready for the next chapter.

13

Working with Text

When working with text in Adobe Flash CS3 Professional, you have many options beyond simply selecting the **Text** tool and typing text on the **Stage**. You can create horizontal or vertical text, change the text attributes such as **kerning** (spacing between characters) and line spacing, apply transformations such as rotation and skew, and much more. As you go through this chapter, you will learn to make text scroll, and you'll create text fields where users can input information. Also included in Flash CS3, **Flash Type** is an improved font-rendering technology that renders smaller text sizes more clearly. Flash CS3 also includes a spelling checker and supports CSS (**C**ascading **S**tyle **S**heets), which lets you create text styles you can apply to HTML (**H**yper**T**ext **M**arkup **L**anguage), making design across HTML and Flash CS3 content more consistent.

Flash CS3 lets you create three types of text elements: static text, dynamic text, and input text. You'll learn about these different types of text elements and try them out with hands-on exercises.

Understanding Text Field Types

The **Text** tool can create three types of text: static text, dynamic text, or input text.

Static text displays information that does not change, such as label buttons, forms, or navigation components. **Dynamic text** shows up-to-date information generated automatically from an external text file or a database. Use dynamic text when you want to automatically show information that gets updated often. **Input text** is text the user inputs, such as a user name and password, forms, and surveys. As you go through the exercises in this chapter, you will get hands-on experience with each of these text types.

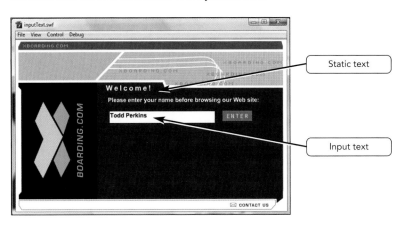

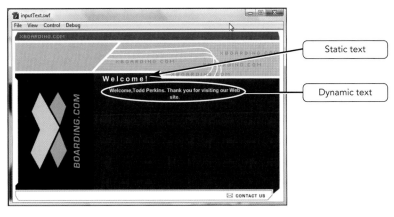

TIP:

Fixing a Text Field Box That Extends Too Far

If, by accident, you create a text field that continues off the **Stage**, don't worry. Just choose **View > Magnification > Fit in Window** to make the entire text field visible. You can then force the text to wrap downward by either placing the cursor in the text block and adding your own line breaks or by dragging the text field handle to create a defined text field that will fit on the **Stage**. When you create a defined text field, the text within that field will wrap to fit the field size.

Creating, Modifying, and Formatting Text

In Flash CS3, you have a lot of control over the attributes of type. By using the **Property inspector**, you can change, preview, and adjust text with a few clicks. This section gives you a close look at most of the available settings.

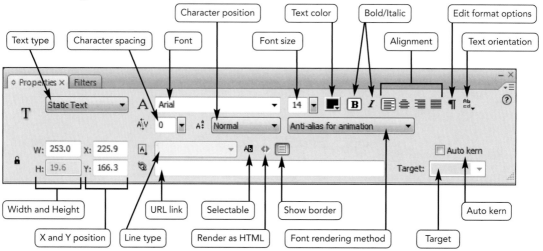

As soon as you select the **Text** tool, the **Property inspector** displays the available text attributes (with the exception of the **Width** and **Height** and **X** and **Y** controls, which require a selection first). The chart that follows details each of these items:

Text Attributes Defined	
Attribute	**Description**
Text type	Lets you choose from one of three text fields (Static, Dynamic, or Input Text). Each text type has its own associated options that will appear in the **Property inspector** when that text field type is selected. **Static Text** is the default.
Font	Displays the name of the current font. The menu lists all the available fonts. As you scroll through the font list, Flash CS3 displays a preview of what each font will look like.
Character spacing	Lets you adjust the space between characters in selected text. Click the arrow next to the **Character spacing** field, and use the slider to increase or decrease the amount of space between characters.
Character position	**Normal**: Resets characters to the baseline. **Superscript**: Shifts characters above the baseline. **Subscript**: Shifts characters below the baseline.

continues on next page

Text Attributes Defined *continued*

Attribute	Description
Font size (font height)	Displays the current font size in points. Click the arrow to the right of the **Font size** field, and use the slider to adjust the size of the font.
Auto kern	Controls the spacing between pairs of characters. Selecting this option will automatically use the font's built-in kerning information. (See the "To Kern or Not to Kern?" sidebar following this chart for more information on kerning.)
Font rendering method	Default text in Flash CS3 is anti-aliased for readability, meaning the edges of the text are smoothed. Five font-rendering options are available in this pop-up menu. **Device fonts** uses fonts that are currently installed on the user's computer, producing a smaller SWF file. **Bitmap text** (no anti-alias) produces sharp text edges, without anti-aliasing, resulting in a larger SWF file because font outlines must be included in the SWF file. **Anti-alias for animation** produces anti-alias text that animates smoothly, and in some cases, faster. This option also produces a larger SWF file size because font outlines are included in the SWF file. **Anti-alias for readability** uses the advanced anti-aliasing engine, which provides the highest-quality, most legible text. This option produces the largest SWF file size because it includes font outlines and also special anti-aliasing information. **Custom anti-alias** is the same as **Anti-alias for readability**, but it provides options for visually manipulating the anti-aliasing to produce the best possible appearance for new or uncommon fonts.
Text color	Lets you change the color of the type. **Note:** For text blocks, you can use only solid colors, not gradients. If you want to use gradients, you have to break the text apart, which will convert it to a shape.
Bold	Bolds the selected type.
Italic	Italicizes the selected type.
Text orientation	Changes the direction of the text. You can choose **Horizontal**; **Vertical, Left to Right**; and **Vertical, Right to Left**.
Alignment	Controls how the selected text will be aligned: **Align Left**, **Align Center**, **Align Right**, or **Justify**.
Rotation	Lets you have more control over vertical text and change its rotation. This option is available only for vertical text.

continues on next page

Text Attributes Defined *continued*

Attribute	Description
Indent	Accessible in the **Format Options** panel. Controls the distance between the margin of a paragraph and the beginning of the first line of a paragraph.
Line/Column spacing	Accessible in the **Format Options** panel. Line spacing (also referred to as **leading**) controls the spacing between lines of type (horizontal text) or between vertical columns (vertical text).
Width and Height	Displays the width and height of a selected text field.
X and Y position	Displays the X and Y position of the top left of a selected text box, relative to the **Stage**. The top left of the **Stage** is 0, 0.
URL link	Creates a hyperlink attached to selected text. In effect, this option creates a button that will link to an internal or external HTML file, without the need to create a button symbol. Flash automatically adds a dotted line under the linked text in the FLA file. Note, however, that hyperlinks created using this feature will not carry any visual feedback (such as an underline) in the SWF file, although when previewed in a browser, the hand icon will appear when the user moves the cursor over the linked text. You learned a better way to create a hyperlink in Chapter 12, *"ActionScript Basics."*
Line type	Lets you choose among **Single line** (displaying the text on one line), **Multiline** (displaying the text in multiple lines with word wrap), **Multiline no wrap** (displaying the text in multiple lines), and **Password**. This option is available only for dynamic and input text. **Password** is only available with input text.
Selectable	Allows a user to select your text and copy it.
Render as HTML	Preserves rich text formatting, including fonts, hyperlinks, and bold with the appropriate HTML tags. You will learn to use this option in Exercise 4.
Show border around text	When selected, displays a white background with a black border for the text field. This option is available only for dynamic and input text fields.
Var (Variable)	For dynamic or input text only, specifies a variable name for the selected text. Variables can be used with ActionScript 2.0.
Target	Used in conjunction with the **URL link** feature. When assigning a hyperlink to selected text, you can also specify a target. Choosing a target lets you specify the URL (**U**niform **R**esource **L**ocator) to load in a new window or to a specific Web page layout that utilizes framesets.

NOTE:

To Kern or Not to Kern?

When font sets are created, the individual characters might look great all by themselves, but some letter combinations may be spaced too close or too far from each other. To solve this problem, many fonts are created with additional instructions about spacing between specific characters. This is known as **kerning** information.

To illustrate this point, I created two text blocks (one blue and one red) and placed them in the same position, with the blue text on top of the red text. I selected the **Auto kern** check box in the **Property inspector** for the blue text, and I left the red text with its default spacing. Notice how the red text shows through in some spots. This indicates that the **Auto kern** feature has changed the spacing of the blue text.

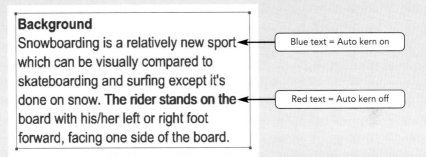

When you create horizontal text, kerning sets the horizontal distance between characters. When you create vertical text, kerning sets the vertical distance between characters.

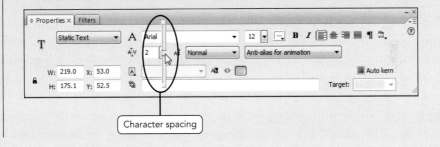

1 | Working with Static Text and Device Fonts

Static text is best used in situations where the text will not change, such as buttons, labels, forms, and navigation. When you add static text to your movie, by default Flash CS3 will embed the font outlines in the SWF file for the font you're using. Depending on the font you choose and the amount of text you use, the font outlines can add to the overall file size of the SWF. If your goal is to keep file sizes as small as possible, use device fonts.

Device fonts are fonts that won't embed themselves in the SWF file. Instead, you choose a device font for the users' machines to display, such as _serif, _sans, or _typewriter, and the users' machines will display that device font for the static text. Using device fonts reduces the file sizes because the font outlines are not embedded in the SWF file. Device fonts can be sharper and more legible than exported font outlines at sizes smaller than 10 points. However, because device fonts are not embedded, text may look different than expected on user systems that do not have an installed font corresponding to the device font. At the end of this exercise, I discuss the pros and cons of using static text and device fonts, but first you'll begin with learning how to check the spelling in your projects.

1 Copy the **chap_13** folder from the **Flash HOT CD-ROM** to your desktop. Open **staticText.fla** from the **chap_13** folder. Read the copy in the interface.

Notice any misspelled words? Next you'll check your project file for any spelling errors and correct them with the spelling checker.

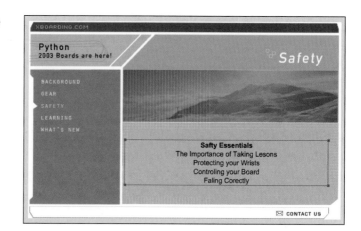

2 Choose **Text > Check Spelling** to open the **Check Spelling** dialog box. Click **Change** to correctly spell the words **Safety, Lessons, Controlling, Falling**, and **Correctly**. Click **OK** when you are prompted with the **Flash CS3** dialog box.

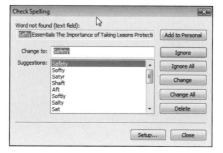

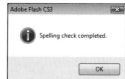

Note: The spelling checker works only with editable text. Because it doesn't work with text that has been broken apart (which you learned about in Chapter 5, "*Shape Tweening*"), be sure to spell-check your movie before you break apart any text.

You can modify the spelling setup by choosing Text > Spelling Setup or by clicking Setup in the Check Spelling dialog box.

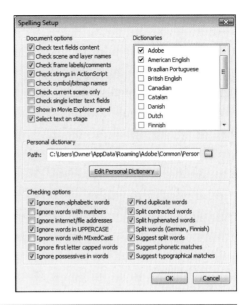

3 Read the copy in the interface again.

Notice all the misspelled words are now spelled correctly! With your movie free of spelling errors, next you will learn about static text and device fonts.

4 Select the **Selection** tool in the **Tools** panel. On the **Stage**, select the block of text. Then choose **Window > Properties > Properties** to open the **Property inspector** (if it is not already open.)

Note that the Font rendering method menu displays Anti-alias for animation.

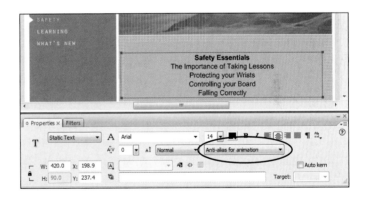

5 Choose **Control > Test Movie** to preview the text. When the preview window opens, choose **View > Bandwidth Profiler**. When you are done viewing the **Bandwidth Profiler**, close the preview window, and return to the project file.

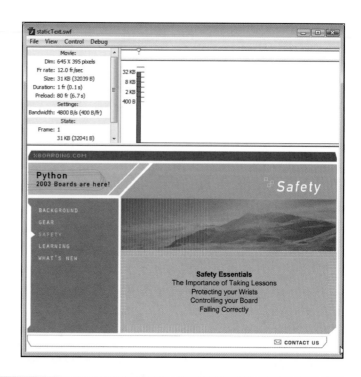

The Bandwidth Profiler appears at the top of the preview window and, among other things, tells you the file size of your SWF file. Currently, the file size is about 30 KB. This file size accounts for all the graphics and font outlines being used in this movie.

In the following steps, you will modify the text block by using a device font to make the file size smaller.

N O T E :

What Is the Bandwidth Profiler?

The **Bandwidth Profiler**, a feature in the **Test Movie** environment, shows useful information including movie dimensions, frame rate, size, duration, preload, bandwidth, and frame.

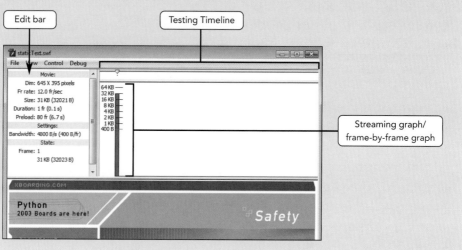

Bandwidth Profiler Information

Option	What It Shows
Dim	The width and height (dimensions) of the movie.
Fr rate	The speed at which the movie plays based on the frames per second.
Size	The file size, in kilobytes (KB), of the movie or scene you are testing. The number in parentheses represents the size in bytes.
Duration	The total number of frames in your movie or scene. The number in parentheses represents the length of your movie or scene in seconds rather than frames.
Preload	The number of frames that need to be downloaded before the movie begins playing.
Bandwidth	The speed used to simulate an actual download when used with the **Simulate Download** command.
Frame	The top number shows the current frame position of the playhead. The bottom number shows the file size for the frame where the playhead is positioned. The number in parentheses represents the total file size. You can get individual frame information by moving the playhead in the **Bandwidth Profiler Timeline**, which is especially helpful for detecting frames that have a lot of content.

6 With the **Selection** tool, click the text block to select it. In the **Property inspector**, choose **Use device fonts** in the **Font rendering method** menu.

Flash includes three device fonts: _sans (similar to Helvetica or Arial), _serif (similar to Times Roman), and _typewriter (similar to Courier). With this selection, during SWF file playback, Flash will select the first device font it locates on the user's system and will render this text using this font. Because device fonts are not embedded, the resulting SWF file should be smaller. Next, you will test the movie again to check for any change in file size.

7 Choose **Control > Test Movie** to preview the text. The **Bandwidth Profiler** should still be visible above the preview window. If it's not, choose **View > Bandwidth Profiler**. Notice the size is now about 26 KB, whereas before setting your text to a device font, the file size was 30 KB, a savings of 4 KB!

Four kilobytes might not sound like much, but if you're designing a banner ad and your target file size is a paltry 10 KB, 4 KB is 40 percent of the total!

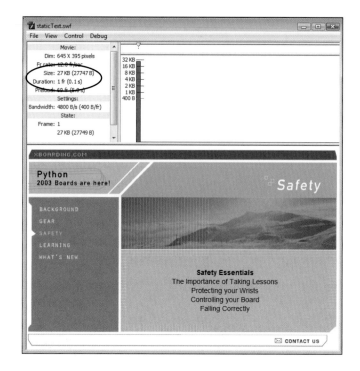

8 Choose **View > Bandwidth Profiler** to hide the **Bandwidth Profiler**, and close the preview window. Close **staticText.fla**. You don't need to save your changes

Embedded Fonts vs. Device Fonts

When you select a specific font for a text block in the **Property inspector**, Flash CS3 automatically takes all the font information (the font's description, kerning, leading, and so on) and embeds it in the exported movie. This is what is known as an **embedded font**. The capability to embed fonts makes Flash CS3 a great platform for using unusual fonts in movies because the user doesn't need to have the same fonts installed on their computers to see the results. Flash CS3 automatically includes all the necessary information.

The downside to using embedded fonts is that they increase the file size of the SWF. Also, some fonts cannot be exported with the movie because Flash CS3 cannot embed the font's outline, which may happen because the font was not installed properly or because the computer has only the screen font. The font may display properly in the production file (FLA) yet falter when the movie is exported (SWF) because the actual font to which the screen font refers cannot be found when the movie is published. To check for this, you can choose **View > Preview Mode > Anti-Alias Text** (which is already selected by default) to preview the text. Rough or jagged text is an indication that the text will not be exported when the SWF file is published.

Because the font outlines will be embedded in the SWF file when you publish your movie, all the fonts in the Flash CS3 document must be installed on your computer. If you receive an FLA from a friend or colleague who uses a font not installed on your computer, an error message informs you that a substitute font will be used in its place. At this point, you have two options. You can allow Flash CS3 to replace the font with a default replacement (click the **Use Default** button), or you can replace the font with a font installed on your computer (click the **Choose Substitute** button).

Device fonts were created as a solution this issue. They are special fonts that will not be embedded in the exported movie, therefore creating smaller SWF files. Rather than using an embedded font, the Flash Player displays the text using the closest match on a user's computer to the device font.

The drawback to device fonts is that when users don't have a similar font installed on their systems, they might see text that bears little resemblance to the text you see on your machine. To combat this concern, Flash CS3 includes three built-in device fonts to help produce results closer to what you expect. These fonts are all available in the **Type** pop-up menu, along with the other fonts:

- **_sans:** Similar to Helvetica or Arial

- **_serif:** Similar to Times Roman

- **_typewriter:** Similar to Courier

Anti-aliasing

Anti-aliasing refers to blurring the edges to make the text appear smooth. Most digital artists prefer the way anti-aliased text looks, but at small sizes the blurred edges make the text appear fuzzy and hard to read. For text that is 10 point or smaller, aliased text is sharper and easier to read because the edges of the text are not blurred.

Aliased Text vs. Anti-Aliased Text	
Aliased Text	**Anti-Aliased Text**
XBOARD	**XBOARD**
Aliased text at large sizes appears jaggy. The edges of the text lack the smoothing effect.	Anti-aliased text at large sizes appears smooth because the edges are blurred to smooth the text. Anti-aliased text works best with large font sizes.
Aliased text at small sizes is sharper and easier to read. Aliased text works best on sizes 10 point or smaller.	Anti-aliased text at small sizes is fuzzy and hard to read because the smoothing effect on the edges causes the text to become blurry.

Flash Type

Flash CS3 provides improved WYSIWYG (**W**hat **Y**ou **S**ee **I**s **W**hat **Y**ou **G**et) or a visual method of text rendering, referred to as **Flash Type**, which is especially effective in making smaller font sizes appear clearer and more readable. Flash Type works in both the Flash authoring application and in Flash Player 9. This improved text rendering is automatically turned on whenever Flash Player 8 or newer is the selected version of the player.

Warning: Flash Type may cause a slight delay when loading movies with a large number of fonts and may also cause an increase in the Flash Player's memory usage.

2 | Using Small Type and Aliased Text

When working with small type (10 point or smaller), the text might become difficult to read because of the anti-aliasing that is automatically applied to vector shapes, including type, in Flash CS3. Anti-aliasing is a blurring, or smoothing, of the edges of vector shapes and text. In most cases, anti-aliasing improves the appearance of a shape because it gives its edges a smooth appearance. However, the blurring generated by anti-aliasing can make small text hard to read. Anti-aliasing has been improved for users with Flash Player 7 or newer for static, dynamic, and input text, especially for very small text.

1 Open the **aliasText.fla** file from the **chap_13** folder. Choose **Control > Test Movie** to preview the text blocks. When you're finished, close the preview window.

Notice the two text blocks side by side. Both text blocks have the same text attributes. Notice that both text blocks look the same and are a little hard to read, which is caused by blurriness generated by the anti-aliasing applied to the text blocks.

2 Select the text block on the right. In the **Property inspector**, choose **Bitmap text (no anti-alias)** in the **Font rendering method** pop-up menu.

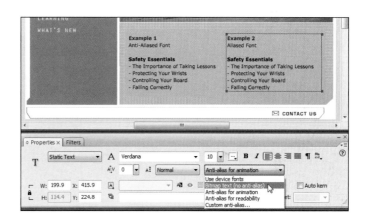

Notice how the text block on the right immediately appears sharper, crisper, and easier to read compared to the text block on the left.

3 Test the movie once more by choosing **Control > Test Movie**.

Notice the text block on the right is still much easier to read! You can use Bitmap text (no anti-alias) with static, dynamic, and input text fields. However, if a user does not have version 7 or newer of the Flash Player plug-in, only static text will appear aliased. Dynamic or input text fields will still appear anti-aliased.

4 Close the preview window. Select the text block on the left. In the **Property inspector**, choose **Anti-Alias for readability** in the **Font rendering method** pop-up menu.

5 Test the movie once more by choosing **Control > Test Movie**.

Notice how the text block on the left appears much sharper, crisper, and easier to read. This is an anti-alias setting in Flash CS3 that is especially useful for making text smaller than 11 point easier to read.

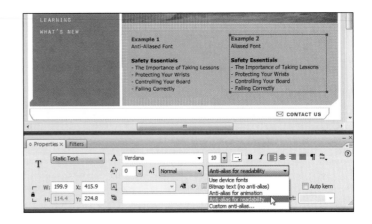

6 Close the preview window, and close **aliasText.fla**. You don't need to save your changes.

3 | Loading Text into Dynamic Text Fields

Dynamic text is best used for information that needs to be updated often, such as news, weather reports, or company information. You can use a bit of ActionScript and a dynamic text field to store an external file holding updated text. Flash CS3 is a robust program for handling this type of data-driven content coming from a database or an external file. This exercise takes you through these steps and teaches you how to load a text file (TXT) directly into a dynamic text field.

1 Open the **textFileLearning.txt** file from the **chap_13** folder.

Notice this is not a Flash CS3 file, but a TXT file, that will open in the default text editor on your computer. (You might need to turn on word wrapping so you can see all the text at once.) I created this TXT file to get you started.

2 Notice this is a simple plain-text file. In previous versions of Flash, you had to give text in an external file a variable name. Using ActionScript 3.0, you can load this text into a text field while your Flash movie is playing.

3 Save and close the text file. Make sure you save it in the **chap_13** folder, because Flash CS3 will be looking for it here in later steps.

4 In Flash CS3, open the **dynamicText.fla** file from the **chap_13** folder.

Notice this file contains one layer with a background image. You will add the dynamic text box next.

5 On the **Timeline**, add a new layer by clicking the **Insert Layer** button, and rename this layer **holder**.

6 Select the **Text** tool in the **Tools** panel. In the **Property inspector**, choose **Dynamic Text**, choose **Multiline**, and click **Show border around text**. Make sure **Font color** is set to **black**, **Font type** is set to **Verdana**, and **Font size** is set to **10**. Choose **Anti-alias for animation** in the **Font rendering method** pop-up menu.

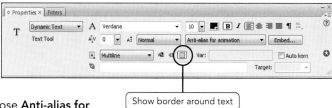

Show border around text

When you draw the text field on the Stage (which you will do next), these settings will create a dynamic text field with a white background and a black border that can support multiple lines of text that will wrap.

7 With the **holder** layer selected, click and drag on the **Stage** to create a text field.

Tip: After you draw the text field, you can drag the handles of the dynamic text field to resize the text field, if necessary.

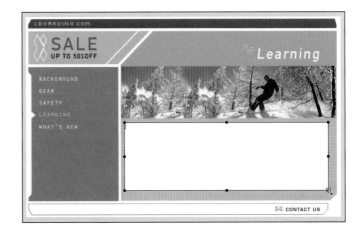

8 In the **Property inspector**, give the text field the instance name **content_txt**. You must give a text field an instance name in order to communicate with it via ActionScript. This is an important step in loading text from an external file.

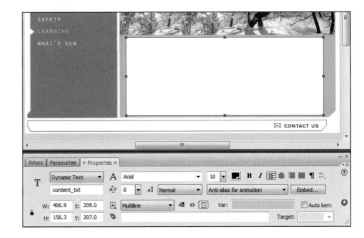

9 Click the **Insert Layer** button below the **Timeline** to add a layer. Rename the layer **actions**. Make sure the **actions** layer is above all other layers. In the **actions** layer, select **Frame 1**. Choose **Window > Actions** to open the **Actions** panel.

10 Click the triangle separating the panes to close the **Actions toolbox** and the **Script navigator** panes. Make sure the tab at the top of the **Actions panel** reads **Actions – Frame**. Make sure **Script Assist** mode is turned **off**. Click in the **Script pane**, and type the following:

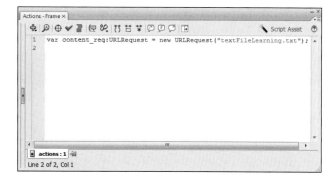

```
var content_req:URLRequest = new
URLRequest("textFileLearning.txt");
```

Don't forget the quotation marks.

This ActionScript tells Flash CS3 to create a variable called **content_req** that has a data type of **URLRequest** and is equal to a new instance of the **URLRequest** class. When you create a new instance of the **URLRequest** class, you need to tell Flash CS3 the name and location (or URL) of the file you want to load, in the form of a String. That is why the file name of the text file is in quotation marks. Essentially, this line of code tells Flash CS3 that textFileLearning.txt is the name of a file.

---

11 Press **Enter** (Windows) or **Return** (Mac) on your keyboard to go to the next line in your code, and then type the following:

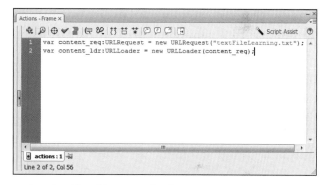

```
var content_ldr:URLLoader = new
URLLoader(content_req);
```

This ActionScript tells Flash CS3 to create a new instance of the **URLLoader** class called **content_ldr**. The **URLLoader** class loads data from a file. When you create an instance of the **URLLoader** class, you must associate it with a file—specifically, a **URLRequest**. Put the name of your **URLRequest** instance inside the parentheses after new **URLLoader**.

---

12 Press **Enter** (Windows) or **Return** (Mac) on your keyboard to go to the next line in your code, and then type the following:

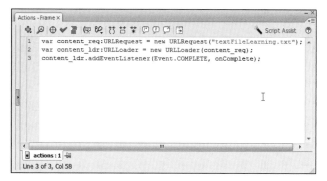

```
content_ldr.addEventListener
(Event.COMPLETE, onComplete);
```

This ActionScript tells the **URLLoader** you created in the previous step to "listen" for when the file is finished loading into the Flash Player and is ready to use. The event for the completion of loaded content is called **Event.COMPLETE**. When the file is loaded and ready to use, Flash CS3 will run the **onComplete()** function.

13 Press **Enter** (Windows) or **Return** (Mac) on your keyboard to go to the next line of code, and then type the following:

```
function
onComplete(event:Event):void
{
  content_txt.text =
event.target.data;
}
```

This ActionScript tells Flash CS3 to create a function called **onComplete**, which will run (as you specified in the previous step) when the text file is finished loading into Flash CS3. The **onComplete** function receives the **COMPLETE** event (as specified in the previous step), which you have called event and has the data type of **Event** (shown in the parentheses of the code). The **onComplete()** function also receives information about the event that triggered it, including the data that was loaded from the text file. This information is accessed using the code **event.target.data**.

---

14 Press **Ctrl+Enter** (Windows) or **Cmd+Return** (Mac) to test the movie.

The text in the text file is loaded into the text field.

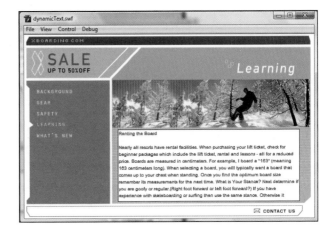

---

15 Close the preview window. Save your **dynamicText.fla** file by choosing **File > Save**. Close the file.

---

16 Minimize Flash CS3 for a moment. Open **textFileLearning.txt** from the **chap_13** folder. After the text **Renting the Board**, type **and Other Accessories**. Save the text file. Now look in the **chap_13** folder on your desktop. Notice the **dynamicText.swf** file.

17 Double-click the **dynamicText.swf** file to open it in the **Flash Player**.

Notice the changes you made to the TXT file in Step 16 have been updated in the SWF file without opening the production file (dynamicText.fla)!

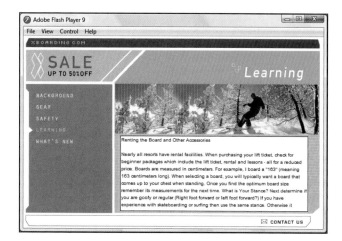

18 When you're done, close the **dynamicText.swf** file, but keep the **textFileLearning.txt** file open. You'll format this text in the following exercise.

So far the text loaded into the dynamic text field has been unformatted (no paragraph breaks, bolding, and so forth). You'll learn how to format the loaded text with HTML next.

NOTE:

Changing Character Attributes

The text that loads into the dynamic text field will take on all the character attributes that are applied to the field within the **Property inspector**. You can quickly change the way the text is displayed in the SWF file by making modifications to the text properties in the **Property inspector**. First, select the dynamic text field. Next, change the font name, the font height, and the font color. You can even deselect the **Show border around text** option to remove the white background from the text. Test the movie again, and you will see a completely different look for your text field!

4 | Working with Dynamic Text and HTML

In the previous exercise, you created a dynamic text field that displayed the content of an external text file. In this exercise, you will go one step further by changing the dynamic text field so that Flash CS3 recognizes and preserves HTML formatting applied to the content in the external text file.

1 If you just completed Exercise 3, **textFileLearning.txt** should still be open. If it's not, open it from the **chap_13** folder.

NOTE:

Dynamic Text HTML Support

Flash CS3 supports the following HTML tags in dynamic and input text fields:
`<a>` = anchor, **`<b>`** = bold, **`<font color>`** = font color, **`<font face>`** = typeface,
`<font size>` = font size, **`<i>`** = italic, **`<img>`** = image, **`<li>`** = list item, **`<p>`** = paragraph,
`<br>` = line break, **`<u>`** = underline, and **`<a href="…">`** = hyperlinks.

Flash CS3 also supports the following HTML attributes in dynamic and input text fields: `leftmargin`, `rightmargin`, `align`, `indent`, and `leading`.

You will add some of these tags in the next few steps.

2 Add bold HTML tags around the words **Renting the Board and Other Accessories**, and add one line break tag so it reads **`<b>Renting the Board and Other Accessories</b>`**. Save your changes, and keep the file open.

By making a small change to the ActionScript you wrote in the previous exercise, you will see the HTML-based text file loaded into the same dynamic text box. You will do this next.

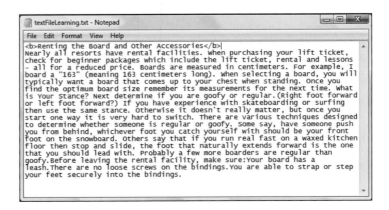

3 Open the **dynamicText.fla** file from the **chap_13** folder. This is the same FLA file you worked with in the previous exercise.

4 Click the first keyframe of the **actions** layer, and choose **Window > Actions** to open the **Actions** panel. Insert your cursor on Line 6 before **content_txt.text**, and change it to **content_txt.htmlText**.

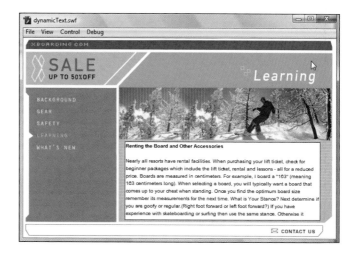

5 Choose **Control > Test Movie** to test your movie. Notice that Flash CS3 recognized the HTML formatting you made in the text file. When you are done viewing your changes, close the preview window.

You will add more HTML formatting to the textFileLearning.txt file next.

Note: In the previous exercise, you previewed the changes you made to the textFileLearning.txt file by opening the dynamicText.swf file. For ease of workflow, you will now preview your changes using Control > Test Movie and creating the SWF file again from the production file (dynamicText.fla). This minimizes going back and forth from the Flash CS3 application to the desktop, and vice versa.

6 In the **textFileLearning.txt** file, add font color HTML tags around the words **lift ticket, rental and lessons** so it reads **<font color="#3399FF">lift ticket, rental and lessons</font>**.

7 Add italic HTML tags around the words **reduced** so it reads **<i>reduced</i>**. Save your changes, and leave the file open.

You will preview your work next.

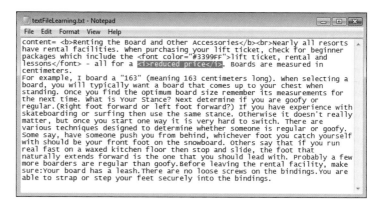

8 Choose **Control > Test Movie** to test your movie again. Notice that Flash CS3 recognized the additional HTML formatting you made in the text file. When you're finished, close the preview window.

You will add a bit more HTML formatting to the extFileLearning.txt file next.

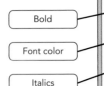

Bold

Font color

Italics

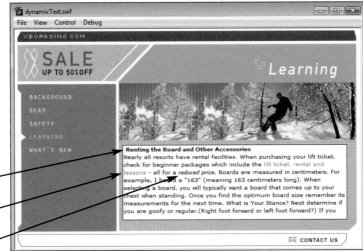

9 To break this large block of text up into smaller, more readable chunks, add five line breaks (**
) to the locations in **textFileLearning.txt, as shown in the illustration here.

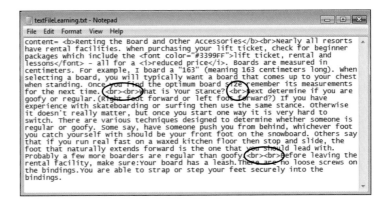

10 To make the last three sentences of the copy more readable, add list item HTML tags (**<li>**) to the locations shown in the illustration here. Save your changes, and close the file.

You will preview your new changes next.

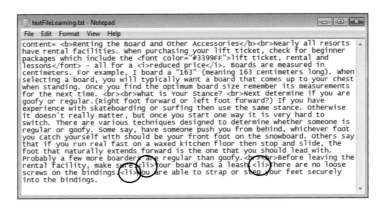

11 Choose **Control > Test Movie** to test your movie.

Notice that Flash CS3 recognized all the HTML formatting you made in the text file! There is, however, some missing content below the edge of the text box.

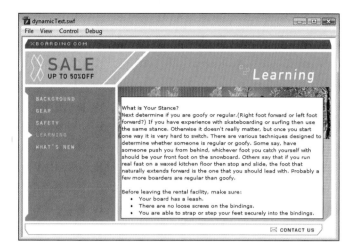

12 Save your changes to **dynamicText.fla**. Keep the file open if you plan to now view the **scrollableText.mov** file and complete the next part of the exercise.

VIDEO: | **scrollableText.mov**

If the user has a scroll wheel mouse, they can click in the text field and scroll down. However, to let the user control this via a scroll bar or other mechanism, you need to add buttons to the interface and then add some ActionScript. To learn how to do this, view the **scrollableText.mov** video in the **videos** folder on the **Flash HOT CD-ROM**.

5 | Working with Input Text

Now that you've worked with static and dynamic text fields, it's time to explore the last remaining text field type: input text. **Input text** fields, as the name implies, let users type text in them, much like an HTML form. If you've ever purchased a product online, you had to give the vendor your name, address, credit card number, and so forth. You typed that information in an input text field. In this exercise, you will learn how to use an input text field to create an area for visitors to type their names. Then you will use that name, in combination with some other text, to populate a dynamic text field.

---

1 Open the **inputText.fla** file from the **chap_13** folder.

Notice this file has one layer with a background image on it.

---

2 Click the **Insert Layer** button four times to add four new layers above the **background** layer. Starting from the top, name the four new layers **actions**, **enter_btn**, **text**, and **name field**.

You will be adding the input text field, some text, a button, and actions to these layers in the following steps. Below the text *Welcome!*, you will enter in a little bit of text and create an input text field. The input text field is where the visitor to your Web site will type his or her name. Later in this exercise, you will use that name in a dynamic text field by adding some ActionScript.

---

3 On the **Timeline**, select the text layer. In the **Tools** panel, select the **Text** tool. In the **Property inspector**, set **Text type** to **Static Text**, **Font** to

Arial, **Font size** to **14**, and **Text color** to **white** and **bold**. Set **Text alignment** to **Align Left**, and select the **Auto kern** option. Set **Font rendering method** to **Anti-alias for animation**.

---

4 Click the **Stage** to create a text block, and type **Please enter your name before browsing our Web site:**. Reposition and resize the text block with the **Selection** tool if you need to do so.

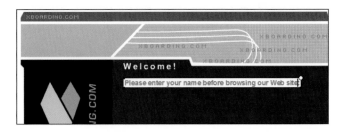

---

5 Lock the text layer, and select the **name field** layer. Select the **Text** tool. In the **Property inspector**, set **Text type** to **Input Text**. On the **Stage**, create a text box (by clicking and dragging) below the **Please enter your name** before browsing our Web site: text.

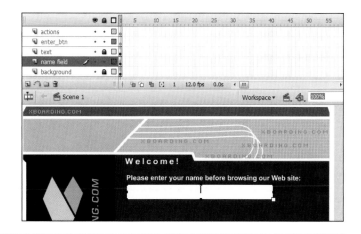

6 With the **Selection** tool, select the input text field you just created on the **Stage**. In the **Property** inspector, make sure **Text type** is set to **Input Text**, Font to Arial, Font size to **14**, and **Font color** to black and **bold**. Make sure the paragraph alignment is set to the left. Set **Line type** to **Single line**, click the **Show border around text** button, and make sure **Auto kern** is deselected. In the **Instance Name** field, type **name_txt** to name this input text field.

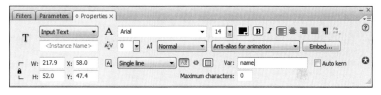

NOTE:

Naming Variables and Instances

ActionScript variable and instance names can contain only letters, numbers, and underscores. Names should begin with a lowercase letter and cannot begin with numbers or underscores. Additionally, words that are used by ActionScript, such as **scroll**, should not be used as variable or instance names. For more information on ActionScript coding standards, visit **www.adobe.com/devnet/flash/whitepapers/ actionscript_standards.pdf**.

NOTE:

Input Text Options

Clicking the **Show border around text** button creates a border and background around the input text box. If **Show border around text** is not selected, a dotted line will surround the text box in the FLA file, although when you publish the movie, there will be no border or background.

The **Maximum characters** setting lets you set the maximum number of characters that a visitor can type in the text box. The default is set to 0, meaning no maximum number of characters.

The **Line type** option lets you set the text box to either **Single line** (displaying the text on one line), **Multiline** (displaying the text in multiple lines), **Multiline no wrap** (displaying the text on one line unless a line break [**Enter/Return**] is used), or **Password** (automatically turns all characters into asterisks as they are typed in the field of either the SWF file or the executable).

The **Var** setting (variable) lets you assign a variable name to the text field for use with ActionScript 1.0/2.0.

---

7 In the **Property inspector**, click the **Embed** button to open the **Character Embedding** dialog box, where you specify the range of characters in the font face you've chosen (Arial, in this example) that will be embedded in the SWF file. In the list box, **Shift-click** to select **Uppercase** and **Lowercase**. Click **OK** to accept these changes.

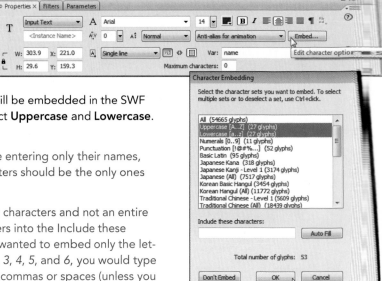

Since visitors to your Web site will be entering only their names, the uppercase and lowercase characters should be the only ones they will need.

Tip: If you want to embed only a few characters and not an entire range, you can type specific characters into the Include these characters field. For example, if you wanted to embed only the letters and numbers *a, b, c, d, e, f, 1, 2, 3, 4, 5,* and *6,* you would type those characters in this box, without commas or spaces (unless you want to embed those as well).

Embedding Font Outlines

When using a static text field, as explained earlier, the font outlines for all the text you used will be embedded in the SWF file. Then you're able to use any font you want in your project, and users will see the font you chose whether they have the font installed on their computers or not.

When using a dynamic or input text field, however, Flash CS3 does not automatically embed the font outline for the font you've chosen. Instead, you must manually specify in the **Property inspector**, as you just did in Step 7, the part of the font face (upper-case characters, lowercase, numerals, and so forth) you want to embed in the SWF file. If you don't do this for each dynamic or input text field, the viewer's computer will treat the text in that field like a device font. Unless the user has the same font face you've chosen for the text field, a substitute will be chosen that comes closest to the one you've picked. This substitute type will be displayed as aliased (jagged edge) instead of anti-aliased (smooth edge)! So unless you're trying to save file size by not embedding font outlines in your SWF file, make sure you specify your font embedding settings for each dynamic or input text field in your project.

Embedding Multiple, Identical Font Outlines

If you have two input text fields and each text field is using the Arial font, you will still need to specify the font embedding options for both input text fields individually. If you embed the uppercase and lowercase characters for both input text fields, does that mean the font outlines for Arial uppercase and lowercase will be embedded twice, increasing your file size even more? No, thankfully it doesn't; the font outlines will be loaded only once.

8 On the **Timeline**, lock the **name field** layer, and select the **enter_btn** layer.

9 Press **Ctrl+L** (Windows) or **Cmd+L** (Mac) to open the **Library** panel. Drag the **btnEnter** button symbol to the **Stage**, and position it below the lower-right corner of the name field.

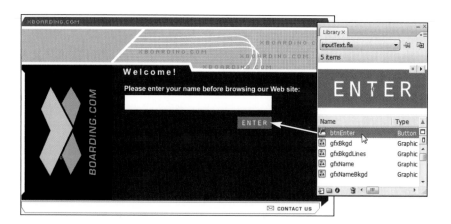

10 Choose the **Selection** tool, and select the **btnEnter** button. In the **Instance Name** field, type **enter_btn**.

11 Lock the **enter_btn** layer, and select the first keyframe of the **actions** layer. Open the **Actions panel** by choosing **Window > Actions**. Click in the **Script** pane, and type the following:

var nameString:String;

This ActionScript tells Flash CS3 to create a new variable called nameString with a data type of String. This variable will receive a value from the **name_txt text** field.

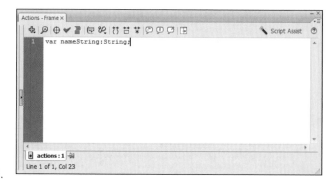

12 Press **Enter** (Windows) or **Return** (Mac) on your keyboard to go to the next line of code, and type the following:

enter_btn.addEventListener (MouseEvent.CLICK, onClick);

This ActionScript tells the button **enter_btn** to "listen" for a mouse click. When a site visitor clicks **enter_btn**, the **onClick()** function will run. You will write the **onClick()** function in the next step.

13 Press **Enter** (Windows) or **Return** (Mac) on your keyboard to go to the next line of code, and type the following:

```
function onClick(event:MouseEvent):void
{
}
```

Make sure to leave a space between the curly braces. This is the skeleton of an event handler. You learned about event handlers in Chapter 12, *"ActionScript Basics."* An event handler is a function that executes when an event (in this case, a mouse click) happens. This event handler receives information about the event that triggered it (as shown in the code **event:MouseEvent**). You will write what happens in this event handler in the next step.

14 Click in the curly braces, and type the following:

```
if(name_txt.text != null)
{
    nameString = name_txt.text;
}
```

This is called a **conditional statement**, which is a block of code that runs if a particular condition is true. The conditional statement begins with the **if** keyword. After the **if** keyword, an expression appears in parentheses. The expression is evaluated as true or false. If the expression is evaluated as true, the code in the curly braces will run. The expression you just typed within the parentheses will be evaluated as true if there is text in the **name_txt** text field when the site visitor clicks the button **enter_btn**. If there is text in that text field, the value of the **nameString** variable will be the same as what is in the **name_txt** text field.

15 Place your cursor at the end of the **nameString = name_txt.text;** line, and press **Enter** (Windows) or **Return** (Mac) on your keyboard to go to the next line in your code. Type the following:

```
gotoAndStop(2);
```

This code will run along with the code in the line before it if the expression you wrote in the previous step is evaluated as true.

16 Shift-click Frame 2 of the **enter_btn** and **actions** layers, and press **F7** to create blank keyframes there. On the **background** layer, select **Frame 2**, and press **F5** to add a frame there.

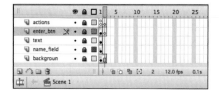

17 Click the **Insert Layer** button. Double-click the layer name, and rename it **message**. Move the layer below **actions** in the layer order. Select **Frame 2** of the **message** layer, and press **F7** to create a new blank keyframe.

18 In the **Tools** panel, select the **Text** tool. Make sure **Frame 2** of the **message** layer is still selected. In the **Property inspector**, set **Text type** to **Dynamic Text**, and then draw a large rectangle below the **Welcome!** text.

This rectangle will be the dynamic text field where the message, incorporating the visitor's name, will be displayed. You will set the remaining options in the Property inspector next.

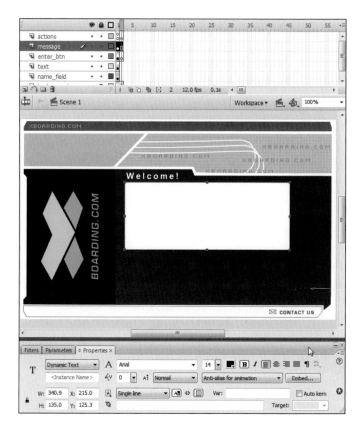

19 With the **Selection** tool, select the dynamic text field you just created on the **Stage**. In the **Property inspector**, make sure **Text type** is still set to **Dynamic Text**. Set **Font** to **Arial**, **12** point, **white**, and **bold**.

Make sure **Text alignment** is set to **Center**, **Line type** is set to **Multiline**, and the **Show border around text** option is deselected. In the **Instance Name** field, type **message_txt**.

You will set the character options for the dynamic text field next.

---

20 In the **Property inspector**, click the **Embed** button. In the **Character Embedding** dialog box, select **Uppercase**, and then while holding down **Ctrl** (Windows) or **Cmd** (Mac), click **Lowercase** and **Punctuation** to select all three options at the same time. Click **OK**.

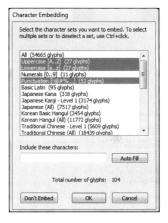

For a simple message that includes the name the visitor typed, these three ranges will work fine. Now that you have all the pieces in place, it's time to put it all together with a little bit of ActionScript.

---

21 Lock the **message** layer. In the **actions** layer, click **Keyframe 2**. Press **F9** (Windows) or **Opt+F9** (Mac) to open the **Actions** panel, if it is closed.

At this point, what you're trying to accomplish with ActionScript is to write a little bit of text that will be combined with the name the visitor typed in the input text field, and then place that name in a dynamic text field (which you gave a variable name of message).

---

22 Click in the **Script** pane, and type the following:

```
message_txt.text =
```

Remember that `message_txt` is the instance name of the text field you just created.

23 After `message_txt.text` =, type the following:

```
"Welcome, " + nameString + ". Thank you for visiting our Web site!";
```

Last, to prevent the movie from initially playing, you need to add a Stop action to the first keyframe.

NOTE:

String Literal vs. Expression

In the text you just entered, notice that some is in quotation marks, and some (such as **nameString**) is not. The text in quotation marks is called a **string literal**. If you want Flash CS3 to display text just as it is typed, put it in quotation marks. Anything not in quotation marks (in this case, **name**), will be treated as an expression. An **expression** is a bit of ActionScripting representing a value. You don't literally want to put the text **nameString** in the dynamic text field; you instead want Flash CS3 to go get the value of the **nameString** (which is whatever the visitor to your site types in the input text field) and insert it into a sentence. To combine string literals with expressions, use **+** (the addition operator).

---

24 Make sure the **Actions** panel reads **Actions – Frame**. Click in the **Script** pane at the end of the last line of code, press **Enter** (Windows) or **Return** (Mac) on your keyboard to go to the next line, and type **stop();**.

Congratulations! You're done! Now it's time to test your handiwork, so cross your fingers....

25 Choose **Control > Test Movie**. When the preview window appears, type your name in the name field, and click **Enter**.

You should now see a simple block of text that incorporates your name into it! Little does the visitor to your site realize the hard work you put into making that block of text seem so simple.

26 When you are finished, close the preview window, and close **inputText.fla**. You don't need to save your changes.

Tip: If you don't see your name in the dynamic text field when you test the movie, go back to the project file, select the dynamic text field in Frame 2 in the message layer, and make sure the Show Border Around Text button is deselected; otherwise, you won't be able to see the white text. Also, click Frame 2 of the actions layer, and in the Actions panel check the ActionScript to make sure you have correctly inserted the code for the frame action. Refer to Steps 20 and 21.

You have successfully made it through the text chapter! Time to take a quick break and get amped up (pun intended) for the sound chapter next!

14

Sound

One of Adobe Flash CS3 Professional's hidden strengths is that it can consistently and reliably play back sound across a wide variety of computer platforms and environments. In fact, this capability may be the best reason to use Flash for projects in which sound is an important component. For example, if you need accurate and consistent sound playback on a Web site, Flash CS3 is an ideal tool for the job.

In Flash CS3, you can use sound for many purposes—including narration, background sound tracks, rollover noises, and sound effects that complement animation. Flash works with a variety of sound formats, including WAV, AIFF, and MP3 files. Under most circumstances, MP3 is the best format because it produces smaller files while maintaining excellent sound quality.

This chapter gives you a solid understanding of how to work with sounds in Flash CS3, including how to import, compress, and control various properties of a sound file. You will learn how to change the format of sound using MP3 compression settings, how to create background sounds, and how to control sound using buttons. The last three exercises are also designed to provide real workflow scenarios where you will learn how to synchronize voice sound clips with an animation and how to control the volume of your sounds.

1 | Importing Sounds

In this exercise, you will learn how to import sound files into Flash CS3. You'll also learn about the types of sound files you can import into Flash CS3 and where they go when you import them.

---

1 Copy the **chap_14** folder from the **Flash HOT CD-ROM** to your desktop. Open a new file, and save it as **basicSound.fla** in the **chap_14** folder.

---

2 Choose **File > Import > Import to Stage**. Navigate to the **sounds** folder (also in the **chap_14** folder), and browse to the **soundsPC** folder if you are using a Windows machine or to the **soundsMac** folder if you are using a Mac.

Note: If you choose File > Import > Import to Stage, the sound files will not be imported to the Stage but instead will be imported into the Library panel.

TIP:

I Don't See Any Files!

If you don't see any sounds in the list, make sure you select **All Files** for **Files of Type** (Windows) or **All Files** for **Enable** (Mac) in the **Import** dialog box rather than **All Formats**.

---

3 To import the sound files from in the **soundsPC/soundsMac** folder, do one of the following:

Windows: Ctrl-click **Free.wav**, **Lektropolis.wav**, and **Space_Jam.wav** to select them, and click **Open** to import the sounds into Flash CS3.

Mac: Cmd-click **Free.aif**, **Lektropolis.aif**, and **Space_Jam.aif** to select them, and click **Import** to import the sounds into Flash CS3.

What Kinds of Sounds Can I Import?

You can import a variety of sound files into Flash CS3, depending on which platform you use and whether you have Apple QuickTime 4 or newer installed on your machine. If you have QuickTime 4 or newer installed on your system, you can import additional sound file formats. The following chart lists the types of sound file formats you can import into Flash CS3:

Sound File Types Supported by Flash CS3		
File Format	**Windows**	**Mac**
WAV	Yes	Yes, with QuickTime 4 or later installed
AIF	Yes, with QuickTime 4 or later installed	Yes
MP3	Yes	Yes
Sound Designer II	No	Yes, with QuickTime 4 or later installed
Sound-only QuickTime movies	Yes, with QuickTime 4 or later installed	Yes, with QuickTime 4 or later installed
Sun Au	Yes, with QuickTime 4 installed	Yes, with QuickTime 4 or later installed
System 7 sounds	No	Yes, with QuickTime 4 or later installed

TIP:

Where Did the Sounds Go?

When you import an image, you will see the image on the **Stage** as soon as you choose **File > Import > Import to Stage**. When you import a sound with this same command, however, it is not visible on the **Stage**. Instead, you must open the **Library** panel to view the sound files. You will do this next.

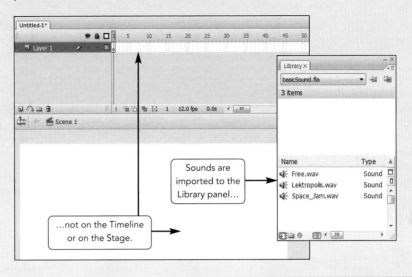

4 Press **Ctrl+L** (Windows) or **Cmd+L** (Mac) to open the **Library** panel. You will see the three sounds you just imported. Select each sound, one at a time, and click the **Play** button to listen to each one.

That's all there is to it! Importing sounds is easy. Working with them on the Timeline can be a bit more challenging. By the end of this chapter, you will get experience working with sounds on the Timeline, modifying and compressing sounds, and controlling sound volume with some simple ActionScript.

5 Save your changes, and leave **basicSound.fla** open for the next exercise. You will learn how to compress sounds in Adobe Flash CS3 next.

2 | Compressing Sound

Now that you know how to import sounds into Flash CS3, the next step is to learn how to compress them. Compressing sounds is especially important for keeping your file sizes as small as possible. Uncompressed sounds increase file sizes drastically, which can lead to a variety of playback problems. In this exercise, you will learn how to compress sound by using the **MP3** compression setting in the **Sound Properties** dialog box.

---

1 If you just completed Exercise 1, **basicSound.fla** should still be open. If it's not, complete Exercise 1, and then return to this exercise.

---

2 In the **Library** panel, click the **Free.wav** sound (**Free.aif** on the Mac) to select it. Click the **Properties** button to open the **Sound Properties** dialog box. (You can also open the **Sound Properties** dialog box by double-clicking a file's sound icon in the **Library** panel.)

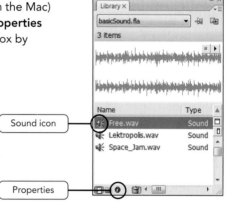

Sound icon

Properties

NOTE:

Sound Compression: Moviewide or Individual?

In Flash CS3, you have two general options for sound compression: You can set compression settings for all sounds in the movie in the **Publish Settings** dialog box, or you can set the compression settings for each sound file individually in the **Library** panel. Next you will learn how to set sound compression in the **Library** panel. You will learn about the **Publish Settings** in Chapter 17, *"Publishing and Exporting."* Whenever possible, you should set compression settings individually for each sound. The individual method usually takes more time and effort, but it produces better results because not all sounds are the same.

3 Notice the sound is large at its default compression setting: **2506.8 kB**. Choose **MP3** in the **Compression** pop-up menu.

The MP3 compression setting offers the best compression rates and sound fidelity. Users with the Flash 4 and newer players can hear MP3 sounds. The following chart defines the sound compression options:

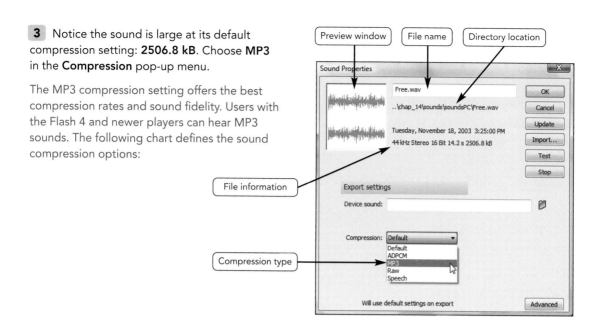

| Preview window | File name | Directory location |

File information

Compression type

Sound Compression Defined	
Option	**Description**
Default	This option uses the global compression settings in the **Publish Settings** dialog box. You will learn about the **Publish Settings** in Chapter 17, *"Publishing and Exporting."*
ADPCM	This compression model is an older method of compression from Flash 3. It sets compression for 8-bit and 16-bit sound data. You should consider using this format only if you need to author movies that are compatible with Flash Player 3.
MP3	Compatible with Flash Player 4 and newer . It offers the best combination of high compression rates with good sound fidelity.
Raw	This format will resample the file at the specified rate but will not perform any compression.
Speech	This option uses a compression method designed specifically for speech sound files. You will work with this compression type in Exercise 5 of this chapter.

4 Choose **8 kbps** in the **Bit Rate** pop-up menu. Click the **Test** button to hear the sound with the new compression applied. Notice the file does not sound very good, but its file size has drastically decreased from the original **2506.8 kB** to **14.2 kB**.

Note: The lower the bit rate, the lower the sound quality and the lower the file size; the higher the bit rate, the higher the sound quality and the larger the file size.

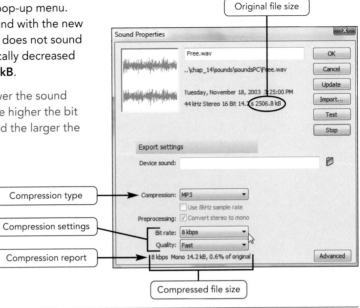

Original file size

Compression type

Compression settings

Compression report

Compressed file size

5 Choose **160 kbps** in the **Bit Rate** pop-up menu, and deselect the **Preprocessing: Convert stereo to mono** option. Click the **Test** button to hear the sound again. Notice how much better the sound quality is at **160 kbps**. However, look at the file size: It has increased to **284.2 kB**. Although this is smaller than the original **2506.8 kB**, it is more than 20 times the size of the file at the **8 kbps** bit rate.

Note: The Preprocessing option is available only for bit rates of 20 kbps or higher. This feature, when selected, converts mixed stereo sounds to mono.

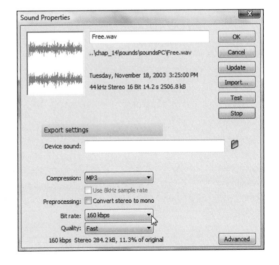

6 Choose **24 kbps** in the **Bit Rate** pop-up menu, and make sure the **Preprocessing: Convert stereo to mono** option is deselected. Click the **Test** button to preview the sound. Notice the sound quality is not as good as before, but it's still acceptable. The file size has dropped to **42.6 kB**.

When you are working with sound files in Flash CS3, you will want to test several bit-rate settings to determine which one offers the lowest file size without sacrificing sound quality. The best procedure is to start at a high or medium setting and to reduce the setting until the sound quality is no longer accept-able for the purpose at hand. Once you reach the point where the sound quality is no longer acceptable, go back one step to the last acceptable setting, and leave it there. You're done. This technique ensures you always achieve the best possible audio quality at the smallest possible file size.

7 Choose **Best** in the **Quality** pop-up menu. Click the **Test** button. This takes a bit longer to convert the file to the MP3 format, but the file will sound better and the file size will be the same. The only trade-off is that it will take longer to convert the file in Flash CS3. However, this is a small price to pay for much improved sound.

Note: Since the file size is the same (between Best and Fast), you will notice no difference in download time, although the Best sound will sound better.

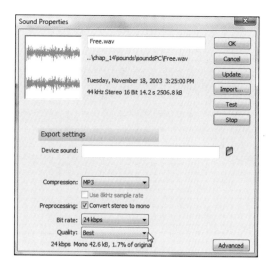

8 When you are finished, click **OK** to accept the settings and close the **Sound Properties** dialog box.

To summarize, remember that the name of the game is to get the best possible sound at the smallest possible file size. Start with larger, better-sounding files, and keep reducing them until you finish with smaller files that still contain acceptable sound quality. Also, use the MP3 compression setting whenever possible because of its superior compression capabilities. With MP3 compression, you have the best of both worlds with no extra effort: small file size with good sound quality.

9 Save your **basicSound.fla** file by choosing **File > Save**. Close the file.

You just learned how to import and compress sounds in Flash CS3. In the next exercise, you will learn how to work with background sound and sound effects.

Note: Once you produce the SWF file, users on both Windows and Mac machines will be able to hear the sound in your Flash CS3 movie, and the sound's original format won't matter. The sound is compressed as ADPCM, MP3, Raw, or Speech when you create the SWF file, and these options are platform-independent.

Creating Background Sound with Sound Effects

As you develop projects in Flash CS3, you will find that some projects really come to life with the addition of some background audio. This exercise shows you how to add background sound, including how to use one of the sound effects in the **Property inspector**. You will also be introduced to the **Edit Envelope** dialog box, which is a handy tool for customizing effects applied to your sound files.

---

1 Open **bkgdSound.fla** from the **chap_14** folder. Choose **View > Magnification > Show All** to see the whole image on the **Stage**.

Notice it contains one layer with a background image.

---

2 Press **Ctrl+L** (Windows) or **Cmd+L** (Mac) to open the **Library** panel.

Notice there are bitmaps, a graphic symbol, and some buttons but no sounds...yet.

---

3 On the main **Timeline**, click the **Insert Layer** button to add a new layer. Rename this new layer **sound**, and make sure it is above the **background** layer.

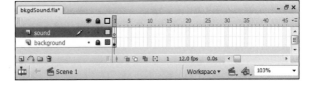

NOTE: | **Audio in the Movie vs. Audio in the Library**

Although the sound file has been successfully imported into the Flash CS3 project file, it does not actually exist in the movie yet—it exists only in the **Library** panel. For the sound to be part of the movie, you must add it to a keyframe on the **Timeline**.

---

4 Choose **File > Import > Import to Library**. Browse to the **mp3** folder in the **sounds** folder in the **chap_14** folder, and select the **Hype.mp3** file. Click **Open** (Windows) or **Import** (Mac) to import the MP3 sound file.

Yet another great aspect of MP3 files is that they work both in Windows and on a Mac.

---

5 Click the **Play** button to test the sound.

You will be adding this sound to the Timeline next.

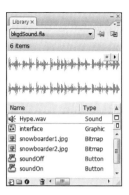

TIP:

Why Am I Making a New Layer for the Sound?

It is good practice to place sound files, such as frame actions, on their own separate layer. This will separate the sound from other artwork and animation, letting you view the waveform (the picture of the sound) better and work with the sound more easily.

---

6 With the first frame on the **sound** layer selected, drag the **Hype.mp3** sound from the **Library** panel, and drop it anywhere on the **Stage**. After you drop the sound, you will not see a representation of that sound anywhere on the **Stage**. However, the sound will appear on the **Timeline** in the form of a blue waveform, providing visual feedback that the sound is located there. If it's hard to see, choose **Medium** in the **Timeline Options** menu to increase your frame size.

NOTE:

Adding Sounds to Keyframes

You can add sounds only to keyframes. The best way to do this is to first create a blank keyframe on the **Timeline** where you want your sound to start playing. Select this keyframe, drag the sound from the **Library** panel, and drop it anywhere on the **Stage**. Without first creating a keyframe, the sound will not go where you want it but instead will attach itself to the last keyframe before the current location of the playhead.

7 Choose **Control > Test Movie** to preview the movie with the new sound added. You will hear the sound play through once and stop. When you are finished, close the preview window.

---

8 On the **sound** layer, click **Frame 1** to select the sound. In the **Property inspector**, notice the name of the sound displayed in the **Sound** pop-up menu and that the **Sync** option is set to **Event**.

The Sync: Event setting causes the sound to start playing when the playhead reaches the frame that contains it. The sound will continue to play all the way to the end, independently of whatever is happening on the main Timeline—even if the main Timeline stops or is only one frame in length.

---

9 In the **Property inspector**, choose **Stream** in the **Sync** pop-up menu.

---

10 Choose **Control > Test Movie** to preview the movie.

This time you will not hear the sound at all. Why? Unlike the Event setting, the Stream setting stops the sound when the movie stops. So if you have only one frame in your movie and you apply a Stream setting to a sound in the main Timeline, the sound will not play. Unlike Event sounds, Stream sounds play only within the frames they occupy.

---

11 Close the preview window when you are done previewing your movie.

Stream sounds have many benefits. I will discuss the benefits in the chart at the end of this exercise and again in Exercise 7, where you will synchronize Stream sounds to animation.

---

12 In the **Property inspector**, choose **Start** in the **Sync** pop-up menu.

The Start setting is most often used for background sounds and is similar to the Event setting. Start causes the sound to begin playing as soon as the keyframe holding it is reached, and the sound will play to the end, independently of the main Timeline, just as an Event sound will. The difference is that if a Start sound is already playing, no new instance of the sound can be played. Only one instance of the sound will play at a time. With the Event setting, if an instance of the sound is playing and another instance is triggered, the two sounds will play over each other.

The Start sound setting is useful when you have a layer with a sound that is already playing and you don't want to introduce a new instance of that same sound until the currently playing sound has stopped. The Start setting prevents the sound from playing over itself. For a more detailed explanation of all the sound settings, see the "Modifying Sound Settings" section following this exercise.

---

13 Choose **Control > Test Movie** to preview the movie. With the **Start** sound setting, the sound will play just as it did with the **Event** setting. When you are finished, close the preview window. You will add basic sound effects in the following steps.

NOTE:

Testing Sounds

You can test all sounds by choosing **Control > Test Movie**. You can also test sounds in the editing environment by pressing **Enter** (Windows) or **Return** (Mac), but this method has its limitations, since certain conditions must be met in order for the sound to play:

- When the main **Timeline** has only one frame, you cannot test sounds by pressing **Enter** (Windows) or **Return** (Mac).

- When the main **Timeline** has more than one frame, you can test **Event** and **Start** sounds by pressing **Enter** (Windows) or **Return** (Mac), and they will play in their entirety (even if there are just two frames on the **Timeline**, but the sound takes 100 frames to play). You will learn more about **Event**, **Start**, and **Stream** sounds in the next steps of the exercise.

- When the main **Timeline** has more than one frame, you can test **Stream** sounds by pressing **Enter** (Windows) or **Return** (Mac). Use caution, however, because if there are not enough frames on the main **Timeline** to play the entire sound or if another keyframe is encountered before the sound finishes, the sound will stop and be cut short. **Stream** sounds are tied directly to the main **Timeline**.

14 In the **Property inspector**, choose **Fade In** in the **Effect** pop-up menu. This will make the sound start out soft and gradually become louder. For the **Sync** setting, make sure **Start** is selected. Choose **Repeat**, and type **1** for the number of times the sound will repeat.

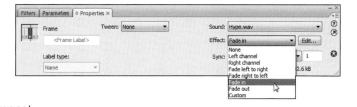

15 Choose **Control > Test Movie** to preview the sound settings you applied. Notice the sound fades in. Keep listening—the sound will repeat once and then stop. When the sound has stopped playing, close the preview window.

16 In the **Property inspector**, choose **Loop** instead of **Repeat**.

This setting will make the sound play over and over continuously throughout the movie. The Start setting will not affect the overall file size, since the file is downloaded only once.

17 Choose **Control > Test Movie** to listen to the sound settings you applied. Notice the sound fades in and continues to play over and over again (**Loop**) for as long as you have the preview window open. When you are done previewing the sound, close the preview window.

18 In the **Property inspector**, click the **Edit** button to open the **Edit Envelope** dialog box.

In the Edit Envelope dialog box, you can edit your sound. Notice the Effect option is set to Fade In. This effect was created when you chose it in the Property inspector.

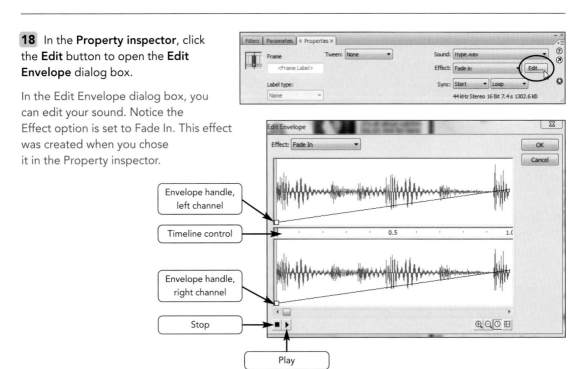

19 In the **Edit Envelope** dialog box, click the **Play** button to test the sound. Notice the sound starts out softly and gradually becomes louder. Click the **Stop** button. Experiment with moving the right and left envelope handles, which will change the way the sound fades in to the right and left speakers. Click the **Play** button again to test it.

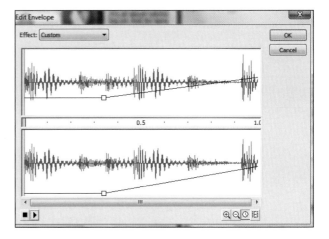

20 To create new left and right envelope handles, click one of the channel's sound wave preview windows once. Note that the **Effect** setting changes from **Fade In** to **Custom** when you move the envelope handles.

21 In the **Edit Envelope** dialog box, drag the **Time In** control to change the start point of the sound. Click the **Play** button again to test it. When you are happy with the way your adjustments sound, click **OK** to accept the settings.

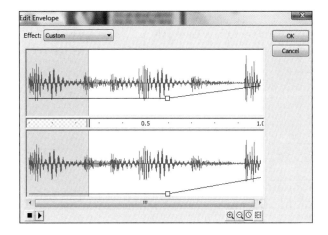

22 Choose **Control > Test Movie** to preview the movie again. You will hear the sound with your custom effects applied to it.

Tip: If you don't like the custom effects you created, rather than clicking OK in the Edit Envelope dialog box, you can click Cancel, or you can choose an Effect option other than Custom in the Property inspector. This will reset the sound to the effect you choose.

23 Close the preview window, save your changes, and leave **bkgdSound.fla** open for the next exercise.

Modifying Sound Settings

After you place an instance of a sound on the Timeline, you can use the settings in the **Property inspector** to control the behavior of the sound, as you learned in this exercise. The following sections provide an in-depth look at the sound settings.

Effect Option

The **Effect** option in the **Property inspector** lets you choose preset effects you can apply to your sound. Choosing the **Custom** setting lets you create your own sound effects, as described in the following chart:

Effect Options Explained	
Option	**Description**
Left Channel	Plays only the left channel of a stereo sound
Right Channel	Plays only the right channel of a stereo sound
Fade Left to Right	Creates a panning effect by playing a stereo sound from the left channel to the right channel (or left speaker to right speaker)

continues on next page

Effect Options Explained *continued*	
Option	**Description**
Fade Right to Left	Creates a panning effect by playing a stereo sound from the right channel to the left channel (or right speaker to left speaker)
Fade In	Makes the sound gradually become louder as it begins to play
Fade Out	Makes the sound gradually become softer as it nears the end
Custom	Lets you create your own effects for the sound

Sync Option

The **Sync** option in the **Property inspector** lets you set the synchronization of the sound file in the movie. Each option controls the behavior of the sound on the **Timeline** and is described in the following chart:

Sync Options Explained	
Option	**Description**
Event	Begins playing the sound when the playhead reaches the frame that holds the sound on the **Timeline**. Event sounds will continue to play independently, even if the **Timeline** stops. If a different instance of the same sound is started, the sounds will overlap. This option is good for short sounds, such as buttons clicks or quick sound effects.
Start	Behaves similarly to an **Event** sound, except that a second instance of the sound cannot be started until any currently playing instances have finished, which prevents the sound from overlapping itself. This option is good for background sound.
Stop	Stops the indicated sound. Use this feature if you have a sound in the main **Timeline** that spans 50 frames, for example, and is set to **Start**. The sound will play from start to finish, no matter what happens in the main **Timeline**. If you need the sound to stop at **Frame 30**, add the same sound to a keyframe in **Frame 30**, and set its sync to **Stop**. This will stop the **Start** sound (or an **Event** sound) from playing.
Stream	Forces the movie to keep pace with the sound. If the movie cannot download its frames fast enough to keep pace, the Flash Player forces it to skip frames. **Stream** sounds stop when the **Timeline** stops or when another keyframe is encountered on the same layer. One advantage to **Stream** sounds is that they begin to play before the entire sound file is downloaded, which is not the case for **Event** and **Start** sounds. **Stream** sounds are ideal for narration and animation.

Repeat/Loop Option

The **Repeat** option in the **Property inspector** sets the number of times the sound will repeat. The **Loop** option sets the sound to play continuously. Repeating or looping **Event** or **Start** sounds has no effect on file size. However, use caution when you choose **Stream** in the **Sync** pop-up menu because repeating or looping a **Stream** sound will cause Flash CS3 to add frames for each loop, thereby increasing the file size significantly.

Edit Button

Clicking the **Edit** button in the **Property inspector** opens the **Edit Envelope** dialog box, where you can edit your sound.

The Edit Envelope Dialog Box

In the **Edit Envelope** dialog box, you can change the effect of the sound, change the start and end points of a sound, modify the envelope handles to change the volume of the sound, test the sound, view the sound using seconds or frames, and zoom in and out to see more or less of the sound wave.

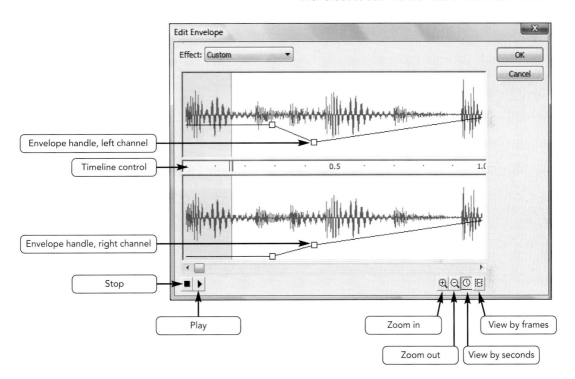

4 | Adding Sounds Using ActionScript 3.0

Being able to play a sound is great, but to make sound start, stop, or change the volume, you need to use ActionScript. In this exercise, you will learn how to use ActionScript 3.0 to add a sound file in your **Library** to a Flash movie.

---

1 Open **soundAS.fla** from the **chap_14** folder.

This file is similar to the bkgdSounds.fla file you worked with in Exercise 3. However, instead of dragging sounds to the Stage from the Library panel, you'll be adding them to the Stage using ActionScript.

2 If the **Library** panel is not already open, open it by choosing **Window > Library**. **Right-click** (Windows) or **Ctrl-click** (Mac) **Hype.mp3**, and choose **Linkage**.

---

3 In the **Linkage Properties** dialog box, select the **Export for ActionScript** check box. Type **SoundTrack** in the **Class** field, and click **OK**.

This step is essential in bringing any item out of the Library panel using ActionScript. Each item brought out of the Library panel with ActionScript needs a unique class name. You learned about classes in Chapter 12, *"ActionScript Basics."* Though it is not necessary, it is a best practice to start your unique class name with a capital letter because all base ActionScript 3.0 class names begin with a capital letter.

The `Base` class field refers to the base, or predefined, ActionScript class that your unique class will extend. In this case, the `SoundTrack` class will inherit all the properties, methods, and events of the `Sound` class.

---

4 A warning dialog box may appear letting you know that the `SoundTrack` class could not be found. This is OK since you are creating a custom class. Click **OK** to dismiss the dialog box.

---

5 Select the first keyframe on the **actions** layer, and open the **Actions** panel by choosing **Window > Actions**.

---

6 Make sure **Script Assist** is turned off. Click in the **Script** pane, and type the following:

`stop();`

This will keep the animation from looping.

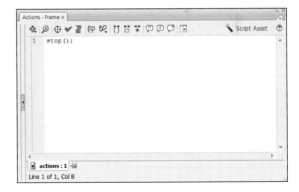

7 Press **Enter** (Windows) or **Return** (Mac) to go to the next line of code, and type the following:

```
var sndTrack:SoundTrack = new SoundTrack();
```

This ActionScript creates a new instance of the custom **SoundTrack** class you defined in the previous step, which will act just like an object in the **Sound** class.

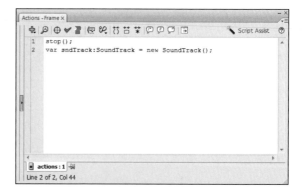

8 Press **Enter** (Windows) or **Return** (Mac) to go to the next line of code, and type the following:

```
var sndControl:SoundChannel;
```

This ActionScript creates a new variable called **sndControl** that has a data type of **SoundChannel**. The **SoundChannel** class is used to control the starting and stopping of a sound.

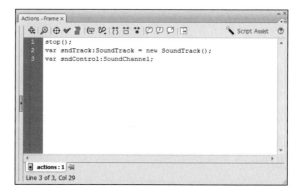

9 Press **Enter** (Windows) or **Return** (Mac) to go to the next line of code, and type the following:

```
sndControl = sndTrack.play(0,999);
```

This ActionScript plays the sound track. This is where you associate the **Sound** (or **SoundTrack**) instance **sndTrack** with the **SoundChannel** instance **sndChannel**. The 0 value represents how long Flash CS3 will wait before the sound starts playing, and the 999 value represents how many times the sound will loop (not forever, but close enough).

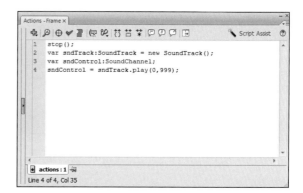

10 Choose **Control > Test Movie**.

Feel the groove. Good job! You just brought a sound out of the Library panel using ActionScript!

If you do not hear any sound playing, check the code you wrote in Steps 6-9.

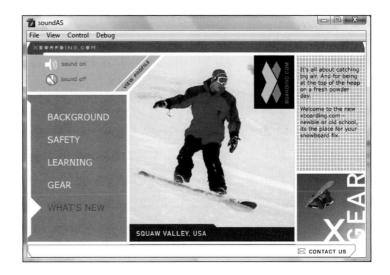

---

11 Close the preview window. Save your **soundAS.fla** file by choosing **File > Save**. Close the file.

---

5 | Controlling Sound with On/Off Buttons

Even though you like the audio you've chosen for the background sound of your movie, certain users may not want to listen to it. It's always good practice to give users as much playback control as possible. This exercise teaches you how to add sound controls to your movie so users can stop and play the sound. Later, you will learn how to add controls for letting users adjust the volume of your sound elements.

1 Open **soundOnOff_Final.fla** from the **chap_14** folder.

2 Choose **Control >Test Movie** to preview the movie. Click the **sound off** button to stop the sound. Click the **sound on** button to start it again. Cool! You will be creating this movie in the steps that follow. When you are finished, close the preview window, and close **soundOnOff_Final.fla**.

3 Open **soundOnOff.fla** from the **chap_14** folder.

This file contains the same contents and ActionScript as the soundAS.fla file you worked with in the previous exercise.

4 Open the **Library** panel, and notice the two buttons inside: one named **soundOn** and one named **soundOff**. These are basic rollover buttons I created ahead of time for you. Select **Frame 1** on the **buttons** layer, and drag an instance of each button to the location on the **Stage** shown in the illustration here.

Now that you have added the buttons to the movie, you will add ActionScript and behaviors to the buttons that make the sound stop playing or begin playing.

5 Select the **soundOn** button on the Stage, and type **on_btn** in the **Instance Name** field in the **Property inspector**. Then select the **soundOff** button on the Stage, and type **off_btn** in the **Instance Name** field in the **Property inspector**.

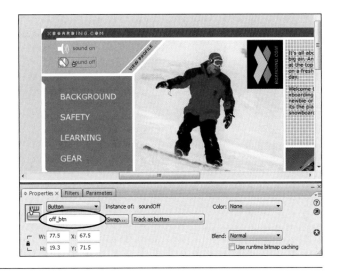

---

6 Select the first keyframe on the **actions** layer on the **Timeline**. Choose **Window > Actions** to open the **Actions** panel.

---

7 Make sure **Script Assist** is turned off. Click in the **Script** pane at the end of the last line of code, and press **Enter** (Windows) or **Return** (Mac) twice to insert two new lines. Type the following:

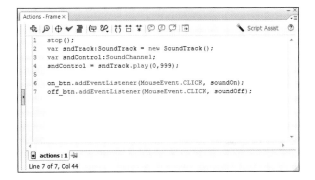

```
on_btn.addEventListener(MouseEvent.CLICK,
soundOn);
off_btn.addEventListener(MouseEvent.CLICK,
soundOff);
```

Make sure to press Enter (Windows) or Return (Mac) after the first line.

This ActionScript tells Flash CS3 to have the **on_btn** and **off_btn** buttons listen for mouse clicks. When a site visitor clicks the **on_btn** button, a function called **soundOn** will run. When a site visitor clicks the **off_btn** button, a function called **soundOff** will run. You will create these functions in the next step.

---

8 Press **Enter** (Windows) or **Return** (Mac) twice, and create a skeleton for the **soundOn()** function by typing the following:

```
function soundOn(event:MouseEvent):void
{
}
```

9 Position your cursor between the two curly braces of the code you just typed, and type the following:

```
sndControl = sndTrack.play(0,999);
```

This is the same as what is written on line 4 in your code.

Now, when you click the **on_btn** button, the sound will begin playing. Because the sound already plays automatically, this button won't do much until you write the code to stop the sound from playing. You will do that in the next step.

10 Now you will create a skeleton for the **soundOff()** function. Click after the closed curly brace of the **soundOn()** function, go to the next line, and type the following:

```
function soundOff(event:MouseEvent):void
{
}
```

11 Position your cursor between the curly braces of the **soundOff()** function, and type the following:

```
sndControl.stop();
```

This ActionScript will stop the sound track. The next step is to test the movie.

12 Choose **Control > Test Movie** to test the movie. Click the **sound off** button to stop the sound, and click the **sound on** button to start it again.

Pretty sweet! If any error messages pop up, check your code in Steps 7–11.

---

13 Close the preview window. Save your **soundOnOff.fla** file by choosing **File > Save**. Close the file.

---

6 | Setting Compression for Narration

You can control sound in Flash CS3 so that it synchronizes with animation, such as narration or a sound effect that matches a character's movement. This exercise shows you how to import and compress sounds using speech compression. You will also learn how to modify the **Timeline** for easier editing.

---

1 Open **soundSync_Final.fla** from the **chap_14** folder. This is a finished version of the file you will create in this and the next exercise. Choose **Control > Test Movie** to preview the movie.

Notice the narration voice is synchronized perfectly with the animation. You will create this same effect in the following steps.

---

2 When you are finished previewing the movie, close the preview window, and close this file.

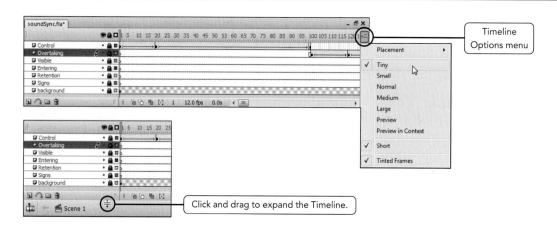

Click and drag to expand the Timeline.

---

3 Open the **soundSync.fla** file from the **chap_14** folder.

I created this file to get you started. Notice the seven layers in the main Timeline. The top six layers hold different parts of the animation, and the bottom layer holds a background image. Scrub (click and drag) the playhead back and forth to see the letters animate.

Tip: Since the main Timeline contains a lot of frames, you can change the frame view temporarily by clicking the Timeline Options menu and choosing Tiny and Short, which will let you see more frames at once on the Timeline.

You can also expand/contract the Timeline by clicking and dragging the bottom of the edit bar below the Timeline.

---

4 On the main **Timeline**, click the **Insert Layer** button to add a new layer. Rename the layer **sounds**. Drag the **sounds** layer so it is on top of all the other layers.

You will import the sound files next.

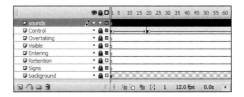

5 Choose **File > Import > Import to Library**. Open the **chap_14** folder. In the **sounds** folder, open the **codeSounds** folder. **Shift-click** to select all six sounds, and click **Open** (Windows) or **Import to Library** (Mac) to import them.

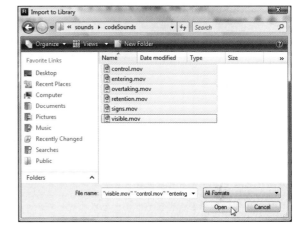

6 Press **Ctrl+L** (Windows) or **Cmd+L** (Mac) to open the **Library** panel. Click **Type** to organize the **Library** panel assets by type instead of by alphabetical order. Notice the six sounds are now in the **Library** panel. Select the **control** sound, and click the **Play** button to test it. Select the other sounds in the **Library** panel, and click the **Play** button to test them.

You will change the compression setting of the sounds next.

7 Select the **control** sound, and click the **Properties** button at the bottom of the **Library** panel to open the **Sound Properties** dialog box.

Tip: You can also double-click a file's sound icon to open the Sound Properties dialog box.

8 Notice the sound is large at its default compression setting: **1517.0 kB**. In the **Compression** pop-up menu, choose **Speech**. In the **Sample rate** pop-up menu, choose **22kHz**. Click the **Test** button to test the sound.

Notice the sound quality is pretty good. However, you may be able to squeeze more audio information out of this file without adversely affecting its sound quality. In the next steps, you'll keep reducing the sample rate until the audio quality is no longer acceptable, and then you'll undo the last reduction.

9 Choose **11kHz** in the **Sample rate** pop-up menu, and click the **Test** button. Notice the file size has been reduced to only **23.7 kB** and that the sound quality is still pretty good. Let's keep reducing.

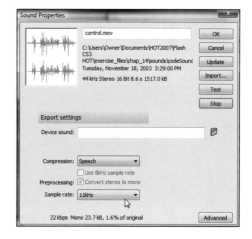

10 Choose **5kHz** in the **Sample rate** pop-up menu, and click the **Test** button. Notice although the file size has been reduced to only **11.9 K**, the sound quality is so bad that it is no longer acceptable. You have gone too far and need to set it back to the last acceptable setting, which was **11kHz**.

You have managed to reduce the file to 23.7 kB from an original size of 1500 kB, which is a substantial savings.

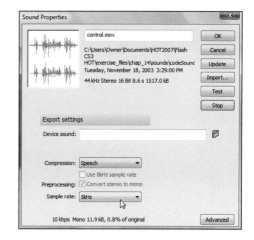

11 Set **Sample rate** to **11kHz**. Click **OK**.

As you heard for yourself, 11kHz is the recommended sample rate for speech, providing the best combination of small file size and acceptable sound quality.

Speech compression is specifically adapted to speech sounds. The sample rate controls sound fidelity and file size; the lower the sample rate, the smaller the file size and the lower the sound quality.

---

12 In the **Library** panel, change each of the remaining five sound's compression settings in the **Sound Properties** dialog box. For each sound, choose **Speech** in the **Compression** pop-up menu, and choose **11kHz** in the **Sample rate** pop-up menu.

---

13 Save your changes, and leave **soundSync.fla** open for the next exercise.

---

7 | Synchronizing Sound to Narration Cues

In the previous exercise, you learned how to compress sounds using the speech compression settings. This exercise shows you how to use the **Stream Sync** option and how to work with the main **Timeline** so that voice sound files synchronize with animation.

---

1 If you just completed Exercise 6, **soundSync.fla** should still be open. If it's not, complete Exercise 6, and then return to this exercise. On the **Timeline**, select **Frame 1** on the **sounds** layer. From the **Library** panel, drag an instance of the **control** sound to the **Stage**. Notice the waveform on the **Timeline**.

Next, you will adjust the height of the sounds layer to make it easier to use.

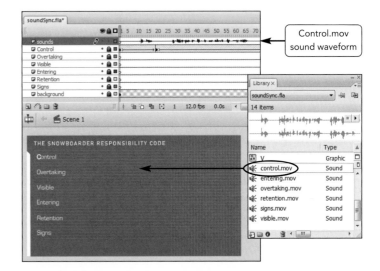

Control.mov sound waveform

---

2 Double-click the layer icon next to the **sounds** layer name to open the **Layer Properties** dialog box.

Sounds layer height at 200%

---

3 In the **Layer Properties** dialog box, choose **200%** in the **Layer height** pop-up menu, and click **OK**. This will make the **sounds** layer taller than all the rest of the layers on the **Timeline**, making it easier to see the waveform.

Tip: You can also access the Layer Properties dialog box by choosing Modify > Timeline > Layer Properties.

---

4 Select **Frame 1** on the **sounds** layer. In the **Property inspector**, choose **Stream** in the **Sync** pop-up menu, and choose **0** in the **Repeat** pop-up menu.

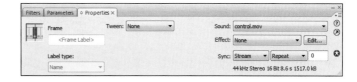

The Stream setting forces the movie to keep pace with the sound. If the movie cannot download its frames fast enough to keep pace, Flash forces it to skip frames.

---

5 Choose **Control > Test Movie** to test the sound and the animation.

The sound will play in synchronization with the animation. You will add the remaining sounds to the Timeline in the following steps, but first you'll learn how to change the appearance of the Timeline to see more layers.

TIP:

Streaming and Looping

Be careful about setting your sound's **Sync** setting to **Stream** and adding loops. Unlike the **Event** and **Start** settings, **Stream** causes the file size to increase for each loop you specify. If you can avoid it, try not to loop sounds that are set to the **Stream** setting.

---

6 Close the preview window. On the **Timeline**, click and drag the **edit bar** down to reveal more of the layers.

---

7 Scrub the playhead back and forth to identify where the **O** animation begins on the **Overtaking** layer. Notice this happens at **Frame 101**.

You want the overtaking sound clip to start where the O animation begins. You will do this next.

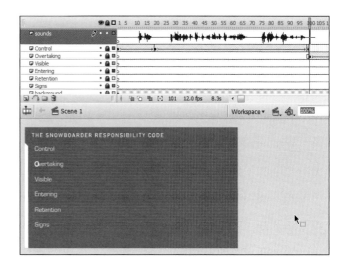

---

8 On the **sounds** layer, select **Frame 101**, and press **F7** to add a blank keyframe.

You will add the overtaking sound next.

---

9 In the **Property inspector,** choose **overtaking.mov** in the **Sound** pop-up menu. This will add the **overtaking** sound to **Frame 101.** Choose **Stream** in the **Sync** pop-up menu, choose **Repeat**, and type **0.**

Flash CS3 lets you conveniently access sounds in the movie's Library panel from the Sound pop-up list in the Property inspector, which lets you quickly access all the sounds in your Library panel. You can even switch the sound located in a keyframe by selecting a different sound in the pop-up list.

NOTE: | **Adding Sound to the Timeline**

In this chapter, you have learned two ways to add sounds to the **Timeline.** You can drag an instance of the sound to the **Stage,** or you can select the frame on the **Timeline** and then choose a sound from the pop-up **Sound** list in the **Property inspector.** Both workflow methods yield the same result—decide which works best for you.

---

10 Repeat Steps 7 and 8 to add blank keyframes on the **sounds** layer where each new letter animation begins.

Tip: Each animation is 100 frames long, so place a blank keyframe at the beginning of each new animation: Frames 201, 301, 401, and 501.

---

11 Repeat Step 9 for each of the blank keyframes you just added to attach the appropriate sound.

Tip: That's Frame 201 (visible sound), Frame 301 (entering sound), Frame 401 (retention sound), and Frame 501 (signs sound).

---

12 Test the movie again. Notice some of the sounds are cut short when a new animation begins. Why? This is because some sound files are longer than others. As you can hear, **Stream** sounds will stop as soon as another keyframe or blank keyframe is encountered in the same layer. When you are finished, close the preview window.

In the following steps, you will fix the sound files so they don't get cut short. Now here's where real workflow issues come into play. Depending on how you plan your project, you can lay out the animation on the Timeline first (as this file has been prepared), or you can lay out the sound on the Timeline first. Either way, you will still have to figure out just where the animations should start and finish according to the sounds. So, from this point forward, not only will you become more acquainted with sounds and their settings, but you will also be much more comfortable moving frames around on the Timeline.

---

13 On the **sounds** layer, click and drag **Frame 201** (with the **visible** sound) to the right to **Frame 240**. Notice as you do, the sound wave in the previous frame (the **overtaking** sound) continues until **Frame 231**. This means the **overtaking** sound is not 100 frames long, as the animation is. Instead, it is 131 frames long. Therefore, in order for the animation and the sound file to span the same duration, you need to make them match. You will do this next by moving the frames on the **Timeline**.

Note: As you learned in Exercise 3, Stream sounds play only within the frames they occupy. So, in order to hear the sound in its entirety, you will extend the Timeline for each sound.

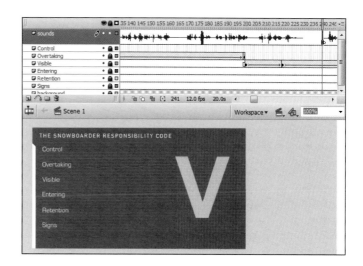

14 Click and drag **Frame 240** back to **Frame 232**, just after the **overtaking** sound wave ends on the **Timeline**, which will start the next sound (**visible**) after the **overtaking** sound ends, without cutting it off.

Note: As soon as the playhead encounters another Stream sound on the Timeline, the previous Stream sound will stop, and the new Stream sound will play.

You will move the frames in the overtaking layer so the animation and sound are in sync next.

Frame 231: Overtaking sound ends

Frame 232: Visible sound begins

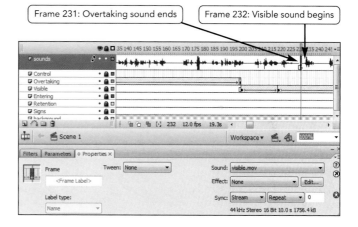

15 Click and drag the last keyframe in the **Overtaking** layer to **Frame 231**, which will make the **Overtaking** animation and the sound narration end together.

You will synchronize the visible animation to the visible sound in the following steps.

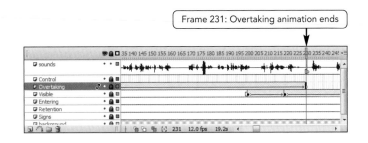

Frame 231: Overtaking animation ends

Note: You can move the frames in the Overtaking layer while it is locked, but you cannot move its artwork on the Stage.

---

16 Notice the **visible** sound begins on **Frame 232**. Click the **Visible** animation layer to select all the frames on that layer. Click and drag the first frame (starting at **Frame 201**) to **Frame 232** so that all the frames move to the right at once. The tween now begins on **Frame 232**, at the same point the **visible** sound begins.

You will move the last keyframe in the Visible layer so that the animation and sound end together next.

---

17 Notice the **visible** sound ends on **Frame 351**. Click the last keyframe in the **Visible** layer, and drag it to **Frame 351**, which will make the **Visible** animation and **visible** sound end together.

You will synchronize the entering animation to the entering sound in the following steps.

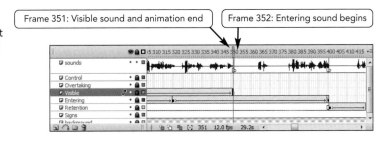

Frame 351: Visible sound and animation end

Frame 352: Entering sound begins

---

18 Notice the **entering** sound begins on **Frame 352**. Click the **Entering** layer to select all the frames on that layer. Click and drag all the frames to the right at once so the tween now begins on **Frame 352**.

You will move the last keyframe in the Entering layer so that the animation and sound end together next.

---

19 Click and drag **Frame 401** on the **sounds** layer to **Frame 452**. Notice the **entering** sound ends on **Frame 451**. Click the last keyframe in the **Entering** layer, and drag it to **Frame 451**, at the same point that the **entering** sound ends, which will make the **Entering** animation and **entering** sound end together.

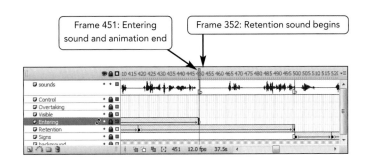

Frame 451: Entering sound and animation end

Frame 352: Retention sound begins

You will synchronize the retention animation to the retention sound in the following steps, but first you'll test your movie.

20 Choose **Control > Test Movie**. Notice the sounds and the animations to the first few letters are now synchronized, and the sounds are not cut short!

You will complete the rest of the movie in the following steps.

21 Close the preview window. Notice the **retention** sound begins on **Frame 452**. Click the **Retention** layer to select all the frames on that layer. Click and drag all the frames to the right at once so that the tween now begins on **Frame 452**.

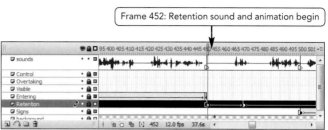

Frame 452: Retention sound and animation begin

You will move the last keyframe in the Retention layer so that the animation and sound end together next.

22 Click and drag **Frame 501** on the **sounds** layer to **Frame 582**. Click the last keyframe in the **Retention** layer, and drag it to **Frame 581**, which will make the **Retention** animation and **retention** sound end together.

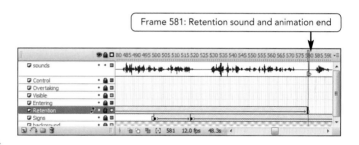

Frame 581: Retention sound and animation end

You will synchronize the Signs animation to the signs sound in the following steps.

23 Notice the **signs** sound begins on **Frame 582**. Click the **Signs** layer to select all the frames on that layer. Click and drag all the frames to the right at once so that the tween now begins on **Frame 582**.

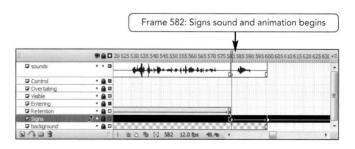

Frame 582: Signs sound and animation begins

Next, you will move the last keyframe on the Signs layer so that the animation and sound end together.

24 Click the last keyframe on the **sounds** layer, and drag it to **Frame 681**. Then click the last keyframe on the **Signs** layer, and drag it to **Frame 681**, which will make the **Signs** animation and **signs** sound end together.

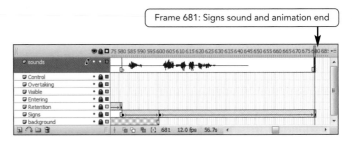

Frame 681: Signs sound and animation end

You will clean up the Timeline next. When you are done, you will have a movie with perfectly synchronized narration and animation!

---

25 On the **background** layer, select **Frame 681**, and press **F5** to add frames, which will make the **background** layer visible throughout the entire movie.

You will delete the extra frames on the Signs layer next.

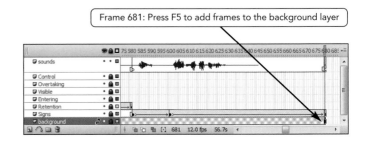

Frame 681: Press F5 to add frames to the background layer

---

26 On the **Signs** layer, click and drag to select all the remaining frames after **Frame 630**. **Right-click** (Windows) or **Ctrl-click** (Mac), and choose **Remove Frames** in the contextual menu, which will clean up the **Timeline** by removing all the selected frames.

---

27 Choose **Control > Test Movie** again to preview the movie and double-check that all the animations and sounds are synced.

---

28 When you are finished, close the preview window, and close **soundSync.fla**. You don't need to save your changes.

Controlling Animation and Sound with Stop and Play Buttons

In the previous exercise, you learned how to sync the sound with the animation. This exercise takes the project file one step further. You will add **Stop** and **Play** buttons from the **Common Libraries** that ship with Flash CS3 and make the animation and the sound stop at the same time.

---

1 Open **SoundAnimCtrl.fla** from the **chap_14** exercise folder.

---

2 In the main **Timeline**, click the **Insert Layer** button to add a new layer. Rename the new layer **buttons**, and place it below the **sounds** layer.

You will add Stop and Play buttons to the Stage from the Common Libraries in the following steps.

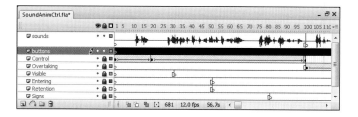

---

3 Choose **Window > Common Libraries > Buttons** to open the **Buttons Library**. Double-click the **playback rounded** folder to expand it.

Note: In the Common Libraries that ship with Flash CS3, you will find premade buttons and sounds you can quickly add to your Flash movies.

4 Select **Frame 1** on the **buttons** layer. Drag an instance of the **rounded grey stop** and **rounded grey play** buttons from the **Buttons.fla Library** to the **Stage**.

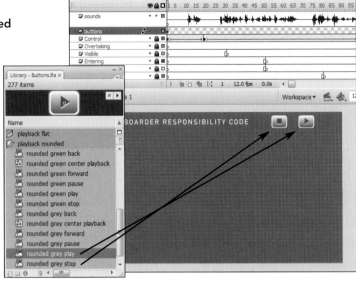

5 Press **Ctrl+L** (Windows) or **Cmd+L** (Mac) to open the **Library** panel. Notice the two buttons you just added from the **Buttons Library** are now in the **Library** panel of your project file.

You will add the ActionScript to the Stop button on the Stage next.

6 On the **Stage**, click the **Stop** button instance to select it. In the **Instance Name** field of the **Property inspector**, type **stop_btn**. Select the **Play** button, and in the Instance Name field of the **Property inspector**, type **play_btn**.

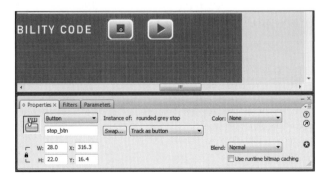

7 On the **Timeline**, select the **sounds** layer, and click the **Insert Layer** button. Name the new layer **actions**, and lock the layer. Select the first keyframe of the **actions** layer, and open the **Actions** panel by choosing **Window > Actions**.

8 Make sure **Script Assist** is turned off. Click in the **Script** pane, and type the following:

```
stop_btn.addEventListener(MouseEvent.CLICK,
stopMovie);
```

This ActionScript tells the Play and Stop buttons to listen for mouse clicks. Depending on which button is clicked, either the **stopMovie()** or **playMovie()** function will run. You will write the **stopMovie()** function in the next step.

9 Press **Enter** (Windows) or **Return** (Mac) twice, and create the **stopMovie()** function by typing the following:

```
function stopMovie(event:MouseEvent):void
{
  stop();
}
```

This ActionScript creates the **stopMovie()** function that will run when a site visitor clicks the **stop_btn** button. When the function runs, the movie will pause, stopping the sound and animation.

10 Close the preview window, and choose **Control > Test Movie** to test the **Stop** button.

Notice when you click the Stop button, the sound and the animation stop at the same time. Cool! You will add the ActionScript to the Play button next.

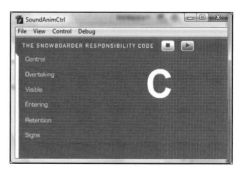

11 Return to the **Actions** panel. Insert your cursor before line 1, and press **Enter** (Windows) or **Return** (Mac) to insert a new line. Go up to the new line, and type the following:
`play_btn.addEventListener(MouseEvent.CLICK, playMovie);`

12 Select lines 5–8, **right-click** (Windows) or **Ctrl-click** (Mac) the selected code, and choose **Copy** in the contextual menu.

13 Click after the closed curly brace on the last line of your code, and press **Enter** (Windows) or **Return** (Mac) to insert a new line. **Right-click** (Windows) or **Ctrl-click** (Mac) in the **Script** pane, and choose **Paste** in the contextual menu.

14 In the pasted code, change **stopMovie** to **playMovie**, and change **stop()** to **play()**.

15 Choose **Control > Test Movie** to test the movie again. Click the **Stop** button, and notice the sound and animation stop at the same time. Click the **Play** button, and notice the sound and animation begin playing at the same time and pick up where they last ended.

The ActionScript you added to the buttons in this exercise instructs the playhead to either stop or play, and since the sound Sync option is set to Stream, the sounds will stop anytime the playhead stops. Stream sounds are dependent on the Timeline.

VIDEO: | **volumeCntrl.mov**

Now that you know how to add sound to your Flash CS3 movies and how to stop and play them, you will expand your Flash CS3 skills by learning how to add volume control through ActionScript 3.0. Controls are an important component for any project containing sound so users can adjust their own volume settings.

To learn more about adding volume control, check out **volumeCntrl.mov** in the **videos** folder on the **Flash HOT CD-ROM**.

16 When you are finished, close the preview window, and close **SoundAnimCtrl.fla**. You don't need to save your changes.

Congratulations! That completes another chapter. A lot of information was covered here, but you should now feel comfortable working with sound in Flash CS3. If you feel like you need more practice, you can always review the exercises again. Working with components and forms is next!

15

Components and Forms

Components in Adobe Flash CS3 Professional help you automate complex tasks, which can be time-consuming and repetitive. For example, rather than building from scratch a scrollable list box offering users choices that are highlighted when a cursor moves over them, you can drag the **List** component to the **Stage** and presto—you have a scrollable list box! All you have to do is add the words you want to appear in the list. This chapter introduces you to working with components in Flash CS3 to create a form. In the following exercises, you will add components to a project file, configure them to display the correct information for the user, and then modify them so they match the interface design.

What Are Components?

Components are like movie clip symbols on steroids—they are a special type of prebuilt movie clip with parameters that let you modify their appearance and behavior. A component can be a simple user interface control, such as a check box or radio button, or it can be a complicated control element, such as a media controller or a scroll pane. Components also contain an ActionScript API (**A**pplication **P**rogramming **I**nterface), which allows you to further customize their appearance and behavior. Since Flash CS3 supports both ActionScript 2.0 and ActionScript 3.0, it supports two component versions.

ActionScript 2.0 uses four categories of components: Data, Media, Video and UI (**U**ser **I**nterface). ActionScript 3.0, new to Flash CS3, contains only two: User Interface and Video. You can use either type of components in Flash CS3, but you can use only one per document. The component version is based on the player and ActionScript versions chosen in the **Publish** settings of your document. Only those component types will show up in your **Components panel**. For example, if you start a new Flash file (ActionScript 3.0) document, your **Components** panel will contain Video components and User Interface components, as shown in the illustration here. User Interface components include a check box, combo box, menu bar, list box, button, radio button, scroll pane, and several others.

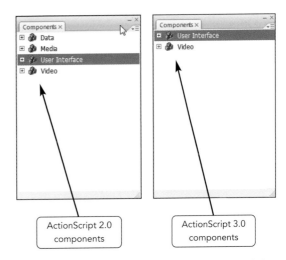

ActionScript 2.0 components

ActionScript 3.0 components

This chapter will concentrate on ActionScript 3.0 components. But whatever version you use to publish your document, you can use the components individually or together to create user interface elements such as forms or surveys. In addition, you can modify the appearance of each component by changing such aspects as the size, font, font size, and font color. A chart listing a sampling of ActionScript 3.0 components follows. For a complete list of ActionScript 2.0 and 3.0 components, visit the "Types of Components" section of Flash Help.

Component Examples	
Type	**Description**
Button	Accepts standard mouse and keyboard interactions. You can program this component to carry out a specific command when the user clicks it or presses **Enter** (Windows) or **Return** (Mac).
CheckBox	Lets users select or deselect this check box.
ComboBox	Displays a single choice with a pop-up menu revealing additional choices.
	continues on next page

Component Examples *continued*	
Type	**Description**
Label	Lets you quickly create a label, similar to using a text field with an instance name assigned to it.
List	Offers a list of all choices in a scrollable menu.
Numeric Stepper	Lets users step through an ordered set of numbers.
ProgressBar	Displays the loading progress while a user waits for content to load.
RadioButton	Lets you add several instances of the radio button to your project file and prevents more than one choice in a group of radio buttons.
ScrollPane	Lets the user view movie clips, JPEGs, and SWF files through a scrollable window.
TextArea	Displays text or lets users type text.
TextInput	Lets users type text (for a user name or password, for example).
UILoader	Loads other movies or JPEGs.
UIScrollBar	Lets the user add a scroll bar to a text field.
Controllers: Back Button, and so on	Provides standard user interface controls (**Play**, **Pause**, and so on) for media playback.
FLVPlayback	Provides a window with a set of prefabricated controllers and skin to display FLV files.

Working with Components

When working with components, you'll go through these phases:

- Adding the components to your project file
- Configuring components
- Modifying the component themes to change their appearances
- Writing ActionScript to gather and submit the data for the form

This chapter concentrates on just the first three phases because the fourth involves more complicated ActionScript and custom server configurations—both subjects that fall outside the scope of this book. To learn more about this topic, check out the resources listed in Appendix B, *"Flash CS3 Professional Resources."*

1 | Creating a Form

The first step in working with components is to add them to your Flash CS3 project file. This exercise shows you how to do just that by creating a form.

---

1 Copy the **chap_15** folder from the **Flash HOT CD-ROM** to your desktop. Open **orderForm_Final.fla** from the **chap_15** folder. Choose **Control > Test Movie** to preview the file. This is the finished version of the form you'll be creating throughout the exercises of this chapter. Test the different form elements to see how they work. When you are finished, close the preview window, and close **orderForm_Final.fla**.

Note: If you click the Submit button, nothing happens because this form is not set up to submit the data to a server.

---

2 Open **orderForm.fla** from the **chap_15** folder.

---

3 On the main **Timeline**, click the **Insert Layer** button to add a new layer. Rename the new layer **components**, and make sure it is on top, above the other two layers.

Tip: You can choose View > Magnification > Show All to see all the Stage at one time.

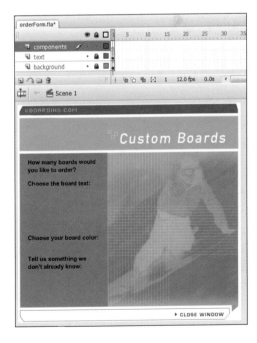

4 Choose **Window > Components** to open the **Components** panel, which is where all the components are stored. Click the **+** (Windows) or **triangle** (Mac) to expand the **User Interface** category. Drag an instance of the **ComboBox** component to the **Stage**, just to the right of the **How many boards would you like to order?** text.

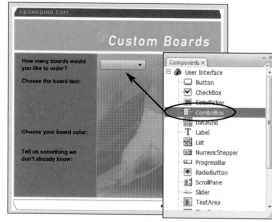

You have just added the first component to your movie! The ComboBox component will display a single choice with a pop-up menu revealing additional choices. You will configure the ComboBox choices in the next exercise.

Tip: You can also double-click a component in the Components panel to add it to your project file. However, doing so adds the component to the center of the Stage; you then have to drag it to the desired position.

5 Press **Ctrl+L** (Windows) or **Cmd+L** (Mac) to open the **Library** panel.

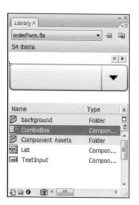

Notice the Library panel now contains the ComboBox component and a folder called background, which I created for you ahead of time; it contains all the files that make up the interface of this project file. For each component you add to your project, Flash CS3 will add the component to the Library panel.

However, also notice that two other components have been added to the Library panel that you did not add to the Stage, List and TextInput, along with a folder called Component Assets. Remember that components can contain other components? Well, List and TextInput are subcomponents of ComboBox. The Component Assets folder contains the skins you will be working with in Exercise 3. For now, you can ignore these items.

6 In the **Components** panel, drag an instance of the **List** component to the **Stage**, just to the right of the **Choose the board text** text.

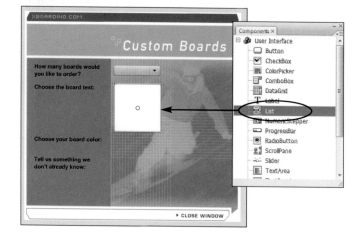

The List component offers a list of all choices in a scrollable menu.

7 In the **Components** panel, drag an instance of the **RadioButton** component to the **Stage**, just to the right of the **Choose your board color** text.

The RadioButton component lets you add several instances of the radio button to your project file (which you will do in the next step). Once you group them by assigning each instance a group name, it will prevent users from selecting more than one choice in that group of radio buttons.

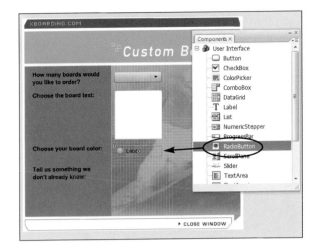

8 In the **Library** panel, drag three more instances of the **RadioButton** component to the **Stage**, and position them below the **List** component. Don't worry about aligning them precisely; you will do this shortly.

Note: Why did you add more radio buttons from the Library panel and not from the Components panel? Once you add a component to your project file, the component is added to the Library panel. From then on, it is convenient to drag additional instances of the component to the Stage from the Library panel (just as you would for any other Library element).

9 In the **Components** panel, drag an instance of the **TextArea** component to the **Stage**, just to the right of the **Tell us something we don't already know** text. With the **TextArea** component still selected, select the **Free Transform** tool in the **Tools** panel, and click and drag to resize the **TextArea** component, as shown in the illustration here.

The TextArea component lets users add comments along with the form submission. It automatically displays a scroll bar if the message becomes longer than the box.

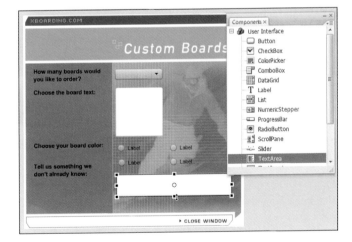

10 In the **Components** panel, drag an instance of the **Button** component to the **Stage**, just below the **TextArea** component.

The Button component accepts standard mouse and keyboard interactions, and you can program it to carry out a specific command when the user clicks it or presses Enter (Windows) or Return (Mac).

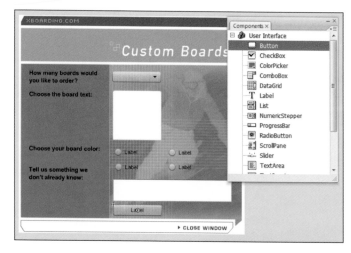

After you add the Button component, take another look at the Library panel. Notice each of the components you have placed on the Stage is now also located in the Library panel. As mentioned previously, you can add instances of each component by dragging them from the Library panel. You may be wondering what the difference is. Dragging instances from the Library panel is important when you make changes to the component skins, since these changes are stored with the component in the Library panel, not with the master copy in the Components panel. You'll learn more about skins in Exercise 3.

11 Choose **Window > Align** to open the **Align** panel. With the **Selection** tool, **Shift-click** all the components that are nearest the white vertical interface line to select each. In the **Align** panel, click the **Align left edge** button to align the selected components vertically. (Make sure the **To stage** option is not selected.)

Note: Because of the Snap Align functionality, the components may already be aligned. But the Align panel is helpful for aligning multiple elements at the same time or for distributing elements evenly across the Stage.

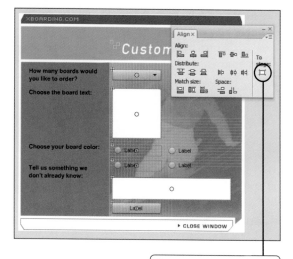

To stage option not selected

12 Click off the **Stage** to deselect everything. **Shift-click** the two right **RadioButton** components. In the **Align** panel, click the **Align right edge** button to align the two components.

13 Press the **Shift** key to select the other two **RadioButton** components. Select the **Free Transform** tool in the **Tools** panel, press the **Shift** key again, and click and drag from the center anchor point on the right to make the components slightly longer.

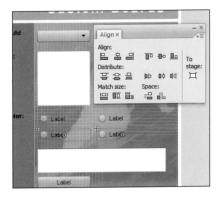

14 Click off the **Stage** to deselect everything. **Shift-click** the top two **RadioButton** components. In the **Align** panel, click the **Align top edge** button to align the top of the components. Click off the **Stage** to deselect everything again. **Shift-click** the bottom two **RadioButton** components. In the **Align** panel, click the **Align bottom edge** button to align the bottom of the **RadioButton** components to each other.

15 When you are finished, save your changes, and leave **orderForm.fla** open for the next exercise.

2 | Configuring Components

Now that you have the components in place, you need to make some adjustments so they display the correct information to the user. This exercise shows you how to do this by setting the parameters for each component.

---

1 If you just completed Exercise 1, **orderForm.fla** should still be open. If it's not, complete Exercise 1, and then return to this exercise. On the **Stage**, click the **ComboBox** component to select it. Choose **Window > Properties > Properties** to open the **Property inspector**. Click the **Parameters** tab.

Notice the Parameters tab looks a little different than normal; this is part of the built-in functionality of the component.

Note: In addition to using the Property inspector, you can also view the parameters for a component by using the Component inspector panel. To do this, choose Window > Component inspector to open the panel. Select a component instance on the Stage to view the parameters associated with that component.

Using the Component inspector panel will give you the same information as using the Parameters tab in the Property inspector; choose whichever workflow works better for you. In this exercise, you will be using the Property inspector to modify the component parameters.

---

2 In the **Property inspector**, type **quantityCB** in the **Instance Name** field, which gives the **ComboBox** an instance name so that you can reference it with ActionScript.

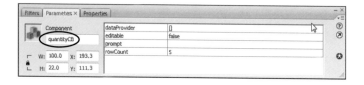

3 Double-click the **dataProvider** parameter to open the **Values** dialog box, where you will type the values users can select in a scrollable pop-up menu.

4 In the **Values** dialog box, click the plus (**+**) button to type a new value. Click in the **label** value field, and type **1**. Leave the **data** field blank. Click the plus (**+**) button again to type the next value. Click in the **label** value field, and type **2**. Repeat this step to add **3**, **4**, and **5** to the list. When you are finished, click **OK**.

5 Choose **Control > Test Movie** to test your **ComboBox** component. The numbers you typed will appear in a pop-up list, making the configuration for this component complete. When you are finished, close the preview window.

Note: You may have noticed that the highlight color when you move your cursor over an option in the ComboBox is light blue. This is the result of the Aeon Halo color scheme built into Flash CS3 components. Unlike previous versions of Flash, ActionScript 3.0 files do not support the external theme files. Instead, you modify the component skins. The default color for most skins is this light blue. In an upcoming exercise, you'll change the color to match the green in the interface design of orderForm.fla.

6 Click the **List** component to select it. In the **Property inspector**, type **textLB** in the **Instance Name** text box, which gives the **List** component an instance name so you can refer to it with ActionScript. Double-click the **dataProvider** parameter to open the **Values** dialog box. Here again, you will type the values users can select in a scrollable pop-up menu.

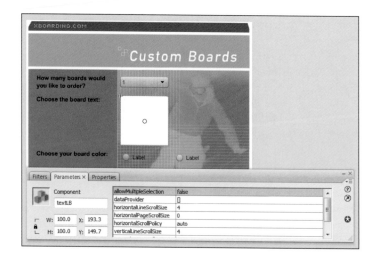

7 In the **Values** dialog box, click the plus (**+**) button to enter a new value. Click in the **label** field, and type **boardThis**. Leave the **data** field blank. Click the plus (**+**) button again to type the next value. Click in the **label** value field, and type **gone boarding**. Repeat this step six more times to add the rest of the text options to match the illustration shown here. When you are finished, click **OK**.

Tip: If you want to move any of your entries higher or lower in the list, you can select the value and use the up or down buttons at the top of the Values dialog box to move them where you want them.

8 Choose **Control > Test Movie** to test the **List** component. Use the scroll bar in the **List** component to see all the options you created for the user. Notice, however, the longer text is cut off. You will change this next. When you are finished, close the preview window.

9 In the **Tools panel**, select the **Free Transform** tool. On the **Stage**, click the **List** component to select it. Press **Alt** (Windows) or **Opt** (Mac), and click and drag the middle handle on the right of the bounding box to the right to resize the **List** component, making all text entries visible.

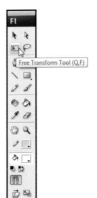

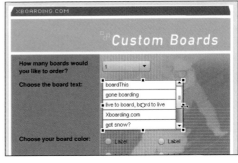

Note: You can modify the width and height of List components in your project file by using the Free Transform tool. However, you can modify only the width of ComboBox components with the Free Transform tool; the height of the ComboBox component is set by the font size of the menu choices and the Row Count parameter that determines the number of choices visible in the pop-up menu at one time.

---

10 Choose the **Selection** tool in the **Tools** panel. On the **Stage**, select the upper-left **RadioButton** component. In the **Parameters** tab of the **Property inspector**, type **redRB** for **Instance Name**. Select the **groupName** parameter, and type **colorGroup**. Select the **label** parameter, and type **firecracker red**. Set the **selected** parameter to **true**. Leave the **labelPlacement** parameter set to **right** (the default value). Leave the **value** field blank.

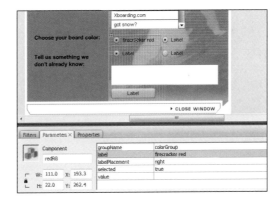

The groupName parameter you set makes this RadioButton part of a group of RadioButton components called colorGroup. The label parameter sets the label that will appear to the right of the RadioButton. A value of true for the selected parameter will make the RadioButton selected by default. (Only one radio button in a group can have the selected state as true.) The labelPlacement parameter sets the location of the RadioButton label text to either the right or the left of the RadioButton component.

---

11 On the **Stage**, select the upper-right **RadioButton** component. In the **Property inspector**, type **greyRB** for **Instance Name**. Select the **groupName** parameter, and type **colorGroup**. Select the **label** parameter, and type **gunmetal grey**. Make sure the **selected** parameter is set to **false**.

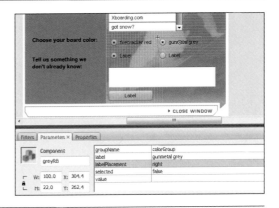

12 On the **Stage**, select the lower-left **RadioButton** component. In the **Property inspector**, type **blackRB** for **Instance Name**. Select the **groupName** parameter, and type **colorGroup**. Select the **label** parameter, and type **lights out black**. Make sure the **selected** parameter is set to **false**.

You need to set the parameters for just one more button.

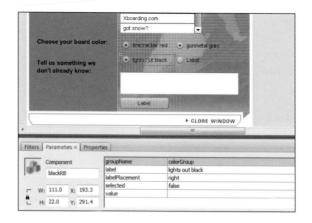

13 Select the lower-right **RadioButton** component. In the **Property inspector**, type **blueRB** for **Instance Name**. Select the **groupName** parameter, and type **colorGroup**. Select the **label** parameter, and type **midnight blue**. Make sure the **selected** parameter is set to **false**. Click any empty area on the **Stage** to deselect the button.

14 Choose **Control > Test Movie** to test the **RadioButton** components.

Notice the firecracker red RadioButton is selected by default. Although you can click to select any of the other RadioButton components, notice you can select only one at a time. This is an example of components at their finest—all the behind-the-scenes work has been done for you. You just placed them where you needed them and set their desired parameters. You now have a fully functional group of RadioButton components. Sweet! When you are finished, close the preview window.

15 On the **Stage**, click the **TextArea** component to select it. In the **Property inspector**, type **messageTxt** for **Instance Name**. Make sure the **wordWrap** parameter is set to **true** and **editable** is also set to **true**. Leave the **text** parameter empty.

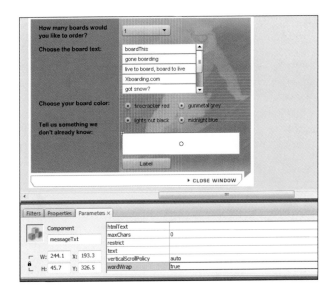

16 Choose **Control > Test Movie** to test the scrolling input text box. Try typing a large amount of text; notice a scroll bar will automatically appear and resize as you type. Cool! When you are finished, close the preview window.

You have one last component to configure next.

17 On the **Stage**, click the **Button** component to select it. In the **Property inspector**, type **submitBtn** for **Instance Name**. For the **label** parameter, type **Submit**, which will be the label that appears on the **Button** component. Click any empty area on the **Stage** to deselect the button.

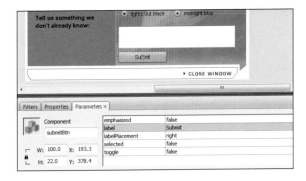

18 Choose **Control > Test Movie** to preview your **Button** component. Notice the label of the button now reads **Submit** instead of **Label**.

Note: To test the functionality of the Submit button, including collecting all the data entered on the form and actually sending it to a server, you would need to add more ActionScript to the movie. You would also need access to a Web server and middleware such as Adobe ColdFusion Server or Microsoft Active Server Pages (ASP). All of this is beyond the scope of this book. You can, however, visit the Adobe Flash Support Center at www.adobe.com/support/flash/applications_building.html to find articles and resources that will teach you how to use ActionScripting to gather and submit data typed in a form like the one you have created here.

---

19 When you are finished, save your changes, and leave **orderForm.fla** open for the next exercise.

For more information about each of the Flash CS3 components, choose Help > Flash Help. In the Help panel, choose Books > ActionScript 3.0 Components.

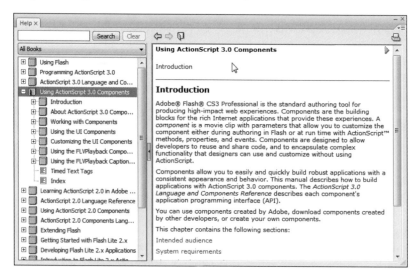

Modifying ActionScript 3.0 Component Skins

In the previous exercises, you learned how to add components to your project and create a form. You may have noticed the light blue tint that appears when you move your cursor over an item or make a selection. Fortunately, you are not stuck with this color.

Unlike ActionScript 2.0, ActionScript 3.0 components do not support **themes**, which are global support files that exist outside the Flash file. Instead of using ActionScript, you modify the appearance of these components directly in Flash, similar to the way you modify the appearance of a symbol. However, components are composed of a number of different skins for each of their different states, and changing them can be time-consuming. In this example, you'll change just one state of one component so that you can see how this works and explore it more in depth on your own.

1 If you just completed Exercise 2, **orderForm.fla** should still be open. If it's not, complete Exercise 2, and then return to this exercise. Choose **Control > Test Movie** to preview the form you have created up to this point. Notice that when you select or move your cursor over a field, the highlight color for the components changes to light blue. You will change this color in the following steps. When you are finished, close the preview window.

2 Double-click the **ComboBox** component on the **Stage**. Notice that you have opened a separate **Timeline** in Flash, consisting of two frames, as shown in the illustration here.

There are skins for different buttons states, such as Up, Down, and Over, but there are also two components listed, a TextInput component and a List component. Components can contain other components, just as other symbols can reside in a movie clip symbol.

3 Double-click the **Down Skin** component on the **Stage** to edit this skin. Notice that you have opened a third **Timeline** in Flash.

The component skin is composed of four layers—one for the border, one for the fill, one for the highlight color, and one for the arrow icon.

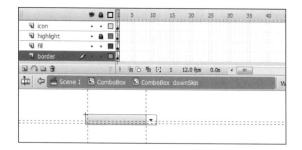

NOTE:

What Are Those Lines?

You may notice that when you open certain movie clip symbol **Timeline** panels in Flash CS3 that four dotted lines appear, cutting the symbol into nine sections. These lines are known as **slicing guides** and are part of a feature called **nine-slice scaling**. Nine-slice scaling has been included in Illustrator for quite some time and has been added to Flash and Adobe Photoshop as part of Creative Suite 3.

Nine-slice scaling slices a symbol into nine distinct sections so that when you resize an object, it scales independently in each of the sections. This really comes in handy when you have an object containing text, as you can see in the illustration shown here. The first object represents the original button. The second object has been set for nine-slice scaling and then scaled using the **Free Transform** tool. The third object was resized without nine-slice scaling.

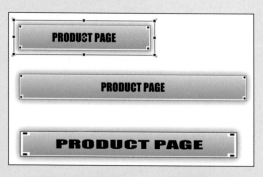

To turn nine-slice scaling on or off, select the symbol (or in this case, the component skin) in the **Library** panel, and choose **Properties** in the **Library Options** menu. Click the **Advanced** button, and select or deselect the **Enable guides for 9-slice scaling** option.

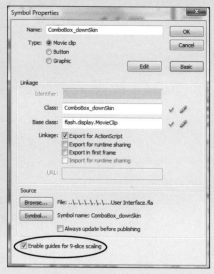

4 Click the **border** layer name on the **Timeline** to select the contents on the **Stage**.

5 Select the **Ink Bottle** tool in the **Tools** panel. Click the **Stroke** color box, and select a green color in the color well. Click the border of the component on the **Stage** to change the stroke color.

Note: You may want to increase the size of the Stage to 200% to make the button easier to work with.

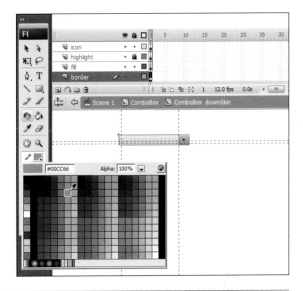

6 Select the **fill** layer on the **Timeline**. Click the **Fill** color box in the **Tools** panel. The **Ink Bottle** tool should still be selected. Choose a light green color, and click the component on the **Stage** to change the fill color.

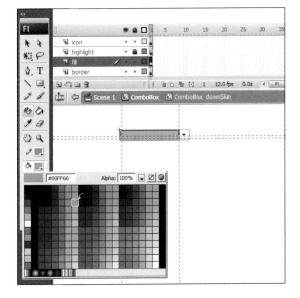

7 Unlock the **highlight** layer by clicking the **lock** icon on the **Timeline**. Click the layer name to select the layer. Click the **Stroke** color box, and choose the darker green color used in Step 5 in the color well.

That's it! Modifying skins is as easy as modifying any other object on the Stage.

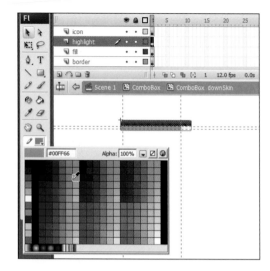

8 Click **Scene 1** in the **edit bar** to exit the component **Timeline** and return to the main **Timeline**.

NOTE:

What Is a Hexadecimal Value?

Hexadecimal values are six-digit number/letter combinations used to identify specific colors in ActionScript and many other programming languages. For a quick glance at which hexadecimal values belong to what colors, you can use the **Eyedropper** tool to sample a color used in the interface or a color swatch in the **Color Mixer**. The hexadecimal value will generate in the **Hexadecimal Value** field.

If you're familiar with HTML (**H**yper**T**ext **M**arkup **L**anguage), you may be more familiar with hexadecimal values in the format #FFFFFF instead of 0x000000. The 0x in front of the hex colors is short for *hexadecimal*.

---

9 Press **Ctrl+Enter** (Windows) or **Cmd+Enter** (Mac) to test the movie.

Hmmm. At first glance, the list box doesn't appear any different.

10 Click the down arrow to display the combo box options.

Did you notice the pop-up menu change to green for moment? That's the point when you clicked, otherwise known as the **down state**. Press and hold your mouse to see the change in the skin, as shown in the illustration here.

Note: You may notice that there is still a narrow blue border around the pop-up menu. That is because of another skin, the focus skin, which you haven't modified from the original blue.

11 Close the movie window. Choose **Window > Library** to open the **Library** panel.

Now you'll examine where these component skins are stored.

12 Double-click the **Component Assets** folder to expand it. Double-click the **ComboBox Skins** folder to expand it as well.

Not only are the components copied over to the project Library panel, but the component assets are as well, which includes the component skins. Notice in the Type column, components are listed as Components, whereas component skins appear listed as Movie Clip Symbols.

So, what happens when you use this component in another project? You'll find out in the next few steps.

13 Choose **File > New**, and select **Flash File (ActionScript 3.0)**. Choose **Window > Components** to open the **Components** panel.

14 Click and drag the **ComboBox** component to the **Stage**. Choose **Window > Properties > Parameters** to open the **Parameters** panel, if it is not already open. Double-click the field next to **dataProvider** to open the **Values** dialog box.

You need to add at least two values to see the combo box in action.

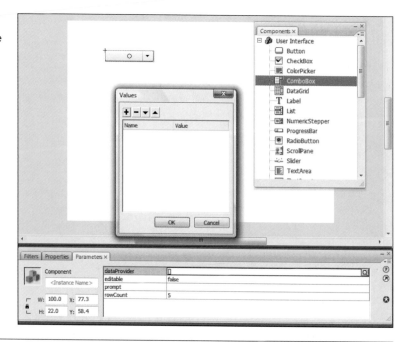

15 Click the **Add** button twice, and change the labels fields to **1** and **2**, respectively. Click **OK** to close the **Values** dialog box.

16 Press **Ctrl+Enter** (Windows) or **Cmd+Enter** (Mac) to test the movie.

17 Press and hold your mouse on the combo box.

Notice that the pop-up menu stays blue when you click. The changes to the Down state weren't carried over to the new document. That's because changes to component skins reside in movies. They are not saved in the Components panel, but in the project Library panel as you saw in Step 12. However, you can share skins between projects. Simply use the Open External Library command, and drag the component or just the skin from one Library panel to the other.

ActionScript 3.0 components also contain a set of styles that specify which skins and icons to use for each component state, and you can modify them using ActionScript. For more information on modifying component skins and styles, check out Appendix B, *"Flash CS3 Professional Resources."*

18 Close the preview window, close the unsaved Flash file, and close **orderForm.fla**; you don't need to save your changes.

Using Adobe Flash Exchange

Now that you're more familiar with components and how beneficial it can be to use them in your movies, take a look at Adobe Flash Exchange. This is a special section of the Adobe Web site that lets users post components and other extensions to a searchable forum. Many of these components were created by Adobe or third-party developers. You can download hundreds of reusable components to build projects, templates for designing Flash content, reusable ActionScript code snippets, additional symbol libraries, and more.

To download these extensions, simply go to **www.adobe.com/exchange/flash**, and search through the various categories to find extensions you find useful or interesting.

Note: To download content from the Flash Exchange, you must have an Adobe account. If you don't already have one, sign up now so you can continue with the download process.

The **Categories** pop-up menu organizes the extensions into a variety of topics for easy access. You can also check out the **Flash Top Ten** sidebar for the highest rated, newest, and most downloaded extensions.

If you select a category in the **Categories** pop-up menu, you'll get a listing of components and other resources. This page gives you useful information about each extension, such as the author,

availability, number of downloads, rating, product compatibility, and date created.

Note: At the time of this writing, few extensions were available for Flash CS3. Be sure to check for an update of available extensions.

Using the Exchange search functionality, you can search by keyword, category, and several other categories to quickly find what you want.

To install an extension, download it to your computer, and follow the onscreen instructions provided by the Adobe Extension Manager. (For more information, search for *Flash Exchange* in Flash Help.)

After installing a component extension, you'll see the extension in the **Components** panel. You can use the downloaded components the same way you would any other components in the **Components** panel—by dragging the component to the **Stage**.

That's a wrap on this chapter. Great work! Now that you are more familiar with components, take a quick break and get ready for the next action-packed (pun intended) chapter: *"Video."*

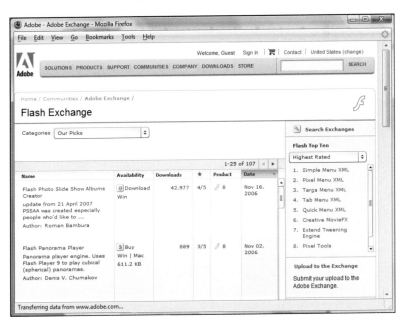

16

Video

The capability to include video in a SWF file was introduced in Adobe Flash MX. This feature opened up many opportunities for Flash developers. Video clips imported into Adobe Flash CS3 can be controlled using very basic ActionScript, can be targeted to let users jump from point to point in the clip, can have alpha transparency effects applied to them, and can be published from within Flash as Apple QuickTime files. In Adobe Flash CS3 Professional, Adobe has added more video compression options, a stand-alone video-encoding application for batch processing multiple files, and the capability to trim and edit video clips and apply color correction. It also includes more options for importing video into Flash projects. The exercises in this chapter lay the groundwork for working with Flash Video.

Importing Video into Flash CS3

Flash CS3 can import video in the most popular file formats. If you have QuickTime 4 or newer (Windows or Mac) or DirectX 7 or newer (Windows only) installed on your system, you can import embedded video clips in a variety of file formats, including MOV, AVI, and MPG/MPEG.

If you attempt to import a file format not supported on your system, a warning message lets you know the operation cannot be completed. In some cases, Flash might import the video but not the audio. For example, audio is not supported in MPG/MPEG files imported with QuickTime 4. In such cases, Flash displays a warning indicating that the audio portion of the file cannot be imported. You can still import the video without sound.

Flash documents with embedded video can be published as SWF files. Flash documents with linked video must be published in the QuickTime format. The following charts list the video formats that QuickTime 4 or newer (Windows and Mac) and DirectX 7 and newer (Windows only) support:

Supported Video Formats with QuickTime 4 or Newer (Windows and Mac)

File Type	Extension
Audio Video Interleaved	.avi
Digital video	.dv
QuickTime video	.mov
Motion Picture Experts Group	.mpg, .mpeg

Supported Video Formats with DirectX 7 or Newer (Windows Only)

File Type	Extension
Audio Video Interleaved	.avi
Windows Media File	.wmv, .asf
Motion Picture Experts Group	.mpg, .mpeg

Understanding On2 VP6 and Sorenson Spark Video Compression

By default, Flash Video Encoder exports encoded video by using the new On2 VP6 video codec for use with Flash Player 8 or newer or by using the Sorenson Spark codec for use with Flash Player 7. A **codec** is an algorithm that controls the way video files are compressed and decompressed during import and export.

The On2 VP6 video codec is the preferred video codec to use when creating Flash content that uses video. On2 VP6 provides the best combination of video quality while maintaining a small file size.

If your Flash content dynamically loads Flash Video (using either progressive download or Flash Media Server), you can use On2 VP6 video without having to republish your SWF file for Flash Player 8, as long as users use Flash Player 8 or newer to view your content. Only Flash Player 8 and 9 supports both publishing and playing back On2 VP6 video. The following chart lists the codecs supported by different Flash versions:

Codecs Supported by Flash Versions		
Codec for Playback	**SWF File Version**	**Flash Player Required**
Sorenson Spark	6	6, 7, 8, 9
	7	7, 8, 9
On2 VP6	6	8, 9
	7	8, 9
	8	8, 9
	9	9

Using the Flash CS3 Professional Video Features

Flash CS3 offers a variety of additional video features not included in Flash 8. The following chart outlines the most important video features found only in Flash CS3 Professional:

Flash CS3 Video Features	
Feature	**Description**
New and improved Flash Video Encoder	The new Flash Video Encoder now includes the ability to deinterlace video during the encoding process. Deinterlacing your video reduces the risk of artifacts appearing in your final video.
Flash 9 skins	Flash CS3 includes new video player skins for Flash Player 9 that work with the new full-screen mode.
Cue points	You can embed cue points directly into an FLV file and trigger events during playback. Cue points can now be exported and imported from other Adobe video-editing applications such as Adobe After Effects.
Better QuickTime exports	Now, you can export ActionScript-generated animations to the QuickTime (**.mov**) format. Also, you can export content with nested movie clips and effects.

Using Adobe Flash Video (FLV)

The Adobe FLV file format lets you import or export a static video stream with encoded audio. This format is intended for use with communications applications, such as video conferencing, and files exported from the Flash Media Server.

When you export video clips with streaming audio in FLV format, the audio is compressed using the **Audio Stream** settings under the **Flash** tab of the **Publish Settings** dialog box. The video content in the FLV file is compressed with the Sorenson Spark codec.

1 | Importing Video

The first step in working with video is importing it into Flash CS3. This exercise shows you how to import a video clip into Flash CS3 as an embedded video using the Flash Import Video wizard.

1 Copy the **chap_16** folder from the **Flash HOT CD-ROM** to your desktop. Open **importVideo_Final.fla** from the **chap_16** folder. This is the finished version of the project you'll be building in this and the next exercise. Choose **Control > Test Movie** to preview the movie. Notice the movie begins in a stopped position. Click the **Play** button to start the video clip, and click the **Stop** button to stop the video clip.

You will add the functionality to the buttons, but first you will learn how to import the video clip into Flash CS3.

2 When you are finished previewing this movie, close the preview window, and close **importVideo_Final.fla**.

3 Open **importVideo.fla** from the **chap_16** folder. I created this file to get you started. Click the **Insert Layer** button to add a new layer on the **Timeline**. Rename the layer **video**, and make sure it is at the top of the layer stack.

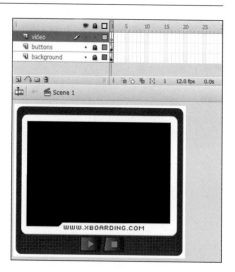

4 Choose **File > Import > Import to Stage**, and select the **jumps.mov** file from the **chap_16** folder. Click **Open** (Windows) or **Import** (Mac).

Note: This is a QuickTime video clip.

5 On the **Select Video** screen in the **Import Video** wizard, make sure the **On your computer** option is selected. Click **Next** (Windows) or **Continue** (Mac).

Flash CS3 gives you the option to import video from a local file on your computer or from a remote Web site or Flash Media Server (formerly known as a FlashCom server).

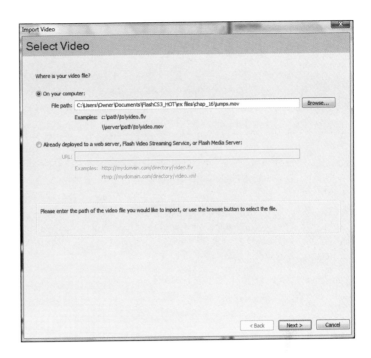

6 On the **Deployment** screen, select the **Embed video in SWF and play in timeline** option, and click **Next** (Windows) or **Continue** (Mac).

Note: You will be given a variety of options for deploying your video, including as a progressive download, streamed from an FVSS or Flash Media Server, or as a linked QuickTime movie.

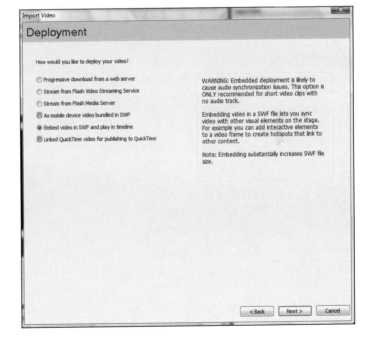

To Stream or Embed or Link?

When you import a QuickTime video clip, you can choose to stream it, embed it, or link it. If you choose to embed a video clip, the video becomes part of the movie, just as a bitmap does when imported into Flash CS3. The embedded video clip will then play in the SWF file in the Flash Player. This is helpful because users do not need any special player to view the video—they just need the Flash Player 8 (or newer) installed on their browsers.

Streaming video requires a server running the Flash Media Server software providing video delivery to each user. With streaming, each user opens a unique connection to the Flash Media Server, which lets you provide different content for users based on their ability to access and download content. For example, a user with a dial-up modem can access your streaming content, requiring much less bandwidth.

You can also choose to link to an external video file. In this case, the video will not be stored in the Flash CS3 document, and when you export the file from Flash CS3, you cannot export it as a SWF file—instead, you have to export it as a QuickTime file (**.mov**). The resulting file will not play in the Flash Player, but it will play in the QuickTime player. The next few exercises concentrate on embedded video.

---

7 On the **Embedding** screen, choose **Movie clip** in the **Symbol type** pop-up menu, select the **Place instance on stage** and **Expand timeline if needed** options, and make sure the **Embed the entire video** option is selected. Click **Next** (Windows) or **Continue** (Mac).

With the Embedding options, you can choose whether to place the video in a movie clip, place an instance on the Stage, import the entire video, or edit the video

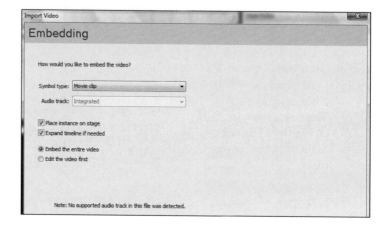

first. Later in this chapter, you will learn how to use the editing capabilities of the Import Video wizard.

Note: The Movie clip option will keep your Timeline less cluttered because all the frames needed to play the video will be nicely self-contained within a movie clip. Also, you may have noticed the audio note at the bottom of the Import Video wizard. This note will appear either if the audio codec used in the audio track is not supported on your system or if there is simply no audio attached to the video file, which is the case in this exercise.

8 On the **Encoding** screen, click the **Encoding Profiles** (Windows) or **Profiles** (Mac) tab, and select **Flash 8 – Medium Quality** in the pop-up menu.

In the encoding profile pop-up menu, you can specify a bandwidth to target. Selecting Flash 8 – Modem Quality, for instance, will compress your video so that a visitor to your Web site on a 56K modem should be able to watch the video—uninterrupted—while it is being downloaded (streamed) to the computer. If you want more control over how the video is going to be compressed, you can set additional options, including the video codec, frame rate, keyframe placement, and more, on the Video tab.

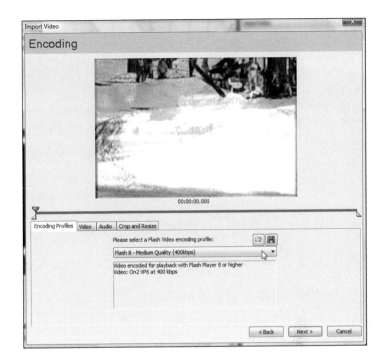

9 On the **Video** tab, make sure the **Encode video** option is selected. Set **Video codec** to **On2 VP6**, **Quality** to **Low**, and **Frame rate** to **Same as source**. In the **Key frame interval** field, type **24** to create keyframes in the video every 24 frames.

When you choose to set your own encoding options, the Video Encoding profile on the Encoding Profiles tab displays Custom. As you can see, this tab has quite a few settings. For more information on the compression settings in the Flash Import Video wizard, check out the chart at the end of this exercise.

10 Click the **Crop and Resize** tab. Make sure the **Resize video** option is not selected.

The Resize video option lets you change the width and height of the imported video.

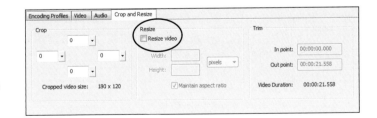

The settings in the Crop section let you crop the left, top, right, and bottom edges of the video. The Trim adjustment sliders, which are located directly below the thumbnail preview, let you trim out footage at the beginning (**In point**) or end (**Out point**) of the video. Experiment with changing these settings.

Notice the results of your adjustments are displayed in the preview window in the wizard.

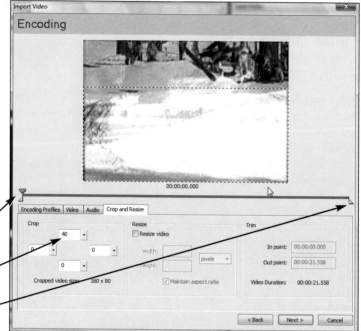

Trim In point adjustment

Cropping the top of the clip

Trim Out point adjustment

11 When you are finished experimenting, set the **Crop** and **Trim** values back to their original settings, and click **Next** (Windows) or **Continue** (Mac). On the **Finish Video Import** screen, click **Finish**.

This screen summarizes the settings you specified.

Note: If you select the After importing video, view video topics in Flash Help option, you'll open the Importing Video section of the Flash CS3 Online Help.

When you click the Finish button, the Flash Video Encoding Progress dialog box appears, providing information about the video clip being imported, including its source file, destination, video codec, video bit rate, audio codec, audio bit rate, and import progress.

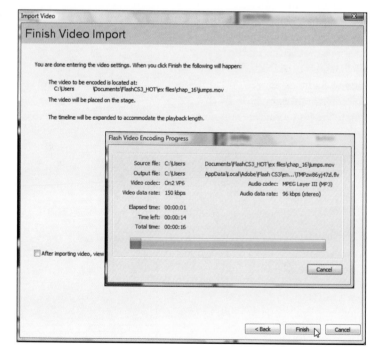

12 When the video import process finishes, the video clip appears on the **Stage**. Click the video clip to select it, and move it slightly higher so it is centered in the background window.

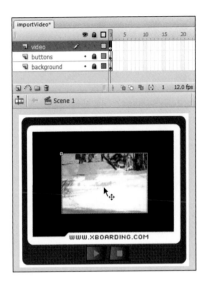

When you imported the video clip into your project, Flash places the video in the Library panel, creates a movie clip symbol, places the video (and all the frames needed to display that video) in the movie clip symbol (because in Step 7 you instructed the Import Video wizard to import your video into a movie clip instance), and places an instance of that movie clip in the center on the Stage.

13 Press **Ctrl+L** (Windows) or **Cmd+L** (Mac) to open the **Library** panel. Notice the **jumps Video** file, which is the video clip you just imported. Flash CS3 has automatically converted it to a movie clip, which is also in the **Library** panel. Select the **jumps Video** file in the **Library** panel. Click the **Properties** button to open the **Video**

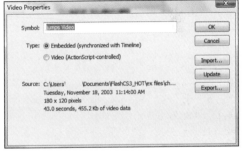

Properties dialog box, which shows the dimensions, duration in seconds, and size in kilobytes of video data. Click **OK** when you are finished.

14 Choose **Control > Test Movie** to see your movie in action in the SWF file!

Note: The buttons will not work yet—you will add ActionScript to them in the next exercise.

15 When you are finished, close the preview window. Save your changes, and leave **importVideo.fla** open for the next exercise.

Compression Settings

The following chart breaks down the compression options you can specify on the **Video** tab in the **Import Video** wizard:

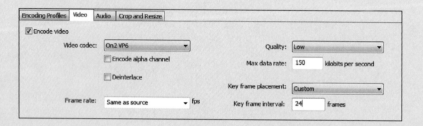

Compression Settings	
Option	**Description**
Video codec	Encodes the imported video file with either the On2 VP6 (default for Flash Player 8 and 9) or Sorenson Spark (default for Flash Player 7) codec.
Frame rate	Sets the number of frames that display for every second of playback.
Key frame placement	Specifies a custom keyframe interval or lets Flash determine the interval based on the source file.
Key frame interval	Specifies the number of keyframes per frame of your actual movie. The more keyframes you have in a video clip (the higher the number), the faster the viewers can fast-forward or rewind through a clip (if you give them that capability). But before you start thinking that's a good thing and adding a bunch of keyframes to your video clip, keep in mind the more keyframes you add to your movie, the larger it will become. For more information about keyframes, see the "Video Keyframes" sidebar following this chart.
Quality	Specifies the quality of all the frames in the video. A lower quality value will lower the quality of the video but will result in a video clip with a smaller file size. The opposite is true for a higher-quality value.

Video Keyframes

Video keyframes are different from the **Timeline** keyframes you've learned about. When you set video keyframes, you are determining how often a full, high-quality frame will be captured and stored in the final file. For example, a keyframe setting of 24 instructs Flash to import in full, every 24th frame. If the computer's processor is too slow to play all the frames, the playback will skip frames until it reaches a keyframe. If the computer can keep up with all the frames, it will play them all.

The lower the keyframe value, the more keyframes there will be in the compressed movie. The frames between keyframes (called **interframes**) will update only based on what has changed in the previous keyframe, thereby reducing file size.

You will not see the video keyframes on the main **Timeline** in Flash CS3. Instead, the video keyframes are part of the compression settings that compress the actual video file itself. Video keyframes are invisible in the project file; they simply affect the playback quality of the embedded video.

2 | Controlling Video with Stop and Play Actions

Now that you know how to import video, you need to learn how to control the video playback. This exercise shows you how to control video on the main **Timeline** by adding ActionScript to buttons to control the video clip.

---

1 If you just completed Exercise 1, **importVideo.fla** should still be open. If it's not, complete Exercise 1, and then return to this exercise.

---

2 On the **Stage**, click the video clip to select it. In the **Property inspector**, type **jumps_mc** in the **Instance Name** field.

Later in this exercise, you will use the instance name to pass ActionScript to the movie clip.

---

3 On the **Timeline**, select the **video** layer, and click the **Insert Layer** button. Name the new layer **actions**. Select the first keyframe on the **actions** layer, and open the **Actions** panel by choosing **Window > Actions**.

---

4 In the **Actions p**anel, click in the **Script** pane, and type **jumps_mc.stop();**. Press **Ctrl+Enter** (Windows) or **Cmd+Return** (Mac) to test the movie.

Notice the **jumps_mc** movie clip does not play, even though it is a MovieClip with many frames. In the next few steps, you will write the ActionScript to control its playback using the Play and Stop buttons.

Note: Another common and acceptable practice to achieve the same effect is to place a **stop()** action on the first frame inside the movie clip.

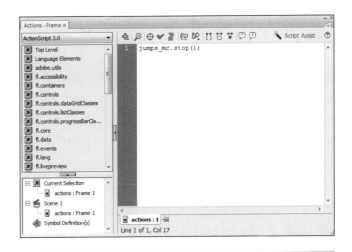

5 Close the preview window, and minimize the **Actions** panel. On the **Timeline**, lock the video layer, and unlock the **buttons** layer. On the **Stage**, click the **Play** button to select it. In the **Property inspector, type play_btn** in the **Instance Name** field. Next, click the **Stop** button to select it. In the **Property inspector**, type **stop_btn** in the **Instance Name** field.

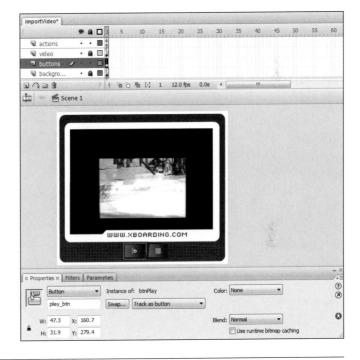

6 On the **Timeline**, select the **actions** layer, and open the **Actions** panel by choosing **Window > Actions**. After the `jumps_mc.stop();` code, you'll write a function called `playMovie` that will play `jumps_mc` when you click the play button. Type the following:

```
function playMovie(event:MouseEvent)
:void
{
    jumps_mc.play();
}
```

When this function runs, the `jumps_mc` movie clip will play. However, the

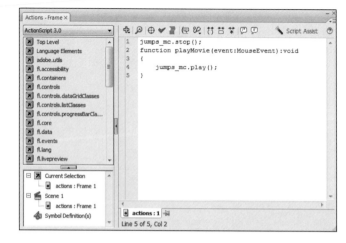

function must first be connected to the play button; otherwise, the function will never be triggered. You will add an event listener to connect the button to the function later. Next, you will create the function that will run when you click the stop button.

---

7 Select the entire `playMovie()` function (don't forget the curly braces!), and press **Ctrl+C** (Windows) or **Cmd+C** (Mac) on your keyboard to copy the code. Paste the code underneath the code you wrote in the previous step. In the pasted code, change `playMovie` to `stopMovie`, and change `jumps_mc.play()` to `jumps_mc.stop()`.

With this code, the `jumps_mc` movie clip will stop. In the next step, you will connect the two functions you just created to the stop and play buttons.

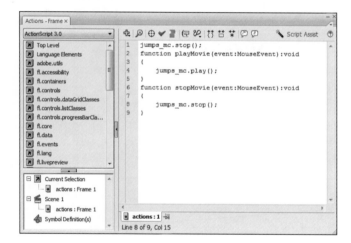

---

8 After the code you wrote in the previous step, write the code to add event listeners to the **stop** and **play** buttons and connect them to the appropriate functions. Type the following:

```
play_btn.addEventListener
(MouseEvent.CLICK, playMovie);
stop_btn.addEventListener
(MouseEvent.CLICK, stopMovie);
```

This ActionScript links the buttons on the Stage to the functions you wrote in Steps 6 and 7. The `playMovie()` function will run

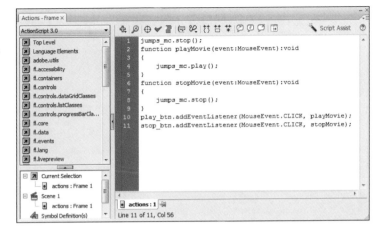

when you click the **play** button, and the `stopMovie()` function will run when you click the **stop** button.

9 Choose **Control > Test Movie** to preview the movie. Click the **play** button to set the video in motion, and click the **stop** button to stop the video again. Sweet! By adding a few basic actions, you give the user complete control over your video. When you are finished, close the preview window.

10 Close **importVideo.fla**. You don't need to save your changes.

Controlling Video by Targeting Frame Labels

Not only can you start and stop a video using ActionScript, but you can also target specific points in the video using frame labels. This exercise shows you how to use the **gotoAndPlay()** and **gotoAndStop()** methods to target different frames within the video sequence. Additionally, you will learn how to use named anchors to navigate through the video.

1 Open **targetVideo_START.fla** from the **chap_16** folder. Select the **buttons** layer, and click the **Insert Layer** button to add a new layer to the **Timeline**. Rename the layer **video**.

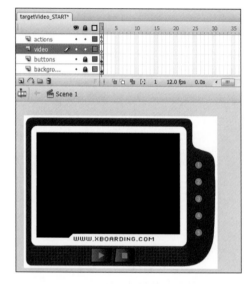

2 Choose **File > Import > Import to Stage**, and select the **catchingAir.mov** file from the **chap_16** folder. Click **Open** (Windows) or **Import** (Mac) to open the **Import Video** wizard.

3 On the **Select Video** screen, select **On your computer** to tell Flash where the video file is located. Click **Next** (Windows) or **Continue** (Mac).

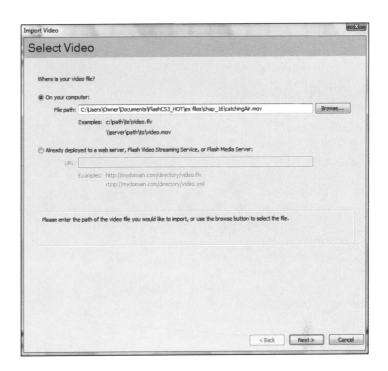

4 On the **Deployment** screen, make sure the **Embed video in SWF and play in timeline** option is selected. Click **Next** (Windows) or **Continue** (Mac).

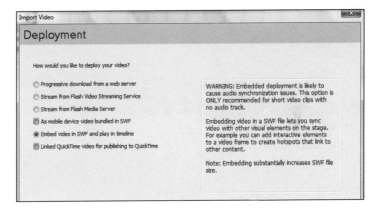

5 On the **Embedding** screen, choose **Embedded video** in the **Symbol type** pop-up menu. Select the **Place instance on stage** and **Expand timeline if needed** options. Make sure the **Embed the entire video** option is selected. Click **Next** (Windows) or **Continue** (Mac).

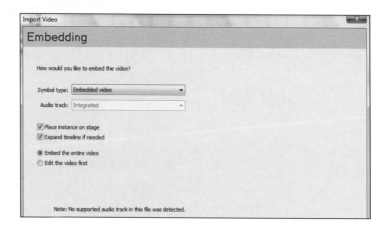

6 On the **Encoding** screen, on the **Encoding Profiles** (Windows) or **Profiles** (Mac) tab, choose **Flash 8 – Medium Quality (400kbps)** in the pop-up menu to encode the video using the ON2 VP6 codec at medium quality and with the keyframe value set to the same as the original video.

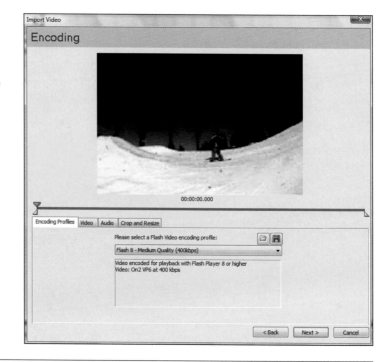

7 On the **Video** tab, choose **Same As FLA** in the **Frame rate** pop-up menu. Click **Next** (Windows) or **Continue** (Mac).

Note: This is important to ensure that the video imports at the same frame rate as the Flash file. Otherwise, the video will be too long.

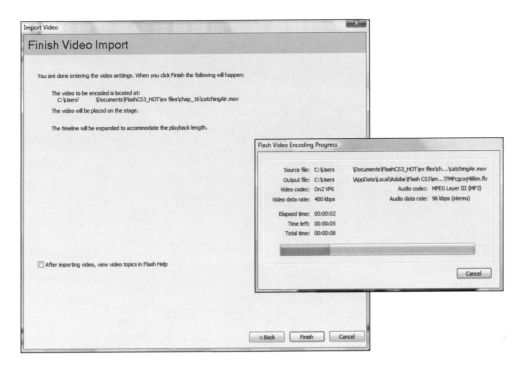

8 On the **Finish Video Import** screen, review your settings, and click **Finish**.

The Flash Video Encoding Progress dialog box appears. When the import process is complete, the video clip will be placed on the Stage.

---

9 Click the video clip to select it. Move it so it is centered in the background window.

Notice the video now occupies 237 frames on the Timeline.

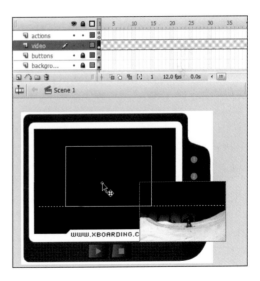

10 On the **Timeline**, move the playhead to **Frame 234**. Scrub the playhead between **Frame 234** and where the video frames stop at **Frame 237**. Notice how the video fades out at about **Frame 234**. The rest of the frames are not necessary because the video has faded to black. Select **Frames 234** through **237**. **Right-click** (Windows) or **Ctrl-click** (Mac) the selected frames, and choose **Remove Frames** in the contextual menu to remove them from the **Timeline**.

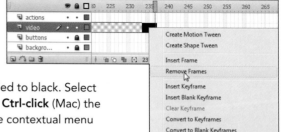

Why remove the frames? In Flash CS3, video on the Timeline is treated just like a sound. Only the frames that exist on the Timeline will be exported with the Adobe Flash movie (SWF file). To reduce the SWF file size, you can remove unneeded frames from the Timeline. In this example, the SWF file will be reduced from 949 KB to about 944 KB by removing those five frames.

Note: Although you deleted frames from the video on the main Timeline, the original full video clip is still in the Library panel.

---

11 On the **buttons** layer, click **Frame 233**. **Shift-click Frame 233** on the **background** layer to select **Frame 233** of both layers. Choose **Insert > Timeline > Frame** to add frames up to **Frame 233** so you can see the background and the buttons throughout the video.

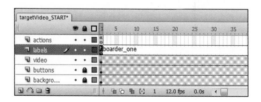

---

12 Move the playhead to **Frame 1**, and click the **Insert Layer** button to add a new layer to the **Timeline**. Rename this layer **labels** and make sure it is positioned below the **actions** layer.

---

13 On the **labels** layer, select **Frame 1**. In the **Property inspector**, type **boarder_one** in the **Frame** field to mark the place where the first snowboarder appears.

14 Scrub the playhead forward to see where a transition occurs, and a new snowboarder appears in the video. Notice a new snowboarder appears at **Frame 47**. On the **labels** layer, click **Frame 47**, and choose **Insert > Timeline > Blank Keyframe** to add a blank keyframe. In the **Property inspector**, type **boarder_two** in the **Frame** field to mark the place where the second snowboarder appears.

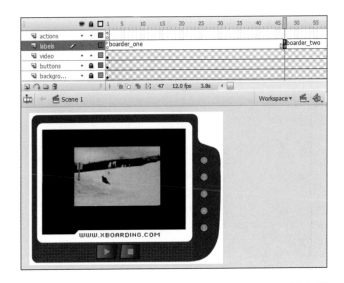

15 Repeat Step 13 to add blank keyframes and frame labels for three more snow-boarders.

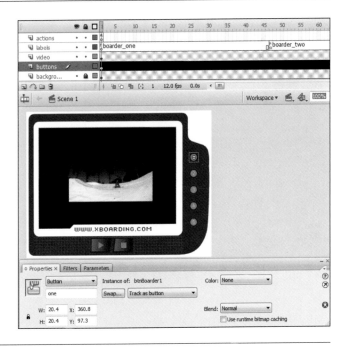

Hint: boarder_three = Frame 96, boarder_four = Frame 118, and boarder_five = 209.

In the following steps, you will add ActionScript to the buttons to target these frame labels.

16 Unlock the **buttons** layer, and select the top button numbered **1**. In the **Property inspector**, type **one** in the **Instance Name** field.

Notice that you didn't end this instance name with **_btn** like you have with every other button instance. Also notice that all the frame labels you created in Steps 12–15 all begin with **boarder_** and end with numbers corresponding to your button instance names. This will let you create one function to control the inter-activity of all your buttons.

17 Repeat Step 16 for the remaining numbered buttons, giving them the instance names **two**, **three**, **four**, and **five**.

18 On the **Timeline**, click the first keyframe on the **actions** layer, and open the **Actions** panel by pressing **F9** (Windows) or **Opt+F9** (Mac).

In the Script pane, notice the code that is already written. This code controls the interactivity of the Stop and Play buttons.

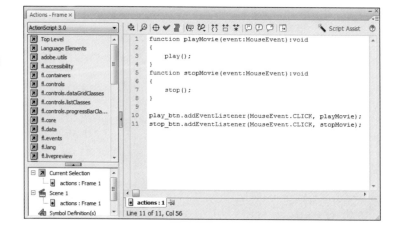

19 After all the prewritten code, create a skeleton for a function that receives a **MouseEvent** event called **gotoLabel** by typing the following:

```
function gotoLabel
(event:MouseEvent):void
{
}
```

This will control the playback of your movie using the buttons on the right side and the frame labels you created in this exercise. You will define what this function does later. Next, you will add listeners to all the buttons.

20 After the code you wrote in the previous step, type the following:

`one.addEventListener(MouseEvent.CLICK, gotoLabel);`

```
1   function playMovie(event:MouseEvent):void
2   {
3       play();
4   }
5   function stopMovie(event:MouseEvent):void
6   {
7       stop();
8   }
9
10  play_btn.addEventListener(MouseEvent.CLICK, playMovie);
11  stop_btn.addEventListener(MouseEvent.CLICK, stopMovie);
12
13  function gotoLabel(event:MouseEvent):void
14  {
15
16  }
17
18  one.addEventListener(MouseEvent.CLICK, gotoLabel);
```

Line 18 of 18, Col 51

---

21 Repeat Step 20 for the rest of the buttons. Don't forget to change the instance names each time!

Tip: The code should look like `two.addEventListener(MouseEvent.CLICK, gotoLabel);`, and so on.

```
5   function stopMovie(event:MouseEvent):void
6   {
7       stop();
8   }
9
10  play_btn.addEventListener(MouseEvent.CLICK, playMovie);
11  stop_btn.addEventListener(MouseEvent.CLICK, stopMovie);
12
13  function gotoLabel(event:MouseEvent):void
14  {
15
16  }
17
18  one.addEventListener(MouseEvent.CLICK, gotoLabel);
19  two.addEventListener(MouseEvent.CLICK, gotoLabel);
20  three.addEventListener(MouseEvent.CLICK, gotoLabel);
21  four.addEventListener(MouseEvent.CLICK, gotoLabel);
22  five.addEventListener(MouseEvent.CLICK, gotoLabel);
23
```

Line 23 of 23, Col 1

---

22 Click between the curly braces of the `gotoLabel()` function you created in Step 19, and type the following:

`var labelName:String = "boarder_" + event.target.name;`

```
5   function stopMovie(event:MouseEvent):void
6   {
7       stop();
8   }
9
10  play_btn.addEventListener(MouseEvent.CLICK, playMovie);
11  stop_btn.addEventListener(MouseEvent.CLICK, stopMovie);
12
13  function gotoLabel(event:MouseEvent):void
14  {
15      var labelName:String = "boarder_" + event.target.name;
16  }
17
18  one.addEventListener(MouseEvent.CLICK, gotoLabel);
19  two.addEventListener(MouseEvent.CLICK, gotoLabel);
20  three.addEventListener(MouseEvent.CLICK, gotoLabel);
21  four.addEventListener(MouseEvent.CLICK, gotoLabel);
22  five.addEventListener(MouseEvent.CLICK, gotoLabel);
23
```

Line 15 of 23, Col 2

This ActionScript tells Flash CS3 to create a new variable called **labelName** that has a data type of String. The value of the **labelName** variable is different depending on which button you click. Here's how it works: Every label you created begins with **boarder_** and ends with a number corresponding to a button. The **gotoLabel()** function runs when a button is clicked and receives information about the button click. The code **event.target.name** is referring to the button click (**event**), the button that was clicked (**target**), and the instance name of that button (**name**). So if the **three** button is clicked, the **labelName** variable will have a value of **boarder_three**. Pretty cool, huh? Now all you need to do is tell Flash CS3 to navigate to the different frame labels. You will do that in the next step.

---

23 After the code you wrote in the previous step, type:

gotoAndPlay(labelName);

This ActionScript tells Flash CS3 to play the movie starting at the label corresponding to the button you click.

Note: Navigating your Timeline with labels is an effective way to control the playback of a movie. You can use labels with **gotoAndPlay** or **gotoAndStop**, but to use a frame label, you must pass in a String. Because the previous code is a variable created with a data type of String, you do not need to use quotation marks. If you put quotation marks around **labelName**, Flash CS3 would attempt to navigate to a frame label called **labelName**.

```
 5    function stopMovie(event:MouseEvent):void
 6    {
 7        stop();
 8    }
 9
10    play_btn.addEventListener(MouseEvent.CLICK, playMovie);
11    stop_btn.addEventListener(MouseEvent.CLICK, stopMovie);
12
13    function gotoLabel(event:MouseEvent):void
14    {
15        var labelName:String = "boarder_" + event.target.name;
16        gotoAndPlay(labelName);
17    }
18
19    one.addEventListener(MouseEvent.CLICK, gotoLabel);
20    two.addEventListener(MouseEvent.CLICK, gotoLabel);
21    three.addEventListener(MouseEvent.CLICK, gotoLabel);
22    four.addEventListener(MouseEvent.CLICK, gotoLabel);
23    five.addEventListener(MouseEvent.CLICK, gotoLabel);
```

actions : 1
Line 16 of 24, Col 25

---

24 Choose **Control > Test Movie** to preview your Flash movie. Click the buttons on the right side, and watch the movie navigate to the appropriate frame labels. Nice!

Now that your movie is navigating properly, in the next few steps you will turn your frame labels into named anchors.

---

25 Close the preview window. On the **labels** layer, click the **boarder_one** frame label on the **Timeline** to select that frame (**Frame 1**). In the **Property inspector**, choose **Anchor** in the **Label type** pop-up menu.

Notice the icon next to the frame label on the Timeline changes. This indicates a named anchor is attached to that frame.

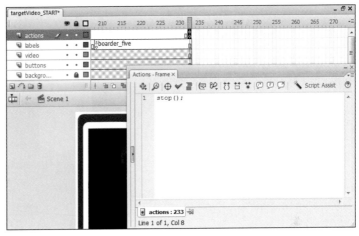

NOTE:

What Is a Named Anchor?

In Flash CS3, you can create movies that work with the **Forward** and **Back** buttons in a browser. This feature is called a **named anchor**, which is a special frame label that resides on the main **Timeline** and has a unique anchor icon. Once the named anchor is played in a browser window, it is registered in a browser's history. Then, when a user clicks the **Back** button in the browser window, the browser will play the previous named anchor position on the **Timeline**.

The **Named Anchor** feature will work in the Adobe Flash Player 6 (or newer) on browsers that support the **FSCommand** command with JavaScript, including Internet Explorer 3 and newer. *Named anchors do not work on browsers running on the Mac operating system.*

26 Repeat Step 25 by selecting each of the remaining four frame labels (**boarder_two**, **boarder_three**, **boarder_four**, and **boarder_five**) and then choosing **Anchor** in the **Label type** pop-up menu in the **Property inspector**.

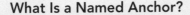

27 On the **actions** layer, select **Frame 233**, and press **F7** to add a blank keyframe.

You will add a Stop frame action to this frame next.

28 In the **Actions** panel, click in the **Script** pane, and type:

`stop();`

This action will stop the playhead at Frame 233, which is the end of the snowboard movie.

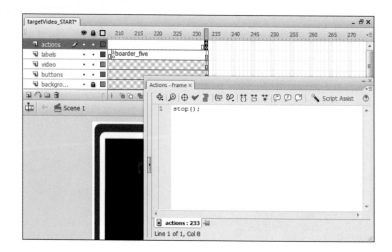

29 Choose **File > Publish Settings** to open the **Publish Settings** dialog box. Click the **HTML** tab, and in the **Template** pop-up menu, choose **Flash with Named Anchors**. Leave the rest of the settings at their defaults, and click **OK** to add JavaScript to the HTML (**H**yper**T**ext **M**arkup **L**anguage) document that will catch the named anchors as they play in the browser.

Note: Because named anchors do not work with most browsers on the Mac, Mac users should skip this step.

Note: You will learn all about the Publish settings in detail in Chapter 17, *"Publishing and Exporting."*

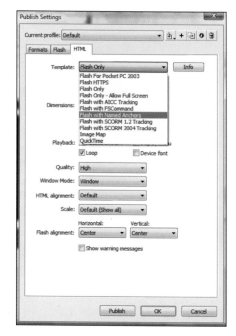

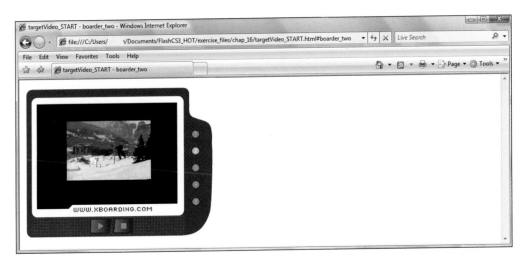

30 Press **F12** (Windows) or **Cmd+F12** (Mac) to publish your Flash CS3 movie and preview it in a browser, where you'll be able to test the named anchors (Windows Internet Explorer users only). As the video plays, notice the end of the URL (**U**niform **R**esource **L**ocator) in the browser window: It changes to reflect the named anchor that is currently playing.

---

31 When the movie reaches the end and stops, Windows users should click the **Back** button in the browser; it will jump back one anchor to **boarder_four**. Click it again, and it will jump back to **boarder_three**. In the browser, click the **Forward** button, and the movie will advance forward to the next named anchor. Neat! When you are finished, close the browser window.

Tip: You can use named anchors with video or with any content on the main Timeline. Because many users will not be accustomed to using the Forward and Back buttons with Flash movies, you may have to add some text to your movie, instructing the users that they can navigate using the browser Forward and Back buttons.

Note: You will learn more about the Publish Preview options in Chapter 17, *"Publishing and Exporting."*

NOTE: | **Other Uses for Named Anchors**

In the past, Flash movies could never utilize the **Back** button of a browser, which created a usability problem because many people built entire Web sites using the SWF file format. The named anchors technique lets you build browser functionality into any Flash CS3 Web site. You learned from this exercise how easy it is to add this feature, so consider this technique for any complete Web site you build in the future. Just make sure the named anchors exist on the main **Timeline** or on the main **Timeline** of other scenes. They have to be placed there in order to work correctly.

---

32 When you are finished, close **targetVideo_START.fla**. You don't need to save your changes.

---

4 | Editing Video

The editing feature in the **Import Video** wizard lets you choose which portions of the video you want to import into your Flash CS3 movie. This is a useful tool if you don't have the budget to purchase a separate video-editing program, such as Adobe Premiere Pro or Apple Final Cut Pro. Instead of opening a separate video-editing program to simply extract a few clips from a larger video clip, you can now streamline your workflow by performing the process right in Flash CS3. In this exercise, you will learn how to select a video file, extract a few clips from that video, and then import *only* those clips into your Flash movie.

1 Open the **importClips.fla** from the **chap_16** folder.

2 Click the **Insert Layer** button to add a new layer to the **Timeline**. Rename it **video**, and make sure it is at the top of the layer stack. Make sure the **video** layer is selected.

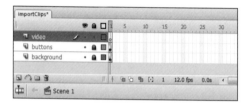

3 Choose **File > Import > Import to Stage**, and select the **jumps.mov** file from the **chap_16** folder. Click **Open** (Windows) or **Import** (Mac) to open the **Import Video** wizard.

NOTE: | **Importing Video**

You can import video into Flash CS3 in two ways. The first way is to choose **File > Import > Import to Stage**, as you have done up to this point in the chapter. This menu option will import the video clip into the **Library** panel and add an instance of it to the **Stage**. The second way is to choose **File > Import > Import to Library**, which will import the video clip directly into the **Library** panel without placing an instance on the **Stage**. These two techniques will work for any media being imported into Flash CS3 as well, including bitmaps, sounds, symbols, and artwork from other programs.

4 On the **Select Video** screen, select **On your computer**, and click **Next** (Windows) or **Continue** (Mac). On the **Deployment** screen, make sure the **Embed video in SWF and play in timeline** option is selected. Click **Next** (Windows) or **Continue** (Mac).

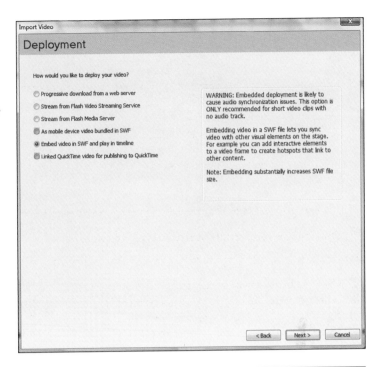

5 On the **Embedding** screen, select **Movie clip** in the **Symbol type** pop-up menu, select the **Place instance on stage** and **Expand timeline if needed** options, and make sure the **Edit the video first** radio button is selected. Click **Next** (Windows) or **Continue** (Mac).

NOTE:

Editing Video in the Import Video Wizard

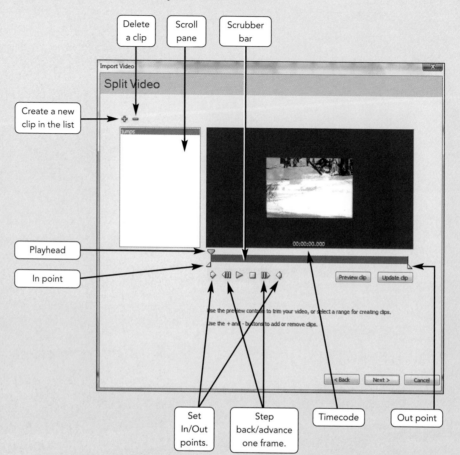

The **Split Video** screen lets you trim the length of your video clips and create multiple clips, simplifying the video-editing process and streamlining your workflow. With this editor, it is easy to select exactly which parts of the video to create clips from. You will do this in the following steps.

6 On the **Split Video** screen, drag the playhead until the time-code reads **00:00:05.546**.

This is the first frame of one of the jumps in this video. You will mark this as the first frame of your soon-to-be clip next.

7 Click the **Set In Point** button to move the **In** point (the beginning marker of your new clip) to the current position of the playhead.

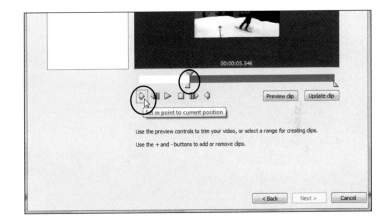

8 Move the playhead to timecode **00:00:07.820** (the last frame of this jump clip). If needed, Windows users can use the left and right arrow keys on your keyboard to fine-tune the time-code setting. Click the **Set Out Point** button to set the **Out** point to the current position of the playhead.

9 Click the **Preview clip** button to review the trimmed clip. Click the **Create new clip in list (+)** button to add a new clip to the scroll pane. Rename the new clip **jumps 1**.

Next, you'll define one more clip and then import both clips into your Flash project.

---

10 Drag the **Out** point slider all the way to the end of the video.

---

11 Move the playhead to timecode **00:00:16.855** (the first frame of this jump clip). If needed, use the left and right arrow keys on your keyboard to fine-tune the timecode setting. Click the **Set In Point** button to define the beginning point of this clip.

The Out point of this clip is the last frame of the video, which you already set in Step 10.

---

12 Click the **Preview clip** button to review the trimmed clip. Click the **Create new clip in list** button to add a new clip to the scroll pane. Rename the new clip **jumps 2**. Click **Next** (Windows) or **Continue** (Mac).

You've selected a video clip on your hard drive and selected two small clips from the larger video. Next, you'll import both clips into your Flash CS3 project.

13 On the **Encoding** screen, on the **Encoding Profiles** (Windows) or **Profiles** (Mac) tab, choose **Flash 8 – Medium Quality (400kbps)** in the pop-up menu. Click **Next** (Windows) or **Continue** (Mac). On the **Finish Video Import** screen, review your settings, and click **Finish**.

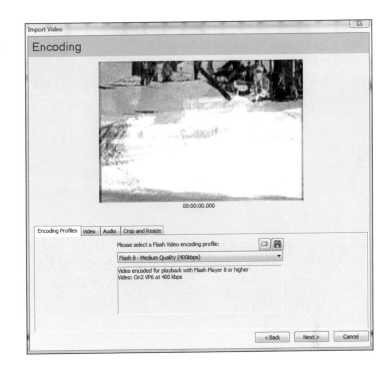

14 When the import is complete, Flash places both video clips in the **Library** panel and one (**jumps 2**) on the **Stage**. Drag the video clip so it is centered in the background window.

Tip: If you want to include the other video clip (jumps 1) in the project, drag it from the Library panel to the Stage.

15 On the **Stage**, click the video clip. In the **Instance Name** field of the **Property inspector**, type **jumps**.

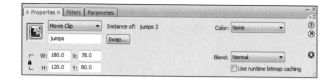

This is now the instance name of the jumps 2 video clip. This name is also incorporated into the ActionScript that has already been added to the Stop and Play buttons at the bottom of the Stage.

---

16 Choose **Control > Test Movie** to preview your new video clip.

As you can see, now instead of the video playing the whole way through, it is playing only the jumps 2 clip you defined in the Import Video wizard!

This is a fast, easy way to trim away unwanted portions of a video clip. In addition, trimming your video clips also decreases the size of the final SWF file.

---

17 When you are finished, close **importClips.fla**. You don't need to save your changes.

---

5 | Using the Flash Video Encoder

As handy as the Flash CS3 **Import Video** wizard is, it has limitations. You can encode only one video clip at a time, which can make the process of encoding multiple video clips very time-intensive. If you work extensively with video-based content, Flash Professional CS3 includes the Flash Video Encoder, a stand-alone video encoding application you can install on a dedicated computer and use to batch process video clips. Batch processing can speed up your workflow by freeing up your production computer and letting you encode multiple clips at a time.

In this exercise, you will get an introduction to Flash Video Encoder by adding several video clips to the encoder, setting encoding options for each clip, and batch encoding all the clips in one process.

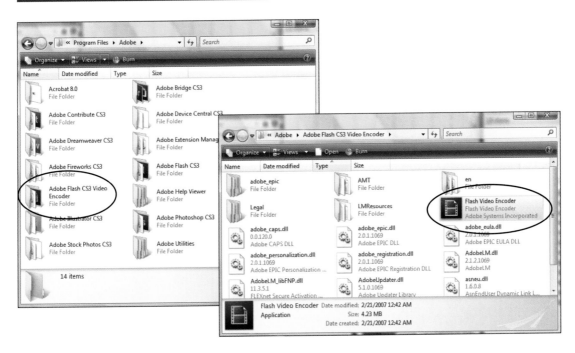

1 Locate the Flash Video Encoder application on your computer. By default, it is installed in a **Flash Video Encoder** folder in the **Adobe** folder in the **Program Files** (Windows) or **Applications** (Mac) folder.

2 Double-click the **Flash Video Encoder** application file to launch the application.

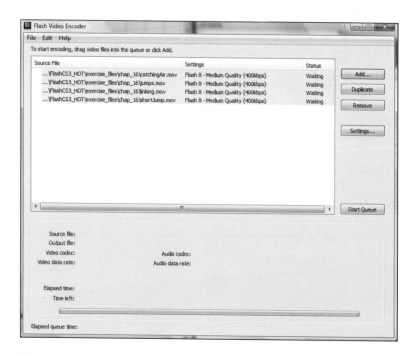

3 Click the **Add** button. Browse to the **chap_16** folder. Hold down **Ctrl** (Windows) or **Command** (Mac), and click the **catchingAir.mov**, **jumps.mov**, **linking.mov**, and **shortJump.mov** video clips to multiple-select all four movies. Click **Open**.

Notice the four video clips are displayed and selected in the video encoder list in the Flash Video Encoder window, and the encoding Status column reads Waiting. The Settings values are all set to the current default setting (Flash 8 – Medium Quality). The encoder is waiting for you to set the encoding settings for each video clip. You can adjust settings for each clip individually or for multiple clips at the same time. You will do each in the next several steps.

4 Click the **catchingAir** clip to select it. Click the **Settings** button.

5 In the **Flash Video Encoding Settings** dialog box, click the **Encoding Profiles** tab, and choose **Flash 8 – Medium Quality**. Click the **Video** tab, and make sure the settings match those shown in the illustration here.

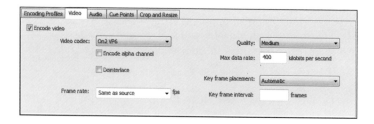

6 Click the **Cue Points** tab. Drag the playhead until the timecode reads **00:00:05.546.** The video preview window lets you visually identify points in the video at which to insert cue points. (Use the left and right arrow keys on your keyboard to fine-tune the timecode setting.) Click the **+** (**Add Cue Point**) button. Type **jump1** in the **Name** field. Leave **Event** for the **Type** setting.

The Flash Video Encoder embeds a cue point on the specified frame of the video and populates the cue point list with a placeholder including the name of the cue point and the time during playback when the event will be triggered. You can also specify the type of cue point you want to embed: navigation or event.

Navigation cue points insert a keyframe at that point in the video clip and are used for navigating or locating the specified point in the video clip. **Event cue points** are used to trigger ActionScript methods at the point the cue point is reached.

You can also establish parameters for each cue point. Parameters are sets of key/value pairs that are passed to the ActionScript method triggered by the cue point. You can use parameters to perform additional work such as indicating which text or graphic content should be displayed for each cue point.

Cue Points

Cue points are established points, or markers, in the video clip that you can use to trigger other actions while playing back the clip. For example, you can create a Flash presentation that has video playing in one area of the screen while text and graphics appear in another area. Cue points placed in the video trigger updates to the text and graphic, keeping them in sync and current with the video.

You can create cue points in either the Flash Video Encoder or the **Import Video** wizard. Each cue point consists of a name and the time at which it occurs. Specify cue point times in the format **hour:minute:second:frame**. You can specify cue point times with any frame rate and also express them in milliseconds rather than frame numbers.

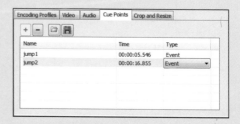

You can also add and remove cue points through ActionScript. For more information, see "Understanding cue points" in the Programming ActionScript 3.0 section of Flash Help.

7 Drag the playhead until the timecode reads **00:00:16.855**. (Use the left and right arrow keys on your keyboard to fine-tune the timecode setting.) Click the **+** (**Add Cue Point**) button. Type **jump2** in the **Name** field. Leave **Event** for the **Type** setting. Click **OK**.

You now have established two event cue points in this video clip that you can use in a script for a variety of duties, such as triggering the display of additional content, playing audio, loading movie clips, and doing much more. You can also change each to a navigation-type cue point and use them with ActionScript to locate and jump to any other navigation cue point in the list. For more information on these techniques, see the "Understanding cue points" topic in the Programming ActionScript 3.0 section of Flash CS3 Help.

8 In the **Flash Video Encoder** dialog box, click the first clip, and **Shift-click** the last file to select each of the last three clips. Click the **Settings** button.

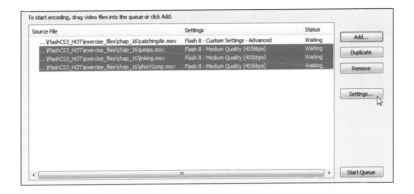

9 The **Flash Video Encoder** dialog box displays a warning that you are about to edit the settings for multiple files and existing settings will be replaced. Click **OK** to acknowledge the warning.

10 In the pop-up menu, choose **Flash 8 – Low Quality (150kbps)**. Click **OK**.

One advantage of using the Flash Video Encoder instead of the Import Video wizard is that you can encode more than one video clip at

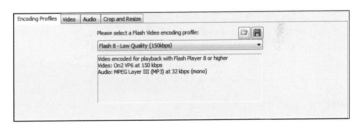

a time, each with different encoding settings. You can also use a single encode setting on multiple clips at the same time and batch process the entire group of video clips with a single click. You will batch process this group of clips next.

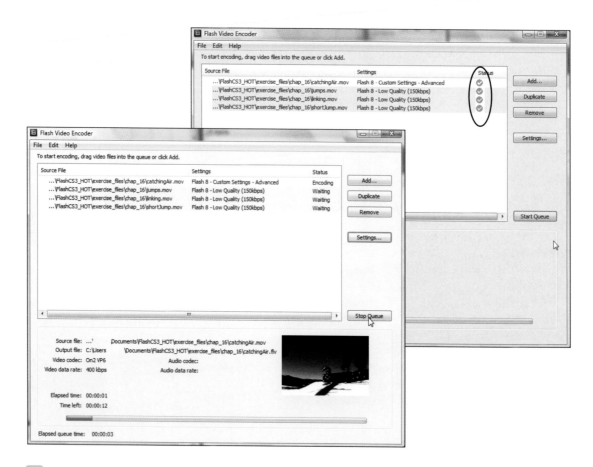

11 Click the **Start Queue** button. The Flash Video Encoder starts batch processing the clips, starting with the first clip. The progress of the encoding appears at the bottom of the screen, together with a preview of the video as it is being encoded. You can stop the batch process at any time by clicking the **Stop Queue** button. When the batch process is finished, a **green check** appears for each clip that was successfully encoded. A **red exclamation point** appears if any errors were encountered during encoding, and an **Errors** dialog box provides more details.

That's it! You have successfully encoded your first batch of video clips using the new stand-alone Flash Video Encoder. This is a fast and easy way to process multiple video clips.

12 The encoded video clips are saved to the **chap_16** folder as Flash FLV files and are ready to be imported into your Flash files. No further processing or encoding is required (or will be performed by Flash when they are imported). Import the video using the same procedure detailed in Exercise 1. Close the Flash Video Encoder by clicking the **Close** button.

Nice job! You have made it through another chapter. Get ready for the next chapter—it is filled with useful information on how to publish your movies using the Publish and Export settings in Flash CS3.

17

Publishing and Exporting

Prior to this chapter, you tested your movies in Adobe Flash CS3 Professional by choosing **Control > Test Movie** to generate a SWF file. This chapter shows you how to publish movies using the **Publish** settings. Testing and publishing both produce SWF files, but publishing offers many more options and greater control over the final output. As well, you'll learn how to generate an HTML (**H**yper**T**ext **M**arkup **L**anguage) file and a projector file from Flash CS3. This chapter also teaches you how to export an image from a project file.

The **Publish** settings in Flash CS3 are complex; the "Learning More About the Publish Settings" section later in this chapter will show you additional settings that are more advanced than those covered by the exercises. In addition, you'll find a chart listing the file types you can export. The chapter concludes with a look at some helpful tips and tricks for optimizing your movies.

What Types of Content Can Flash CS3 Publish?

In addition to the SWF file, Flash CS3 can publish to several file formats. The following chart describes many of the available publishing options:

Flash CS3 Publishing Options	
Format	**Description**
Web delivery	If you plan to publish Web content, you can create an HTML file to embed the Flash CS3 movie in. You'll learn how to generate this HTML code, and establish how the movie will appear, in this chapter.
CD-ROM delivery	If you want to run Flash CS3 on a CD-ROM or other physical media, you can create a projector file, which you'll learn to do in this chapter.
E-mail attachment	If you want to create a Flash CS3 movie you can easily attach to an e-mail, you can create a projector file, which you'll learn how to do in this chapter.
QuickTime	You can generate a Flash track for Apple QuickTime, which offers the opportunity to create Flash CS3 controllers or buttons for QuickTime content. You learned how to do this in Chapter 16, *"Video."*
Image file	If you want to publish an image file, such as a JPEG, PNG, or GIF, from your project file, you can use the **Publish** settings to create an image, which you'll learn how to do in this chapter.

1 | Using Flash CS3 with HTML

This exercise walks you through the **Publish** settings interface to show how to create the necessary HTML files for Web delivery of Flash CS3 content. The following steps show you how changes you make in the **Publish** settings affect the way your movie is viewed in a browser.

---

1 Copy the **chap_17** folder from the **Flash HOT CD-ROM** to your desktop. Open **publish.fla** from the **publishTesting** folder in the **chap_17** folder. Choose **Control > Test Movie** to preview the movie. This is the finished version of the effects movie you created in Chapter 9, *"Working with Bitmaps."*

Notice the title publish.swf at the top of the window. A movie report will also open in the Output panel.

2 Close the preview window. Leave Flash CS3 for a moment, and open the **chap_17** folder on your desktop. Open the **publishTesting** folder.

Inside, you will see three files: one FLA file, one SWF file, and one text file. When you chose Control > Test Movie, Flash CS3 created the SWF file and the report file in the folder as well.

---

3 Return to Flash CS3. Choose **File > Publish Preview > Default – (HTML)**, or press **F12** (Windows) or **Cmd+F12** (Mac), to launch the default browser on your computer.

Notice the browser displays an HTML page with the SWF file embedded in it. When you choose the Publish Preview command, the Publish settings determine how Flash CS3 decides to publish the documents. You will work with the Publish settings in just a few steps.

WARNING:

Publish Preview vs. Test Movie

The **Publish Preview** command gives you the most accurate representation of how your movie will look on the Web. The preview you see when you choose **Control > Test Movie** does not always appear exactly the same as the published movie appears on a Web server. For example, sound in your movie may vary slightly, and complex animations may animate slightly slower when using the **Test Movie** command. To be safe, use the **Publish Preview** or **Publish** command to view the movie before you upload it to the Web.

4 Look in the **publishTesting** folder.

Inside you will now see five files: the FLA file, the SWF file, the text file, the HTML file, and a JavaScript file. When you preview your movie in a browser, Flash CS3 creates HTML and JavaScript files in the same folder where you saved your FLA file. Notice the HTML, FLA, and SWF files have similar names. By default, Flash CS3 names the additional files with the same name as the FLA file. You will learn how to change these names in the next few steps.

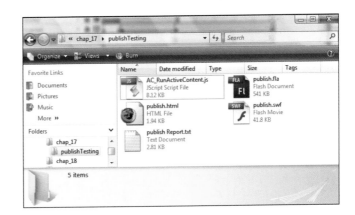

5 Return to Flash CS3, and choose **File > Publish Settings** to open the **Publish Settings** dialog box. Make sure the **Formats** tab is selected.

You use the Formats tab to specify which file formats Flash CS3 will create when you publish the movie. Other tabs will appear or disappear according to which check boxes you select.

Tip: You can also access the Publish Settings dialog box by clicking the Settings button in the Property inspector.

---

6 Make sure the **Flash (.swf)** and **HTML (.html)** boxes are selected. Notice all the file names are set to have the prefix **publish**. By default, Flash uses the name of the FLA as a basis for naming the other file types. Type **movie.swf** in the **File** field for **Flash (.swf)** to change the name of the published SWF file. Type **webPage.html** in the **File** field for **HTML (.html)**.

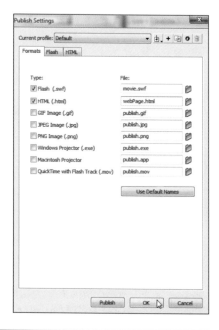

---

7 Click the **Flash** tab. Choose **Top down** in the **Load order** pop-up menu to load each layer in the movie from the top layer first and continue downward. Don't click **OK** or **Publish** just yet; you will change another setting in the next step.

Choosing the Top down option is a good habit to get into since (as you learned in Chapter 12, "*ActionScript Basics*") you should always place your actions on the top layer. When you choose Top down, your ActionScript layer will always load first in the Adobe Flash Player.

---

8 Ensure the **Generate size report** option is still selected.

---

9 Click the **Publish** button to publish the SWF and HTML files with the names you just specified in Step 6. Click **OK** to exit the **Publish Settings** dialog box.

Flash CS3 creates these new files and saves them in the same folder as the original FLA file.

10 To make sure the new files have been published, look in the **publishTesting** folder.

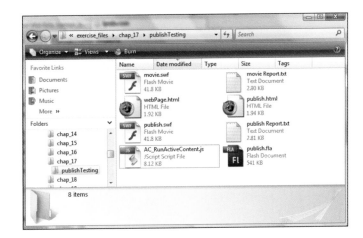

Inside you will now see *eight* files: the five files that were already there, each with the *publish* name, and three new files named publishReport.txt, movie.swf, and webPage.html. Each time you click the Publish button in the Publish Settings dialog box (or choose File > Publish), Flash CS3 writes and creates all the files you selected in the Publish Settings dialog box (in this case, SWF and HTML). If you publish more than once with the same settings, Flash CS3 will overwrite the existing files each time.

11 Return to Flash CS3. Choose **Control > Test Movie**. Because you will be looking at the size report in a different manner, close the preview window and the **Output** panel for now.

12 Look in the **publishTesting** folder again.

Notice the movie Report.txt file. When you generate a size report, Flash creates a detailed report about the most current SWF file.

13 Double-click the **movie Report.txt** file to open it. When you are done reviewing the file, close it.

The Generate size report option breaks down the file size contributions of all the symbols, fonts, and other elements in the movie. This is a handy tool when you want to know, frame by frame, how big the movie is, how many elements are present in the movie, and even which font faces you used and which font characters were embedded in the SWF file!

41	1	42852
42	1	42853
43	1	42854
44	1	42855
45	1	42856

Scene	Shape Bytes	Text Bytes	ActionScript Bytes
Scene 1	918	0	0

Symbol	Shape Bytes	Text Bytes	ActionScript Bytes
origImage	0	0	0
boarder	261	0	0

Bitmap	Compressed	Compression	
air.png	41165	1080000	JPEG Quality=80

14 Return to Flash CS3, and choose **File > Publish Settings** to open the **Publish Settings** dialog box. Click the **Flash** tab, and select the **Protect from import** option.

Selecting this box prevents others from importing your SWF movie file into Flash and converting it back to a project file. Selecting the Protect from import option is not 100 percent secure. You can still import a protected movie into an Adobe Director movie, and people "in the know" can also use third-party utilities to break into your Flash movie. To be safe, don't put highly sensitive information into Flash CS3 movies, but do select the Protect from import option.

15 Click the **HTML** tab. Make sure **Match Movie** is selected for **Dimensions**. Click **Publish** to publish these changes, and then click **OK** to close the **Publish Settings** dialog box.

The Match Movie option determines the movie's dimensions in the HTML tags. This value can be in pixels or can be a percentage of window size. As you will see in the next step, the Match Movie option publishes the movie at the same dimensions as the Stage and will not allow the SWF file to scale.

---

16 In the **publishTesting** folder, double-click **webPage.html** to open it. Click and drag the lower-right corner of the browser window to resize it.

Notice the SWF file doesn't scale with the browser window and, as you make the window smaller, the image cuts off. You'll fix this in the next step.

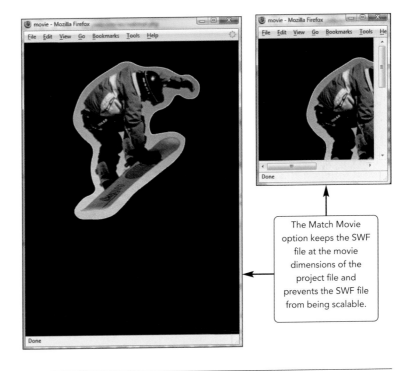

The Match Movie option keeps the SWF file at the movie dimensions of the project file and prevents the SWF file from being scalable.

---

17 Close the browser window, and return to Flash CS3. Choose **File > Publish Settings**. In the **Publish Settings** dialog box, click the **HTML** tab, and choose **Percent** for **Dimensions**. Notice the default settings read **100%** for both **Width** and **Height**, which will keep both the width and height of the SWF file at 100 percent of the size of the browser. Click **Publish**, and then click **OK** to close the **Publish Settings** dialog box and to replace the **webPage.html** file you created in Step 11.

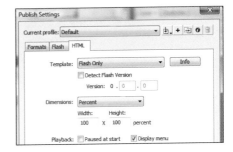

You need to click the Publish button if you want to preview the new settings you specified. Flash CS3 will update the HTML document with the new settings only if you click the Publish button or choose File > Publish.

18 To see the difference this setting makes, open the file **webPage.html** file from the **publishTesting** folder. Resize the browser window. Notice the SWF file always matches the dimensions of the browser window.

So the SWF file scales this time! With the Percent setting at 100 percent by 100 percent no matter how you resize the browser window, the movie will scale to fit the entire browser window and will not be cut off.

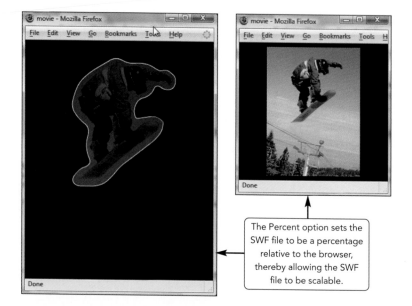

The Percent option sets the SWF file to be a percentage relative to the browser, thereby allowing the SWF file to be scalable.

NOTE: | **Important Uploading Advice!**

Flash CS3 publishes the HTML file with the assumption the SWF file will be located in the same folder as the HTML file, so when you upload the HTML file to a Web server, make sure you put both files in the same directory.

19 Close the browser window, and close **publish.fla**. You don't need to save your changes.

This exercise showed you many of the common Publish settings on the Flash and HTML tabs in the Publish Settings dialog box. For a more in-depth look at what each of the settings on these tabs can do, refer to the charts later in this chapter.

NOTE:

Scalable Bitmaps and Vector Art

Flash CS3 is known for its vector capabilities, but its support of bitmap images is superb and far exceeds the support offered by HTML. Flash CS3 lets you scale, animate, and transform (skew, distort, and so on) bitmaps without much image degradation. As a result, you can combine bitmap and vector images in your movies. When you create scalable content with bitmaps, make sure you import the bitmap at the largest size (although this can dramatically increase the final size of your SWF file) you plan to display it in your movie to ensure the best image quality without degradation.

No matter how you size the browser window, the bitmap and vector content scale proportionally.

2 | Creating Projectors

Have you ever received an e-mail attachment with an **.exe** or **.app** extension and found when you opened it that it was a Flash movie that played right in its own window without a browser? If you have, you may be more familiar with projector files than you think. Projector files are often sent via e-mail because they are stand-alone files that can play without the Flash Player on most computers. You can also distribute projector files via floppy disks or CD-ROMs, or you can show them from your hard drive without a browser (as a great Microsoft PowerPoint substitute). This exercise teaches you how to create a projector file using the **Publish Settings** dialog box.

1 Open **projector.fla** from the **chap_17** folder.

In the following steps, you'll turn this Flash movie into a stand-alone projector file.

2 Choose **Control > Test Movie** to preview the movie and to create and save the SWF file in the same folder as the FLA file.

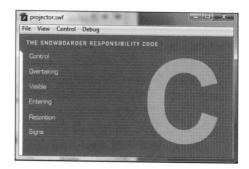

3 Close the **Preview** window. Choose **File > Publish Settings** to open the **Publish Settings** dialog box.

4 Choose the **Formats** tab, and deselect the **Flash** and **HTML** options. Select the **Windows Projector (.exe)** and **Macintosh Projector** options. In the **File** field for **Windows Projector (.exe)**, type **wProjector.exe**. In the **File** field for **Macintosh Projector**, type **mProjector.app**. Click **Publish**. Click **OK** to close the **Publish Settings** dialog box.

When you click Publish, Flash CS3 automatically saves the projector files to the same folder as your FLA file.

NOTE:

Missing Tabs in the Projector Publish Settings?

When you select the projector file types on the **Formats** tab in the **Publish Settings** dialog box, no additional tabs are available for you to alter the settings. However, you can control the way your projectors behave by using ActionScript and FSCommands.

5 Open the **chap_17** folder on your desktop. Inside you'll see the two files you just generated, **mProjector** and **wProjector**.

Note: Although you can create projectors for both Windows and Mac platforms, you can't open a Mac projector (APP) on a Windows machine, and likewise, you can't open a Windows projector (EXE) on a Mac computer. The format that works on your computer will display the icon shown in the illustration here.

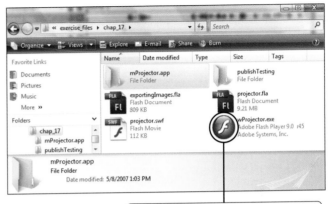

Look for this icon on either platform as visual feedback that you can open the projector.

6 If you're using Windows, double-click the file named **wProjector** to open it. If you're using a Mac, double-click the file named **mProjector** to open it.

You have just created your first projector file. Notice that the sound and animation play. This is because the projector file takes the entire movie, sound and all, and displays it in its own player.

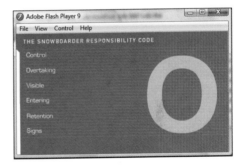

7 Close **wprojector** and **mprojector**, but leave **projector.fla** open for the next exercise.

3 | Modifying Projectors with FSCommands

In the previous exercise, you learned how to create a projector file. This exercise shows you how to modify the original project file by adding ActionScript to control the stand-alone projector file. You'll also learn how to use FSCommands to force the movie to take up the full screen of the computer and to turn off the menu so that users cannot **right-click** or **Ctrl-click** the movie and see a list of menu items.

---

1 If you just completed Exercise 2, **projector.fla** should still be open. If it's not, complete Exercise 2, and then return to this exercise. Choose **File > Save As** to save a copy of the file. Name the file **fsProjector.fla**.

---

2 Click the **Insert Layer** button to add a new layer to the movie. Rename the new layer **actions**. Make sure this layer is on top of all the other layers.

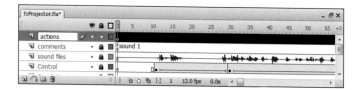

---

3 Click the first keyframe on the **actions** layer, and press **F9** (Windows) or **Opt+F9** (Mac) to open the **Actions** panel.

Next, you will add the ActionScript to control the stand-alone projector file in this keyframe.

NOTE:

FSCommands as Frame Actions

It is usually most effective to add the FSCommands that control the window behavior to one of the first keyframes in the movie so your commands take effect immediately after the player opens.

FSCommands are actions that invoke JavaScript functions from within Flash CS3. They include a command that is similar to an instruction and an argument that checks to see whether the command should be allowed (**true**) or not (**false**). A chart at the end of this exercise describes the FSCommands for the stand-alone projector.

---

4 In the **Actions** panel, make sure **Script Assist** is turned off. Click in the **Script** pane, and type the following:

```
fscommand("fullscreen", "true");
```

When the `fscommand` action is triggered (because it is on the first frame of the movie, it will be triggered when the movie is first launched), it will make the projector launch and completely fill the user's screen. The `fullscreen` command makes the player take up the whole screen and prevents screen resizing when the parameter is set to `true`.

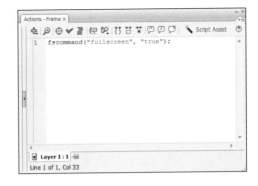

5 Minimize the **Actions** panel, and choose **File > Publish Settings**. In the **Publish Settings** dialog box, rename the projector files **fsWprojector.exe** and **fsMprojector.app**, which will publish two new files without replacing the old projector files you created in the previous exercise. When you are finished, click **Publish** to publish the projectors with the FSCommands added. Click **OK**.

6 Open the **chap_17** folder on your desktop. Inside you will see all the files you have created thus far. If you are using Windows, double-click **fsWprojector.exe** to open it. If you are using a Mac, double-click **fsMprojector.app** to open it. Now the projector will launch in full-screen mode! To exit full-screen mode, press the **Esc** key.

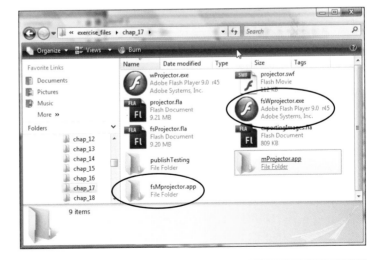

7 Return to Flash CS3. Make sure **Frame 1** is still selected on the **actions** layer, and maximize the **Actions** panel. Click after the last line of code, and press **Enter** (Windows) or **Return** (Mac) to go to the next line. Type the following:

```
fscommand("showmenu", "false");
```

While a projector file plays, users can either right-click (Windows) or Ctrl-click (Mac) to view a list of menu items. If the projector is set to full-screen, you may not want users to zoom in or out or manipulate the way the movie is presented. By disabling the menu (setting `showmenu` to `false`), you can limit the control users have.

8 Choose **File > Publish** to publish the changes you made to the files you specified in the **Publish Settings** dialog box.

9 Open the **chap_17** folder on your desktop. If you are using Windows, double-click the **fsWprojector.exe** file to open it. If you are using a Mac, double-click the **fsMprojector.app** file to open it. Try to **right-click** (Windows) or **Ctrl-click** (Mac) to access the shortcut menu and see the full list of menu items.

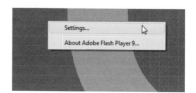

You can't do it! You should see only the About Adobe Flash Player 9 and Settings menu items. Because you set `showmenu` to `false`, you're preventing users from seeing the full menu and using any of the options.

10 When you are finished testing the projector file, close any open files.

Understanding the Stand-Alone Projector FSCommands

Command	Arguments	Function
fullscreen	`true/false`	Sets the movie to fill the full screen when **true** and returns the movie to a normal window when `false`. Setting the movie to `fullscreen` without also setting `allowscale` to `false` can result in the movie changing scale in some cases.
allowscale	`true/false`	Controls the user's ability to scale the movie. If the argument is set to `false`, the movie will always be presented at the original size and can never be scaled. It also prevents the scaling that occurs when the movie is set to `fullscreen`. It is important to note that this option refers to the Flash movie itself and not the stand-alone projector window, since the user can still scale the player window larger or smaller by dragging an edge of it. However, the movie will remain at the original size if `allowscale` is set to `false`. Note also that if `showmenu` is not set to `false`, the user can still scale the movie by **right-clicking** (Windows) or **Ctrl-clicking** (Mac) to access the contextual menu, which includes **Zoom In** and **Zoom Out** options.
showmenu	`true/false`	Lets a user **right-click** (Windows) or **Ctrl-click** (Mac) the projector and have access to the full set of context menu items when **true**. When this command is set to `false`, it means the user can't access any of the menu items except for the **About Flash Player** and **Settings** items.
trapallkeys	`true/false`	Lets the movie capture keystrokes that the user presses on the keyboard when **true**.
exec	Path to application	Lets you launch another application file on the local system. For this to work properly, you must know the correct path and name of the application. You must type the correct path and name of the application in the **Parameters** field. If you are calling a file in the same directory, all you need is the file name.
quit	None	Quits the projector.

Knowing When to Publish and Export

In addition to publishing files from Flash CS3, you can also export files into other editable formats. Why would you want to do this? Sometimes you might want to use a frame of something you created in Flash CS3 in another application, such as Adobe Photoshop or Adobe Illustrator. Many of the **Export** settings are similar to the **Publish** settings, but the workflow for exporting files is different from publishing files. The following chart documents the file formats you can export from Flash CS3:

Export File Types Supported by Flash CS3			
File Format	**Extension**	**Windows**	**Mac**
Adobe Illustrator 6.0, Adobe Illustrator sequence	.ai	x	x
Animated GIF, GIF image, GIF sequence	.gif	x	x
Bitmap and bitmap sequence	.bmp	x	
AutoCAD DXF image or DXF sequence	.dxf	x	x
Enhanced metafile and enhanced metafile sequence	.emf	x	
EPS 3.0 and EPS 3.0 sequence	.eps	x	x
Flash movie	.swf	x	x
JPEG image and JPEG sequence	.jpg	x	x
PICT and PICT sequence	.pct	x	
PNG image and PNG sequence	.png	x	x
QuickTime video	.mov	x	x
WAV audio	.wav	x	
Windows AVI	.avi	x	
Windows metafile and Windows metafile sequence	.wmf	x	

4 | Exporting Image Files

In the previous three exercises, you worked with the **Publish** settings in Flash CS3 to publish different types of files. This exercise shows you how to use the **Export** settings to produce different image file types from your project file. If you know you want to export only an image from your project file so you can work with it in another application, using the **Export** settings can be a great solution. You will learn how to export content from Flash CS3 to create an Illustrator file in the following steps.

1 Open **exportingImages.fla** from the **chap_17** folder. Choose **Control > Test Movie** to preview the movie. When you are finished, close the preview window.

What if you also want to use the boarding logo as a static image for various printed pieces, such as a business card, letterhead, and envelope? In the following steps, you will learn how to export the logo as an Illustrator file.

2 On the **Stage**, click the logo to select it. Notice the setting in the **Property inspector**—this is an instance of the movie clip named **mcOverAnim**.

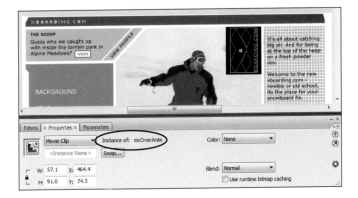

3 Double-click the movie clip instance to open the movie clip's **Timeline**. Scrub the playhead to **Frame 20** of the animation, where the logo is in full color.

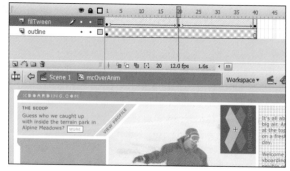

When you choose Export Image, you have several ways to decide what you're going to export. Flash CS3 lets you export the frame the playhead is over (and all layers under that frame), export a selected frame (and all layers under and over that frame), or export a selected image (including the frame the image is on and all layers under and over that frame). Therefore, Flash CS3 will export artwork based on what is selected or where the playhead is in the Timeline.

---

4 Choose **File > Export > Export Image**. In the **Export Image** dialog box, navigate to the **chap_17** folder on your desktop, name the file **logo**, and choose **Adobe Illustrator** in the **Save as type** (Windows) or **Format** (Mac) pop-up menu. Click **Save**.

---

5 In the **Export Adobe Illustrator** dialog box, select the **Adobe Illustrator 6.0** option, and click **OK**.

Illustrator 6.0 is the latest version Flash CS3 can export to as an Illustrator file. Fortunately, you can open the exported file in Adobe Illustrator 6.0 and newer.

---

6 Navigate to the **chap_17** folder on your desktop. Double-click **logo.ai** file to open it in Illustrator.

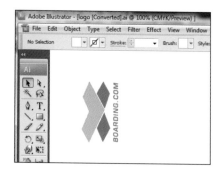

You will see the logo all by itself, without any other images from the project file. Handy!

---

7 When you are finished, close **logo.ai**, and close Illustrator. Close **exportingImages.fla**. You don't need to save your changes.

Learning More About the Publish Settings

The first three exercises in this chapter taught you firsthand how to use some of the Flash CS3 **Publish** settings. I'm sure you noticed many settings that weren't covered in the exercises. You can change these settings at any point while developing or editing your project file (FLA).

Formats Tab

The first tab is the **Formats** tab. It lets you select the file formats that Flash CS3 will publish. As each format is selected, additional tabs will appear to the right of the **Formats** tab, with the exception of the **Windows Projector (.exe)** and **Macintosh Projector** types. Each tab contains settings specific to the selected format. The **Formats** tab also lets you modify the file name of each selected format that Flash CS3 will publish.

Type: In the **Type** section on the **Formats** tab, you can select the type of files you want to publish. Each of the types is covered in the following pages.

File: As you saw in Exercise 1, the default behavior is that all file formats will have the same name as the original project file. You can easily change the default by simply typing a new file name to

the right of the corresponding file type. To revert to the default name(s), simply click the **Use Default Names** button. You can also publish to another directory by targeting it in the name field, like this: **..:swfs/movie.swf**. By doing so, you can save and separate the project files (FLAs) from the movie files (SWFs) in their own folders and prevent clutter in your main directory.

Flash Settings

The **Flash** tab contains all the settings that will be used for the SWF file, which is the file you have been viewing when you choose **Control > Test Movie**. The SWF file is embedded in the HTML document so that the movie can be seen properly in a browser. The following charts give a detailed description of each option:

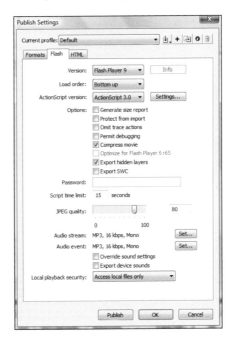

Flash Publish Settings

Name	Description
Version	Lets you export earlier formats of Flash SWF files. The real value of this feature is that it provides you with the means to import (but not edit) work you did in Flash CS3 into earlier versions of Flash, such as Flash 8.
Load order	Sets whether the layers will be loaded from the top down or the bottom up. For example, **Bottom up** means the lowest layer will be shown first, the second lowest next, and so on. The reverse is true of **Top down**. This load setting takes place only when you have multiple elements loading in different layers in the same frame slot, and on a fast connection you may never see this happen. However, as you learned in Chapter 12, *"ActionScript Basics,"* you should always place your actions on the top layer. For this reason, you should select **Top down** so that your ActionScript layer will load first. The frames (not layers) will always load in numeric order.
ActionScript version	In this pop-up menu, choose what version of ActionScript you used in your movie.
Generate size report	Creates a text file that contains detailed information about the size of all the elements in your movie. It will be published to the same directory as the rest of the files.
Protect from import	Prevents anyone from importing your SWF movie file into Flash and converting it back to a project file (FLA). This lets you protect your work. However, these protected files can still be imported into Director, and certain third-party applications can break into any Flash movie. So, to be on the safe side, don't put sensitive information in your Flash movies.
Omit trace actions	Blocks the **Trace** action (a debugging tool) from being exported with your movie. Select this option if you are using **Trace** actions and are producing a final cut of your movie.
Permit debugging	Activates the debugger and allows the Flash CS3 movie to be debugged remotely.
Compress movie	Compresses the Flash CS3 movie to reduce file size and download time. This option is selected by default and works best when a movie has a lot of text or ActionScript.
Optimize for Flash Player 6 r65	If you're publishing a version 6 Flash movie, select this option to increase the playback performance of your movie. This performance increase will be realized only by those viewers who have Flash Player 6 r65 or newer.

continues on next page

Flash Publish Settings *continued*

Name	Description
Export hidden layers	Exports layers marked as hidden in your Flash project file. Deselecting this option means hidden layers will not be visible in the final movie.
Export SWC	Exports an **.swc** file. An **.swc** file contains information about a component, including a compiled movie clip and ActionScript, which allows you to distribute it to other Flash users.
Password	Lets you set a password that prevents unauthorized users from debugging your movie.
JPEG quality	Lets you set the default image quality **Export** setting for all the bitmap graphics in your movie. To retain greater control over your image fidelity and file size, ignore this setting, and set the individual settings for each file in the **Library** panel instead.
Audio stream	Lets you set separate audio compression types and settings for all sounds in the movie that have a **Stream** sync type and that have a compression type of **Default**.
Audio event	Lets you separately set the audio compression type and settings for all sounds in the movie that have a **Start** or **Event** sync type and whose compression type is set to **Default**.
Override sound settings	Selecting this option lets you force all sounds in the movie to use the settings here, instead of using their own compression settings.
Export device sounds	Exports sounds in formats suitable for mobile devices.
Local Playback Security	**Access local files only:** Allows the SWF file to interact only with files and assets stored on the local machine. **Access network only:** Allows the SWF file to interact with files and assets on a network, but not on a local system.

HTML Settings

The **HTML** tab lets you set values that determine how the HTML file is created for your movie. The HTML file is needed as a container to embed the SWF file if you plan to publish to the Web. By changing the settings on the **HTML** tab, you can change the appearance of your SWF file when viewed from a browser. The following chart describes the available options:

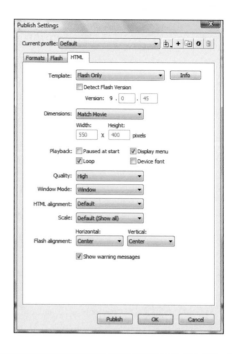

HTML Publish Settings	
Name	**Description**
Template	Lets you choose from a list of HTML templates. Each of these templates was constructed to provide different types of support for the movie. If you don't choose a template, the default template will be used.
Detect Flash Version	Selecting this option will embed a Flash plug-in version detector in the HTML page. If the specified player is not found, users will be taken to an HTTPS server to download the required plug-in.
Dimensions	Lets you set the dimensions (in pixels or as a percentage of window size) the Adobe Flash movie will be set to in the HTML tags. **Match Movie:** Does not allow the SWF file to scale in the browser. **Percentage:** Allows the SWF content to scale if the user resizes the browser window.
Playback	Lets you define how the movie will act in the browser. You can select **Paused at start** to force the movie to start in a stopped position, without using a **Stop** action in the first keyframe. You can deselect the **Loop** check box to make the movie play only once. If you deselect the **Display menu** option, the **Control** menu will be turned off in the browser window. If you select **Device font**, the movie will use the local anti-aliased system font on the user's system instead of the font(s) embedded in the movie.

continues on next page

HTML Publish Settings	*continued*
Name	**Description**
Quality	Sets whether the movie will be played back with emphasis on graphics quality or playback speed. **High:** Emphasizes graphics quality over speed. **Low:** Emphasizes playback speed over appearance.
Window Mode	Determines how the movie interacts in a DHTML (**D**ynamic **HTML**) environment. This setting affects only those browsers that are using absolute positioning and layering.
HTML alignment	Sets the horizontal alignment of the Flash movie within the HTML page in a browser window.
Scale	Determines how the Flash movie resizes within the movie window on the HTML page.
Flash alignment	Determines how the movie is aligned within the Flash movie window. This determines how the movie will look if it is zoomed or cropped.
Show warning messages	Toggles whether the browser will display error messages that occur within the **Object** or **Embed** tags.

GIF Settings

You can use the GIF file format to produce animated graphics and static graphics, such as an icon you want to save to use in other applications. By default, Flash will output the first frame of the movie as a GIF unless you specify a particular keyframe by typing the frame label **#Static** on the keyframe you select. Use caution, because Flash CS3 will publish all the frames in the current movie as an animated GIF unless you designate a range of frames by typing the frame labels **#First** and **#Last** in the corresponding keyframes. The following chart explains the GIF settings in detail:

GIF Publish Settings

Name	Description
Dimensions	Lets you set the size of the GIF by entering the width and height into the corresponding fields. Selecting the **Match movie** option will generate a GIF that has the same dimensions as those in the **Movie Properties** dialog box in the project file.
Playback	Determines whether the GIF will be static or animated. If you select **Static**, the first keyframe of the movie will be used as the GIF image. If you want a different keyframe to be used as the GIF image, you can add the label **#Static** to the selected keyframe, and Flash CS3 will export the labeled keyframe instead. If you select **Animated**, Flash CS3 will export the whole project file as an animated GIF. If you want to export only a selection of frames, add **#First** and **#Last** labels to the first and last keyframes. If you select **Loop continuously**, the GIF will repeat the animation over and over. If you select **Repeat**, you can manually type the number of times you want the animated GIF to loop before it stops.
Options	**Optimize colors** removes unused colors to decrease file size. **Interlace** makes the image appear in stages as it is downloaded. **Smooth** makes the GIF anti-aliased, which can increase file size. **Dither solids** matches colors that are not part of the 256-color palette as closely as possible by mixing similar colors. **Remove gradients** changes all gradients to solid colors, thereby reducing file size.
Transparent	**Opaque:** Makes the image's background appear solid. **Transparent:** Makes the background of the image appear invisible. **Alpha:** Controls the background and all shapes that have an alpha setting applied to them. This lets you set the threshold so that all colors greater than the specified amount will be solid, and all colors with an alpha setting less than the specified amount will be transparent.
Dither	**None:** Matches any color that is not within the 256-color palette with the closest color from within the 256 colors, rather than using dithering. **Ordered:** Matches any color that is not within the 256-color palette by using dithering from a pattern of colors. **Diffusion:** Matches any color that is not within the 256-color palette by using dithering from a random pattern of colors. This creates the closest match of colors but also creates the greatest increase in file size of these three options.

continues on next page

GIF Publish Settings *continued*

Name	Description
Palette Type	**Web 216:** Creates a GIF file using the 216 Web-safe colors.
	Adaptive: Creates a custom color palette for this specific image. This palette type yields an image that is closest in appearance to the original thousands-of-colors or millions-of-colors image, but it also has a larger file size than the other palette types.
	Web Snap Adaptive: Similar to **Adaptive**, except Flash will substitute colors for Web-safe colors when possible.
	Custom: Lets you use a custom palette for the GIF file. When you select this option, the **Palette** option becomes active as well.
Max colors	Determines the maximum number of colors created within the palette when you select either the **Adaptive** or **Web Snap Adaptive** option. The smaller the number, the smaller the file size, but this option can degrade the image quality by reducing the colors.
Palette	Lets you select your own custom color palette from your hard drive.

JPEG Settings

You can use the JPEG file format for images that have more detail than GIF images generally do, such as photographs. Although JPEG images cannot be animated (like an animated GIF), they can have an unlimited number of colors, rather than being limited to 256 colors. By default, Flash will output the first frame of the movie as a JPEG unless you specify a particular keyframe by typing the frame label **#Static** on the keyframe you select. The following chart describes the available options for publishing a JPEG image:

JPEG Publish Settings

Name	Description
Dimensions	Lets you set the size of the JPEG by typing the width and height in the corresponding fields. If you select the **Match movie** option, the JPEG will have the same dimensions as the project file's **Movie Properties** settings.
Quality	Sets the amount of compression, from **0** (lowest quality and smallest file size) to **100** (highest quality and largest file size).
Progressive	Lets the image appear in stages as it is downloaded.

PNG Settings

You can use the PNG file format to produce static graphics. Similar to the GIF format, the PNG format supports transparency. By default, Flash will output the first frame of the movie as a PNG unless you specify a particular keyframe by typing the frame label **#Static** on the keyframe you select. The PNG settings, which are similar to the GIF settings, are explained in detail in the following chart:

PNG Publish Settings	
Name	**Description**
Dimensions	Lets you set the size of the PNG image by typing the width and height in the corresponding fields. Selecting the **Match movie** option will generate a PNG with the same dimensions as those set in the **Movie Properties** dialog box in the project file.
Bit depth	Sets the number of colors (bits per pixel) that will be used in the published file. As the bit depth increases, the file size increases as well. **8-bit:** Creates a 256-color image. **24-bit:** Creates an image using millions (16.7 million) of colors. **24-bit with Alpha:** Creates an image with millions of colors and allows transparency. (The higher the bit depth, the larger the file.)
Options	**Optimize colors** removes unused colors to decrease file size. **Interlace** makes the image appear in stages as it is downloaded. **Smooth** makes the PNG anti-aliased, which can increase file size. **Dither solids** matches colors that are not part of the 256-color palette as closely as possible by mixing similar colors. **Remove gradients** changes all gradients to solid colors, thereby reducing file size.

continues on next page

Name	Description
PNG Publish Settings *continued*	
Dither	This option is available if the **Bit depth** is set to **8-bit**. **None:** Matches any color that is not within the 256-color palette with the closest color from within the 256 colors, rather than using dithering. **Ordered:** Matches any color that is not within the 256-color palette by using dithering from a regular pattern of colors. **Diffusion:** Matches any color that is not within the 256-color palette by dithering from a random pattern of colors; this creates the closest match of colors but with the greatest increase in file size of these three options.
Palette Type	**Web 216:** Creates a PNG file using the 216 Web-safe colors. **Adaptive:** Creates the PNG using a custom color palette for this specific image. This palette type yields an image that is closest in appearance to the original thousands-of-colors or millions-of-colors image, but it also has a larger file size than the other palette types. **Web Snap Adaptive:** Similar to **Adaptive**, except Flash will substitute colors for Web-safe colors when possible. **Custom:** Lets you use a custom palette for the PNG file. When you select this option, the **Palette** option becomes active as well.
Max colors	Determines the maximum number of colors created within the palette when either the **Adaptive** or **Web Snap Adaptive** option is selected.
Palette	Lets you select your own custom color palette (in the ACT format) from your hard drive.
Filter options	Lets you choose a filtering method that produces an image at the best quality and smallest file size.

Projector File Settings

You can also use Flash CS3 to produce stand-alone applications for Windows or Mac machines.

Although there are no additional settings to choose from in the **Publish Settings** dialog box, you can select **Windows Projector (.exe)** and **Macintosh Projector** in the **Type** options on the **Formats** tab. These projectors are self-contained files that can run on any computer, regardless of whether the user has the Flash CS3 Player installed. You learned about projector files in depth in Exercises 2 and 3.

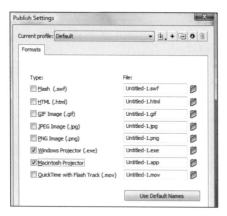

QuickTime Settings

The QuickTime settings let you publish the Flash CS3 project file as a QuickTime movie (MOV) if you are targeting Flash 5 or earlier. The layers of the Flash CS3 file will be converted to what is called the **Flash track** within the QuickTime movie. To publish to a newer version of QuickTime, you have to use the **File > Export** command. The following chart explains the QuickTime tab options in detail:

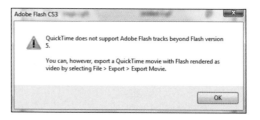

QuickTime Publish Settings

Name	Description
Dimensions	Lets you set the size of the QuickTime movie by typing the width and height in the corresponding fields. Selecting the **Match movie** option will generate a QuickTime movie that has the same dimensions as those set in the **Movie Properties** dialog box in the project file.
Alpha	Controls the transparency (alpha) of the Flash track in the QuickTime movie.
	Auto: Makes the Flash track opaque if it is the only track in the QuickTime movie or if it is located on the bottom of the other tracks. Makes the Flash track transparent if it is located on the top of other tracks.
	Alpha Transparent: Makes the transparent areas within the Flash track transparent. Other tracks below the Flash track will show through the transparent areas of the Flash track.
	Copy: Makes the Flash track opaque. Tracks below the Flash track will be masked.
Layer	Determines where the Flash track will reside relative to other tracks in the QuickTime movie.
	Top: Positions the Flash track on top of all other tracks.
	Bottom: Positions the Flash track below all the other tracks.
	Auto: Positions the Flash track in front of the other tracks if Flash CS3 content is placed in front of QuickTime content in the Flash CS3 movie. Positions the Flash track behind the other tracks if Flash CS3 content is placed in back of QuickTime content in the Flash CS3 movie.
Streaming sound: Use QuickTime compression	Lets you convert all streaming audio in the Flash CS3 project file into a QuickTime sound track.
Controller	Specifies the type of QuickTime controller that will be used to play the QuickTime movie.
Playback	When the **Loop** option is selected, the movie starts over at the beginning after the end is reached. When **Paused at start** is selected, the movie will start paused. When the user clicks a Play button, the movie will play. When **Play every frame** is selected, all sound is turned off, and each frame plays without skipping.
File: Flatten (Make self-contained)	Combines Flash CS3 content and video content in one QuickTime movie. If this option is not selected, the Flash CS3 file and video file will be referenced externally.

Saving Publishing Profiles

In the **Publish Settings** dialog box, you can set up the **Publish** settings the way you want and then save them as a **publish profile**. The benefits of saving your publishing settings is that you can easily use them later or even pass them on to co-workers so that everyone has the same publishing settings as you do.

Current profile: Lets you choose from a list of profiles you have created or imported.

Import/Export Profile: Lets you import a publish profile. You can also export (save) your current profile as an XML file you can store for later use or pass on to co-workers.

Create New Profile: Lets you save your current **Publish** settings as a new publish profile.

Duplicate Profile: Duplicates your currently selected profile. Duplicating a profile lets you use the profile settings as a starting point to make changes, while leaving the original profile unaltered.

Profile Properties: Lets you change the name of the currently selected publish profile.

Delete Profile: Deletes the currently selected profile.

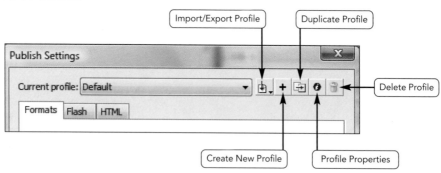

Optimizing Movies

All movies in Flash CS3 are not created equal. You can, however, use a few tricks and follow some simple guidelines to reduce the file size and increase the playback performance of your movie. The following list provides helpful tips to generate the best performance in your Flash CS3 files:

Use symbols: Convert your artwork to a symbol, which makes it easier on a computer's processor since there is no raw data on the **Stage**. Also, if you use artwork multiple times in your project file, the symbol will have to be downloaded once, and you can use it over and over without having any significant impact on file size.

Use solid lines wherever possible: Try to avoid using the dashed, dotted, or jagged line styles. Each dot, dash, or squiggle in these lines will be tracked as an independent object when the file is published. The jagged line style is the worst of the three. Lines using the jagged style contribute more than 100 times more bytes to the file size of your movie than do plain lines.

Use alpha sparingly: The more alpha, or transparency, you have in the movie, the slower the playback performance will be. Using alpha will not increase file size, but it can have a dramatic impact on playback performance. If you do use alpha, try not to have too many transparent elements stacked on top of one another.

Use gradients sparingly: Although their impact is not as serious as alpha, gradients can also slow down playback performance. Additionally, gradients that use alpha settings and are animated will significantly slow down playback performance. This combination of techniques is demanding on users' computer processors.

Use the Optimize command on your vector artwork: By selecting a vector object and using the **Modify > Shape > Optimize** command, you can reduce the file size of your movie.

Use vector graphics rather than bitmaps wherever possible: Vector graphics are usually significantly smaller than bitmaps, which can keep the file size down.

Be aware of complex objects in animation: The more complex your object is, the slower the playback performance of the animation will be.

Use device fonts where appropriate: When you use device fonts, Flash CS3 will not embed the outlines for your movie's fonts, as it otherwise does by default. Instead, Flash CS3 will display the text using a font on the user's machine that is closest to the specified font, saving file size.

Be cautious when looping streaming sound: When a sound's **Sync** option is set to **Stream**, it will play the sound at the same rate the animation is played. If you loop the streaming sound, Flash CS3 will multiply the file size by the number of times you loop the sound; when the **Sync** is set to **Stream** and you specify a number of loops, Flash CS3 actually adds frames to the **Timeline**— so be careful when adding looping to streaming sound.

Turn layers into guide layers: To prevent unwanted content from being exported, convert unwanted layers into guide layers. For example, if you have artwork you don't want to delete just yet but also don't want a particular layer to end up in the movie, turn the layer containing the content into a guide layer. Guide layers are not exported with the final movie, which may also save file size.

Use the individual compression settings: Use individual compression settings to compress imported bitmap graphics and sound files. By compressing each file individually, you can control the file size and image/sound quality, and often you can drastically reduce the image/sound file size from the original while keeping the image/sound quality relatively high.

Use the Load Movie command: Use the **Load Movie** command to break one large movie up into smaller pieces that display content only when needed or requested. With this command, rather than having one huge movie, you can create several smaller SWF files and load them into the main movie when the user requests the content by clicking a button.

Use the Generate Size Report and the Bandwidth Profiler features: Use these features to look at the breakdown of the SWF file, frame by frame. The report helps you identify places where you may be able to reduce the file size by compressing an image further, for example; the **Bandwidth Profiler** lets you spot a frame that is significantly larger than other frames.

Be aware of platform performance: Flash CS3 plays slightly faster (frames per second) on a Windows machine than it does on a Mac. Ideally, before you distribute Flash CS3 files or upload them to a live Web site, test the files on both a Windows-based machine and a Mac-based one to make sure the movie performs to your expectations on both platforms.

You have completed another chapter and should be ready to distribute your Flash CS3 movies all over the world! Before you do, you may want to hang on and finish the last two chapters— *"Putting It All Together"* and *"Integration"*— because they contain some valuable information.

18

Putting It All Together

You may not realize it, but after working through the exercises in the previous chapters, you have actually created all the parts that make up a full, working Web site. This chapter takes you through the completed xboarding.com Web site and points out the elements in the site you've already created. You will then have a chance to rebuild sections of the site to enhance it even further, such as adding a preloader and creating draggable movies. Additionally, you will learn about several features in Adobe Flash CS3 Professional that allow you to maximize your production efficiency, including the **Movie Explorer**. Finally, you'll learn about the program's print capabilities.

1 | Understanding the Big Picture

This exercise introduces you to the completed xboarding.com Web site, which includes many of the exercise files you created in previous chapters in this book. As you look through the site, you'll see references to previous chapters where you used the associated technique. You might find you know more than you think you do!

---

1 Copy the **chap_18** folder from the **Flash HOT CD-ROM** to your desktop. Open **xboardingSiteFinal.fla** from the **final** folder in the **chap_18** folder.

I created this fully functional project file ahead of time for you by using many of the techniques you learned in this book.

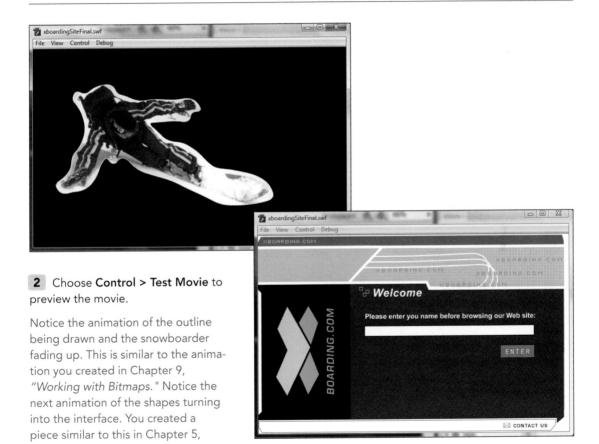

2 Choose **Control > Test Movie** to preview the movie.

Notice the animation of the outline being drawn and the snowboarder fading up. This is similar to the animation you created in Chapter 9, *"Working with Bitmaps."* Notice the next animation of the shapes turning into the interface. You created a piece similar to this in Chapter 5, *"Shape Tweening."*

NOTE:

Missing Fonts

When you choose **Control > Test Movie**, you may see a dialog box that says, "One or more of the fonts used by this movie are not available. Substitute fonts will be used for display and export. They will not be saved to the Adobe Flash authoring document." This message tells you that your computer does not have some of the fonts used to create the artwork in this file. Click **Use Default** so your computer will pick a default font to replace the unrecognizable fonts in the movie.

When creating your own projects, you can avoid this missing font issue altogether by working with your designer to select fonts, such as Arial, Verdana, or Helvetica, that are common across multiple platforms. If you choose fonts that are likely to be included on

all platforms, you will not see the "missing font" warning message. Also, please note that the user will not encounter this problem, because the font outlines are embedded in the movie to be viewed with the Adobe Flash Player. The only time this error message will occur is when you try to view an FLA project file containing a font that is not installed on your computer.

3 On the **Welcome** screen, type your name, and click **ENTER**. On the next screen, click the **CLICK TO ENTER THE SITE** button to enter the Web site. You built a similar **Welcome** screen in Chapter 13, *"Working with Text."*

4 Click the **sound off** and **sound on** buttons to stop and start the sound. You created similar buttons to control sound in Chapter 14, *"Sound."*

Notice the snowflake slowly falling down the screen. Does it look familiar? It is the same motion guide you created in Chapter 8, *"Motion Tweening and Timeline Effects."* Notice the logo animating near the top of the screen. You created this in Chapter 11, *"Movie Clips."*

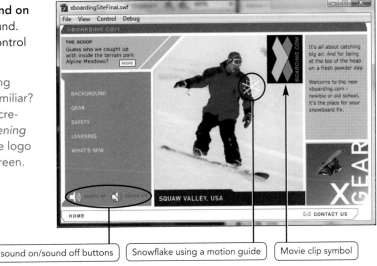

sound on/sound off buttons   Snowflake using a motion guide   Movie clip symbol

5 In the upper-left corner of the interface, click the **MORE** button.

This opens a browser window with the thescoop.html file embedded in it. You created this file in Chapter 12, *"ActionScript Basics."* Close the browser window when you are finished previewing the file.

6 In the preview window, in the lower-right corner of the interface, click the **XGear** button to load an order form in the Flash Player. This form is similar to the file you created in Chapter 15, *"Components and Forms."* Test the components, and click the **drag** button to drag the form around the window. When you are finished, click the **CLOSE WINDOW button** to unload the form from the Flash Player.

You will learn how to make the form draggable and make the CLOSE WINDOW button work in a later exercise in this chapter.

7 In the navigation menu, click the **SAFETY** button. You'll see the same drop-down menu you built in Chapter 12, *"ActionScript Basics."* On the **Safety** page of the Web site, click **PLAY** on the **Watch the RC Movie** button to load the **Responsibility Code** movie you made in Chapter 14, *"Sound,"* into a level above the main **Timeline**. Click the **drag** button to drag the movie around the screen, and click the **CLOSE WINDOW button** to unload the movie from the Flash Player.

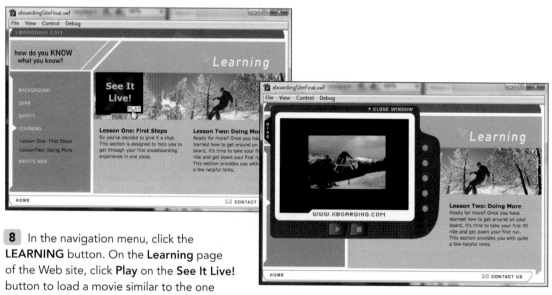

8 In the navigation menu, click the **LEARNING** button. On the **Learning** page of the Web site, click **Play** on the **See It Live!** button to load a movie similar to the one you made in Chapter 16, *"Video,"* into a level above the main **Timeline**. Click the **drag** button to drag the movie around the screen, click the buttons in the movie to see the different snowboarders, and click the **CLOSE WINDOW button** to unload the movie from the Flash Player.

9 In the navigation menu, click the **WHAT'S NEW** button. On the **What's New** page of the Web site, click the **Check Out Our CLIP OF THE DAY** button to load a movie that has features similar to the file you made in Chapter 16, "*Video*," into a level above the main **Timeline**. Click the **drag** button to drag the movie around the screen, click the **Start** and **Stop** buttons to play and stop the movie, and click the **CLOSE WINDOW button** to unload the movie from the Flash Player.

Explore this Web site to see how many other sections you recognize from exercises in this book. In later exercises of this chapter, you'll re-create parts of this project file to learn how to add some of the new sections, such as the draggable movies and CLOSE WINDOW button. When you are finished, keep the preview window open—you have one more area to look at next.

10 With the preview window still open, choose **View > Bandwidth Profiler**. Choose **View > Simulate Download**, which lets you see the preloader for the xboarding.com site.

A **preloader** is a short animation that plays while ActionScripting checks to see how many frames from the main movie have downloaded to the user's computer. This technique is often used as a "loading" screen while a large Flash movie downloads. You will build this preloader in Exercise 5 of this chapter. The Bandwidth Profiler is a feature in the test movie environment that lets you see how the movie streams based on different connection speeds.

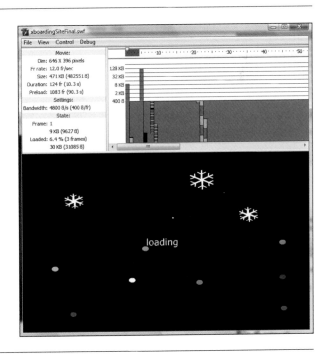

11 When you are finished, close the preview window, but leave the project file open for the next exercise.

It is now time to take a closer look at the FLA file to see how the Web site was put together. The next several exercises show you how the xboarding.com site was created, highlight certain workflow techniques, and introduce you to a few tools, including the Movie Explorer.

2 | Examining the Timeline

You can use frame labels to organize large projects into smaller, more manageable pieces. This exercise also demonstrates how frame labels were employed in the **xboardingSiteFinal** project file.

1 If you just completed Exercise 1, **xboardingSiteFinal.fla** should still be open. If it's not, open **xboardingSiteFinal.fla** from the **chap_18 > final** folder. On the **Timeline**, notice there are three frame labels: **intro**, **welcome**, and **home**.

At each frame label in this movie, there is one frame on the main Timeline. Each of these frames has a movie clip. Each movie has many layers and frames. Using frame labels in conjunction with movie clips is an effective way to organize your Flash movies, because the content of the site is in a few manageable pieces, instead of having many hard-to-manage frames and layers on the main Timeline.

2 Select **Frame 1** on the **movie clips** layer, and then double-click the **mcIntroAnim** movie clip on the **Stage** to enter its **Timeline**. Notice that there are many layers, many frames, and some frame labels. Select **Frame 2** on the **actions** layer, and choose **Window > Actions** to open the **Actions** panel. Take a minute to examine the code.

```
1  if(framesLoaded >= totalFrames)
2  {
3      gotoAndPlay("Start");
4  }
5  else
6  {
7      gotoAndPlay(1);
8  }
```

Notice the conditional, or **if/else**, statement. You learned about conditional statements in Chapter 12, *"ActionScript Basics."* This conditional statement causes the movie to play if enough frames are loaded, and if not enough frames are loaded, the movie will play in a loop. This is called a preloader. You will learn more about preloaders and create one yourself later in this chapter.

3 At the bottom of the **Timeline**, click the **Scene 1** button to return to the main **Timeline**.

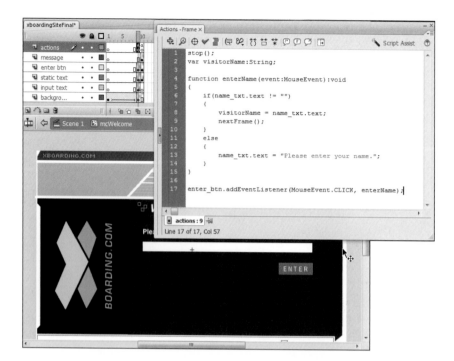

4 At the **welcome** frame label, double-click the **Welcome** movie clip to enter its **Timeline**. Note that this movie clip contains all the **Welcome** movie animations, layers, and ActionScript. In the **Welcome** movie clip, select **frame 9**, and choose **Window > Actions** to open the **Actions** panel and review the ActionScript that controls the **Welcome** menu.

5 Select **Frame 10**, and look in the **Actions** panel to review the code.

```
function enterSite(event:MouseEvent):void
{
    this.parent.gotoAndStop("home");
}

enterSite_btn.addEventListener(MouseEvent.CLICK, enterSite);
message_txt.text = "Welcome, " + visitorName + ". Thank you for visiting our Web site!";
```

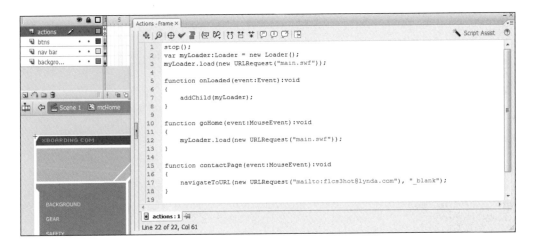

```
1   stop();
2   var myLoader:Loader = new Loader();
3   myLoader.load(new URLRequest("main.swf"));
4
5   function onLoaded(event:Event):void
6   {
7       addChild(myLoader);
8   }
9
10  function goHome(event:MouseEvent):void
11  {
12      myLoader.load(new URLRequest("main.swf"));
13  }
14
15  function contactPage(event:MouseEvent):void
16  {
17      navigateToURL(new URLRequest("mailto:flcs3hot@lynda.com"), "_blank");
18  }
19
```

6 At the bottom of the **Timeline**, click the **Scene 1** button to return to the main **Timeline**. At the **home** frame label, double-click the **Home** movie clip to enter its **Timeline**. Select **frame 1** on the **actions** layer, and choose **Window > Actions** to open the **Actions** panel. Review the code that controls this movie clip.

The navigation movie clip on the Stage may look familiar to you. You created a similar navigation system in Chapter 12, *"ActionScript Basics."* The navigation system uses the **Loader** class to load several external SWF files.

7 When you are finished, leave **xboardingSiteFinal.fla** open for the next exercise.

Managing Layers

Layers in Flash are similar to transparent sheets stacked on top of each other. Layers help you organize the content of the frames in the project file. For example, in Chapter 12, *"ActionScript Basics,"* you learned to get in the habit of adding an action layer on top of all other layers so that you can always find your frame actions in the same place. In Chapter 14, *"Sound,"* you learned to add a sound layer to the **Timeline** to keep the sounds consistently on the same layer and separate from others. Layers also play an important role in animation in Flash CS3. For instance, you learned in Chapter 5, *"Shape Tweening,"* that if you want to tween multiple elements, each tweened element must be on its own layer. By default, all movies in Flash CS3 have at least one layer, although you can add as many layers as you need.

Understanding Types of Layers

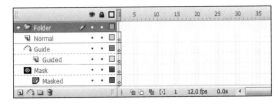

Throughout this book, you have worked with several kinds of layers in addition to standard layers. There are three special types of layers:

- **Guide layers:** Guide layers come in two flavors: motion guide layers (guide layers) and guided layers. The difference between the two is that motion guide layers serve as a path for an object to follow, and guided layers contain the objects that follow the path.

Motion guide layers are special layer types that are not exported when the movie is published or tested, and therefore they do not add to the size of the SWF file. These layers are visible only in the development environment. However, although artwork on a guide layer is not exported, actions on the layer are.

- **Mask layers:** Mask layers come in two flavors as well: mask layers and masked layers. A mask layer is a special layer that defines what will be visible (and invisible, or masked) on the layer (or layers) below it. The layers that are attached or indented under the mask layer are masked layers. Only layers beneath the shapes in the mask layer will be visible.

- **Layer folders:** A layer folder is a special kind of layer that can hold other layers inside it.

Layer folders cannot contain artwork—the layer folder's sole purpose is to hold other layers so you can keep your **Timeline** compact and organized.

In the next exercise, you will see an example of both a motion guide layer and a layer folder in the **xboardingSiteFinal.fla** project file.

Adding and Removing Layers

You can add a new layer by choosing **Insert > Timeline > Layer** or by clicking the **Insert Layer** button. You can click the **Add Motion Guide** button to add a guide layer. You can click the **Insert Layer Folder** button to add a layer folder. You can remove a layer by clicking the **Delete Layer** button (the **Trash** icon).

Organizing the Library

Throughout your production work on Flash CS3 projects, you will frequently use the **Library** panel for a variety of purposes, including opening files, dragging sounds or movie clips to the **Timeline**, renaming elements, finding elements within a project, and doing much more. Since you'll often use the **Library** panel, you need to keep it organized and use consistent naming schemes.

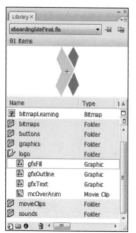

Organized Library pane

Disorganized Library panel

These two examples show an organized **Library** panel and a disorganized **Library** panel. Would you rather search for a movie clip symbol in the **Library** panel on the left, which has consistently named elements, or in the **Library** panel on the right, which is disorganized and uses many different naming schemes, as well as inconsistently placed items in the folders?

In addition to helping improve your efficiency, organizing your **Library** panel can also help others working on the project with you. Here are several basic "**Library** etiquette" guidelines to keep in mind:

Be consistent in your naming conventions: There is no right way to name the items within your project file, but once you decide on a structure to follow, stick to it. Since the **Library** panel sorts elements alphabetically, I recommend using prefixes at the beginning of the item name. For example, use the prefix **btn** for buttons (as in **btnHome**), and use **mc** for movie clips (as in **mcMenu**). Again, there is no perfect way to name your elements. Instead, consistency is what matters.

Choose brief, descriptive names, such as mcEffects: Use descriptive names rather than meaningless letters, such as **mef**. By doing so, you can find your asset a lot easier, knowing you have given it an accurate, descriptive name.

Use folders to organize the Library elements: Also stay consistent with the folder names. You can create a folder by clicking the **New Folder** button. Short, descriptive names will help you navigate through the **Library** panel faster, and you will know what to expect in each folder before you open it.

3 | Investigating the Library

This exercise will give you additional practice in working with the more important features of the **Library** panel.

1 Press **Ctrl+L** (Windows) or **Cmd+L** (Mac) to open the **Library** panel. Double-click the folders to view the elements in them. Notice all the elements are named consistently and are located in the corresponding folders. Double-click a **Library** panel item to open its **Timeline**, or select an item and click the **Properties** button to open the **Properties** dialog box to learn more about the element.

2 Continue to click items, expand and collapse folders, and examine other elements in the **Library** panel.

3 Click the **Library** panel's **Option** button, and choose **Collapse All Folders** to collapse all the folders in the **Library** panel.

4 Notice the **btnWhatsnew** button is not in a folder. Click the **buttons** folder once to expand it and reveal the files inside. Drag the **btnWhatsNew** file to the **buttons** folder.

5 In the **Resolve Library Conflict** dialog box, select **Don't replace existing items**, and click **OK**.

The library conflict resolution feature detects when you try to put two items with the same name in the same Library folder. If you choose not to replace the existing item, the new item will be given a slightly different name, keeping the original name and adding the word *copy* at the end.

Notice Flash CS3 automatically renames the file btnWhatsNew copy. This feature is a great safeguard against accidentally writing over files!

6 When you are finished, save your changes, and leave **xboardingSiteFinal.fla** open for the next exercise.

Using the Movie Explorer

The **Movie Explorer** is a handy tool that provides you with a visual representation of every aspect of the project file, organized into a hierarchical structure. You can use the **Movie Explorer** to view and locate just about every type of element within the project, including graphic symbols, button symbols, movie clip symbols, text, ActionScripts, frames, and scenes. This exercise introduces you to the basic features of the **Movie Explorer** while looking at the **xboardingSiteFinal.fla** project file.

---

1 In **xboardingSiteFinal.fla,** choose **Window > Movie Explorer** to open the **Movie Explorer**.

TIP:

Why Use the Movie Explorer?

You can use the **Movie Explorer** for a variety of purposes. For example, it can display a customized map showing all the text within a movie that uses the Verdana font, a list of all the graphic symbols in the project, or even all the sounds within a scene. Additionally, it can search for and locate a particular element when you know its name but not its location. The following steps take you through some of these examples.

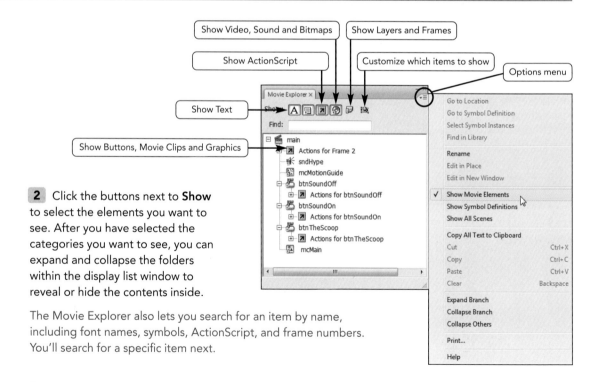

2 Click the buttons next to **Show** to select the elements you want to see. After you have selected the categories you want to see, you can expand and collapse the folders within the display list window to reveal or hide the contents inside.

The Movie Explorer also lets you search for an item by name, including font names, symbols, ActionScript, and frame numbers. You'll search for a specific item next.

3 In the **Movie Explorer** panel, click the panel **Options** button, and check the **Show Movie Elements**, **Show Symbol Definitions**, and **Show All Scenes** items to reveal the categories for all the symbols in the movie.

Now you can see all the symbols in your movie and what is within each symbol by clicking the + buttons to the left of the symbol names.

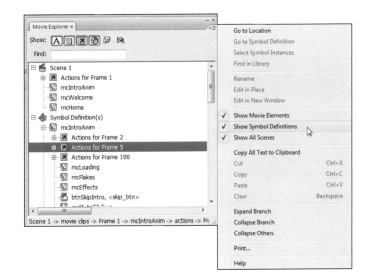

4 In the **Find** text box, type the item name **btn** to search for any elements within the project file starting with **btn**. If Flash finds an item, it will display it in the window.

Tip: Make sure the Show Buttons, Movie Clips, and Graphics filter button is selected.

The Movie Explorer will also reveal ActionScript applied to frames and objects within the project file. You will see this next.

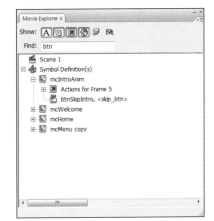

WARNING:

Finding Files in the Movie Explorer

When you use the **Find** feature in the **Movie Explorer**, Flash CS3 will search all the currently selected categories, not all the categories in the project file. If, for example, you are searching for a button, make sure you have the second button (**Show Buttons, Movie Clips, and Graphics**) selected. Otherwise, the **Movie Explorer** will not find the item you want. When you open the **Movie Explorer** for the first time, by default, the first three buttons (including the **Show Buttons, Movie Clips, and Graphics** category) are selected for you.

5 Find the button called **btnSkipIntro**. If it is not already expanded, click the **+** sign next to the **Actions for Frame 5** text to reveal actions related to that object.

In this case, the Movie Explorer will reveal the actual ActionScript attached to the button instance. Using the Movie Explorer is a great way to learn how projects were built because you can drill down to the actual ActionScript on any object in the movie.

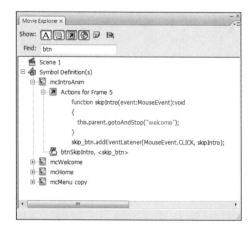

TIP:

Viewing the Full Path

You can view the full path to the object selected at the bottom of the **Movie Explorer** panel. Also, if the layer is not locked in the project file, Flash CS3 will select the element on the **Stage** when you select it in the **Movie Explorer**.

6 When you are finished investigating the **Movie Explorer**, close the **Movie Explorer** panel, and close the **xboardingSiteFinal** project file. You don't need to save your changes. You will be re-creating the preloader in the xboarding.com Web site in the next exercise.

What Is a Preloader?

SWF is a streaming format, meaning the movie can begin playing before it is completely downloaded. In many cases, streaming is good for users because they don't have to wait for the whole movie to load before they see the beginning of the movie. On the other hand, sometimes you may not want the movie to begin until all the frames have been downloaded—to assure smooth playback or synchronization with sound and the animation, for example. Additionally, there is no way of knowing the users' bandwidth, which could be dial-up, broadband, T1, or T3. Therefore, you may want to give users on a slower connection some type of visual feedback that the movie is being downloaded while they wait. One method of achieving both proper playback and giving visual feedback is to use a **preloader**.

A preloader can exist in the very first frames of the movie, in the first scene of the movie, or even at different points within the movie. It uses ActionScript to detect the progress of the SWF file download. After the whole movie (or an amount you specify) has downloaded onto the user's machine, the movie will play. You can put different artwork or animation into your movie to be displayed while the preloader is doing its detection work. The animation or artwork can keep users interested while they wait for the movie to download. The following exercise shows you how to create a simple preloader.

5 | Building a Preloader

As you build more complex projects in Flash CS3, users may see the movie differently depending on their connection speeds. Rather than allowing users to view a choppy animation or click a button that doesn't work yet because the movie is not completely downloaded, you can add a preloader that permits playback only after all the necessary frames have downloaded. This exercise shows you how to create a basic preloader so you can take control over what your users see and when they will see it.

1 Open **xboardingSite.fla** from the **site_in_prog** folder in the **chap_18** folder.

The siteInProgress folder contains all the files you need to re-create the xboarding.com Web site. Some files are already complete, and others have been partially created to get you started. You will complete these in the next few exercises.

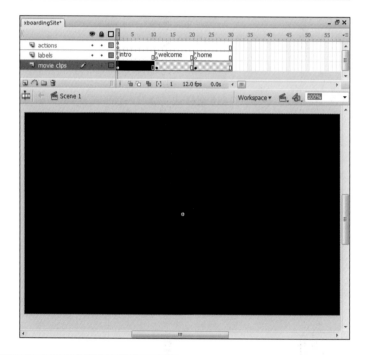

2 Select **Frame 1** on the **movie clips** layer on the **Timeline**. Double-click the **Stage** to open the **mcIntroAnin** movie clip's **Timeline**. Notice there are two layers: **bg** and **actions**. The **bg** layer has a black rectangle background, and the **actions** layer has some script written for you. You will create the preloader in this movie clip.

3 Select the first keyframe of the **actions** layer and open the **Actions** panel by pressing **F9** (Windows) or **Opt+F9** (Mac) on your keyboard. Examine the code written for you.

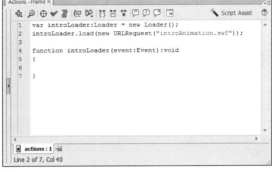

The code written in the actions layer creates an instance of the Loader class called introLoader, which loads an external SWF file called introAnimation.swf. The skeleton of a function called introLoaded is already written for you as well.

Later in this exercise, you will add to this code and tell Flash CS3 to display the loaded SWF file once it is finished loading.

---

4 Close the **Actions** panel. Open the **Library** panel. In the **movieClips** folder, click the **mcLoading** movie clip to select it. In the **Library** panel's preview window, click the **Play** button to preview the movie clip.

This movie clip will serve as the part of the looping animation that will play over and over until all the frames you specify are loaded.

---

5 In the **movieClips** folder, click the **mcFlakes** movie clip to select it. In the **Library** panel preview window, click the **Play** button to preview the movie clip.

Notice the falling snowflakes. This clip will serve as the background of the looping animation that will play until all the frames you specify are loaded.

---

6 Select the **bg** layer, and then click the **Insert Layer** button to add a new layer to the **Timeline**. Name the new layer **flake**.

---

7 From the **Library**, drag an instance of the **mcFlakes** movie clip onto the center of the **Stage**.

Tip: You can use the Align panel (Window > Align) to center the mcFlakes movie clip instance on the Stage. You can also use the Free Transform tool to stretch the mcFlakes movie clip instance so that it covers more of the Stage.

---

8 Click the **Insert Layer** button to add a new layer to the **Timeline**. Name the new layer **loader**. Make sure the **loader** layer appears above the **flake** layer.

---

9 From the **Library**, drag an instance of the **mcLoading** movie clip onto the center of the **Stage**.

Tip: You can use the Align panel to center the mcLoading movie clip instance on the Stage.

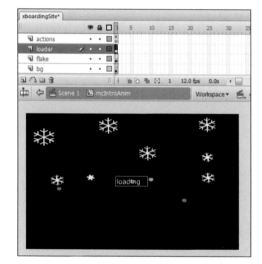

---

10 Select the first keyframe of the **actions** layer and open the **Actions** panel by choosing **Window > Actions**.

---

11 In the **Script** pane, insert your cursor at the end of Line 2, press **Enter** (Windows) or **Return** (Mac) to enter a new line, and type:

```
introLoader.contentLoaderInfo.
addEventListener(Event.COMPLETE,
introLoaded);
```

This ActionScript tells the information object of `introLoader` (`contentLoaderInfo`) to listen for the `COMPLETE` event, which is triggered when the SWF file finishes loading. When the file is completely loaded, the `introLoaded` function will run. You learned about the `contentLoaderInfo` property and the `COMPLETE` event in Chapter 12, *"ActionScript Basics."*

```
1   var introLoader:Loader = new Loader();
2   introLoader.load(new URLRequest("introAnimation.swf"));
3   introLoader.contentLoaderInfo.addEventListener(Event.COMPLETE, introLoaded);
4
5   function introLoader(event:Event):void
6   {
7
8   }
```

Line 3 of 8, Col 77

12 Click inside the `introLoaded` function and type:

```
addChild(introLoader);
```

This ActionScript places the loaded movie on the Stage using the `addChild()` method. Because this code is inside the `introLoaded` function, you will not see the `introAnimation` SWF file on the Stage until it is completely loaded. Until then, you will see the `preloader` movies.

```
1   var introLoader:Loader = new Loader();
2   introLoader.load(new URLRequest("introAnimation.swf"));
3   introLoader.contentLoaderInfo.addEventListener(Event.COMPLETE, introLoaded);
4
5   function introLoader(event:Event):void
6   {
7       addChild(introLoader);
8   }
```

Line 7 of 8, Col 24

13 Choose **Control > Test Movie** to preview the movie.

You may not see the preloader just yet. Why? Because the SWF file may load so fast you can't even see the preloader in action. The next step will show you how use the Bandwidth Profiler to simulate the way the movie will appear on the Internet, so you can test the scripts by seeing the preloader hard at work.

Note: When you choose Control > Test Movie, you may see the "missing font" warning message. Go ahead and choose Use Default so your computer will pick a default font to replace the unrecognizable fonts in the movie.

What Is the Bandwidth Profiler?

The **Bandwidth Profiler** is a component in the test movie environment. It lets you see how the movie streams based on different connection speeds. You can use the Bandwidth Profiler to simulate how a user would view your movie using a a 56K modem, for example. You can also use the Bandwidth Profiler to view the preloader before the movie plays.

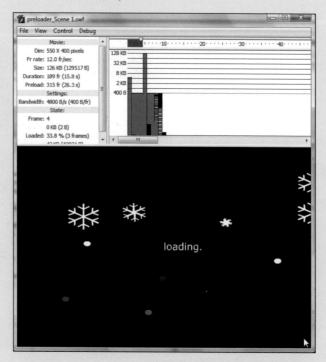

14 Keep the preview window open, choose **View > Bandwidth Profiler**, and choose select **View > Download Settings > 56K (4.7 KB/s)**. Choose **View > Simulate Download** to see your preloader work!

This setting lets you see the movie as it will appear when streamed on a live 56K connection. Notice the loading animation loops until all the frames are loaded (you will see *Loaded: 100%* in the State section of the Bandwidth Profiler), and then the intro animation begins.

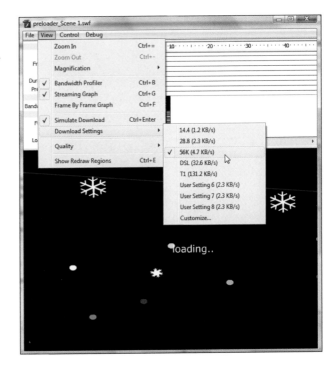

---

15 When you are finished previewing the preloader, choose **View > Bandwidth Profiler** to close the Bandwidth Profiler, and then close the preview window.

---

16 Nice work—you have made your first preloader! Save your changes, and leave **xboardingSite.fla** open for the next exercise.

6 | Printing from the Project File

Many Flash CS3 users are unaware of the capability to print from the project file (the FLA file). You can use this feature to show a client the page layouts for a Web site or even your progress on a project. In the project file, you can choose to print all frames in the movie or just the first frame. This exercise shows you how to set up the parameters and print a section of the movie from the project file. Then, the following exercise shows you how to set up printing from the Flash Player.

---

1 If you just completed Exercise 6, **xboardingSite.fla** should still be open. If it's not, complete Exercise 6, and then return to this exercise. Choose **File > Page Setup** (Windows) or **File > Print Margins** (Mac) to open the **Page Setup** (Windows) or **Print Margins** (Mac) dialog box.

---

2 In the **Frames** pop-up menu, choose **First Frame Only** to print the first frame of the movie.

Tip: The other option, All Frames, will print all the frames in the movie.

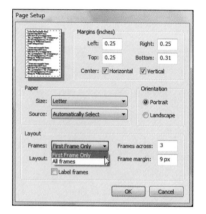

---

3 In the **Layout** pop-up menu, choose **Storyboard – Boxes**, which determines how the frames will appear on the printed page. Click **OK**.

---

4 In Windows, choose **File > Print** to preview how the printed page will look based on the settings you selected in the previous steps. On a Mac, choose **File > Print**, and then click the **Preview** button, which generates a PDF of the preview page.

Note: Not all systems will have a preview option.

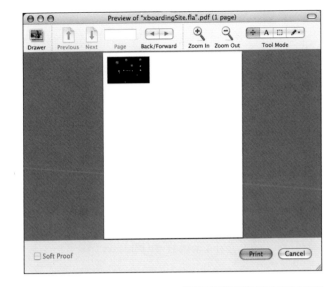

5 Click the **Print** button in the **Print Preview** window to print the first frame of the movie from the project file.

This is a great way to quickly show a client the page layouts for a Web site or even your progress on a project without having to show your client the entire project file.

6 You have just printed your first document from Flash CS3! Save your changes, and leave **xboardingSite.fla** open for the next exercise.

Setting Layout Options

The **Layout** settings allow you to select from five layout options, which are described in the following chart:

Printing Layout Options	
Option	**Description**
Actual Size	Prints the frame at full size
Fit On One Page	Increases or decreases the size of each frame so it fills the print area of the page
Storyboard – Boxes	Prints multiple thumbnails on one page and creates a rectangle around each thumbnail

continues on next page

Printing Layout Options *continued*	
Option	**Description**
Storyboard – Grid	Prints multiple thumbnails inside a grid on each page
Storyboard - Blank	Prints multiple thumbnails on one page and prints only the artwork inside each thumbnail

NOTE:

Printing Flash CS3 Content from a Browser

When a user is viewing a Web site created using Flash CS3, different results occur when the user attempts to print the Web site, depending on the method used:

- If the user clicks the **Print** button in the browser window, the page of the Web site that he or she is currently viewing will be printed. Since you cannot control the user's browser, there is no way to completely control or disable printing in the user's browser using Flash CS3.

- If the user **right-clicks** (Windows) or **Ctrl-clicks** (Mac) and chooses **Print** in the contextual menu, every frame in the movie will print. However, you can change this by labeling certain keyframes as printable in the project file and thus restricting users to print only the frames you specify. You will learn to do this in the next exercise.

- If the user clicks a **Print** button created in the Flash movie, all the frames to which you have added a **#p** on the **Timeline** will print. (You will learn how to add this in the next exercise.)

TIP:

Disabling Printing

You can also disable printing entirely in the Flash Player by adding the label **!#p** to a keyframe. This label will make the entire movie nonprintable from the contextual menu in the Flash Player.

NOTE:

Printing Platforms Supported by the Flash Player

Flash Player 6 and newer can print to both Adobe PostScript and non-PostScript printers. This includes most common printers, such as black-and-white and color printers, laser and ink-jet printers, and PostScript and PCL (**P**rinter **C**ommand **L**anguage) printers.

7 | Printing from the Flash Player

In addition to printing files from within the project file, you can let users viewing the movie in the Flash Player print Flash content. By default, all the frames on the **Timeline** will print unless you either specify certain frames as printable by a user viewing the movie or disable printing altogether. This exercise shows you how to control printing by adding a special label to the chosen printable frames. It also shows you how to add ActionScript to a button and set up the printing parameters for your users.

1 If you just completed Exercise 7, **xboardingSite.fla** should still be open. If it's not, complete Exercise 7, and then return to this exercise. Make sure you are in **Scene 1** on the main **Timeline**. Select **Frame 20** on the **movie clips** layer, and double-click the **Stage** anywhere to open the **mcHome** movie clip's **Timeline**.

Note: If you receive the "missing font" message, click Use Default so your computer will pick a default font to replace the unrecognizable fonts in the movie.

2 Click the **Insert Layer** button to add a new layer to the **Timeline**. Name the layer **labels**, and place it below the **actions** layer.

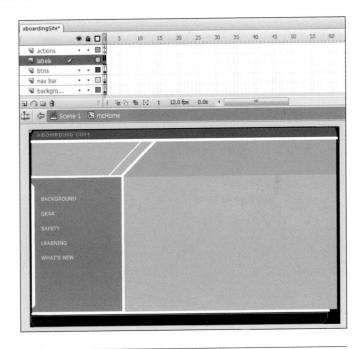

3 On the **labels** layer, select the first frame. In the **Property inspector**, type **#p** in the **Frame Label** field to define that keyframe as printable.

NOTE: | **Printing from the Contextual Menu**

You can permit your users to access the **Print** command from the contextual menu. The contextual menu will appear in the Flash Player when a user **right-clicks** (Windows) or **Ctrl-clicks** (Mac) the movie.

By default, this **Print** command will print every frame in the movie. However, by labeling certain keyframes as printable in the project file (as you did in Step 3 by adding the **#p** label to the keyframe), you can restrict the users to printing only the frames you specify.

Further, you can also disable printing entirely in the Flash Player by adding the label **!#p** to a keyframe. This label will make the entire movie nonprintable from the Flash Player. Note that although you disable printing from the Flash Player, the user can still choose the **Print** command in the browser. Since you cannot control the user's browser commands, there is no way to disable printing in the user's browser using Flash.

4 Choose **Control > Test Movie**. Type your name after the intro animation, and click the **enter site** button to see the **mcHome** movie clip. **Right-click** (Windows) or **Ctrl-click** (Mac) the movie to access the contextual menu. Choose **Print** to print the frame you labeled in Step 3.

Note: After you have defined a keyframe as printable, when a user accesses the contextual menu and chooses Print, Flash will print only the frames labeled as #p.

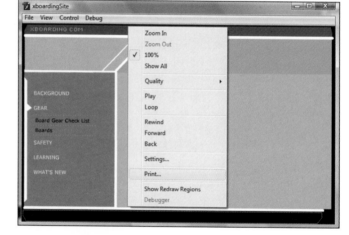

In addition to allowing access to the contextual menu, you can allow the user to print frames within the movie by attaching ActionScript to a button that will print the frames you specify. To do this, you must first create the printable frame labels, as you did in the previous steps, and then you can create the button, which you will do in the following steps.

5 When you are finished, close the preview window, and close **xboardingSite.fla**. You don't need to save your changes.

The following chart explains the print action parameters:

Print Action Parameters

Option	Setting	Description
Print	As Vectors	Prints frames that do not use transparency (alpha) or color effects.
Print	As Bitmap	Prints frames that contain bitmap images, transparency, or color effects.
Location	Level	Specifies the level in the Flash Player to print. By default, all the frames in the level will print unless you specify otherwise. You can assign a **#p** frame label to print only specific frames in the level, rather than all the frames.
Location	Target	Identifies the instance name of the movie clip or **Timeline** to print. By default, all the frames in the movie are printed. However, you can designate frames for printing by attaching a **#p** frame label to specific frames.

8 | Creating Draggable Movies

When you load movies using the **Loader** class, you can add functionality so that they not only will load but can also be dragged around the interface by the user. This exercise shows you how to do that. This exercise also shows you how to add the ActionScript to allow the user to close the window when finished with it.

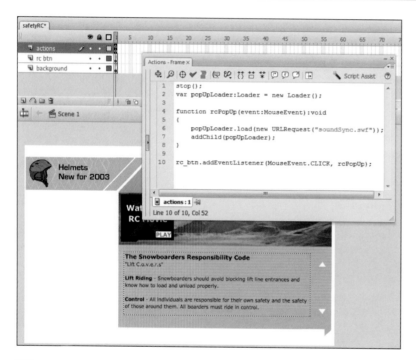

1 Open the **safetyRC.fla** file from the **site_in_prog** folder. Select the first keyframe on the **actions** layer, and press **F9** (Windows) or **Opt+F9** (Mac) to open the **Actions** panel. Look at the code that is written for you already, and make a special note of the name **popUpLoader**, an instance of the **Loader** class. You will refer to this instance later. When you are finished looking at the code, close the file.

This file is already set up to load the draggable movie. The **popUpLoader** instance loads the external Flash movie using its load method and a **URLRequest**. You learned about loading external movies in Chapter 12, *"ActionScript Basics."* The **popUpLoader** instance places the loaded content on the Stage using the **addChild()** function. In this exercise, you will write code to make the loaded movie draggable and use a function called **removeChild()** to make it disappear when the user clicks a button.

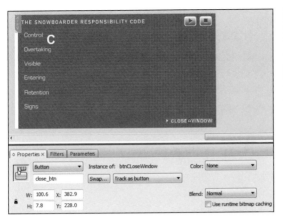
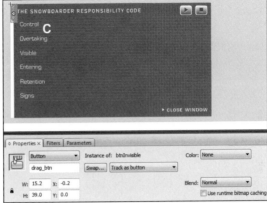

2   Open the **soundSync.fla** file from the **site_in_prog** folder. On the **Stage**, notice the **CLOSE WINDOW button**. Click that button, and note its instance name in the **Property inspector: close_btn**. Notice the other button near the top left of the **Stage** that says **drag**. The button is a semitransparent cyan color, indicating it is an invisible button. Click the **Invisible** button on the **Stage**, and note its instance name in the **Property inspector: drab_btn**.

Invisible buttons are buttons with only a hit state. They act as hot spots you can use to trigger ActionScript. Invisible buttons are excellent tools because you can recycle them easily.

3   Select the first keyframe on the **actions** layer, and press **F9** (Windows) or **Opt+F9** (Mac) to open the **Actions** panel. Look at the code that is written for you already. Some of the code may be familiar to you, because you wrote similar code in Chapter 14, "Sound."

Near the bottom of the code, you will see a few skeletons of functions written for you. These functions are already linked to the buttons on the Stage. In the next step, you will learn how to make this movie draggable.

```
1  play_btn.addEventListener(MouseEvent.CLICK, playMovie);
2  stop_btn.addEventListener(MouseEvent.CLICK, stopMovie);
3  function playMovie(event:MouseEvent):void
4  {
5      play();
6  }
7  function stopMovie(event:MouseEvent):void
8  {
9      stop();
10 }
11
12 function dragMovie(event:MouseEvent):void
13 {
14
15 }
16
17 function dropMovie(event:MouseEvent):void
18 {
19
20 }
21
22 function closeMovie(event:MouseEvent):void
23 {
24
25 }
26
27 drag_btn.addEventListener(MouseEvent.MOUSE_DOWN, dragMovie);
28 drag_btn.addEventListener(MouseEvent.MOUSE_UP, dropMovie);
29 close_btn.addEventListener(MouseEvent.MOUSE_DOWN, closeMovie);
```

4 In the **dragMovie** function, click in the curly braces, and type the following:

`this.startDrag();`

The **startDrag()** method allows you to drag visible objects. Because the **this** keyword is written in ActionScript on the main Timeline, **this** is referring to the main Timeline. In this case, you are dragging **this**, meaning the main Timeline, or the entire Flash movie. So when this file (soundSync.swf) loads into the safetyRC.swf file, the whole soundSync.swf file will be draggable.

```
Actions - Frame ×                                    Script Assist
1  play_btn.addEventListener(MouseEvent.CLICK, playMovie);
2  stop_btn.addEventListener(MouseEvent.CLICK, stopMovie);
3  function playMovie(event:MouseEvent):void
4  {
5      play();
6  }
7  function stopMovie(event:MouseEvent):void
8  {
9      stop();
10 }
11
12 function dragMovie(event:MouseEvent):void
13 {
14     this.startDrag();
15 }
16
17 function dropMovie(event:MouseEvent):void
18 {
19
20 }

actions : 1
Line 14 of 29, Col 19
```

5 Choose **Control > Test Movie** to preview the file. Notice if you try to drag the movie, you can. But when you release the mouse, the movie doesn't drop. Close the preview window when you are finished.

You will write the code to drop the movie using the **stopDrag()** method in the next step.

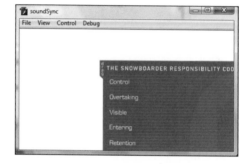

6 Return to the **Actions** panel. Click in the curly braces of the **dropMovie** function, and type:

`this.stopDrag();`

This ActionScript tells Flash CS3 to stop dragging the movie when you release the mouse.

Note: The area that you tell Flash CS3 to respond to a mouse down or a mouse up event is in the same the line of code where you use the **addEventListener** function. Look at the **addEventListener** lines of code for the different buttons to see the mouse events for which the buttons are listening.

```
Actions - Frame ×                                    Script Assist
1  play_btn.addEventListener(MouseEvent.CLICK, playMovie);
2  stop_btn.addEventListener(MouseEvent.CLICK, stopMovie);
3  function playMovie(event:MouseEvent):void
4  {
5      play();
6  }
7  function stopMovie(event:MouseEvent):void
8  {
9      stop();
10 }
11
12 function dragMovie(event:MouseEvent):void
13 {
14     this.startDrag();
15 }
16
17 function dropMovie(event:MouseEvent):void
18 {
19     this.stopDrag();
20 }

actions : 1
Line 19 of 29, Col 18
```

7 Choose **Control > Test Movie** to preview the file. Drag the movie. Drop the movie. Nice! Close the preview window when you are done.

Now all you have left is to make the movie disappear when you click the CLOSE WINDOW button. You will write the code to close the movie window in the next step.

8 Return to the **Actions** panel. In the `closeMovie()` function, click in the curly braces, and type the following:

`this.parent.parent.removeChild(this.parent);`

This ActionScript will make the window disappear, but only after it is loaded in from the safetyRC file. Notice that the code uses the **removeChild()** function. This function does the opposite of **addChild()**; it removes a visual element.

Take a second to analyze how this code is working. What does **this** mean? What does **this.parent** mean? The **this** keyword means this Timeline, or this movie. The phrase **this.parent**, in this case, is referring to the parent of this movie.

Because this movie will be loaded in through the **popUpLoader** instance of the **Loader** class, the parent of this movie is the **popUpLoader** instance. Then what does **this.parent.parent** mean? The parent of the **popUpLoader** instance is referring to the main Timeline of the safetyRC file.

Remember in step 1 when you looked at the code in that file? In that file, the **addChild()** function was used to place the **popUpLoader** instance on the Stage. Since the **popUpLoader** instance is a child of the safetyRC movie's Timeline, the main Timeline of the safetyRC movie is considered its parent. That is why that particular object (the main Timeline of the safetyRC movie, which is referred to in the soundSync movie as **this.parent.parent**) is using the **removeChild()** function to make the pop-up window disappear.

In the parentheses of the **removeChild()** function, you wrote **this.parent**. The code **this.parent** is referring to the **popUpLoader** instance on the main Timeline of the safetyRC movie. So, essentially what this code is telling Flash CS3 to do is to take the **popUpLoader Loader** instance out of its display list, thus making the soundSync movie invisible.

Note: This code will not work if you simply test this movie. This line of code will work only when this file is loaded into another file using the **Loader** class. The reason for that is until this movie gets loaded into another file, it has no parent.

9 Open **safetyRC.fla** from the **site_in_prog** folder. Test the movie by choosing **Control > Test Movie**. Click the **drag** button to drag the movie. Click the **CLOSE WINDOW button** to make the movie disappear.

Yeah! The changes you made to soundSync.fla carry over to safetyRC.fla when the movie is loaded.

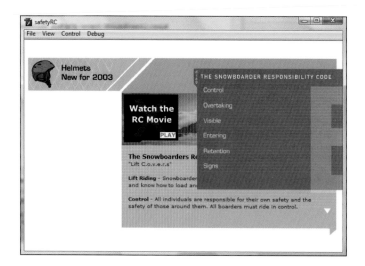

10 When you are finished, close the preview window. Close **safetyRC.fla** and **soundSync.fla**. You don't need to save your changes.

You have conquered another chapter! You should now have a more solid understanding of how the different pieces in this book come together to make a whole. Now there is only one more chapter left: Chapter 19, "*Integration.*"

19

Integration

Although many designers work exclusively in Adobe Flash CS3 Professional, the program doesn't have to be an island unto itself. You have many opportunities to combine it with other tools. The following hands-on exercises show how to use Adobe Fireworks, Adobe Illustrator, and Adobe Photoshop content with Flash CS3. They also show you how to incorporate Flash CS3 content into a Web site designed in Adobe Dreamweaver CS3. Keep in mind that in order to try these exercises, you must have these programs installed on your system. If you don't have the applications, you can download trial versions of them at **www.adobe.com**.

Importing Vector Files

You can import several file types into Flash CS3. The following chart lists the supported file types:

Vector File Types Supported by Adobe Flash CS3			
File Type	Extension	Windows	Mac
Adobe Flash movie	.swf	X	X
Adobe Illustrator	.ai	X	X
Adobe Photoshop	.psd	X	X
AutoCAD DXF	.dxf	X	X
Bitmap	.bmp	X	X
Enhanced Windows metafile	.emf	X	
Adobe FreeHand	.fh8, .ft8, .fh9, .ft9, .fh10, .fh11	X	X
FutureSplash Player	.spl	X	X
JPEG	.jpg	X	X
PNG	.png	X	X
Windows metafile	.wmf	X	X

1 | Importing Fireworks Content

As you continue to develop your skills, you may want to use content created outside Flash CS3. Although you can choose from many applications for creating artwork, you'll enjoy using Fireworks content because colors and text can remain editable when you import the Fireworks CS3 file into Flash CS3. Or, if you choose to import flattened images, you can edit the artwork in Fireworks without ever leaving Flash CS3! This exercise takes you through some basic techniques for importing and working with Fireworks PNG files as editable objects and text and as rasterized, flattened images.

Note: You must have Fireworks CS3 installed in order to complete this exercise. You can download a trial version of Fireworks CS3 from Adobe's Web site at **www.adobe.com**.

---

1 Copy the **chap_19** folder from the **Flash HOT CD-ROM** to your desktop. Open **fireworksFlash.fla** from the **chap_19** folder.

---

2 Choose **File > Import > Import to Stage**. Select the **gearSale.png** file in the **chap_19** folder, and click **Open** (Windows) or **Import** (Mac) to open the **Import Fireworks Document** dialog box.

Flash CS3 automatically detects you are trying to import a Fireworks PNG file.

---

3 Choose **Page** for **Import**, **New Layer** for **Into**, **Keep all paths editable** for **Objects**, and **Keep all text editable** for **Text**. Click **OK** to import the PNG image onto a new layer. The text and paths will remain editable.

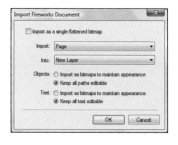

Note: Importing a PNG file with editable paths and editable text allows all the vector information to remain as vector information and allows text to be editable. However, you will lose bitmap effects, such as bevels and glows. Also, if you are using an older version of Fireworks, you may notice some of the artwork aligns incorrectly upon importing.

Notice Flash CS3 places the Fireworks PNG file on its own layer in a layer folder and even names it for you. Although you may not have realized it, you instructed Flash CS3 to do so when you chose the New Layer option for Into in the Import Fireworks Document dialog box.

NOTE:

Understanding the Fireworks Import Settings

The **Import Fireworks Document** dialog box offers a number of options. The following chart outlines each option:

Fireworks Import Settings	
Option	**Settings/Description**
Import as a single flattened bitmap	Turns the PNG file into a single flattened image.
Objects	**Import as bitmaps to maintain appearance:** Maintains the appearance to preserve Fireworks fills, strokes, and effects **Keep all paths editable:** Keeps all objects as editable vector paths, but fills, strokes, and effects may be lost on import
Text	**Import as bitmaps to maintain appearance:** Maintains the appearance to preserve Fireworks fills, strokes, and effects applied to text **Keep all text editable:** Keeps all text editable, but fills, strokes, and effects may be lost on import

4 Select the **Selection** tool in the **Tools** panel. On the **Stage**, double-click the **GEAR** text, which will allow you to edit the text. Type the word **BOOT**. See how easy it is to make changes? Select the **Selection** tool in the **Tools** panel again, and reposition the **BOOT** text so it is centered above the **SALE** text.

5 Click the upper-right corner of the background artwork movie clip.

6 Double-click the movie clip to enter its **Timeline**. In the **bg** movie clip, select the shape on the **Stage**. Notice in the **Property inspector** that it is a **drawing object**. In the **Property inspector**, choose a new color in the **Fill Color** box to change the background color.

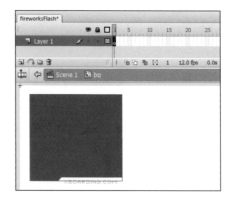

7 Below the **Timeline**, click **Scene 1** to return to the main **Timeline** and see your changes!

You just learned how to import a Fireworks PNG file as a new layer using editable paths and editable text, which lets you modify object attributes such as the type and object color. Next, you will learn how to import the same Fireworks document as a flattened bitmap. However, with that method, you lose the ability to edit the object as a vector because it is imported as a bitmap graphic.

8 In the main **Timeline**, lock the **gearSale.png** layer, and select **Frame 1** on **Layer 1**.

9 Choose **File > Import > Import to Stage** to open the **Import File** dialog box. In the **chap_19** folder, select the same **gearSale.png** file you imported previously in this exercise. Click **Open** (Windows) or **Import** (Mac) to open the **Import Fireworks Document** dialog box.

Again, Flash CS3 automatically detects you are trying to import a Fireworks PNG file.

10 Select the **Import as a single flattened bitmap** option. Click **OK** to import the PNG image onto **Layer 1** as a flat, bitmap graphic.

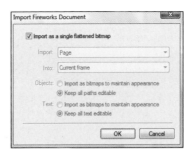

---

11 Select the new bitmap graphic, and drag it to the right of the **Stage** so you can see it better.

Tip: By default, Flash CS3 automatically places imported artwork in the upper-left corner on the Stage. Since Layer 1 is below the Fireworks PNG layer, it will appear behind it in the stacking order.

---

12 Select the bitmap you just imported.

In the Property inspector, notice the image you just imported is a bitmap. Also notice the glow around the artwork; this is visual feedback that the artwork has been imported as a bitmap. You imported the same file earlier in the exercise, but there was no glow. Why? When you import a Fireworks PNG file using editable paths and editable text, some fills, strokes, and effects may be lost. However, when you import a Fireworks PNG file as a flattened bitmap, you lose the ability to edit the text and

paths, but glows and bevels are preserved. What's best? It depends on what you want to do with the imported content. If you need to edit the vector artwork in Flash, import it using the technique you learned in Steps 2 and 3. If you want the image to look the same as it did in Fireworks, use the technique you learned in Steps 9 and 10. What if you need to edit the content? Fortunately, you can edit the bitmap using Fireworks CS3 without ever having to leave Flash CS3. You'll learn how in the next steps.

---

13 Press **Ctrl+L** (Windows) or **Cmd+L** (Mac) to open the **Library** panel. Select the **gearSale** bitmap.

14 Click to open the **Library** panel's **Options** menu, and choose **Edit with Fireworks** to open **gearSale.png** in Fireworks CS3 automatically.

Note: You must have Fireworks CS3 installed on your computer in order to perform this step.

15 In Fireworks CS3, select the **SALE** text. In the **Property inspector**, click **white** for the text fill color. When you are finished, click the **Done** button to close Fireworks CS3 and return to Flash CS3.

Note: The Editing from Flash text provides a visual clue that you are editing directly from Flash.

Back in Flash CS3, notice your file has been updated! As you can see, you can edit and update content created in Fireworks CS3 easily!

16 Close **fireworksFlash.fla**. You don't need to save your changes.

2 | Integrating with Dreamweaver CS3

Many designers create SWF files using Flash and then use Dreamweaver to integrate the SWF file with HTML documents. Dreamweaver CS3 is also a great tool for managing large numbers of Web site files, and it provides a way to transfer the files to a Web server. This exercise shows how to combine HTML (**HyperText Markup Language**) and Flash content using Dreamweaver CS3. Why not just use the publishing features of Flash CS3 for your HTML? It's fine for simple pages with only Flash content, but Dreamweaver CS3 offers more control if you plan to integrate Flash content with more complex HTML pages or if you want to add content to a number of different pages. After you import the SWF file into Dreamweaver, you can alter many attributes of the Flash CS3 file, such as its size and positioning. You can even insert Flash content inside frames, tables, or layers within a Dreamweaver HTML document. The process is quite simple—this exercise shows you how.

Note: You must have Dreamweaver CS3 installed in order to complete this exercise. You can download a trial version of Dreamweaver CS3 from Adobe's Web site at **www.adobe.com**.

---

1 Open **homePage.fla** file from the **chap_19** folder.

---

2 Choose **Control > Test Movie** to produce the SWF file you will need in later steps for this exercise. Notice the animated logo.

---

3 Close the preview window. Keep Flash open.

---

4 Open Dreamweaver CS3. Choose **File > Open**, select the **index.html** file from the **chap_19** folder, and click **Open**. The HTML file is an empty file with a black background.

5 In the **Insert** bar, choose **Common**. In the **Common** panel, click the **Media** button, and then choose **Flash** in the menu.

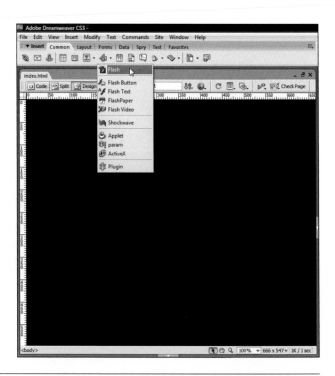

6 In the **Select File** dialog box, locate the **chap_19** folder, select **homePage.swf**, and click **OK** (Windows) or **Choose** (Mac). Make sure you choose the SWF file and not the FLA file.

Note: If Dreamweaver opens the Object Tag Accessibility Attributes dialog box, just click OK to ignore it for this exercise.

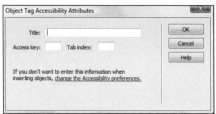

7 In the **Property inspector**, click the small arrow in the lower-right corner to expand the **Property inspector** (if it's not already expanded). Notice the green **Play** button. Click the **Play** button to preview the Flash file in Dreamweaver.

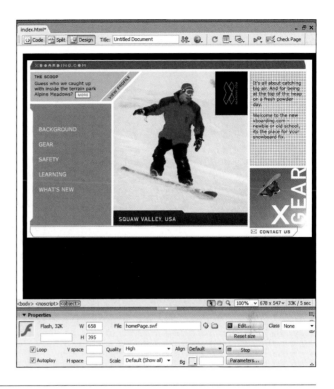

8 Notice the rollover functionality of the buttons (the caret appears to the left of the text when you move your cursor over the buttons). Notice the logo is animating also.

Using the Play button, you can have Adobe Dreamweaver CS3 preview graphic, button, and movie clip symbols in your Flash CS3 movie.

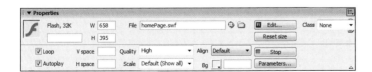

9 When you preview the file, notice that the green **Play** button in the **Property inspector** changes to a red **Stop** button. When you're done previewing the file, click the **Stop** button to return to your work environment. The Flash content will turn gray.

10 Make sure the SWF file is still selected, and then click the **Edit** button in the **Property inspector**. If you see a pop-up window, click **OK**.

Tip: You can also right-click (Windows) or Ctrl-click (Mac) the SWF in Dreamweaver and then choose Edit with Flash in the contextual menu to open the file in Flash CS3.

---

11 Dreamweaver prompts you to locate the original source FLA file. Select **homepage.fla** from the **chap_19** folder, and click **Open**.

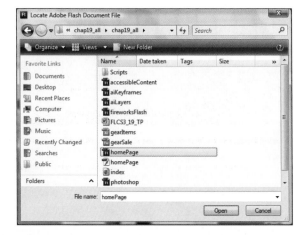

---

12 Select the **Free Transform** tool, and click and drag to rescale the logo smaller. When you are finished, click the **Done** button to return to Dreamweaver CS3.

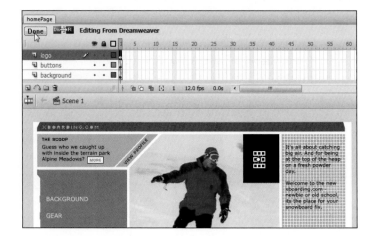

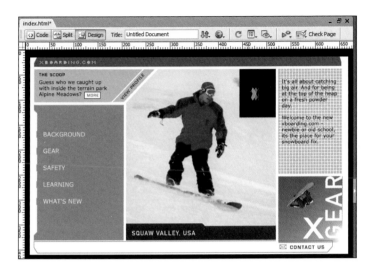

13 In Dreamweaver CS3, click the **Play** button in the **Property inspector**.

Notice that Dreamweaver CS3 automatically updates the SWF file in the document to reflect the change you made to the logo. Cool!

Note: Using the Property inspector in Dreamweaver CS3 is an easy way to edit the FLA file, change the background color, change how the content will be aligned or how the movie will scale, and change plenty of other useful properties. Dreamweaver CS3 offers a lot of control over how the content is displayed.

---

14 When you are finished, close all files in Dreamweaver CS3 and Flash CS3. You don't need to save your changes. Close Dreamweaver CS3, and return to Flash CS3 for the next exercise.

---

3 | Importing Illustrator Content

Many digital artists are familiar with Illustrator and prefer to use its drawing capabilities over other vector illustration tools. Flash CS3 supports direct import of Illustrator files and has improved integration since Flash 8. This exercise walks you through the process of importing an Illustrator file as keyframes into Flash CS3 and importing Illustrator content as separate layers in Flash CS3.

Note: Illustrator CS3 is not necessary to complete this exercise. However, you can download a trial version of Illustrator CS3 from Adobe's Web site at **www.adobe.com**.

---

1 Choose **File > New** to create a new document. Select **Flash File (ActionScript 3.0)**, and click **OK**. Choose **Edit > Preferences** (Windows) or **Flash > Preferences** (Mac) to open the **Preferences** window. Select **AI File Importer** in the **Category** list.

The AI Importer preferences allow you to specify how Illustrator files are imported into Flash CS3. In the next few steps, you will learn about the different options in the AI Importer menu.

---

2 Select **Exclude objects outside crop area** for **General**, and select **Editable paths** for **Import paths as**. Deselect **Show import dialog box**. When you are finished, click **OK**.

Notice all the other options below the options you selected. There are many ways to import an Illustrator file. How do you know which options to choose? As a general rule, if you need something to look exactly as it does in Illustrator, a bitmap is the best choice. If your content needs to be editable, select the Editable text and Editable paths options. Use the Create movie clips option if you want to store particular elements within movie clips.

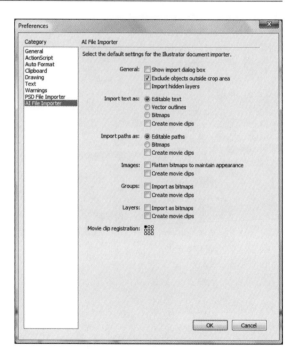

3 Choose **File > Import > Import to Stage**, and select the file **gearItems.ai** from the **chap_19** folder. Notice the elements from the Illustrator file are placed on the **Stage**. Also notice Flash CS3 creates four layers for you and even names them! Sweet!

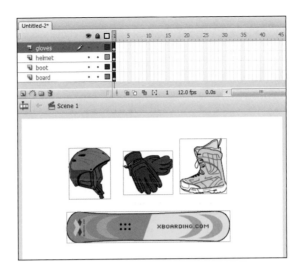

Using these options, Flash CS3 imports Illustrator layers as Flash CS3 layers with names identical to the layer names in Illustrator. The Illustrator files have many different paths, and they come into Flash CS3 as grouped objects. You can edit any of the vector paths by double-clicking a group, which you will do next.

4 On the **Stage**, double-click the **board group**. In the **board group**, there are some groups and some shapes. Click the **board shape**, and notice in the **Property inspector** that it is a shape. Change the color of the board in the **Property inspector**. Below the **Timeline**, click the **Scene 1** button to return to the **main Timeline** and view your changes. Nice!

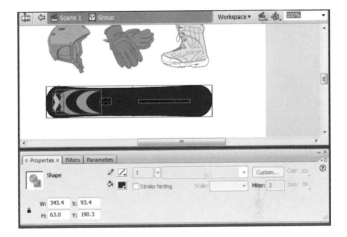

This is a great way to quickly import Illustrator files. Using this technique, you have a lot of control as to how specific elements are imported. In the next steps, you will learn a technique that will give you even more control over the files you import by selecting specific layers and paths!

5 Choose **File > New** to create a new document. Select **Flash File (ActionScript 3.0)**, and click OK. Choose **Edit > Preferences** (Windows) or **Flash CS3 > Preferences** (Mac) to open the **Preferences** window. Select **AI File Importer** in the **Category** list.

6 Select **Show import dialog box** for **General**. When you are finished, click **OK**.

The import dialog box is the tool that lets you import any combination of layers or paths from an AI file. You will learn how to do this in the next step.

7 Choose **File > Import > Import to Stage**, and select the file **gearItems.ai** from the **chap_19** folder. Notice all the layers and paths of the Illustrator file on the left side of the dialog box. Also notice how all the paths are organized into groups and layers. Nice!

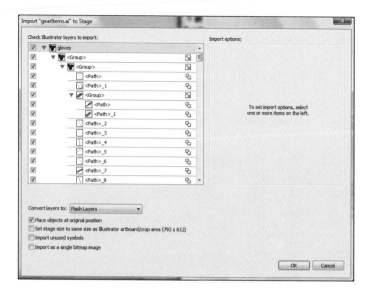

8 Select **<Group>** in the layers area on the left side of the dialog box. Notice the options on the right side. Then, select **<Path>** in the left menu, and notice how the options on the right have updated to include **Editable path** for **Import as**. Select or deselect the boxes for each of the paths and groups to choose which paths and groups you want to import.

Notice the option to create a movie clip out of any path or group, with the registration and instance name of your choice.

Note: Remember that importing as a bitmap will preserve the path's appearance, while importing as an editable path will keep the path editable.

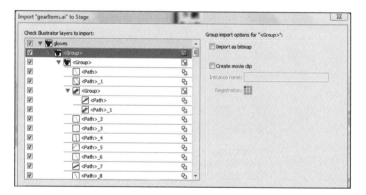

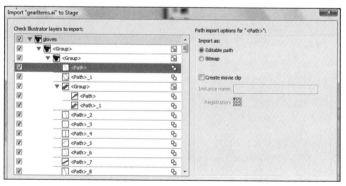

9 Set the following options at the bottom of the dialog box, and click **OK**:

- Choose **Flash Layers** in the **Convert layers to** pop-up menu.

- Select **Place objects at original position**.

- Select **Set stage size to same size as Illustrator artboard/ crop area**.

Note: The Place objects at original position and Set stage size to same size as Illustrator artboard/crop area options make the Stage size and positioning of elements in Flash match those in the Illustrator file. That way, you can create art in Illustrator exactly how you want it in Flash and never worry about rearranging your art. Nice!

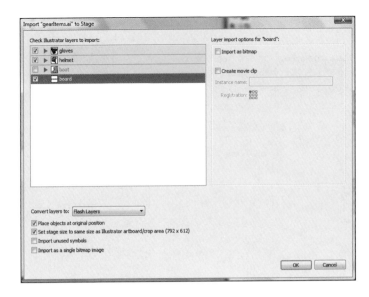

10 On the **Timeline**, notice you see only the elements you selected to import. Flash has also created and named layers, resized the **Stage**, and placed all the paths and groups to match the Illustrator file. Sweet!

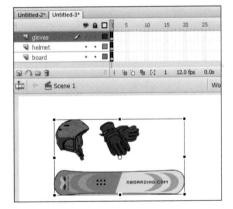

11 Close the files. You don't need to save your changes.

Note: Illustrator 10 and newer and Adobe Photoshop CS and newer can now export in the SWF file format, allowing you to import Illustrator and Photoshop content as SWF files. These versions provide you another possible workflow when integrating content from Illustrator and Photoshop.

Import Dialog Box for Illustrator Files

Flash can import Illustrator files in version 6 or newer. The following chart options explains the options settings in the Import dialog box:

Note: Flash CS3 no longer supports importing of PDF or EPS files. To import a PDF or EPS file into Flash, open the file in Illustrator and then copy and paste the object into Flash. You can also save it as an Illustrator (.AI) file and then import it in Flash.

Illustrator Import Dialog Box	
Option	**Description**
Convert layers to: **Layers/Keyframes/** **Single Flash Layer**	Controls how individual layers are imported into Flash CS3 from your Illustrator file. Selecting **Layers** allows the layers in your file to remain as layers when imported into Flash. Selecting **Keyframes** allows Flash to convert the layers into keyframes. Selecting **Single Flash Layer** converts multiple layers into one layer in Flash.
Place objects at original position:	With this option selected, Flash will insert all the objects in the same positions they had in Illustrator.
Set stage to same size as Illustrator artboard/crop area:	With this option selected, Flash will preserve the text blocks in your Illustrator file so that they remain editable in Flash.
Import unused symbols:	Flash will import symbols in the Illustrator project's **Library** panel even if they aren't on the document **Stage**.
Import as single bitmap image:	Selecting this option flattens layers, rasterizes text, and disables options for converting layers or maintaining text blocks.

4 | Importing Photoshop Content

In previous versions of Flash, importing Photoshop content required many tedious and challenging workarounds. In Flash CS3, you have options to import layers, layer styles, editable text, and even vector paths. In this exercise, you will learn how to import and edit Photoshop content in Flash CS3.

Note: Photoshop CS3 is not necessary to complete this exercise. However, you can download a trial version of Photoshop CS3 from Adobe's Web site at **www.adobe.com**.

---

1 Open **photoshop.fla** from the **chap_19** folder.

---

2 Choose **Edit > Preferences** (Windows) or **Flash CS3 > Preferences** (Mac) to open the **Preferences** dialog box. Select the **PSD File Importer** in the **Category** list.

Notice there are many options similar to the options in the AI File Importer. Just like importing an AI file, you have many options to import a PSD file into Flash CS3. In the next steps, you will learn how to use these options.

---

3 Select the following options, and click **OK**:

- **Editable text** for **Import text layers as**

- **Editable paths and layer styles** for **Import shape layers as**

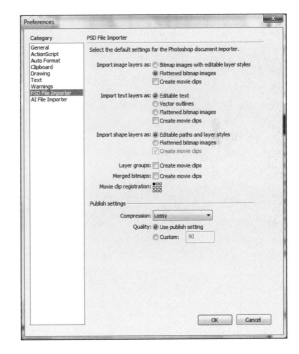

4 Choose **File > Import > Import to Stage**, and select the file **snowboard.psd** from the **chap_19** folder. Notice the layers menu and importing options in the dialog box are similar to the options you see when importing an AI file.

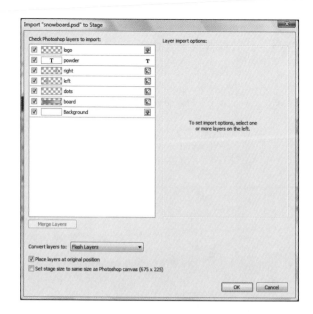

5 Select the **powder** layer. Notice on the right side of the dialog box that the **powder** layer will be imported as editable text. Nice! Select any other layer, and note that it will be imported into a movie clip. You can even choose an instance name and registration!

Notice the icons to the right of each layer name. Flash CS3 is telling you how each layer will be imported. The T symbol represents editable text, and the movie clip symbol means Flash will place that element inside a movie clip.

Note: Using the Publish Settings area of the dialog box, you have the option to set the bitmap compression setting for each layer. You can also check what the file size of the layer will be as a bitmap by clicking the Calculate File Size button. Cool! This saves you the step of having to manually set the compression of each layer in the Library panel.

6 Select the **logo** layer, press **Shift** on your keyboard, and select the **powder** layer. Click the **Merge Layers** button.

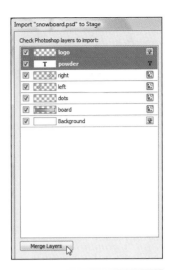

7 Select the **Merged Bitmap 1** layer group, and click the **Separate** button.

Using the Merge Layers button, you can import multiple Photoshop layers as one bitmap in Flash. This is a great option if there are many bitmaps in your Photoshop document that you do not need to edit or move separately. Merging layers can also make it easier for you to manage large amounts of Photoshop content.

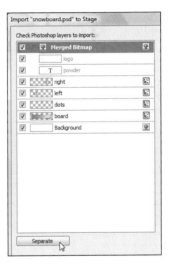

8 Choose the following options, and click **OK**:

- **Flash layers** for **Convert layers to**
- Place layers at original position
- Set stage size to same size as Photoshop canvas

These options work much like the same options used when importing an Illustrator file. When you import the Photoshop file, Flash will create and place layers and change the Stage size for you.

9 Notice that Flash has created, named, and placed the layers for you. Also notice the size of the **Stage** has changed to match the size of the Photoshop canvas. Nice!

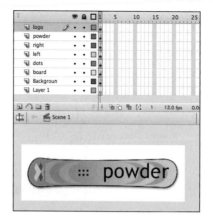

10 On the **Timeline, right-click** (Windows) or **Ctrl-click** (Mac) the **left** layer, and choose **Lock Others** to lock the other layers. Select the shape on the **left** layer, and look in the **Properties inspector**. Flash has created and named a movie clip for you! Double-click the shape on the **left** layer to enter its **Timeline**.

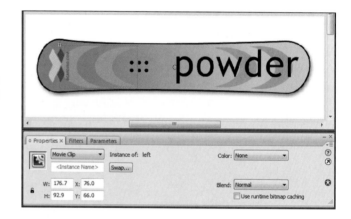

11 In the **left** movie clip's **Timeline**, notice how the layers are set up. There is a mask layer with a vector shape, with a bitmap solid fill.

This is similar to how vector shapes are created in Photoshop. In the next step, you will edit the fill color of this shape.

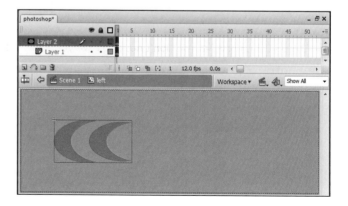

12 Select the tan bitmap fill on the **Stage**, and press **Delete** on your keyboard to delete the graphic. Make sure **Layer 1** is selected. Using the **Rectangle** tool and any fill color, draw a rectangle roughly the same size and position of the bitmap you just deleted.

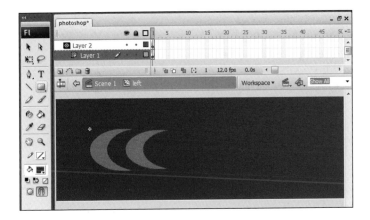

13 Below the **Timeline**, click the **Scene 1** button to return to the main **Timeline**. Notice the graphic on the **left** layer has updated according to your change. Cool!

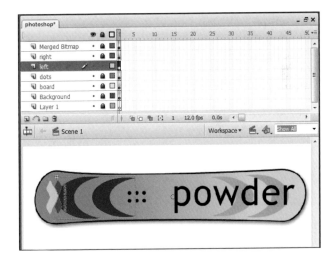

14 Close **photoshop.fla**. You don't need to save your changes.

5 | Creating Accessible Content

An increasing number of Web sites require accessible content, which means the content must be accessible and navigable by people who have disabilities. In Flash CS3, you can make the content in your movie accessible to visually impaired people who have access to screen reader software. Screen reader software uses audio to describe what is on the screen. For the screen reader to read your content properly, you must set up the content in a certain way. This exercise shows you how to make content in your Flash CS3 project files accessible.

---

1 Open the **accessibleContent.fla** file from the **chap_19** folder.

This file contains a background image, buttons, and text.

2 In the **Property inspector**, make sure nothing is selected in the project file, and click the **Edit accessibility settings** button to open the **Accessibility** panel.

3 Select the **Make movie accessible** option. In the **Name** field, type **Safety**, and for **Description**, type **This page offers information about snowboarding safety.**

The Make Movie Accessible option makes the whole movie (which resides on one frame in the main Timeline) accessible to screen readers. The following chart describes the options in this panel.

Accessibility Panel Options

Option	Description
Make movie accessible	Makes the movie readable by screen readers; this includes all static text, input text fields, buttons, and movie clips. If this option is deselected, the movie will be hidden from screen readers.
Make child objects acessible	Makes the accessible objects (text, input text fields, buttons, and movie clips) located in movie clips readable by screen readers. If this option is deselected, accessible objects within movie clips cannot be accessed by screen readers.
Auto label	Uses text objects, such as buttons or input text fields contained in the movie, as automatic labels for accessible content. If this option is deselected, screen readers will read text objects as text objects, not labels. (You will learn how to label individual items later in this exercise.)
Name	The title (name) for the movie, which the screen reader will read even if there is no other accessible content in the movie. This option is available only if you select the **Make movie accessible** option.
Description	The description of the movie, which will be read by the screen reader software. This option is also available only if you select the **Make movie accessible** option.

4 When you are finished, close the **Accessibility** panel.

NOTE:

Accessible Objects

Flash Player 9 will include dynamic text, input text fields, buttons, movie clips, and entire movies as accessible objects that can be read by screen readers. However, individual graphic objects are not included as accessible objects, because graphics can't be easily turned into spoken words. On the other hand, movie clips are included as accessible objects, as are the objects inside movie clips, as long as they are dynamic text, input text fields, buttons, or other movie clips.

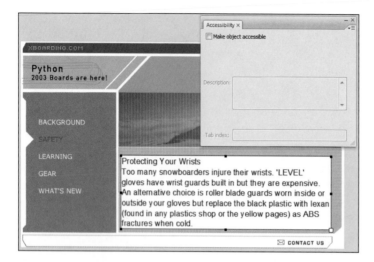

5 On the **Stage**, double-click the dynamic text field to select the content. Choose **Window > Other Panels > Accessibility** to open the **Accessibility** panel again.

Even though you made your movie accessible in Step 3, you can have more control over what the screen reader will read by filling out the fields in the Accessibility panel for this static text field, which you will do next.

Tip: You can open the Accessibility panel either by choosing Window > Other Panels > Accessibility or by clicking the Edit accessibility settings button in the Property inspector.

6 In the **Accessibility** panel, select the **Make object accessible** option. In the dynamic text field on the **Stage**, select all the text below **Protecting Your Wrists**, and press **Ctrl+C** (Windows) or **Cmd+C** (Mac) to copy it. In the **Description** field, press **Ctrl+V** (Windows) or **Cmd+V** (Mac) to paste the content.

Screen readers will read the description you just pasted.

---

7 On the **Stage**, select the **BACKGROUND** button. In the **Accessibility** panel, make sure the **Make object accessible** option is selected. Type **Background button** for **Name** and **This button takes you to the background page** for **Description**. Close the **Accessibility** panel.

Again, rather than leaving it up to Flash to name your buttons (to avoid names like button 17), you should name your buttons individually.

Note: Even if you test your movie, unfortunately it is not possible to test your movie's accessibility content using the Flash CS3 Test Movie command. If you have access to a screen reader, however, you can test the movie's accessibility by playing it in a screen reader. Additionally, demonstration versions of screen reader software are available, so you can download one and test your movie that way.

TIP:

Learning More About Accessibility

If you are interested in learning more about Adobe applications and accessibility, a section on Adobe's Web site will tell you all about it: **www.adobe.com/accessibility/**.

---

8 Save and close this file. You are finished with the book!

Congratulations! You did it! I really hope this book helped you learn Adobe Flash CS3 quickly and you are now armed and ready to create your own animated and interactive projects. I wish you the best of luck with all your future Flashing!

A

Troubleshooting FAQ
and Technical Support

If you run into problems while following the exercises in this book, you might find the answers to your questions in the "Troubleshooting FAQ" section. If you don't find the information you're looking for, use the contact information provided in the "Technical Support Information" section.

Troubleshooting FAQ

Q On a Mac, why can't I see any FLA files when I choose **File > Open**?

A If an FLA file was created in Windows, you might experience a problem seeing the file when you try to open it on a Mac. You can correct this problem by changing the **Show** option to **All Files**.

Q On a Mac, an FLA file won't open when I double-click it. Why?

A If the FLA file was created in Windows, you might not be able to double-click it to open the file. If this is the case, open Adobe Flash CS3, and choose **File > Open** to open the FLA file. If you don't see the FLA file listed when you choose **File > Open**, see the previous question. After you save the FLA file (originally created on in Windows) on your Mac, you will be able to double-click the FLA to open it.

Q My Tools panel has disappeared. What should I do?

A Choose **Window > Tools** to show/hide the Tools panel. Chapter 2, *"Understanding the Interface,"* explains the Tools panel in detail.

Q All of my panels have disappeared. What should I do?

A Press the **Tab** key to show them and even hide them again. If you don't like their arrangement, you can restore them to their default onscreen positions by choosing **Window > Workspace > Default**. This command is especially helpful when someone else has undocked and changed the combination of your panels. Chapter 2, *"Understanding the Interface,"* describes each of the panels in detail.

Q I undocked one of the panels, but I can't redock it again. Why?

A To redock a panel, make sure you drag it over the location where you want to dock it. When the blue outline appears, release the mouse. Chapter 2, *"Understanding the Interface,"* explains docking and undocking in detail.

Q Why does Flash create extra files when I press **F12** (Windows) or **Cmd+F12** (Mac)?

A Pressing **F12** (Windows) or **Cmd+F12** (Mac) is a shortcut for the **Publish Preview** command, which publishes a SWF file and an HTML file. Flash CS3 creates these files in the same directory as the FLA file. If you want to preview your movie without publishing any other files, choose **Control > Test Movie** or **File > Publish Preview > Flash** to create only the SWF file. Chapter 17, *"Publishing and Exporting,"* explains the publish features in detail.

Q I tried to create my own shape tween, but it won't work, and the **Timeline** has a broken line. What does this mean?

A A solid line with an arrow indicates that the tween is working properly. A dashed line in the **Timeline** indicates a problem with the tween, which could be caused by several issues. First, you cannot create a shape tween using symbols, groups, or text blocks (text that hasn't been broken apart). Make sure you are using only objects that work with shape tweens. Second, make sure you have at least two keyframes in the layer you are trying to tween. In Chapter 5, *"Shape Tweening,"* you will find a detailed list of the objects you can use to create shape tweens.

Q Why do all the objects on my **Stage** appear faded?

A This occurs when you double-click a symbol instance or **right-click** (Windows) or **Ctrl-click** (Mac) a symbol instance and choose **Edit in Place**. This is a quick way to make changes to a symbol without having to access the **Library** panel; however, it can be confusing if that's not what you intended to do. In the **edit bar**, click **Scene 1** to exit this editing mode and return to the main **Timeline**.

Q I tried to create my own motion tween, but it won't work. And the **Timeline** has a broken line. What does this mean?

A You cannot create a motion tween using shapes or broken-apart text. A solid line with an arrow indicates that the tween is working properly. A dashed line in the **Timeline** indicates that there is a problem with the tween. Make sure you are using only objects that work with motion tweens. In Chapter 8, *"Motion Tweening and Timeline Effects,"* you will find a detailed list of the objects you can use to create motion tweens.

Q I tried to motion tween multiple objects, but it's not working. What could be wrong?

A Motion tweening multiple objects requires that each different object exist on a separate layer. If you have all the objects on a single layer, the tween will not behave as expected. You can use the **Modify > Distribute to Layers** command to quickly distribute each object to its own layer. Also, make sure you are trying to tween objects that are capable of being motion tweened. Objects such as shapes and broken-apart text cannot be motion tweened. In Chapter 8, *"Motion Tweening and Timeline Effects,"* you learned how to motion tween multiple objects; refer to that chapter for a review.

Q I tried to change the alpha transparency of a shape using the **Property inspector**, but Flash doesn't allow me to do so. What could be wrong?

A To change the alpha transparency of a shape (dotted mesh), you need to use the **Color** panel. To change the alpha transparency of a symbol instance, you need to use the **Property inspector**. You learned how to do this in Chapter 6, *"Creating Symbols and Instances."* Refer to that chapter for a review.

Q Why won't my movie clips play when I click the **Play** button?

A You can preview your movie clips on the main **Timeline** within the Flash CS3 authoring environment. You can preview movie clips in their own **Timeline**, in the **Library** panel, or in the Flash Player (by choosing **Control > Test Movie**).

Q I made an input text field, but when I test it by choosing **Control > Test Movie** and trying to type in it, nothing happens. Why?

A When you created the text box, you most likely set the text color to the same color as the background of the movie. Try changing the text color and testing the movie again. Also, make sure you have **Input Text** set for the text type.

Q I want to learn more about the many actions in the **Actions** panel. How do I do this?

A In the **Actions** panel, type any action or keyword you need more information about. Then choose **Help > Flash Help** to open the content-sensitive **Help** menu. A complete description of the action or keyword will appear in the window.

Technical Support Information

The following is a list of technical support resources you can use if you need help.

lynda.com

If you run into any problems as you work through this book, check the companion Web site for updates:

www.lynda.com/books/HOT/flcs3

If you don't find what you're looking for on the companion Web site, send an email to **books-errata@lynda.com**.

We encourage and welcome your feedback, comments, and error reports.

Peachpit Press

If your book has a defective CD-ROM, please contact the customer service department at Peachpit Press:

customer_service@peachpit.com

Adobe Technical Support

If you're having problems with Flash Professional 8 unrelated to this book, please visit the following Web site to access the Adobe Flash Support Center:

www.adobe.com/support/flash/

To contact Adobe Technical Support, use the e-mail form at the following Web site:

www.adobe.com/support/email/cscontact/

Adobe Technical Support can help you with typical problems, such as an expired trial version.

You can also try to contact Adobe directly by phone:

United States and Canada:
1-800-470-7211 (toll-free)

Outside the United States and Canada:
+1-415-553-7186

Flash CS3 Professional Resources

Adobe Flash CS3 Professional users have a great many resources for finding information about Flash. You have ample choices among a variety of newsgroups, conferences, and third-party Web sites that can really help you get the most out of the new skills you've developed by reading this book. In this appendix, you'll find a list of the best resources for further developing your skills with Flash CS3.

lynda.com Training Resources

lynda.com

lynda.com is a leader in software books and video training for Web and graphics professionals. To help further develop your skills in Flash, check out the following training resources from lynda.com.

lynda.com Books

The **Hands-On Training** series was originally developed by **Lynda Weinman**, author of the revolutionary book, *Designing Web Graphics*, first released in 1996. Lynda believes people learn best from doing and has developed the Hands-On Training series to teach users software programs and technologies through a progressive learning process.

Check out the following books from lynda.com:

Adobe Dreamweaver CS3 Hands-On Training
by Garrick Chow
lynda.com/books and Peachpit Press
ISBN: 0321509854

ActionScript 3.0 for Adobe Flash CS3 Professional Hands-On Training
(September 2007)
by Todd Perkins
lynda.com/books and Peachpit Press
ISBN: 0321293908

Designing Web Graphics 4
by Lynda Weinman
New Riders
ISBN: 0735710791

lynda.com Video-Based Training

lynda.com offers video training as stand-alone CD-ROM and DVD-ROM products and through a subscription to the lynda.com **Online Training Library**.

For a free, 24-hour trial pass to the lynda.com Online Training Library, register your copy of *Flash CS3 Professional HOT* at the following link: **www.lynda.com/register/HOT/flcs3**

Note: This offer is available for new subscribers only and does not apply to current or past subscribers of the lynda.com Online Training Library.

To help you build your skills with Flash, check out the following video training titles from lynda.com:

Flash CS3 Professional Essential Training
with Rich Schupe

ActionScript 3.0 in Flash CS3 Professional Essential Training
with Todd Perkins

Illustrator CS3 and Flash CS3 Professional Integration
with Mordy Golding

Flashforward Conference and Film Festival

The Flashforward conference and film festival is an international educational conference dedicated to Adobe Flash. Flashforward was first hosted by Lynda Weinman, founder of lynda.com, and Stewart McBride, founder of United Digital Artists. Flashforward is now owned exclusively by lynda.com and strives to provide the best conferences for designers and developers to present their technical and artistic work in an educational setting.

For more information about the Flashforward conference and film festival, visit **www.flashforwardconference.com**.

Online Resources

The following are online resources for Flash information.

Adobe Flash Developer Center

www.adobe.com/devnet/flash
Adobe has created a section of its Web site called the Adobe Flash Developer Center. This is a one-stop shop for everything Flash. For example, you can read tutorials and articles on Flash CS3, download sample applications, access links to other Flash resources, and even read the white papers written on topics related to Flash CS3. This is the perfect link to use if you want to learn more about components or even video in Flash CS3.

Adobe Online Forums

www.adobe.com/cfusion/webforums/forum/
Adobe has set up several Web-based online forums for Adobe Flash. This is a great place to ask questions and get help from thousands of Flash users. These online forums are used by beginning to advanced Flash users, so you should have no problem finding the type of help you need, regardless of your experience with the program. The following list describes several of Adobe's online forums:

Flash General Discussion: Online forum for general issues related to using Adobe Flash.

Flash Site Design: Online forum for design feedback on your Flash animations. This forum is dedicated to discussing Flash design and animation principles and practices. Other issues not specific to the Flash tools yet important to Flash designers are also discussed here.

Flash ActionScript: Online forum for discussing creating interactive Flash projects using ActionScript.

Flash Remoting: Online forum that discusses issues involved with Flash Remoting, which supplies the infrastructure that allows users to connect to remote services exposed by application server developers and Web services. Examples of these are message boards, shopping carts, and even up-to-the-minute stock quote graphs.

Flash Exchange Extensions: Online forum for issues relating to Flash extensions, including how to use them and how to troubleshoot any problems with them. (See also the "Adobe Exchange for Flash" section next.)

Adobe Exchange for Flash

www.adobe.com/exchange/flash/
Adobe has set up another section of its Web site, called the Adobe Flash Exchange. Here you'll find hundreds of free extensions written by third-party users and developers that can help you build new features into your Web site. These features are not part of the Flash CS3 product, but you can download them when you need them. Many of these extensions have features that would otherwise require an advanced level of ActionScript skills. For example, some of these behaviors let you password-protect areas of your site and create pop-up menus, scroll bars, complex text effects, and so on.

The Adobe site is not just for developers but for any Flash user who wants to take Flash to the next level. If you are a developer, this is a great place to learn how to write your own behaviors to share with the rest of the Flash community.

You can also visit **www.adobe.com/cfusion/webforums/forum/** and click the **Flash Exchange Extensions** link to access the online forum for Flash extensions.

Adobe TechNote Index

www.adobe.com/support/flash/technotes.html
This section of the Adobe Web site lists all the issues that have been reported and answered by the Flash staff members.

Third-Party Web Sites

The following are helpful third-party Web sites:

www.flashkit.com/

www.ultrashock.com/

http://virtual-fx.net/

www.actionscripts.org/

www.flzone.net/

http://flashmove.com/

http://flazoom.com/

www.were-here.com/

www.popedeflash.com/

Index

Symbols

– (minus) sign, Remove Shortcut button, 20
. (dot syntax). *see* dot syntax
. (period), naming conventions and, 118
/ (slashes), naming conventions and, 118
; (semicolon), ending statements, 288
▶ (arrow sign in Macs), drilling down into additional
    commands, 20
" (quotation marks)
    string data types and, 288
    string literal vs. expression syntax, 358
+ (addition operator), combining string literals and
    expressions, 358
+ (plus) buttons
    Add Filter button (+), 158, 207
    Add Shortcut button (+), 20
< (less than), moving playhead backward, 169
= (equals), 302
== (equal to), 302
> (greater than), moving playhead forward, 169

A

A *see* Subselection tool (A)
accessibility options, 554–557
    accessible objects, 555
    overview of, 554–555
    working with Accessibility panel, 556–557
accessible objects, 555
Actions panel, 285–287
    accessing, 294, 444
    adding actions to keyframes, 293–294
    buttons, 287
    controlling movie playback, 292
    modes, 285–286
    reviewing ActionScript code, 504–505
    Top down option for loading actions, 468
ActionScript, 284–324
    Actions panel, 285–287
    addChild( ) function, 317
    classes, 291
    coding standards, 351

component skin modifications, 415–420
component support, 401
conditional statements, 291, 300–305
dot syntax and, 299
draggable movies, 526–530
dynamic text and, 341
dynamic text and HTML and, 346–349
elements, 288
events, event handlers, and event listeners, 290–291
file extension (.as), 8
frame labels and, 310
functions and methods, 289–290
instances and instance names, 289
JavaScript used together with, 10–11
layer added for, 293
Loader class, 316
loading actions (Top down), 468
loading movies using **Loader** class, 318–324
loading text into dynamic text fields, 343–345
movie clip controls, 297–299
Movie Explorer for viewing actions, 512
navigateToURL( ) function, 306–310
online resources, 564
overview of, 284
pop-up menu, creating using frame labels, 311–316
preloader construction and, 517
projector controls, 476–479
properties, 289
sound controls (on/off buttons), 380–383
sound controls (stop/play), 397–399
sound effects added with, 376–379
Timeline controls, 292–296
training resources, 563
URLRequest class, 305
variables, 288–289
version setting, in Publish settings, 483
video control using frame labels, 443–449
video controls (stop/play), 434–437
Add Filter button (+), 158, 207
Add Motion Guide button, Timeline, 182
Add Shortcut button (+), 20
addChild( ) function, ActionScript, 317
addition operator (+), combining string literals and
    expressions, 358
Adjust Color filters, 156
Adobe Device Central, 6

B

E

N

O

Publish settings *(continued)*
   saving profiles, 494
   scalable bitmaps and vector art and, 473
   sound compression, 364
   SWF file options, 483

Q

Q *see* Free Transform tool (Q)
.qtf (QuickTime), 214
quality
   Drop Shadow settings, 209–210
   HTML Publish settings, 487
   JPEG Publish settings, 489
   sound options, 367
   video compression settings, 432
QuickTime
   bitmap file types, 214
   importing sounds and, 362
   Publish settings, 492–493
   publishing content via, 465
   video formats supported, 423
QuickTime export, new features in Flash CS3, 6
QuickTime movie (.mov), 423, 425, 480
quit, FSCommands, 479
quotation marks (")
   string data types and, 288
   string literal vs. expression syntax, 358

R

R *see* Rectangle tool (R)
radial gradients, 54
RadioButton
   as component, 402
   modifying, 412
   working with, 405
radius settings, Property Inspector
   creating inner circle, 30
   rounding corners as you draw, 32
   setting corner radius, 31
raster graphics. *see* bitmap images (.bmp)
raw, sound compression, 365
Rectangle Primitive tool, 32
Rectangle tool (R)
   exercise using, 29–33
   fly-out menu, 29
   keyboard shortcuts for, 33
   strokes or outlines created with, 25
   what it does, 24
registration points
   center crosshair indicating, 242
   changing with Free Transform tool, 136

Info panel, 191–192
   motion guides and, 184
   for symbols, 123
Remove Frames option, context menus, 269, 394
Remove Shortcut button, 20
Repeat option, Property inspector, 375
repeat/loop options, sound, 375
resizing
   handles for, 342
   objects, 162
   panels, 16–17
   shapes, 109–110
   video, 429
Resolve Library Conflict dialog, 509
resources
   Flashforward conference and film festival, 564
   online resources, 564–565
   technical support, 561
   third-party Web sites, 565
   training, 563
result objects, blend modes and, 147
Retention layer, on Timeline, 392–393
Return (Mac), previewing animation on Stage, 73
Revert command, files, 123
RGB values, 132–133
RIAs (Rich Internet Applications), 9–10
right clicking (Windows), accessing context menus, 228
rollover buttons
   button types, 240
   creating, 241–245
   creating animated rollover button, 275–280
   creating rollover buttons with text, 246–249
   putting animated rollover button into action, 281–283
rotate cursor, Free Transform tool (Q), 135
rotation
   CCW (counter clockwise) option, 174
   letters, 193
   text attributes, 329

S

S *see* Ink Bottle tool (S)
.sai (Silicon Graphics), bitmap file types, 214
Sample rate pop-up menu, sounds, 386–387
scalability, benefits of Flash CS3, 4
scale
   HTML Publish settings, 487
   image instances, 173–174
   letters, 193
   shapes, 109
scale cursor, Free Transform tool (Q), 135
Scene Timeline, 119
Screen blend mode
   applying, 154
   overview of, 150

T

T see Text tool (T)
tangent handles
  drawing circles with Pen tool, 60–61
  reshaping using anchor points or tangent handles, 62–65
  selecting, 62
target, text attributes, 330
technical support, 561
Template, HTML Publish settings, 486
Test button, Bitmap Properties dialog, 219
Test Movie feature
  overview of, 92–95
  previewing movie clips, 265
  Publish Preview compared with, 467
  testing sounds, 371
  Timeline and, 143
text, 326–359
  alignment, 350
  animating text, 189–194
  anti-aliasing, 338
  attributes, 328–330
  character attributes, 345
  color, 350
  dynamic text and HTML, 346–349
  field types, 327
  Flash Type, 338
  importing Fireworks content, 535
  input text fields, 350–359
  kerning, 331
  loading text into dynamic text fields, 341–345
  motion tweening, 190
  overview of, 326
  rollover buttons with text, 246–249
  small type and anti-aliasing, 339–340
  spell checking, 332–333
  static text and device fonts, 332
text blocks
  comparing motion tweening and shape tweening, 165
  motion tweening, 195
text boxes, breaking apart, 190
text color attribute, 329
text orientation attribute, 329
Text tool (T)
  adding text to buttons, 246
  shape tweening and, 100
  types of text created with, 327
  what it does, 23
text type
  setting, 350–351
  text attributes, 328

TextArea
  as component example, 402
  modifying components, 413
  working with, 405
TextInput component, 402
.tgf, bitmap file types, 214
themes, ActionScript not supporting, 421
third-party Web sites, resources, 565
this keyword, 321, 528
thumbnails, of keyframes, 76
.tiff, bitmap file types, 214
Timeline
  Add Motion Guide button, 182
  adding layers, 266
  adding sound layer, 368–369
  adding sounds, 390
  button symbols, 239
  controlling, 292–296
  Edit Multiple Frames button, 177–179, 221
  expanding or contracting, 384–385
  fixing broken tweens, 102
  frame rate and, 78
  frames and keyframes and, 71
  how it works, 67–68
  inserting/deleting frames, 79–82
  interface components, 14
  layer controls, 113
  layer folders for organizing, 506
  making changes on, 75
  power of movie clip symbols and, 298
  sound indicator on, 257
  Test Movie feature and, 143
  testing sounds, 371
  types of, 119
Timeline effects
  animating with Blur filter, 204–206
  animating with Drop Shadow filter, 207–210
  Copy to Grid, 200–203
  Distributed Duplicate, 196–200
  editing effects and editing symbols that have effects, 199
  Timeline effects assistants, 196
  what happens when adding, 198
  what they are, 195
Timeline effects assistants
  Copy to Grid, 200–203
  Distributed Duplicate, 196–200
  overview of, 164, 196
Timeline independence, movie clips and, 265, 274
Timeline Options menu, 384
Tint option, Color pop-up menu, 132, 137
Tiny and Short option, frames, 384
To Stage button, in Align panel, 255
Tool modifiers, Tool panel, 25
tool tips, disabling, 15
toolbox, showing/hiding, 287

V

W

U

X

Y

Z